Algeria in France

New Anthropologies of Europe
Daphne Berdahl, Matti Bunzl, and Michael Herzfeld, editors

Algeria in France

Transpolitics, Race, and Nation

Paul A. Silverstein

Indiana University Press

Bloomington and Indianapolis

This book is a publication of

Indiana University Press
601 North Morton Street
Bloomington, IN 47404-3797 USA

http://iupress.indiana.edu

Telephone orders   800-842-6796
Fax orders   812-855-7931
Orders by e-mail   iuporder@indiana.edu

© 2004 by Paul A. Silverstein

The paper used in this publication meets the minimum
requirements of American National Standard for
Information Sciences—Permanence of Paper for Printed
Library Materials, ANSI Z39.48-1984.

Manufactured in the United States of America

Library of Congress Cataloging-in-Publication Data

Silverstein, Paul A., date
Algeria in France : transpolitics, race, and nation / Paul A.
Silverstein.
    p. cm. — (New anthropologies of Europe)
  Includes bibliographical references and index.
  ISBN 0-253-34451-4 (cloth : alk. paper) — ISBN
0-253-21712-1 (pbk. : alk. paper)
      1. Algerians—France—History. 2. Algerians—
France—Attitudes. 3. Algerians—France—Ethnic identity.
4. Algerians—France—Cultural assimilation. 5. Algerians—France—Social conditions. 6. Algerians—France—
Economic conditions. 7. France—Emigration and
immigration—History. 8. Algeria—Emigration and
immigration—History. 9. Immigrants—Cultural assimilation—France. 10. Islam—France. I. Title. II. Series.
  DC34.5.A4S58 2004
  944'.00492765—dc22
                                            2004002655
       2   3   4   5   09   08   07   06

In loving memory of my father

Contents

Preface and Acknowledgments

The paradigmatic narrative of entry into a field site follows that of Bronislaw Malinowski (1922: 4): "Imagine yourself suddenly set down surrounded by all your gear, alone on a tropical beach close to a native village, while the launch or dinghy which has brought you sails away out of sight." While it is tempting to translate this scene to the not-so-remote location of an Algerian neighborhood on the outskirts of Paris, to do so would belie the realities of conducting urban anthropological fieldwork in the New Europe of the 1990s. Indeed, my own story of arrival began well before the actual research project when, as a young college student, I spent a summer as a cabana boy on a French beach along the English Channel resort city of Deauville. Often referred to as the "21st *arrondissement* of Paris" (Paris proper has twenty districts), Deauville attracts a mixed company of vacationers during its summer peak season, with bourgeois Parisians and Londoners who own property in the area rubbing shoulders with the more diverse weekend crowd escaping the heat of France's landlocked capital. The two groups regard each other with a certain amount of disdain, and as an employee of the beach, I often found myself caught in the middle of their often racialized disputes.

One glorious Saturday morning in August, as the beach was filling up to capacity, one of the beach's regulars, Madame Rosenzweig, an older Parisian Jewish woman who grew up in colonial Algeria, approached me with a somewhat unusual request. While she always asked to be given a parasol where she could be left *tranquille*—by which we were to understand distant from Arab or African vacationers—on this day her demands were more emphatic, in no small part in reaction to the previous day's faux pas of a new beach employee who had parked a large, dark-skinned family next to her. "I'm not a racist," she explained. "But those people make lots of noise and cook strong foods. In any case, you're from America so you understand. They are the racist ones, not us." I was particularly struck by the seeming disconnect between her words and her personal trajectory of migration. Her words continued to resonate several years later as I began formulating a research project to explore the intimate relationship between France and Algeria.

If my arrival in the "field" predated my actual fieldwork, so too did my presence in the field long outlast the official period of sponsored research. While I closed my twenty months of on-site research in Paris and its surrounding areas in November 1996, I remained (and remain) closely connected to my Algerian interlocutors' lives and struggles. Since then, I have made several shorter trips to Paris, revisiting friends and sites of research, re-establishing my propinquity to the community of Beur and Berber activists I studied. And even when I have been physically absent, I have been able to stay communicatively present, directly exchanging electronic mail with my prior interviewees, actively participating in on-line discussion groups, and following local events through regular visits to Internet web sites dedicated to Algerian issues. As I write these words, I am listening to Beur FM —a Paris-based radio station dedicated to North African news and music— through my university office's high-speed data connection, imagining that I am participating in some ritual communion with the thousands of other listeners across North Africa and the diaspora. While these forms of long-distance fieldwork by no means replace the direct observation of and participation in the lived everyday realities of Algerian immigrant life in and around Paris, they do underline the fact that anthropological research is always (or at least should be) a multiply mediated endeavor. This realization is central to the transpolitics—to the formation of Franco-Algerian political subjectivities across localities and through multiple genres of cultural production—that this book seeks to unravel.

The research project from which the book emerges was formulated over many years while I was an undergraduate and graduate student at Princeton University and the University of Chicago, and my many teachers at these two institutions are owed my deepest gratitude for their insights and wisdom in putting a hapless student on the right track. Nadia Abu El-Haj, Arjun Appadurai, Andrew Apter, Leora Auslander, James W. Fernandez, Michael Geyer, John Kelly, Rashid Khalidi, Jorge Klor de Alva, Saree Makdisi, André Maman, and Terence Turner deserve special thanks for guiding me through the vagaries of project preparation and accomplishment. Jean Comaroff was an inspiring mentor throughout; she set the highest of standards that I can only hope to one day live up to.

Research in Paris and its environs was made possible by generous grants from the National Science Foundation, the Jennings-Randolph Program of the US Institute of Peace, and the MacArthur Scholars' Program of the Center for Advanced Study in Peace and International Conflict of the University of Chicago. While in Paris, I was graciously hosted as an exchange scholar by the École des Hautes Études en Sciences Sociales. Jocelyne Dakhlia, Nancy Green, Lucette Valensi, Tassadit Yacine, and the staff of this formidable institution deserve my utmost thanks for the warm welcome (and generous research stipend) I received. René Gallissot and Marguerite Rollinde of the Institut Maghreb-Europe of the Université de Paris-VIII, Saint-Denis, likewise offered generous hospitality, allowing me to take part in their research workshop on "Social Movements in the Maghreb." Much of my archival work was conducted in the libraries of the Institut du Monde Arabe and the Centre des Informations et Études sur les Migrations Internationales (CIEMI), and I want to thank the staff of these institutions—and particularly Christine Pelloquin and Lorenzo Prencipe—for welcoming a foreign researcher in their midst. My fieldwork was likewise only made possible by the doors that were opened for me by countless individuals and associations. The staffs and members of the Association de Culture Berbère (Paris), Tamazgha (Paris), and MCB-France (Argenteuil) deserve my particular gratitude, as do a number of other people who I promised would remain nameless. Hopefully they will find themselves and their aspirations faithfully reflected in the text that follows.

Writing and rewriting the manuscript has taken more years than I could possibly have imagined when I began the project. My age-mates, colleagues, and students at the University of Chicago, Barnard College, Columbia University, and Reed College have been supportive and stimulating interlocutors throughout the long process. They have set examples of academic integrity and commitment that I hope to take with me to future projects. I would like to thank the series editors of "New Anthropologies of Europe" for believing in and supporting the book project, and particularly Rebecca Tolen for being the editor that any young author would dream of having. John Bowen, Abdellah Hammoudi, Susan Terrio, and several anonymous reviewers provided extremely helpful comments and suggestions on the manuscript; their shrewd advice notwithstanding, I am solely responsible for the scope and contents of the resulting text. Brian Keith Axel, to quote him back, has been "a dear friend, a persistent critic, and an enduring interlocutor" from the beginning of the project to the end; without his support and engagement, the book would not have been what it is. My family has been a pillar of love and confidence throughout my entire life, all the more so when I have been distant from them. Lastly, Genevieve Bell deserves more love and gratitude than I could possibly give her; she is an inspiration as a scholar and a human being, and I am very lucky to have met her.

An earlier, shorter version of Chapter 2 appeared under the title "The Kabyle Myth: The Production of Ethnicity in Colonial Algeria," in *From the Margins: Historical Anthropology and Its Futures*, ed. Brian Keith Axel (Durham, N.C.: Duke University Press, 2002). Sections of Chapter 4 were included in "Sporting Faith: Islam, Soccer, and the French Nation-State," *Social Text* 65 (2000).

Note on Translation and Transliteration

All translations throughout the text are mine except where otherwise indicated. In transcribing from Arabic and Berber (Tamazight), I have used French approximations whenever the names, terms, or phrases are of common everyday or scholarly usage (ex. *tajmaât*). Otherwise, I have generally employed a simplified system of Romanization for Arabic words, using a circumflex diacritic to lengthen vowels (ex. *kitâb*), and apostrophes to indicate the 'ayn and the hamza. For Tamazight words, whenever possible I have employed the orthographic conventions established by scholars at the Institut National des Langues et Civilisations Orientales (INALCO) (ex. *axxam*).

Algeria in France

Introduction

        In the summer of 1995, a series of bombs exploded in subway stations and public markets in Paris and Lyon. Attributed to the Armed Islamic Group (GIA) that had been fighting a guerrilla war against the military government in Algeria since 1992, the bombings testified to France's lack of immunity in the postcolonial struggles over the future of its former colony. Moreover, they renewed widespread fears that France's large Algerian immigrant population represented a fifth column of a global Islamist insurgency that stretched from Kabul to Chechnya to Algiers to France's own working-class suburbs (*banlieues*). Already, these anxieties had come to the fore in fierce national debates over the place of Muslim headscarves in France's public school system, headscarves that, for many, indexed the growth of an integralist Islam in France incompatible with French state secularism (*laïcité*). Such fears appeared confirmed when a 26 August failed attack on a high-speed train line from Paris to Lyon was linked to Khaled Kelkal, a second-generation Algerian immigrant (or Franco-Algerian) from a housing project (*cité*) in the Lyonnais *banlieue* of Vaulx-en-Velin. In response, French authorities initiated a series of anti-terrorist measures that particularly targeted the Algerian immigrant community: reinforcing its policing of the *cités,* conducting a series of roundups of suspected Islamist militants, and instituting a policy of de facto racial profiling that resulted in hundreds of thousands of identity checks against North Africans in train and subway stations. In the wake of the 11 September 2001 attacks on the World Trade Center, this war on terror has continued apace, particularly after Zacarias Moussaoui, a French-born-and-raised child of Moroccan immigrants, was identified as the twentieth al-Qaeda hijacker.

Algeria in France plumbs the postcolonial predicament that unites Algeria and France into a single transpolitical space. It understands the struggle over the future of Algeria in France to be part of a larger transnational politics that takes place within and about the "West," rather than relying on the popular discourse of a putative "clash of civilizations"—in which a secular-Christian modernity associated with Europe and North America finds itself set against an Islamic modernity associated with large parts of Africa and Asia (cf. Huntington 1996). Political Islam and late capitalist *laïcité*, rather than alternate global futures, must be understood as equally important elements within a larger historical dialectic in which universal models of social and political behavior (e.g. citizenship, cosmopolitanism, secularism) derived from late-eighteenth-century European nationalism transform, and are transformed by, particular, incommensurable cultural logics. Making sense of these dialectics requires a nuanced understanding not only of the historical and demographic specificities of Algeria in France, but also of the broader formations in which these dialectics are embedded: the production and consumption of immigrant ethnic and religious subjectivities, the ongoing construction and reconstruction of the French nation, the dynamics of everyday life in the urban built environment, and the multiply mediated dimensions of Algerian transpolitics. The pages that follow introduce these broader conditions of Algerian immigrant life in France.

A New France?

As a locus of transnational violence and deterritorialized culture wars, France has increasingly had its capacity to socially reproduce the nation called into direct question. Throughout the 1990s, European unification continued apace, opening new avenues for physical mobility, economic cooperation, and cultural exchange between previously hostile states and populations. Intra-European borders that had been constructed across several centuries through multiple continental wars and treaties found themselves withering away with each successive phase of European economic and political integration. At the same time, as internal borders disappeared, extra-European borders became increasingly more stringent, with European states bringing their policing and immigration policies into conformity—resulting in what has often been referred to as "Fortress Europe."

In spite of such increased barriers to international movement, the civil war in Algeria proliferated in France during this same period, with Islamist and Berberist politics transecting the French metropole. After the Algerian army took power in 1992 and canceled the second round of legislative elections that the newly legalized Islamist parties were likely to have won, Islamist armed factions turned to guerrilla warfare, perpetrating attacks on government and civilian targets in the name of *jihad*. By century's end, an estimated 100,000 people had been killed in the fighting that took the form of car bombings, political assassinations, roadside shootings, and village massacres throughout Algeria. While political reforms and elections continued gradually, many journalists, intellectuals, feminists, and political activists fled the country under threat of death. The resulting situation became increasingly non-transparent, with the true power brokers—military generals and their Islamist militia leader counterparts—shrouded behind a facade of democratic political institutions (Quandt 1998; Roberts 2003; Silverstein 2002a).

The escalating violence of the Algerian civil war dovetailed with emerging demands of Berber speakers primarily residing in the eastern province of Kabylia for increased cultural and linguistic rights. During the colonial period, colonial military ethnographers identified the Kabyles as culturally distinctive from the Arab majority, as more hard-working, more democratic, less religious, and hence more potentially assimilable to Frenchness. After Algerian independence, the ruling National Liberation Front attempted to gloss over internal cultural differences, seeking to unite the Algerian populace under the banner of Arabic language and Islamic religion. Since 1980, Kabyle activists in Algeria and France have militated for the official recognition of Berber language (Tamazight) and culture as an integral part of Algerian national identity. On several occasions in 1980, 1998, and 2001, this activism resulted in violent encounters between Kabyle youth and the military that added to the larger chaos of the civil war (Maddy-Weitzman 2001; Silverstein 2003). Through these struggles, the war reinvigorated a set of colonial antagonisms turned postcolonial anxieties over the exact relationship between Algeria's Arabo-Islamic national ideology, its multiethnic and polyglot citizenry, and its ongoing economic and cultural dependency on Europe.

The book charts how these struggles over Algeria's future spread to France, Algeria's colonial ruler from 1830 until the first Algerian war of 1954–62. Postcolonial France served as both a space for and target of civil war politics enacted by immigrant, expatriate, and refugee Algerians. Through electioneering and public demonstrations as well as more violent means, Berberist and Islamist groups put pressure on France to force one resolution or another to the war in Algeria. Moreover, they sought electoral support, financial aid, and recruits among France's large Algerian immigrant population, attempting to reproselytize Algerians born and raised in France (or Franco-Algerians) into essentialized forms of Berber and Islamic identities. In the process, France and Algeria became once again united into a single, transnational political terrain.

The France in which such extra-territorial politics were occurring was by no means the simple result of a unilinear transformation of "peasants into Frenchmen," *pace* Eugen Weber's famous formulation (1976). As a number of studies have detailed, France has become a de facto multicultural nation whose diverse ethnoracial, religious, and class makeup shatters all myths and stereotypes of baguette-carrying, beret-donned peasants and aristocratic aesthetes sipping fine Bordeaux at Chez Maxim (cf. Amselle 2003; Beriss 1992; Gross et al. 1994; Grillo 1985; Hargreaves 1995; Hargreaves and McKinney 1997; Horowitz and Noiriel 1992; Lamont 2000; Lebovics 1992; MacGaffey and Bazenguissa-Ganga 2000; MacMaster 1997; Noiriel 1988; Raulin 2000; Rosello 2001; Silverman 1992; Terrio 2000; Ungar and Conley 1996). The cathedrals and cafés for which Paris is world-renowned now occupy an urban landscape dotted with synagogues, mosques, couscous restaurants, curry houses, Chinese supermarkets, and African hair salons. Emblematic of such transformations, France's victorious 1998 World Cup football team boasted elite players sporting names (Zidane, Trezeguet, Djorkaeff, Karembeu, Lizarazu, Barthez) of Arab, Kabyle, African, Antillean, Eastern European, Breton, and Basque derivation, attesting to a former colonial empire come home to score.

The multiracial character of France that the book explores derives from a century-long process by which France has become a center of migration, with large immigrant populations harking from its former African and North African colonies. In particular, Algerian migration to France derives from the expropriation of Algerian lands under French colonialism that sent many villagers—primarily from Kabylia—into emigration to colonial farms, Tunisian mines, and eventually to France. This emigration was boosted by the government recruitment of Algerian soldiers and laborers to work on short-term contracts during the First World War and in its aftermath. After World War II, as many as 350,000 Algerian men worked in the French manufacturing and construction industries in Paris, Lyon, and Marseille, contributing greatly to France's thirty years of spectacular postwar growth known as the *Trente Glorieuses*. During the 1954–62 anti-colonial war in Algeria, the families of many laborers came to France to escape the escalating violence. Immigration continued apace after the war until the global economic downturn of 1973, at which point the French government enacted legal barriers to future labor migration. Nonetheless, benefiting from allowances for family reunification and political refuge, the Algerian population in France continued to grow, reaching as many as 1.5 million men, women, and children by the mid-1990s (Costa-Lascoux and Temime 1985; Gillette and Sayad 1976; Hargreaves 1995: 4–17; Liauzu 1996: 115–131; Noiriel 1988; Sayad 1999; Talha 1989).

France's immigration policies have been subject to national debate at various historical junctures, particularly during moments of economic crisis in the 1930s and 1970s. In the 1980s and 1990s, when France faced national unemployment as high as 13 percent, the debate focused less on border policies than on state security, on immigrants' access to French nationality, on social integration and exclusion in the (sub)urban *cités* in which many immigrants and their children lived, and on the legitimacy of signs of

Muslim difference—particularly group prayer, mosque building, and women's headscarves—in the French public sphere. These various anxieties have been the subject of endless polemics for French politicians and lay residents alike, with "immigration" remaining a prominent platform issue in election campaigns throughout the 1990s and the early twenty-first century. With both its avatars and its anathemas, its Zinedine Zidanes (the Franco-Kabyle hero of the 1998 World Cup side) and its Khaled Kelkals, the blade of France's multiracial present is seen to cut both ways, simultaneously toward national grandeur and national disaster. It is this ambivalent character of a postcolonial France vacillating between republican logics of universalist citizenship and localizing concerns over the demise of national particularity—what Zygmunt Bauman (1991) has broadly termed the "ambivalence of modernity"—that is at the center of this book.

Transpolitics

Algeria in France focuses on the contemporary situation and the historical roots of the "New France" through an examination of transformations of ethnoracial difference among Algerians and Franco-Algerians in France. The production and consumption of various Algerian immigrant subjectivities in the colonial and postcolonial periods point to the changing nature of the French national identity from one based in empire to one now centered on Europe. Algerian subject formation, in this sense, is more than the residue of commodity fetishism and state discourses that transmuted Algerians into mobile laborers and their children into a potentially hostile mass of unemployed Muslims. It is, following Michel de Certeau (1984), the result of immigrant actors' tactical manipulation of the sociopolitical environment of the *cités,* both in their everyday social and religious practices of headscarving and Berber domestic organization, as well as in their overdetermined cultural productions of novel writing and hip-hop artistry. These two sides of subject formation—state representation and immigrant practice—operate in dialectical relation, each responding to the other, and together constituting the base on which the multiracial hopes and fears of a New France are built.

Drawing on more than ten years of anthropological experience in France and North Africa, including twenty months of sustained ethnographic fieldwork and archival research in Paris and its northeastern suburbs between 1995 and 1997, the study investigates the aporias of what Gérard Noiriel (1988) has famously called "the French melting pot" (*le creuset français*). It details with firsthand observation and historical evidence the connection between a burgeoning anti-immigrant racism within both popular and governmental circles, and the simultaneous rise of equally essentialist Islamist and Berberist movements among second-generation Algerian immigrants themselves. These latter ethnic and religious movements have created new spheres for political engagement that have provided marginalized immigrant groups with effective means of locally contesting state authority. As Berberist and Islamist oppositions have developed in both France and Algeria, and as the two contexts are closely tied through the reciprocal flows of people and information across the Mediterranean, Algerian politics have become mapped ever more mimetically onto French soil. In this sense, the book addresses transnational political formations based in ethnic and religious solidarity that call into question universalist ideologies of citizenship underwriting modern nation-states.

While the book draws directly on nearly two years of participant observation and ethnographic interviews conducted in *cités* and Berber associations located in the northeastern districts (*arrondissements*) and *banlieues* of Paris, it should by no means be read as a community study of Algerians in France. Rather, the study is organized topically, with each chapter focusing on a particular category of Franco-Algerian belonging: ethnicity, religion, gender, and generation. Tracing the elaboration of these categories to the colonial encounter and their contemporary transformations in the postcolonial metropole, the chapters thus outline a historical anthropology of Algeria in France. In order to understand this intimate relationship between colonial Algeria and postcolonial France, the study focuses on two intersecting genealogies. The first narrative charts the arrival of Algerians in France alongside the development of political discourses concerning immigration, integration, and citizenship. The second genealogy traces the cultural mapping of the Algerian space during the colonial period, a mapping that occurred in dialectical relation to the constitution of a national body within metropolitan France. In the postcolonial period, the multiracial *banlieues* have become the colonial space against which new French national imaginaries are formulated.

The double history of categorization and knowledge production involves more than the constitution of a New France via an Algerian other, of a (post)colonial national order in and through (post)colonized alterity. Immigration and cultural difference, as categories of knowledge and ideology, are appropriated by the colonial subjects and immigrant actors themselves for their own purposes, with counter-discourses of identity emerging that borrow from, but as often re-edit, the colonial narratives. In the contemporary era, this process is often mediated by a set of local and contested memories that target key events in colonial and postcolonial history: resistance to colonialism, the war of national liberation, the moment of immigration, and recent struggles for civil rights. Such memories themselves are portrayed in a number of commodified forms: novels, songs, posters, comic books, videos, and films. These objects become vital elements to the production and consumption of Algerian and Franco-Algerian subjectivities that underline a transnational politics connecting the Mediterranean, the New

France, and the New Europe, and as such are objects of detailed inquiry in this study.

Algerian identity politics in France, beyond a set of commodified narratives, is directly linked to a set of violent processes that surround and, to a large extent, enable it: from racist attacks and forced deportations in France to the extreme violence of the civil war in the Algerian postcolony. These terrors pervade the everyday lives of Algerians and Franco-Algerians, both in the actual physical occurrences of violence and in the symbolic ways by which the media has increasingly equated both Algeria and Algerian immigrant neighborhoods in France with sectarian violence and terrorism. On the one hand, racialized violence in France, along with more general socioeconomic marginalization, has disempowered immigrant communities and made a mockery of republican ideologies of sociocultural integration. On the other hand, the second Algerian war has destroyed community solidarity, pitting brother against brother, family against family, village against village, in an extreme binary politics of partisanship.

The binary politics of the civil war has appropriated essentialized cultural forms and identity diacritics. Islamic religious practices, once encouraged by colonial administrations as a means of ensuring docile native workers, have been reinterpreted in reified forms, commodified, and proffered by transnational Islamist militant groups to younger generations of Algerians. For Algerians in France, this is particularly problematic as Islam has been represented as aligned with terrorism since the beginning of the Algerian civil war, and even more acutely in France's post–11 September war on terror. Likewise, a similar process has occurred in the constitution of a Berberist ethnic movement in France, with many second-generation Algerian immigrants today militating for the official recognition of Tamazight on both sides of the Mediterranean. The opposition between various ethnic and religious subjectivities—between Islamist and Berberist groups—is often constituted by both their purveyors and critics as absolute, and it is through the lens of such violent, ideological conflict that alternate conceptions of belonging and allegiance are today being formed among Algerians and Franco-Algerians. This ethnopolitical opposition is played out simultaneously at the domestic, urban, national, and transnational levels.

The processes of collusion and contention, of appropriation and transformation, that link Algeria and France—Algerians and Franco-Algerians—constitute what I refer to as *transpolitics*, a central theme of the book. Transpolitics indicates two parallel characteristics of the postcolonial predicament of contemporary nation-states. Firstly, it points to how processes of and debates over postcolonial immigration and identity cross national borders and chart new spaces of conflict and cosmopolitanism. A growing number of recent theorists have termed such migratory situations "*transnational*," as pointing to and depending on processes of globalization that defy if not destroy the nation-state framework (Appadurai 1996; Schiller et al. 1994). While it would be premature to declare the end of the nation-state as the hegemonic form of global political sovereignty, transpolitics illuminates the fissures that transnational migration opens in nationalism's bundling of people, territory, and politics. It underlines, in other words, the translocal dimensions of all local cultural processes.

Transpolitics further implies that questions of migration and identity not only cross geographic boundaries, but also *transcend* the formal political institutions of state bureaucracies, political parties, and labor unions. The constitution of Berberist and Islamist political subjectivities among second-generation immigrants in France, for instance, depends upon various media and popular cultural forms—from television coverage of the French World Cup victory to Kabyle activist folk songs to Francophone rap albums to Franco-Algerian (or "Beur") novels—that find themselves deterritorialized and subsequently reterritorialized into the cultural politics of the Parisian *cités*. As such, events occurring within the formal political arena join discourses and debates within public institutions, as well as highly informal cultural practices, as equally salient spaces where sentiments of allegiance and loyalty are constituted, where political forms and subjectivities are contested. In other words, rap and graffiti artistry operate alongside urban planning measures and debates over the place of Muslim headscarves in French schools as realms of politics of equal or greater importance in the everyday lives of Franco-Algerians as the official French and Algerian presidential elections of 1995 and 1996. Such forms of transpolitics infuse not only the situation of Algeria in France, but any cosmopolitan context—indeed any cultural form—of contemporary anthropological study.

Coloniality and Postcoloniality

Algerian transpolitics in France engages larger anthropological queries into the cultural logic and social organization of urbanity, transnationality, nationalism, ethnicity, and history. As a historical anthropology, *Algeria in France* extends the historical frame of an ethnographic enterprise that has traditionally prided itself on its presentist stance, on its ability to describe cultural forms and practices as they actually and presently occur. While one can trace the use of historical methods within anthropology back to the discipline's forebears (e.g. Franz Boas, Ruth Benedict, E. E. Evans-Pritchard, and Edmund Leach), only more recently have scholars interrogated the disciplines and methods of anthropology and history as themselves products and instruments of colonial rule (Asad 1973; Axel 2002; Cohn 1987; Comaroff and Comaroff 1992; Etienne and Leacock 1980; Fabian 1983). In the case of Algeria, French sociologists and military ethnographers played essential roles in the incorporation of the colony and the postcolonial integration of the *cités* into a single spatiotemporal structure in the realms of economics, politics, and culture, the elaboration of which has been the condition of possibility for French national construction and reconstruction. At the same time, these scholars—using the techniques of enumeration and categorization (mapping, cadastral surveys, genealogy) employed to consolidate rule and centralize authority—have paradoxically reified the distinctiveness of the groups they studied, establishing their various origins in time and space, and, in so doing, fixing their proximity to or distance from French norms. In the postcolonial period, government integration programs have sought to disaggregate insular immigrant groups by parsing out migrant families according to "generations," focusing on Franco-Algerians of the second generation as the particular objects and agents of cultural mediation and eventual assimilation.

These efforts have provided the fodder for the construction of various non-national immigrant subjectivities in France endowed with their own value and authority. In the early 1980s, Franco-Algerians began to argue in literary productions and political demonstrations that their position was one of permanent liminality between French and Algerian cultures: as postmodern mutant hybrids, or "Beurs." Their declarations of ethnic particularity dovetailed with neo-racist pundits associated with the xenophobic Front National political party, which utilized essentialized models of cultural identity to underwrite calls for exclusion and repatriation. In the contemporary period, Berberist activists have returned to colonial sources to argue for their privileged status simultaneously as autochthones of Algeria and as ur-Mediterraneans sharing an ethnoracial genealogy with the French, and thus as the potential cultural mediators within the Algerian immigrant community. These claims point to the perduring legacy of French colonialism in the contemporary, postcolonial setting.

Nation and Infranation

Tracing postcolonial transformations of colonial categories of ethnic and religious subjectivity, *Algeria in France* builds on theories of nation, ethnicity, and religion as constructed entities (Anderson 1991; Gellner 1983; Hobsbawm 1990; Smith 1986). Pointed national debates over the place of the Islamic headscarf in French schools, or over the construction of mosques in suburban *cités,* for example, indicate not the intolerance of religious difference in France, but rather the production of two particular visions of immigrant religious identity, a production over which the French state and transnational Muslim associations have both collided and colluded. On the one hand, with regard to the Algerian civil war, the government and media have bolstered the image of an internal Islamic terrorist threat. This Islam, associated with the delinquency, petty crime, and drugs of the *banlieues,* is represented by journalists and social scientists as pathological and incommensurable with *laïcité,* capable of erupting at any moment into a full-scale *jihad*. On the other hand, the government has worked with "moderate" Muslim leaders to build a second Islam, an Islam based in individual conviction and private faith that is consonant with the strictures of *laïcité*. This "French Islam" poses no threat to the nation-state because it imposes no boundaries to its adherents becoming fully participating citizens in French public life and, in the end, poses itself as commensurable with any other form of individualized philosophical belief. While neither of these two Islams corresponds exactly to the heterogeny of religious practices in immigrant France, they both outline possibilities for the construction of future religious subjectivities.

In this respect, the ongoing process of French national construction is predicated as much on the production as on the erasure of infranational differences. The ambivalence over the avowal and disavowal of cultural difference has rested at the heart of France's national imaginary, from its imperial heyday to the eve of European integration. This ambivalence is tied to what Michael Herzfeld (1997: 109) has termed "structural nostalgia," the longing for a "time before [national] time" that infuses nationalist ideologies and diacritics. French nationalism, in this respect, has rested not only on invocations of universalist citizenry, but also on particularist social memories of "our ancestors, the Gauls." Policies of assimilation are thus always balanced by nostalgic practices of cultural preservation. As a result, infranational and national categories of belonging remain in permanent dialectical relationship in the historical articulation of the French nation.

Transnational Social Formations

In addition to national and infranational categories of belonging, *Algeria in France* also illuminates how transnational social formations serve to underwrite the production of new political subjectivities that play on the ambivalence of the nation-state's negotiations of local and global dimensions. Diasporic groups and transnational communities have been the subject of important anthropological inquiry since the early 1990s (cf. Appadurai 1996; Clifford 1994; Hannerz 1992; MacGaffey and Bazenguissa-Ganga 2000; Raulin 2000; Rouse 1991; Schiller et al. 1992, 1994; Swedenburg and Lavie 1996; Van der Veer 1995). These studies have acutely demonstrated how the contemporary movements of peoples, commodities, and ideas have called into question the hegemonic authority of the spatially and ethnically bounded nation-state. In the case of Algeria in France, elaborated infranational differences of ethnicity and religion provide the framework for the outlining of new modes of political contestation and new possibilities for the enactment of civil society. From the creation of a charter for a supranational Berber political entity (Tamazgha) to the joint petitioning of the Council of Europe for collective rights by French immigrant and linguistic minority groups of diverse origins, contemporary social movements in France have consciously challenged a state national model predicated on the fungibility of state, territory, and ethnos.

The play, challenge, and flexibility within the nation-state model highlighted by migrant and diasporic groups indicate as much an internal transformation within existing structures—a late nationalism—as they do to a transition to a new mode of sovereignty *tout court*. While the Algerian civil war certainly transcends state borders and reproduces itself in the Algerian diaspora in France, it is more directed at establishing hegemony over the political field of the Algerian nation-state than in elaborating a new, transnational formation. Indeed, the border-crossing war has provided the French state with the excuse to establish even more stringent border controls, as occurred in the aftermath of the 1995 bombings. In the end, the French nation-state has from its foundational moment been in a constant state of negotiation between local and global dimensions of authority.

Urban Anthropology

As transnational social formations challenge the ability of nation-states to control locality, they are themselves constantly sited and resited in identifiable and inhabited places. One of the key sites for Algerian transpolitics has been the urban centers of France. Anthropologies of urban spaces pose particular methodological challenges. Unlike in archetypical ethnographic studies of French village life (Chevallier 1934; Pitt-Rivers 1960; Rogers 1991; Wylie 1957; Zonabend 1980), the Algerian diaspora in France does not constitute a single community bounded in space and time. While there do exist habitation patterns to immigration trends, even the so-called "Arab quarters" in Paris and its environs—e.g. the Goutte d'Or or Saint-Denis—tend to be multiethnic in character and non-contiguous across the urban landscape. This diffusion of immigrant groups has largely resulted from a conscious state urban policy designed to break down communitarian structures and foster socioeconomic integration, as well as from larger tendencies toward neo-local dispersion that broke up multigenerational immigrant households during the 1980s and 1990s.

Following recent studies in urban anthropology (cf. Beriss 1992; Hannerz 1980; Low 1999), *Algeria in France* addresses this methodological problem by focusing on social institutions that underwrite forms of group belonging at a distance. It particularly highlights cultural associations as a salient space where larger identity discourses and transpolitical practices take place. While only a small percentage of the actual Algerian population of Paris are official members of these bodies, Algerian cultural associations in and around Paris are nonetheless privileged forums for the expression of community identity and unity. The associations function as centers of ritual performance, with the associations acting as sponsors of celebrations of 'Aid, Yennayer, and other Muslim and Berber holy days. They further act as self-appointed political agents for Algerians in France, rallying people in marches, demonstrations, elections, and commemorations of historically significant dates. At the same time, the associations play a social role in local neighborhood development, acting as mediators between residents and municipal officials and providing after-school day care, adult education, and sports clubs. In the end, these institutions exist as nexuses where various kinds of identity based on culture and locality are expressed and demonstrated. As such they have served as key sites for the emergence of immigrant actors onto the public stage.

The book's attention to associations and public cultural displays exists alongside a larger ethnographic attention to quotidian and domestic spaces in which Algerian subjectivities are produced and consumed in and around Paris. Visits to informants' homes, discussions in cafés or over prepared meals, participation in local sports activities, and personal interviews balanced the more institutionalized aspects of the field research. As a foreign researcher, my belonging to the neighborhoods in Paris, Aubervilliers, and Pantin where I lived and researched was always circumspect and ambivalently accepted. For as much as I became a regular presence, if not an active participant, in local cafés, gyms, and association meetings, my outsider status was occasionally made viscerally clear. On more than one occasion I was excluded from strategic political or minutely personal discussions and, in one case, even violently attacked by several youths hailing from the *cité* adjoining where I lived in Pantin. As a male outsider, my access to domestic spaces, particularly those with older fathers and unmarried daughters, was limited; it is not by pure chance that the vast majority of my interviewees were either age-mates, men, or married women. Moreover, as many of my interlocutors were politically active on one or another side of the Mediterranean, or were residing in France in a tenuous immigration status, interviews often had to overcome a thick patina of initial suspicion. During one interview with a Berber cultural activist, a Kabyle friend who happened to be present upbraided me for writing the actual nickname of my interviewee rather than a pseudonym. The latter, however, laughed off my faux pas, bragging that I could feel free to use his name, "as everyone knows what I have to say."

In this respect, being American—and thus an *étranger* to France like many of the immigrants with whom I was working—actually proved to facilitate my research, as it tangibly distinguished me from the panoply of French sociologists studying the *cités*, whom many residents believed to be agents of the state. Indeed, in spite of the recent media hype over the rise of anti-Semitism among France's North African populations (cf. Brenner 2003), being *Jewish*-American in the end proved to be an unexpected boon. I had been initially reluctant to divulge my Jewish background to my Muslim interlocutors, less because of any presumption of their incipient anti-Semitism than because of my fears of being associated with a Zionist history that had proved historically detrimental to Arab nationalist aspirations. Only later did I realize that Berber cultural activists in France actually deployed Israel as a positive example of an ethnolinguistic movement that succeeded in territorializing itself into a nation-state. Indeed, when I finally revealed my ancestry to Mounir, a Kabyle friend and key interlocutor, during a well-lubricated dinner in his Argenteuil apartment, he smiled knowingly. "I knew it all along. I could tell in how you talked and thought. I could sense that we had certain Oriental traits in common, unlike the French."

The book, while not an ethnography of Franco-Algerian associations or domestic life per se, does nonetheless draw directly on my participant observation in these sites. It explicitly attempts to link these local sites for the production and consumption of subjectivity to the larger transpolitical discourses and processes in which they are embedded. As a result, it tacks back and forth between formalized expressions of political agency and the everyday practices in which such cultural politics is diffused, attempting to reach the overdetermined "cultural complexity" that Ulf Hannerz (1992) identifies with world cities like Paris. In its conscious addressing of material and sources—including media reports, academic treatises, billboard advertising, and novels—that transcend the realms of immediate ethnographic expertise, and in its continual movement between the historical past and the ethnographic present, *Algeria in France* seeks to provide a historically informed, urban anthropology of such cultural complexity.

Organization of Chapters

With its focus on the production and consumption of Algerian and Franco-Algerian subjectivities, the book is organized topically, elaborating on individual categories of belonging—citizenship, ethnicity, locality, religion, and generation—as embedded within larger transpolitical discourses and practices. It thus refrains from the unilinear narrative that is characteristic of many earlier works on "Algerians in France" that trace the historical evolution of the immigrant community from Algerian villages to the French *cités* (cf. Costa-Lascoux and Temime 1985; Gillette and Sayad 1976; Zehraoui 1994). While these works are invaluable in providing the groundwork from which a critical analysis of French immigration and integration policies can be accomplished, they tend to elide the perduring colonial character of French postcoloniality as well as the density of physical and ideological connections that unite Algeria and France transnationally. Attempting to account for this larger situation of transpolitics, each chapter in this book traces a particular genealogy of Algerian belonging in France. In order to illustrate how these categories of belonging inform individual lives, each chapter likewise begins with a brief character sketch drawn from interviews conducted over the course of fieldwork. All names, except where otherwise indicated, are pseudonyms.

Chapter 1 presents the story of Algerian subjectivity in France as one of a historical production of "immigration" as a political category within a changing Europe. It details how Algerian migration became a point of widespread public debate in France after the economic downturn of 1973, and how since 1981 the public discourse on immigration has shifted from unemployment to multiculturalism to Islam and, with the outbreak of the Algerian civil war, to terrorism. With a more general focus on the intersection between academic studies of migration and national policies of immigrant integration, the chapter traces the development of alternative models of universal and cultural citizenship. Indeed, it argues that immigration is a prime site on which debates over the future of the nation-state within a unifying Europe take place.

Chapter 2 examines Algerian subjectivity in respect to the colonial constitution of ethnic and national divides within France and Algeria, paying particular attention to the reification of a Berber/Arab dichotomy that has conditioned contemporary identity politics. Taking the colonial elaboration of the "Kabyle Myth" as its starting point, the chapter interrogates the relationship between colonial, national, and regional integration projects. From 1830 to Algerian independence in 1962, military ethnographers and linguists collaborated with the colonial state in detailing a particular Berber tribal identity independent of the larger Arab polity in Algeria. Since independence, conflicting interest groups in Algeria and France have appropriated this identity alternately to justify politics of Arabization, national integration, and Kabyle autochthonous rights. The chapter argues that the production of the national and transnational formations has always entailed the elaboration rather than the erasure of ethnic, racial, and religious differences.

Chapter 3 explores how Algerian subjectivity in France has been determined in and through spatializing practices of domestic arrangement and urban planning that produce locality. Beginning with a discussion of the *axxam*, Pierre Bourdieu's "Kabyle House," as a space of structural nostalgia, the chapter analyzes urbanization policies in the colony and metropole that have produced peripheral neighborhoods in the French suburbs and endowed them with a particular cultural distance from French social norms. In the postcolonial period, the ultra-modern built environment of the *banlieues*, the product of ordering and hegemonic spatializing practices, replaced the *axxam* as the foil against which French conceptions of order and civilization posit themselves. This movement reflects a dialectic of centralization and peripheralization, of circulation and containment, by which categories of town and country, metropole and periphery, become structurally valorized. Within this history of capital- and nation-building processes, Algerian immigrants and Franco-Algerians have constructed alternate spatial totalities on the embers of built and destroyed forms, endowing them with frameworks of value and hierarchy not necessarily isomorphic with those projected by grand-scale urbanization plans.

Chapter 4 focuses on how Algerian subjectivity in France is gendered and embodied through two conflicting modes of integration *qua* social reproduction—religion and sports—over which the state, immigrant actors, and multinational corporations compete and collude. Conflicts over the legitimacy of sports and religious practices simultaneously involve localizable debates concerning the place of Muslim headscarves in French *laïcité,* as well as larger fears over the rise of a global Islamist insurgency operating in the French *banlieues.* However, in deploying sports programs to combat this Islam deemed incommensurable with the French nation-state, the French state ironically provides the practical means through which immigrant groups can reproduce themselves and attract new adherents. Rather than being erased in the social reproduction of the French nation, alternate categories of religious belonging are continually mobilized for the engendering of social totalities and hierarchies constituted largely through bodily practice.

Chapter 5 approaches Franco-Algerian subjectivity through an exploration of generational identity and conflict between immigrant parents and children. It demonstrates how agnatic ties, both actual and symbolic, are produced and reproduced in Algeria and France, and how such modes of generation have not been simply replaced by the socializing institutions of the modern French state, but rather operate alongside them. Elaborating a particular liminal second-generation identity, the Beur Movement of the early 1980s outlined a space for Franco-Algerian political agency. In the process, it challenged the ties between parents and children, resisting and even reversing processes of cultural transmission. In the 1990s, Beur social actions and cultural associations have been replaced by ones based in Islamist and Berberist political projects, forging explicit transnational links between Algeria and France.

Chapter 6 recounts the same history of generational identity and agency through the lens of Beur and post-Beur writing. Through their semi-autobiographical literary productions, Franco-Algerian authors narrated their cultural identity and outlined political subjectivity. In gradually coming to terms with their parents' original immigration and the colonial experience in Algeria, these writers by the 1990s narratively realigned their identity politics away from a localized culturalism and toward an embracing of their diasporic situation. With this shift, they radically redefined their subject position in postcolonial France, becoming spokespeople for the Algerian transnation as a whole. Writing thus constitutes one of the central practices in the contemporary articulation of challenges to the hegemonic political and cultural authority of the French and Algerian nation-states.

Finally, Chapter 7 discusses the implications of these new narrations for the expression of a political culture that increasingly premises itself on a critique of the nation-state as the hegemonic form of geopolitical sovereignty. On the one hand, the enactment of the Algerian civil war in France by Islamist and Berberist groups has resulted in the foundation of a transnational social formation that traverses the Mediterranean. On the other hand, Franco-Algerian transnational political projects have turned toward Europe, with Algerians in France forging reciprocal ties of solidarity with other migrant and regional groups to petition the supranational institutions of the "New Europe" for cultural and linguistic rights. While these struggles have not implied the end of the French nation-state, they have nonetheless challenged the unilineal ties that bind French citizens to French territory under the French republic. In this sense, the terms through and about which the contemporary French *Kulturkampf* is waged must be viewed as a particular historical moment in a paradigmatic ambivalence by both states and citizens over the espousal and disavowal of cultural heterogeneity.

Of course, no study, in spite of its attention to the historical dimensions of the present, can fully capture the changing reality that marks contemporary France. While the flows that unite Algeria to France are a particularly salient transnational dimension to the postcolonial cultural predicament facing the French nation-state, they are by no means the only elements at play. With the establishment of a borderless and single-currency Europe, French transpolitics are increasingly aligned to its European partners and further distanced from its imperial legacy across the Mediterranean. Likewise, the post–11 September global war on terror—in spite of clear divergences between American and European interests—threatens to make a reality of reified and essentialist notions of a "clash of civilizations" and create tangible as well as ideological borders between the "West" and "the rest." Nonetheless, even these geopolitical transformations remain enmeshed in a *longue durée* of colonial violence and postcolonial ambitions, and, as the pages that follow elaborate, these structural and historical conflicts weigh, as Marx (1963: 15) would have it, "like a nightmare on the brain of the living."

As anthropologists, we are in a privileged position to study the global present, to trace the colonial roots and everyday enactments of contemporary struggle. While we may be tempted to retreat to our boweries of areal specialization, we can no longer escape the fact that our objects of study are in every case influenced, if not determined, by events and processes of a world magnitude. If the globe has not become the village of Marshall McLuhan's fantasies, anthropology's villages have certainly become global. The particular Franco-Algerian transpolitics studied in *Algeria in France* are but one reflection of larger struggles between various cosmopolitan and particularist modes of belonging that mark the ambivalence, as well as violence, of modernity.

1 /

Immigration Politics in the New Europe

Siblings Gilles-Salah and Sonya were born and raised in France to foreign-born parents. Their mother Monique was born in England to a French mother and British father, but moved to Paris to work as a translator after finishing her university education. Farid, their father, was born in Algeria and came to France to attend university at the end of the war in Algeria and had stayed on to work as an economist at the Organization of Economic Cooperation and Development in Paris. It was there that he and Monique met and married. After ten years of marriage the couple divorced. Farid returned to Algeria and married a woman from his natal village; Monique moved to Geneva with the couple's two children. After their parents' divorce, Gilles-Salah and Sonya spent their school years in France and later Geneva with their mother and their summer vacations in Algeria with their father and his family, until his premature death from cancer in 1990. Gilles-Salah and Sonya were still living in Geneva when I last saw them together in June 1995.

I first met Gilles-Salah in 1993 while I was studying Arabic in Damascus, Syria. In his late twenties, he had just moved to Beirut and was seeking work as a French teacher; he spent his weekends in Damascus visiting my German housemate Kristina. He and Kristina had lived together the previous year in Cairo where he had been working at the French consulate and she had been a student. At that time, he introduced himself to people as "Gilles," and it was only much later that I learned that his family called him "Salah." On his weekend visits to Damascus, he would spend time with Kristina; me;

a fellow Franco-Algerian student, Franck; Franck's Moroccan girl-friend Salima; and Gilles's best friend Mohammed, an Algerian political refugee in Cairo. It was an intimate group and we spent many summer weekend evenings embroiled in animated discussions in French on the politics of France and North Africa over numerous packs of cigarettes and bottles of beer. At the end of the summer, the mini-salon broke up. Mohammed returned to Cairo, Franck and Salima returned to Paris, Kristina went on to London for a master's degree in Middle Eastern studies, and Gilles moved back to live with his mother in Geneva, having tried unsuccessfully to find work in Beirut.

While the group never reformed, Gilles and I stayed in touch. He regularly came to Paris where I was living to visit me and his French cousins. I likewise visited him in Geneva and met his family. His mother was working for the United Nations High Commissioner on Refugees and had remarried a Jewish-American man who worked as an engineer for a technology company in Geneva. Together they had a daughter, who was the only one in the household to hold Swiss citizenship. In similar fashion, Gilles-Salah's older sister, Sonya, also living in Geneva, had married a Russian man who had migrated to Switzerland with his parents and brother as a young child, and had a young daughter with him. Inspired by their multinational family situation and an around-the-world honeymoon, Sonya and her husband had founded an umbrella cultural association in 1993 to foster intercultural dialogue among the various national and ethnic communities living in Geneva. "Upon returning from our trip, we were struck that Geneva—a city with 50 percent of the population coming from elsewhere—had hundreds of functioning immigrant associations but no communication between them. What relation-ships that existed were marked by stereotypes and mistrust." In addition to maintaining a newsletter and electronic mailing list to apprise association members of various changes in municipal laws of relevance to the larger migrant and refugee community, the associa-tion hosts a yearly cultural festival. Supported with municipal funds, the festival highlights the cultural diversity of Geneva, with partici-pating associations presenting their national heritage and local struggles in the form of informational lectures, music, material cul-ture, and food and drink for sale to a visiting public. The June 1995 event I observed and participated in hosted forty different associa-tions representing migrant and refugee communities from Morocco, Turkey, Kurdistan, Western Sahara, Eritrea, Brazil, Vietnam, Tibet, Galicia, Andalusia, Portugal, and Lebanon, among others. Although the festival was primarily a money-making activity through which associations could fund their yearly activities, many of the groups also treated the event as having a pedagogical purpose, alerting passersby to their efforts at rain forest conservancy, school building, and orphanage funding in the regions they represented.

The association has continued to operate since 1995, though

Sonya and her husband have passed on its organization to younger activists. Gilles-Salah, in spite of incredible efforts, failed to find permanent work in Geneva, in part because of the economic situation, in part because of his lack of Swiss citizenship. He became increasingly disenchanted with everyday life in Geneva, which, in spite of its large foreign population, struck him as a cold, bourgeois, "Germanic" city. This feeling was exacerbated by several episodes of anti-Arab racism he experienced while looking for a job and apartment. Depressed, he became increasingly attracted to the discipline of Muslim orthopraxy. He stopped drinking, started referring to himself exclusively as "Salah," and for the first time in his life began to pray. In the meantime, he sought a job as a French teacher abroad, and the last I heard from him had accepted a posting in Cambodia.

In late May 2000, on the eve of France's accession to presidency of the European Union (EU), a minor political scandal erupted that laid bare a set of tensions between national identity and supranational governance in the New Europe. Responding to German Foreign Minister Joschka Fischer's project for a "federal Europe," French center-left Interior Minister Jean-Pierre Chevènement accused Germany of "still dreaming of a German Holy Roman Empire," of having "not been cured of the derailment that Nazism represented in its history." Chevènement continued his 21 May public address on France 2 television by invoking a stereotyped distinction between French and German national identity: "Germany has a conception of the nation that is that of the *Volk,* that is, an ethnic conception. We need to help it forge another idea of the nation, the idea of a citizen's nation." "It's the republican identity against the ethnic conception," Chevènement added later that day, speaking at a conference organized by his Citizens Movement (*Mouvement des Citoyens*) political party (*Le Monde* 23 May 2000).

These statements, needless to say, drew deep criticism from across the French political spectrum, with Chevènement's leftist allies (including Socialist Prime Minister Lionel Jospin and the former May 1968 militant turned Green Party representative to the EU, Daniel Cohn-Bendit) and conservative opponents (including ex-President Valéry Giscard d'Estaing and former Interior Minister Charles Pasqua) alike espousing pro-Europe positions and forcing Chevènement to submit a public apology within twenty-four hours. However, the speech and the swift reaction it provoked are telling of a set of unresolved issues over the place of France in a unified Europe. More than historically grounded fears over German economic, political, and territorial aggression, Chevènement's Euroskeptic statements reflected a more profound set of anxieties over the political cultural makeup (or breakup) of the French nation-state. While the invocation of German ethnic nationalism and French republican citizenship as binary opposites represents a hegemonic, taken-for-granted idea in the French popular political imaginary, it actually belies internal tensions between particularist and universalist formulations of Frenchness. In other words, worries over the nature of citizenship and sovereignty in the New Europe mask equally profound concerns over the nature of cultural and political belonging in France—concerns that are intimately tied to the "problem" of postcolonial immigration and identity.

In order to understand the contemporary transpolitics of Algerians in France, it is necessary to trace larger transformations of immigration and national identity across Europe since the end of the Second World War. For the postcolonial politics surrounding the status of Algerians as French citizens (juridical and cultural) is mirrored by similar predicaments of "Blacks" in Britain, Turks in Germany, and "Asians" in the Netherlands. Issues of racism and anti-racism, integration and multiculturalism, state intervention and minority activism, that are central to this book are themselves transnational phenomena, occurring simultaneously across a larger space that unites European metropoles to their former colonial peripheries. Not operating in isolation, Algerians in France—as immigrants, ethnic minorities, and Muslims—have maintained an open dialogue with other groups across this transnational space in the formulation and enactment of their political and economic struggles. And as the internal borders of Europe are erased, such transpolitical solidarity becomes all the more tightly drawn. In this respect, questions regarding immigration and citizenship, regarding particularist ("ethnic") and universalist ("republican") conceptions of the nation-state within a New Europe, are both the necessary background to and the ultimate site of inquiry of this book.

Immigration and European Identity

As the last pieces of the Maastricht Treaty fall into place and the possibilities of an economically, socially, and politically unified Europe, first envisioned in 1956, approach proximate reality, the question of transnational, north-south migration takes on an increasingly pressing importance. Although labor immigration was officially halted in most Western European countries following the 1973–1974 oil embargo and subsequent economic crisis, migrations in the forms of tourism, political asylums, and clandestine border crossings have continued apace. European states for decades considered "countries of emigration," such as Italy and Spain, found themselves by the 1990s joining the ranks of Germany, France, and Britain as "countries of immigration," although even these latter states, notably Germany, were reluctant to admit their relatively new (post-WWII) status.

Moreover, these demographic concerns quickly leapt into the political arena. Since the early 1980s, with the political and cultural mobilizations of those immigrants and their children already settled in the territories, issues concerning the place of ethnicity and race in European countries have entered into political debates as a "problem" of national importance. Constructed as a zero-sum game of "control or invasion" or "integration or crisis" (cf. Böhning 1991), immigration has attained an almost unprecedented status as the one issue on which every viable political candidate must have an opinion, if not a well-formulated policy. For instance, the 1996 and 2002 displacement of the French Socialist Party (PS) in favor of conservative and extreme right political candidates—with the xenophobic Front National leader Jean-Marie Le Pen advancing to the second round of the latter election ahead of outgoing PS Prime Minister Jospin—represents not only the populace's anxieties concerning France's place in a post–Cold War, unified Europe, but also its discontent with the PS's continual vacillations on questions of border controls, internal security, and national (cultural) integration. Despite the rhetoric to the contrary, political rivals have found themselves curiously converging on most immigration policies when it comes to putting them into practice (Hammar 1990; Schnapper 1992).

Furthermore, these concerns have not remained solely on an official or political level, but have manifested themselves in the everyday practices of housing, education, and, above all, racism. Although neo-Nazi attacks on interned political refugees in a reunited Germany have received heavy media attention on both sides of the Atlantic, most incidents of racism (violent or not) across Western Europe are approached with a quasi-total institutional reticence.[1] In a parallel manner, "anti-racist" groups have burgeoned throughout Europe, allying themselves with church, socialist, and human-rights organizations that assert the rights of immigrants to civil liberties and cultural expression. However, these groups have found themselves walking on dangerous ground as a cultural "new racism" has co-opted their discourse on the "right to difference" (the well-known slogan of Harlem Désir's French SOS-Racisme movement) to promulgate ideologies of ethnic absolutism and repatriation (Barker 1981; Balibar and Wallerstein 1991; Gilroy 1991; Schain et al. 2002; Taguieff 1991). In response, many of these groups have fallen back on the "right to resemblance," thus reworking the ground of assimilation and acculturation they had previously criticized. In this atmosphere of strange bedfellows and appropriated discourse, anti-racism has perhaps reached its end as an effective political strategy (Gilroy 1990).

Likewise, the scholarly literature on the immigration phenomenon has found itself trapped in a similar set of dichotomies. As Maxim Silverman (1992) has suggested, works that pose the issues in terms of binary oppositions between individual and collective immigration/integration, between universalistic and particularistic official responses, risk reinforcing an either/or proposition which poses the migrants as either perpetrators or victims of the "problem." Indeed, the literature on migration has been largely structured by common tropes and oppositions of security/insecurity and

European Passport Against Racism. Produced by the
associations France-Libertés and the Fondation
Danielle Mitterrand. The information inside the
"passport" defines racist acts and provides instruc-
tions on what to do should one be a victim of racism.
It also includes an oath: "I . . . , citizen of Europe,
wish to live in a Europe of Citizens, a space of
tolerance and hospitality where the law of the
European Convention on Human Rights applies."

natural/artificial that have served as often as not to situate immigrant populations as external challenges to the nation-state in question.

Moreover, such scholarly works are often appropriated by political
agents to lend support to certain policy decisions. Since the early 1960s, the
International Labor Office, World Bank, and Organization of Economic
Cooperation and Development (OECD) have focused a large part of their

efforts on the "problem" of international labor migration. These supranational institutions have funded research projects, organized conferences, and published statistical yearbooks to provide data to their member nations to aid regulation and policy decisions. In this respect, scholarly works on migration represent timely interventions into an overdetermined polemic, and deserve treatment as historical documents in and of themselves.

A genealogy of the category of "migration" is thus a necessary prelude to any understanding of the political stakes of migration in general. While bureaucratic state structures generally make a distinction between "immigration" and "immigrant" policies (cf. Hammar 1985), this dichotomy fails to account for immigration as a total social phenomenon and tends to result in a historical narrative antipathetic to contemporary struggles by immigrant and minority groups in Europe today. Questions of nationalism and racism, issues of paramount importance given the number of violent conflicts in the name of "culture" and "nation" throughout contemporary Europe and its postcolonial periphery, transcend categories that separate "immigrant" from "native" populations. If nothing else, the apocalyptic linkage of immigration to terrorism, disease, and economic catastrophe within the popular political imagination indicates that a veritable crisis is perceived in the presumed natural progression of universal history as defined by the political and economic ideals of Euro-American modernity. Immigration, in other words, is a primary site on which the putative "clash of civilizations" takes place (Huntington 1996).

"The Immigration Problem"

Since the mid-1970s, international migration to Europe has been a phenomenon of substantial political and economic importance to politicians and their constituencies. More often than not, these movements of peoples, commodities, and ideas from the postcolonial periphery to metropole have been represented, within party programs and scholarly literatures alike, as novel, unnatural, and potentially threatening to European host societies. Government policies have moreover tended to treat immigration as an economic factor that can be controlled, manipulated, or even embraced—as an economic problem to be solved.

Since the late 1960s, immigration has been largely approached in terms of state policy through a macro-model of economic factors, a push-pull system resulting from income differentials. According to this schema, development in peripheral countries created a situation of overurbanization (especially in terms of a disproportionately large tertiary sector) characterized by overpopulation and unemployment, thus reproducing the countries' poverty. At the same time, until 1973, postwar Europe experienced a situation of both high growth and underemployment. Labor migrants merely responded to these factors, being driven from their home countries in the postcolonial periphery and drawn to Western metropoles, a "permanent attraction of higher living standards and earning power" (Power 1979: 24).

According to this schema, migrants act implicitly as rational actors, as homo economicus *par excellence*. Migrants approach their migration as purely instrumental, a means to economic and political ends—"a means to gather income, income that can be taken back to his or her home community and used to fulfill or enhance his or her role within that social structure" (Piore 1979: 54). Working under these economistic assumptions, European states established a number of international institutions to quantify and predict the workings of this system of economic exchanges that migrants represented. A 1983 World Bank project, for instance, developed an "Integrated Computer-Based Manpower Forecasting Model" which could compile worldwide data into an easily accessible format (Serageldin et al. 1983). Likewise, the OECD, a supranational agency bringing together industrialized nations in North America and Western Europe, has established a migration-watch group that bills itself as a "permanent observation system" (*système d'obsérvation permanente*) and provides annual data on recent migration developments to each of its member states (SOPEMI 1992). These elaborated technologies and techniques have not only reinforced the notion of immigrant populations as immanently external and exchangeable (as "birds of passage" [Piore 1979]), but also, in their establishment of an expanded system of surveillance, construed the immigrant as a potential threat to the economic and political health of the modern nation-state.

Yet immigration takes place within a larger "world system" of economic exchange and exploitation. From this perspective, international migration does not merely represent the sum total of the calculated decisions made by individual actors, but rather needs to be understood as a structural feature of late capitalism. Rather than free choice, migration is the end result of a succession of colonial and neo-colonial economic and political violences inflicted upon the poorest populations, "uprooted" from their lifestyles and displaced from their homes (Bourdieu and Sayad 1964; Castles 1984; Jacques 1985). Labor migration thus proves integral to processes of capital accumulation, as it allows for the reproduction of labor power to occur outside of capital's concern, in the periphery of "developing" nations, hence making immigrant labor more profitable than domestic labor (Meillassoux 1981). Moreover, the flexibility of labor provided by the temporary worker migrations provided European industries with an "industrial reserve army," allowing them to quickly Taylorize their production processes while at the same time disempowering the workers by minimizing skills and wages through "tasking." Immigrant labor arguably provided the conditions of possibility for France's postwar boom (Castles 1984; Talha 1989).

Approaching migration through the lens of capitalism provides a particularly salient and critical way to understand the place of the "immigrant" within larger (political economic) structural anxieties affecting the French nation-state today. It offers a critique of taken-for-granted rational choice models that assume a universal capitalist actor across all societies. However, such a structural Marxist approach tends to deny migrants agency, treating them as pawns of larger-than-life structural forces (Silverman 1992). It tends, in other words, to reproduce the very categories of capitalist ideology: capital and labor, as transhistorical actors. As Marshall Sahlins has argued, "World Systems theory becomes the superstructural expression of the very imperialism it despises" (1988: 3). Immigration, while clearly a central factor within larger economic and political configurations, needs to be understood as a structured form of cultural practice accomplished by social actors with their own, non-universalizable intentions.

"The Immigrant Problem"

Since the early 1980s, the European discourse on immigration has shifted in accordance with the growing settled nature of Europe's immigrant populations due to the increase in family reunification and the decrease in voluntary return migration in the 1960s and 1970s. European governments have increasingly focused on immigrants alternately as social actors or victims within the metropole. While this has not signaled the end of economistic approaches to immigration per se, it does indicate that immigration is now more generally regarded in relationship to society as a whole, and not just to its economic health. In fact, the first controls placed on immigration were not solely or directly in response to the economic slowdown of the late 1960s, but rather they were created out of a concern over the "ethnic balance" and social tensions surrounding the settled immigrants (Silverman 1992). These controls were established according to notions of a "tipping point" (*seuil de tolérance*) above which a class, ethnic, or racial minority would provoke a negative psychological reaction from the host population (MacMaster 1991). Government policies, newspaper stories, and academic studies focused on immigration through related issues of worker relations, housing conditions, and, for anti-racists, violence directed against the immigrants. In France, such topics have underwritten contemporary concerns over the creation of "ethnic minorities" and their "isolation" in Anglo-American-style "ghettos" (cf. Schnapper 1992).

By the 1980s, however, the crux of the immigration debate in France had shifted once again, this time centering on the second-generation immigrant youth who, for both the right and left, became a potent symbol for the "problem" of immigration. A series of official governmental reports were directed at questions of delinquency, education, and identity "crises" among immigrant youth, issues which were simultaneously addressed by a number of scholarly studies (Abou-Sada and Millet 1986; Aïssou 1987; CCI 1984; Gaspard and Servan-Schreiber 1984; Jazouli 1986). The overriding image within this discourse was the North African immigrant youths (or "Beurs"), caught between the culture of their parents and that of the surrounding society, unable to achieve the latter without forgoing the former. Such an assumed process of acculturation always seemed to involve psychological if not physical violence.

Since the 1990s, these concerns over societal health were expanded to encompass the nation-state as a cultural form and a political unit of sovereignty: it was not just the immigrant youth but the nation writ large that was in the midst of an identity crisis. In France, such formulations were prompted by the so-called "headscarf affair" (*l'affaire du foulard islamique*), the 1989 expulsion of three French-Moroccan girls from a public school outside Paris for wearing Islamic *hijab*s to class, as well as similar controversies that questioned the place of Islam in French society (Beriss 1990). The media uproar and public debate which ensued surprised observers less than the ideological reshuffling which this event prompted; traditional liberals rubbed shoulders with arch-conservatives and the most outspoken antiracists found their arguments co-opted by ideologues of the "new racism." In this climate, "nationality," "nationalism," and "citizenship" became salient keywords in a public debate that engaged politicians, pundits, and intellectuals alike (cf. Safran 1991). In the end, what was at issue was the role of the nation-state in a unifying Europe.

One important way to approach this tension between nationalism and citizenship is through an examination of the relationships between "immigrant policies" and juridical definitions of nationality in the broader European context. These relationships have generally been characterized by a set of ideologically charged distinctions: the nationalism of German romanticism as opposed to the republicanism of the French revolution, *jus sanguinis* citizenship policies as opposed to *jus soli* models (cf. Bauböck 1991; Brubaker 1992; Hammar 1990, 1985). Internally more ambivalent and differentiated than they first appear, these national distinctions have been progressively challenged by the new hegemony of a transnational regime of migrant incorporation based on notions of cultural rights and underwritten by the European Union (Soysal 1994). Nonetheless, differences in citizenship policies still persist and remain salient as markers of national tensions within the new Europe. Germany and Switzerland, Britain and Sweden, and France in this respect pose three competing models for the future European nation-state.

Germany and Switzerland have generally followed a juridical model that treated all foreign populations resident on their soil as temporary. Both Germany and Switzerland established well-organized labor recruitment policies in the post–World War II years based on a system of rotation. In West Germany, this consisted of a series of bilateral agreements beginning in 1955 with a number of southern European and Mediterranean countries (Italy, Spain, Greece, Turkey, Morocco, Portugal, Yugoslavia) for short-term contracts. This guest-worker (*Gastarbeiter*) system replaced the industrial labor force either coerced during the Nazi war effort or supplied by refugees from Soviet-controlled East Germany in the immediate postwar years (approximately twelve million crossed the relatively permeable border). Likewise, in Switzerland, government officials supported and encouraged a system of cross-border day and seasonal workers. In both cases, then, the presence of "foreigners" was designed to accord directly with the economic needs of the countries; the guest workers were not legally allowed to become part of the permanent population.

For this reason, even in the contemporary situation where migrant workers have taken up permanent residence in the countries, the German and Swiss states have generally refused to acknowledge that they have become "countries of immigration." Both governments have been slow to institute "immigrant policies" as such, relying on employers to provide housing and subsistence wages according to Taylorist models of economic organization (Hammar 1985). Moreover, despite the plethora of social categories and distinctions in legal membership in Germany (*Gastarbeiter, Arbeitnehmer, Ausländer, Migranten, Asylanten*), concepts of "immigrant community" and "ethnic minority" are largely missing. Operating according to the racialized ideology of *jus sanguinis* (the right of blood legitimated in Article 116 of the Basic Law), Germany officialized the overriding distinction between ethnic Germans (*Volksdeutsch*) and others.

In this respect, recent popular fears over "*Überfremdung*" (overforeignization) have been framed in terms of the oft-heard racialized statement: "There will soon be too many people, but too few Germans" (quoted in Wilpert 1991). On the one hand, migrations of *Aussiedler* (ethnic Germans from Eastern Europe) and *Übersiedler* from the former East Germany have generally been supported by the German government with housing subsidies, language-training programs, and assured access to German citizenship. On the other hand, long-term "foreign" residents of Germany (notably Turks) have been consistently denied most civil rights and voting privileges. "There is no recognition of a right to membership for persons who were invited as guest workers and who have lived over three generations in the country" (Wilpert 1991: 58). The government of Chancellor Helmut Kohl even introduced schemes for the repatriation of non–European Community (EC) migrants in 1982–83, though these programs were considered more of a symbolic move to appease an anxious electorate than a sound economic measure.

By the 1990s, however, this *jus sanguinis* system showed signs of liberalization. In 1990, the center-right coalition government introduced a new "Foreign Law" that eased the path to naturalization for second- and third-generation foreign residents (Bischoff and Teubner 1990). In 1999, the newly elected socialist government of Chancellor Gerhard Schröder amended the laws on citizenship to allow for the automatic granting of citizenship to third-generation residents, the easing of the residence requirements for naturalization, and the allowance for double nationality.[2] In the meantime, however, these "foreigners" have continued to suffer overt racial attacks from extreme right groups, incidents which have increased since unification and have often gone unprosecuted (Wilpert 1991). This anti-foreigner climate was reinforced by the government's 1993 tightening of the Basic Law's liberal Article 16 that formerly gave right of political asylum to all those reaching Germany. In this respect, if Germany is indeed moving toward a transnationally generalized *jus soli* approach to migrant incorporation (Soysal 1994), it has not relinquished the paramount distinction between *Volksdeutch* and others.

By contrast, Britain and Sweden appear to be diametrically opposed to Germany. While the two countries differ greatly in terms of the role of the state in migrant incorporation (Soysal 1994: 66–75), neither of them pursued a formalized system of worker recruitment nor tied immigration policy directly to economic concerns (Hammar 1985). They both favored granting permanent status to immigrants and generally allowed for family reunification. As early as the 1960s, Sweden had developed a sophisticated "immigrant policy" which provided for basic living necessities and took steps toward assuring equality for all the country's residents. Britain as well has been praised by anti-racists for its tough anti-discrimination laws (cf. Sivinandan 1993). Moreover, both Sweden and Britain have taken steps to preserve the ethnic differences of their immigrant populations. While both countries have allowed the ethnic groups to develop more or less independently, Sweden has progressed beyond Britain in taking active, state-directed measures to either teach immigrant languages in public schools or establish special schools for immigrant children. Finally, both countries have pursued relatively liberal enfranchisement programs, granting many non-citizens voting rights in local, state, and even, in the case of Britain, national elections after only three to five years of residence.

Britain and Sweden have nonetheless remained entrenched in a scheme which has traditionally linked nationality to citizenship in European nation-states. The vast majority of immigrants to Sweden come from neighboring Nordic countries (primarily Finland), thus largely eliding anxieties around purportedly incommensurable "racial" and religious differences that have provided fodder for the "neo-racist" cannon in other Western European countries. Nonetheless, a series of racialized attacks against Africans, Asians, and Arabs in the 1990s did provoke a national debate over the future of the country's policies. Similarly, Britain's liberal policies of free migration and access to civil rights have generally only applied to those migrants from the Commonwealth, the so-called "patrials." The 1971 Immigration Act officially ended the right of entry for citizens of ex-colonies, requiring them to obtain special visas. In addition, the 1981 Nationality Act further differentiated the levels of belonging in British society, effectively creating three classes of citizenship which reified *jus sanguinis* as the basis of nationality. Finally, the 1988 Immigration Act strengthened this revision, making deportation a more readily available option for immigration officials (Allen and Macey 1990). In this way, Britain and Sweden are also caught in the polemics of supporting democracy while defending racialized constructions of "British" or "Swedish" national identity.

Finally, the French state generally portrays itself as pursuing an immigration policy somewhere between the German and Swedish models. While France has had a longer history (since the beginning of the twentieth century) of organized recruitment of colonial labor, it was never able to set up a state-directed guest worker system in the post–World War II era. Instead, its employers tended to directly recruit workers themselves or use undocumented laborers (*les sans-papiers*). Furthermore, while at first relying on employers to provide housing and services for the putatively temporary workers, the government later responded to the growth of permanent shantytowns (*bidonvilles*) on the outskirts of its metropolises with the building of public housing (HLM) blocks and the establishment of various "immigrant" services. Moreover, unlike either Germany (which virtually refuses to acknowledge permanent immigrant communities) or England and Sweden (which underwrite ethnic differences), France has to a great extent maintained an assimilationist approach in its immigrant policies. Fleeting experiments in multicultural education and pro-immigrant quota systems, despite their initial support by the socialist government in the early 1980s, have since received volatile criticism from almost all fronts, with most politicians fearing that any support given to immigrant community–based initiatives will result in the creation of ethnic ghettos, if not ethnic separatism.[3]

While generally following a *jus sanguinis* approach to nationality, French laws have implicitly supported *jus soli* by granting automatic citizenship at birth to all third-generation immigrants born in France to parents born in France, and at the age of eighteen to all second-generation immigrants born in France who have lived there uninterruptedly for the previous five years and who have not previously revoked their rights (either through a verbal statement or by committing a felony).[4] However, this automatic granting of citizenship has been variously endangered. During the conservative governments of Edouard Balladur and Alain Juppé (1993–96), the Code of Nationality was revised to require that second-generation immigrants make a formal request of citizenship between their sixteenth and eighteenth birthdays, as well as to provide the means whereby such requests could be denied on the basis of a criminal (especially drug-related) record.[5] Likewise, in a similar spirit of institutional ambivalence, while naturalizations have been much more liberal in France than in Germany, and all immigrants, regardless of generation, could potentially obtain citizenship after a requisite stay, no voting privileges have been granted to non-citizens along the lines of those in Sweden or Britain. In fact, François Mitterrand's original 110 propositions promised upon his election in 1981 included such a feature, but intense political pressure kept it from being implemented. France's approach to immigration and immigrant policies has thus tended to vacillate between temporary and permanent migration preferences, between non-recognition and overrecognition of ethnic minorities, between *jus sanguinis* and *jus soli* approaches to citizenship.

New Nationalisms, New Citizenships

Ambivalences and instabilities in immigrant policies and citizenship laws have exacerbated widespread political debates concerning the future of state nationalism in a united Europe. In these debates, the romantic foundations of European nationalism expressed in integralist notions of rooted cultural belonging—present from Herder's historical philosophy through contemporary neo-fascist cant—run headlong into parallel republican and scientific modernist discourses of a social body united in organic solidarity that underlie Durkheimian sociology as appropriated by the architects of European federalism (Holmes 2000: 19–36). The ambivalence between these two powerful discourses indicates a fundamental conflict between representative democracy and the nation-state, a conflict which plays on the notion of representation (Bauböck 1991; Hammar 1990). In a national context, democracy assures political representation to all residents of the country, while, in an international context, it seeks to represent the interests of those members of the nation. In this respect, given the existence of a large number of "denizens" (long-term adult residents without political rights) in countries like France, Germany, and Britain, one can constitute two non-congruent levels of citizenship currently operating in Western Europe: internal and external (Hammar 1990: 191).

"Internal citizens" or denizens do not enjoy the same rights as full, "external citizens," but this does not necessarily imply that they are entirely passive or voiceless; they engage in housing protests, labor strikes, etc. In France, these "minority politics" are often understood as leading primarily to ethnic strife and political conflict (cf. Wieviorka 1996). With this in mind, many European sociologists and political scientists have argued against a laissez-faire approach to citizenship that would formally maintain the unequal levels while simultaneously providing for means of upward mobility and equalities of opportunity (cf. Bauböck 1991: 44). Instead, they envision a transnational notion of citizenship for a future united Europe, one which would deny individual governments the right of exclusion based on their own nationalistic models (Neveu 2000; Soysal 1994). "The formidable chal-

June 1995 demonstration of French anti-racist groups,
Place de Trocadéro, Paris. Photograph by author.

lenge which a radically democratic outlook must face, is how to dissociate these rights from their ties to nationhood" (Bauböck 1991: 46).

This formulation of a "new citizenship" seeks to sublate "the conflict between the universalistic principles of constitutional democracies on the one hand and the particularistic claims of communities re-enacted by new pressures from European unification and immigration from the East and South" (Habermas 1992: 1). Instead of rejecting the nation-state, pundits of the new citizenship—including such diverse intellectuals as Jürgen Habermas, Julia Kristeva, and Dominique Schnapper—wish to preserve those political elements which emphasize tolerance and equality. The true nation, the one derived in the French Revolution, is understood as a "nation of citizens" which derives its identity from the "praxis of citizens who exercise their civil rights" (Habermas 1992: 3) and not from cultural properties or ethnic particularities.

From this perspective, immigrants can only be admitted to the burgeoning transnational political culture outlined by the European Union as rationally defined individuals. Anglo-American-type multiculturalism has no part in the future of Europe, for, in such a view, it can only lead to the "ghetto-ization" of immigrant groups and the perpetuation of ethnic and religious conflicts.[6] This should not be understood by the new citizens as a violation of their right to diversity, for they are perfectly free to practice their individual cultural and moral values as long as they do not interfere with the proper functioning of the public sphere: "Respect for the private sphere is one of the democratic principles" (Schnapper 1992: 145). Rather, such a universalist ideology protects the immigrants from the anarchies and totalitarianisms of Eastern European "balkanism" and Islamic "fundamentalism" from which they had generally fled (Kristeva 1993: 47). Only by searching into the history of the European nation and expunging those nationalistic elements, then, can Europe "develop a new political self-confidence commensurate with the role of Europe in the world of the twenty-first century" (Habermas 1992: 12). Europe, accordingly, must become, as the title to Julia Kristeva's 1993 essay insists, a set of "nations without nationalism."

But the success of such a project can be only limited, for promulgations of universalistic notions of citizenship are always already culturally particular. The nation of German romanticism and that of the French Revolution —integralism and state republicanism—are not separable choices, but rather determined opposites (Balibar and Wallerstein 1991), part of Zygmunt Bauman's characterization of the "ambivalence of modernity" (1991). "Universalism, assimilation, and individualism are not opposites of particularism, difference, and collectivity, the former constituting the French model, the latter constituting the Anglo-Saxon model. Instead, these concepts form part of a more complex whole: that of a tension within the fabric of Western nations" (Silverman 1992: 5). Ambivalently expressed, both sets of concepts are part of the same anthropological project of the Enlightenment in which France, as well as all the states in Western Europe, are engaged. Both are contained within the production of a new, unified Europe that simultaneously projects itself as the sublation of nationalism and searches nostalgically for a rooted cultural unity to define its borders.

In this respect, the project of new citizenship and the call for the French nation to be built on universalism and individuality (rather than particularism and community) tread very close to assimilation models that, as Etienne Balibar has demonstrated, are deeply implicated with French ethnocentrism and racism (Balibar and Wallerstein 1991: 94). The elision of racism from discussions of the French nation, or its attribution to differentialist, anti-discrimination laws (cf. Schnapper 1992: 160), runs the risk of playing into the hands of the extreme right, which for years has itself been calling for a similar separation of citizenship from nationhood in favor of the latter (Allen and Macey 1990: 388). In this sense, it is necessary to re-examine genealogically the French national imaginary of republican universalism as a historical product of colonialism, to show how its definitions of "nation," "nationality," and "citizenship" are themselves historically linked to a series of ongoing exclusions of particular peoples and cultural features. The nation, Ernest Renan (1990) reminds us, is defined as much by what is included as by what is left out.

So how can we fathom the challenge posed by postcolonial immigration to the hyphen linking nation and state in the France of a New Europe? On the one hand, we need to rethink immigration and citizenship rights as lying somewhere between the individual and the collective, as deriving from a complex "multi-dimensionality of identity" (Silverman 1992). Simple dichotomies of insider/outsider or native/foreigner or national/immigrant no longer can account for a present situation where Algerians in France simultaneously identify with and participate in the public life of a number of distinct localities (of national, infranational, and transnational dimensions). On the other hand, we must approach issues of immigration and integration as transpolitical processes that transcend the individual nation-states in question. More and more, organizations like the United Nations, the Council of Europe, and the Organization of Islamic States, endowed with a burgeoning degree of power to intercede in the internal affairs of individual states, have become the prime locus to which French immigrant and minority populations have taken their issues and claims, thus bypassing municipal and national authorities (Kastoryano 1994; Soysal 1994). In such cases, issues of French citizenship and nationality become less important than regional or religious or even continental affiliation.

However, it would be a danger to overemphasize these globalizing tendencies. While a number of authors have made great strides in detailing the "global ecumene" that transcends the economic, cultural, and political particularities of individual societies (Hannerz 1992), we need to continue to pay attention to the local level (e.g., the housing project or immigrant neighborhood), where worldwide phenomena are interpreted and appropriated into situated discursive traditions, where global tensions are recreated in local conflicts and struggles. Likewise, claims of our entrance into a "postnational" era characterized by "nations unbound" (Appadurai 1996; Schiller et al. 1994) need to be qualified by the realization that nation-states like France, while rife with internal conflicts and contradictions (of which the current immigration "problem" is but one of many), continue for the present time to dominate the geopolitical landscape and control (with varying degrees of efficiency) the permeability of their borders. In this respect, attempts to disassociate citizenship from nationality and theorize about "nations without nationalism" in the New Europe must be viewed as nostalgic efforts to underwrite the viability of individual nation-states within a world of increasing global diversity and, as Jean-Pierre Chevènement's statements from the beginning of this chapter indicate, fear of the loss of national sovereignty. However, such efforts are ultimately doomed to fail, for nationality and citizenship—ethnic and republican, integralist and federal modalities of political subjectivity—exist quite literally as two sides of the same euro. Each implies the existence of the other within the historical construction of the nation-state and its attendant cultural intimacy and structural nostalgia for a "time before time" (Herzfeld 1997: 109).[7] It is this nostalgic ambivalence—between nationality and citizenship, between universalism and particularism—as both a historical construct and a contemporary dilemma in France, that this book seeks to interrogate.

2 /

Colonization and the Production of Ethnicity

Yunis is a Kabyle activist in the Berber cultural movement who was living in the Parisian suburb of Saint-Denis when I met him in April 1996. He is a consummate storyteller and relished the opportunity to tell me about his life over a plate of chouk-chouka stew he cooked in the small apartment he shared with his Italian *copine* (long-term girlfriend). As he recounted it, he was born in 1962, during the last days of the Algerian war of national liberation, in a village in the Soummam Valley in the eastern province of Kabylia. In a last-ditch effort to preserve the French colony in Algeria, colonial extremists had formed the Organization of the Secret Army (OAS) to assassinate Algerian revolutionary leaders and undermine the French government's efforts to bring the war to a peaceful end. His older brother was killed as a child in a drive-by attack perpetrated by the OAS in his village. On the day of Yunis's birth, the OAS had condemned his parents to death. Fleeing before their assassins, Yunis's father and mother became separated. His father was caught and was about to be shot, but at the last moment he was spared by a French lieutenant "whose life he had apparently saved earlier." Yunis's mother succeeded in evading her captors by "skipping from rooftop to rooftop across the village until she reached the surrounding fields. She ran across the fields and streams to an olive tree at the base of which was a wolf's den where she lay down to hide and give birth. As I was born, my mother fell into a coma. An old woman happened to be passing by on a road that bordered the fields. She heard my cries, and not seeing the wolf she approached. She cut the umbilical cord, carried my mother and myself to her village, and brought my mother back to consciousness. It's for this reason that they call me *le sauvage* (the wild one), and to this day I do not know the exact date of my birth."

As a child, Yunis stayed true to his nickname. "I adored and still adore nature. One day I almost killed my brother while protecting some ants from his cruel games." Yunis avoided school whenever possible and spent the better part of his youth in the gardens and fields of the village, in what he referred to as the *école buissonière et forestière* (the school of the bushes and forests). "I hated school, even if I was very good at it. I experienced school as a great injustice, as a prison run by a professor who made me talk like him. I had long hair, and the principal insisted that I cut it. Every time I had my hair cut I became ill. So I refused and stopped coming to class. Several times I was expelled for playing hooky." On one occasion, after his parents forced him to return to school, Yunis went on strike, refusing to speak for thirty-three days. "People came from all over to see the mute child."

Yunis's initiation to Berber cultural difference, as he related it, was similarly mediated by this predilection for resistance. When he was eight years old, his cousin wrote out his name in the Berber alphabet, Tifinagh. "I didn't even know that Tifinagh existed!" Afterwards, he gradually learned more and more from his cousin and others about the history of Berber peoples. "I came to realize that the Berber 'Z' is the symbol for liberty. In learning that, I became conscious of Berber culture. The symbol cost me my first arrest." In 1975, at the age of twelve, he painted the Z on the back of his jeans jacket. "I was the first one in T. to openly wear the symbol." Several days later he was arrested by the military gendarmes. "I resisted, I insulted them. Through this action I entered into the Berber movement. My first dive into the cultural struggle was wearing that Z."

This experience was reinforced by his first voyage away from home. At the age of fifteen he went by train to visit his uncle in Algiers to see a football match played by the Sporting Youth of Kabylia (JSK), a club based in Tizi-Ouzou and founded by the French colonial administration as part of its avowed mission to civilize Algerian natives (*indigènes*). Having been educated primarily in French and not speaking a word of Arabic, Yunis quickly got lost and got off the train fifty kilometers before Algiers. "When I finally got to Algiers, I asked an old man I met on the street directions to the stadium. He hit me for speaking in Kabyle. I then asked a police officer, who threatened me with his baton. These were the so-called 'civilized' I had heard about. After this I began to differentiate between 'Arabs' and 'Kabyles.' When I returned home ten days later, everyone was ecstatic that I had gone to the land of the 'Arabs' (*chez les Arabes*) and come back alive."

Not deterred by his first venture "abroad," Yunis developed a thirst to see the world. As a child, he grew up watching Westerns that were continuously being played at his village's movie theater. "I was completely absorbed by the Indians who I related to as *sauvages* like me. Afterwards, I absolutely wanted to travel." Seeing an announcement in the newspaper, he took the national naval examination, and at the age of eighteen enrolled in the Maritime Superior Institute at Bousmaïl (approximately forty-five kilometers west of Algiers). Within a year he received his diploma and spent the next six years as an engineer on a variety of boats, mostly crossing the Atlantic between Algiers and Montreal. "But I never wore a dress tie, and I never saluted the Algerian flag."

In the meantime, Yunis had become increasingly active in the Berber cultural movement and a number of demonstrations and protests for the recognition of Berber culture that were occurring across Algeria in the late 1970s and 1980s. Already in 1978 he was arrested at a demonstration in Algiers. In 1980 he took a leading role in organizing the various marches and confrontations with police in March and April in Tizi-Ouzou that would later become known as the "Berber Spring" and during which Yunis and the other organizers were summarily arrested and beaten. "Throughout the 1980s I ran around night and day distributing tracts, giving talks, organizing people, etc. My role was not only to demonstrate, but to structure the movement, to give it political and cultural guideposts so that people weren't taking the streets for nothing." His round trips to Montreal were particularly pertinent, as they put him into direct communication with the burgeoning diasporic Berber cultural movement occurring there. "The voyages permitted me to distribute and gather information. It put cultural associations in Kabylia and Canada in touch with each other." Gradually the movement gained strength as the younger activists convinced the older generation of the necessity of the struggle for cultural rights in a country with a monolithic "Arabo-Islamic" national ideology. "At first the parents didn't understand. They didn't want another war. But little by little they began to understand. As did the government authorities who increasingly treated the Kabyles as troublemakers, if not enemies within." In 1985 Yunis was arrested in Tizi-Ouzou and sentenced to death.

Somehow Yunis escaped and made his way to Italy where he lived for several years before moving with his *copine* to France. The intimate details that marked his recounting of his early years quickly faded when the story got to his life in Europe. There was a boat accident off the coast of Spain that made him give up his life at sea. And a brush with the Italian police while hitchhiking across the country convinced him to come to France. But otherwise, his account of his life and activism since leaving Algeria was vague at best. It was clear that he remained very active and well-connected in Berber politics into the 1990s, but that his role had not been nearly as public as the singer-activists and leaders of political parties and associations who marked the mature movement. His reticence and occasional aside indicated that he had more stories to tell about himself, but could not do so at that moment.

He was, however, more than happy to talk about Berber history, culture, and language (Tamazight), subjects on which he was a self-taught virtuoso. At the time I knew him, Yunis was completing a textbook on Berber linguistics, and would often stop our conversation to provide etymologies of various terms. For instance, he derived the term "Africa"—which he preferred to the Arabic term "Maghreb" generally used in France as a designator for the geographical region of North Africa—from the Berber "Tafrika," claiming that it spread from the Berbers to the rest of the continent. Likewise, he had an encyclopedic knowledge of early Berber history and had been invited on European television on several occasions as an expert in the field. When I first met him in Paris in April 1995, after a demonstration for Berber language rights in front of the Algerian embassy in Paris to mark the fifteenth anniversary of the Berber Spring, he lectured to me and several Franco-Kabyle friends for thirty minutes about the early colonization of North Africa by the Phoenicians and Romans. In his version, the king of Berberia welcomed Phoenician refugees from Tyr who then took away the Berbers' land and established the city of Carthage. The king's grandson, Massinissa, allied with the Romans against Carthage but was again betrayed after the Roman victory. Massinissa's nephew Jugurtha, whose life and struggles were later recorded by the Roman historian Sallust, fought valiantly against the Romans, only to be captured and brought back to Rome. Yunis, on his first trip to Italy, had made a pilgrimage to Jugurtha's grave and was happy to show us the pictures.

The moral of the story, for Yunis, was that the hospitality and generosity of the Berbers was their fatal flaw. Moreover, the history highlighted for him the Berbers' eternal spirit of resistance that was evident in their historical and present struggles against the French and Arabs. "France was afraid of the Kabyles. The Kabyles never accepted colonization; they were rebels. The French admired us as a proud people, but they saw us as dangerous at the same time." Yunis likewise perceives such an ambivalence in the Algerian government's fears of Berber separatism. "The Arab/Berber difference was a difference imposed on us. At the same time, the authorities have wanted to erase all Berber difference."

One of the major ambivalences associated with the "problem" of immigration, identity, and citizenship in contemporary Europe concerns the management of ethnicity within the contemporary nation-state. Nation-states like France have consistently wavered between the acceptance and erasure of social (which variously includes ethnic, racial, class, and religious) differences within their populations throughout their histories. While European states have generally battled against the perceived divisiveness of internal cultural diversity in an effort to integrate (if not assimilate) their populations, they have simultaneously made use of such cultural differences in strategies of conquest and control, and in doing so have tended to underwrite reified versions of them. In other words, while immigrants from North Africa have been in France since the end of the nineteenth century, it is only in recent years, with the problematization of Islam, that the "North African" (*Maghrébin* or *Arabe*) has emerged as a particular category of ethnic identity that glosses over internal tribal, national, and religious distinctions.

This process of social *qua* ethnic production is not new, and indeed, as Jean-Loup Amselle (1998, 2003) has averred, has been a perduring feature of French colonial and postcolonial history. In the case of Algeria, one can trace it to the initial days of French colonization in the mid-nineteenth century, when military officials and scholars collaborated with the colonial state in detailing a particular Berber identity independent of the larger Arab polity in Algeria. This preoccupation with marked forms of social difference both reflected a growing racialized consciousness within nineteenth-century European social thought and dovetailed with a colonial strategy of direct rule in which intellectuals (from Alexis de Toqueville to Maurice Halbwachs, passing through Arthur de Gobineau) were themselves often involved. Seeking an ally in their colonial endeavors, French officials produced a privileged image of the Berber as culturally and genetically proximate to European civilization, and proceeded to invest financially and educationally into Berber-speaking areas (Colonna 1975). Berberophones, however, never became the Francophiliac toadies imagined by certain colonial ideologues and indeed played a central role in anti-colonial resistance throughout the 132 years of French conquest from 1830 to 1962. Nonetheless, stereotypes of the democratic, free-spirited, assimilable Berber have persisted since Algerian independence, utilized by conflicting interest groups in the postcolony to justify policies of Arabization and to underwrite Berber ethnonationalism. Drawing on primary source material from the colonial period in North Africa—consisting primarily of published ethnographic, geographic, and linguistic studies—this chapter demonstrates that the production of Franco-Algerian national and transnational formations has always entailed the elaboration rather than the univocal erasure of ethnic, racial, and religious differences.

In this light, it is important to take insight from the contemporary scholarship on the place of ethnicity in nationalist movements and contemporary nation-states (Anderson 1983; Gellner 1983; Hobsbawm 1990; Smith 1986). Employing a constructivist approach, this literature has convincingly argued that the nation is an invented entity, a recently formulated "imagined community" of compatriots separated by great distances, unaware of each other's physical existence, united through institutions of education, the military, and print capitalism. While some scholars have differentiated between constructed nations and the primordially authentic *ethnies* upon which they are built—with Eric Hobsbawm, for instance, making a stark distinction between the "invented" nation of Algeria and the "genuine" nations of Berbers and Arabs (1991: 179; cf. Gellner 1983: 48–49)—others have insisted on the basic continuity of these levels of belonging as equally historically constituted social formations (Handler 1988; Handler and Segal 1993).

Increasingly, a number of anthropologists and historians have called attention to the "colonial genealogies of nationalism" (Segal and Handler 1992: 2; cf. Comaroff and Comaroff 1997: 365–404; Stoler 2002). The Algerian colony, as a site of innovation and experimentation with the norms and forms of modernity, provided the tools for the French state to monopolize its authority at home, slough off its undesirable masses, and gain a rotating reserve army of laborers necessary for building up the metropole (Rabinow 1989; Talha 1989; Wright 1991). Such labor was buttressed by the cultural work of military scholars who reified the boundaries of the French nation through a detailed elaboration of the cultural differences encountered in the colony's indigenous populations. While maintaining an explicit republican ideology of universal citizenship, the French state during the colonial and postcolonial periods thus abetted the production of ethnicity within and among its colonial and later immigrant populations. In the process, it established certain parameters outlining the "right to difference," parameters that effectively categorized particular cultural features as commensurable or not with the French nation-state. Today, fears over tribalism—coded as the rise of Islam in France—remain tempered by overt declarations of culture as an essential human right. This ambivalence over the avowal and disavowal of ethnicity, as the book as a whole seeks to demonstrate, has rested at the heart of France's social imaginary, from its imperial heyday to the eve of European integration.

Colonialism and National Integration

The interplay between metropole and colony in the entrenchment of a state national regime of sovereignty and the putative elimination of social tensions arising from extant heterogeneous class and cultural loyalties is greatly illustrated in the military conquest of Algeria. Algeria, prior to the arrival of the French, consisted of three Ottoman provinces, each governed by a dey answerable directly to the Sublime Porte in Istanbul. Primarily responsible for collecting taxes and maintaining the peace, the deys were supported by minimal armies of *janissaries*—troops recruited from throughout the Ottoman Empire, but largely from the Balkans—essentially stationed in the urban centers of Algiers in the center, Constantine in the east, and Oran in the west. They oversaw an economy that relied historically on grain production and export, but had increasingly turned to the piracy of European vessels in the Mediterranean by the infamous "Barbary corsairs" in the ultimate employ of the dey of Algiers.

This military force ruled over a heterogeneous population consisting of Muslims, Christians, and Jews, the latter two numerically smaller groups persisting as officially recognized communities under the Ottoman *millet* system, subject to a special tax (the *jizya*). The Muslim community was primarily unified under the Sunni *melkkite* interpretation, with the exception of a small group of Ibadi Shi'a in the Mzab southeastern region. Nonetheless, the former group was itself split into the orthopraxy of the urban faith, a set of Sufi brotherhoods (*tariqât* or *ikhwan*) including the Rahmaniyya and Qadiriyya orders, and the various rural heteropraxies of ancestor/"saint" veneration and religious leadership of marabouts—lineages claiming descent from the Prophet.[1] These religious communities were further transected non-isomorphically by cultural and linguistic differences between Arabophones living primarily in urban areas and in the north-central plains and speakers of several dialects of Berber living in the mountainous region of Kabylia just east of Algiers, the neighboring Aurès mountains, Mzab, and Tassili/Ahaggar in the southern Sahara. This cultural, religious, and linguistic heterogeneity served as a testament to a long history of migrations and invasions that had brought various waves of Phoenician, Roman, Vandal, Arab, Bedouin, and Andalusian conquerors and settlers to the region, each having left their imprint on the social, linguistic, and physical landscape.

In this respect, France's attack on Algiers in July 1830 functioned as part of a longer set of interactions between Europe, North Africa, and the Middle East, mediated by particular historical moments of (Roman/Moorish) expansionism and (Carthaginian/Spanish) reconquest. Narrowly, the invasion by the naval fleet of restoration monarch Charles X was understood by most contemporary observers as a punitive expedition for insults made by the dey of Algiers to the French consul during an 1827 diplomatic visit to negotiate trade relations that had stagnated since two shipments of wheat had been confiscated without payment by Marseille port authorities in 1798.[2] Moreover, the mission had, in the words of one observer, its "secret goal," the elimination of Algerian piracy and the various tributes France had to continually pay to keep its Mediterranean fleet functioning (Société de l'Afrique 1836).

Furthermore, the attack was situated historically within the imperial competition of European powers, occurring within recent memory of Napoleon's loss of his outpost in Egypt to the British in 1801. Many of those participating in the expeditionary force to Algiers were veterans of the Egyptian campaigns. Military plans were largely developed on the basis of the French army's experience in Egypt, from health precautions to institutions designed to govern the natives (the *bureaux arabes*) once conquest had been achieved (Lorcin 1995: 19). Since this earlier defeat, France had consistently set its sights on a reconquest of the Mediterranean, in part to facilitate the burgeoning trade with the East Indies (whose shipping lines were threatened by the British on the one hand and the Barbary corsairs on the other), in part to restore the Napoleonic empire and the national prestige that had accompanied it (Cobban 1961: 41–42). Additionally, the popular media of the time would link the new African colony to the Belgian and German territories west of the Rhine River, which had been annexed by France by 1799 and subsequently amputated by the 1815 Treaty of Vienna after the defeat of Napoleon. It was even rumored that Great Britain had offered to reconstitute these former provinces if French forces agreed to leave Algeria (Guiral 1955). Whether this rumor actually held any validity proves less relevant than the fact of its reception, that the colonization of Algiers served in part to reanimate the imagination of "national glory" (Guilhaume 1992: 61–62; Addi 1996).

This issue of national unity was of particular concern at the time of the expedition to Algeria given the high degree of political turmoil within Charles X's government. In a series of political blunders, the monarch had managed to offend both the "liberal" and "conservative" political factions, as he simultaneously reinstated clerical control of the educational system—a feature of the *ancien régime* to which the bourgeois, professional classes were particularly opposed—and minimized the indemnity paid to returned aristocratic émigrés who had fled France during the 1789 Revolution. In 1827, the minister of war wrote to Charles that an invasion of Algiers would be a "useful distraction from political trouble at home" which would allow the government "to go to the country at the next election with the keys of Algiers in its hand" (Ageron 1991: 5). With the dey's insult as a pretext, the king initiated a naval blockade of the port of Algiers, and then, when that did not quiet the parliamentary opposition, he dissolved the chamber of deputies and ordered General Bourmont to attack Algiers.

The final political result of Charles's actions was a dismal failure, as the monarchy was toppled within a month of the Algiers attack. Nonetheless, the conquest of Algiers, originally conceived as an expeditionary mission to remove the dey from power, soon took on a life of its own. While the Ottoman government quickly fell to the superior military force of the French, the occupation met stiff resistance from the native elite, particularly from the Emir Abd al-Qadir, who mobilized the Qadiriyya brotherhood to a protracted and bloody uprising (*jihad*). By the time his rebellion was finally laid to rest in 1847, the French were firmly ensconced not only in Algiers, but in the surrounding countryside as well.

In the years that followed, the French gradually expanded their control across the entirety of Algeria, finally conquering the last remaining holdouts in Kabylia in 1856. With their military presence firmly established, the French created a set of civilian-military colonial governments, with the alternate goals of assimilating or integrating the "colony" into the political and economic structures of France.[3] Following the establishment of the Second Empire, Emperor Louis-Napoleon initiated a policy of indirect rule, creating an Algerian "Arab kingdom" (*royaume arabe*). Operating under ultimate French military governance, Muslim and Jewish populations were incorporated as formal political "subjects" (*sujets*), with their interests represented by advisory *conseils généraux* made up of indigenous elites, and their tribal (*arch*) landholdings protected by senatorial decree. As subjects, they enjoyed most civic rights, but were excluded from full citizenship, voting, and mandatory military service unless they abandoned their religious "personal status" (*statut personnel*) and accepted the French civil code concerning marriage and property. In this respect, what had begun as a regime change had become a cardinal example of imperial rule.

Moreover, the 1830 attack was not only the condition of possibility for the establishment of the Algerian colony, but it also set the precedent of employing foreign policy as a strategy of national unification. If the conquest largely responded to the imperative of forging a national consensus around a decaying Bourbon monarchy, of recovering a lost imperial prestige, the 1871 military expedition to Kabylia followed a similar logic of national integration for the nascent Third Republic in France formed in the wake of the spectacular defeat of the Second Empire in the 1870 Franco-Prussian war. In March 1870, the colonists in Algeria pushed through a new constitution to establish a civilian regime of direct rule even more closely tied to the metropole than the *royaume arabe*. In October 1870, the Crémieux Decree responded to the lack of indigenous naturalizations and the pressing need for military conscripts by granting full French citizenship to Algerian Jews but not Muslims (Bodley 1926: 39).

Following the Prussian victory, the European powers allowed the colonial expansion in Algeria to continue apace in order to divert French attention from the lost territories of Alsace and Lorraine (Cobban 1965: 91). Indeed, such expansion greatly served the interests of the nascent Third Republic to defuse the urban social tensions that would poignantly surface in the 1871 Paris Commune. Laws enacted by the new civilian government in Algeria eliminated the influence that Muslim elites had garnered, suspending the protection of tribal landholdings, expanding the territory under direct French administration, dismantling the *conseils généraux,* and instating a special "Arab tax" (*impôt arabe*) on Muslim subjects. Reacting largely to these new measures, a number of tribes in Kabylia (amounting to an estimated 200,000 armed fighters under the leadership of the Rahmaniyya brotherhood) rose up in February 1871 against the colonial government in a bitter insurrection which would last for nearly a year (see Mahé 2001: 190–203). Finally, by February 1872, the French colonial army had crushed the uprising with absolute vehemence. The military imposed an impossible indemnity, confiscating more than 400,000 hectares of tribal lands, a quarter of which was redistributed to 1,183 Alsatian families who had fled to Paris before the invading Prussian armies and had joined the burgeoning, unemployed urban swell and unrest of the Paris Commune (Julien 1963: 65; Talha 1989: 31). Meanwhile, the Kabyle resistance fighters and their families were forcibly exiled to the newly acquired Pacific colony of New

Caledonia, and thousands of other Kabyles expropriated from their land were forced into a situation of migrant labor, bringing them to Tunisia, Algiers, and eventually France in search of work.

Having consolidated its rule in both Paris and Kabylia, the Third Republic began to use the colony as a proving ground for national integration policies and, in so doing, further incorporate it into the metropole. In 1880, the Third Republic accommodated the loss of Alsace-Lorraine by legislatively assimilating the Algerian colony as three administrative departments, thus expanding France's effective territory fourfold. In the early 1880s, Prime Minister (previously Education Minister) Jules Ferry of France drafted a series of laws that put all local Algerian public services under the direct control of the respective French ministries (Collot 1987: 10–11). Kabylia was particularly affected by these measures. Mountain villages destroyed by French army troops during the 1856 and 1871 campaigns had their villagers relocated to model government villages built according to a logic of European social organization and surveillance. In 1874, autonomous legal jurisdiction in the remaining Kabyle villages (regulated by local, oral laws, or *qanoun*) was abolished and regional courts were established. Economically speaking, the government sought to subsume village markets into the greater economy and, through the recruitment of local *fellahin* (peasants) into colonial plantations or industrial concerns abroad, introduce money (in the form of remittances) as the uniform standard of value (Sayad 1977).

The establishment of the Algerian colony thus dovetailed with the larger production of a uniform spatial and temporal structure in the realms of politics, economics, and law, at the root of French national construction. Rather than simply peripheral regions to which national standards were exported, the colonies reciprocally functioned as an integral element in the consolidation of a republican national regime. Education in particular was viewed as the most important instrument or "armament" in this process of colonial *qua* national integration (Anon. 1924), with colonial military leaders like Maréchal Lyautey painting themselves as first and foremost teachers (*instituteurs*) and calling for an army of soldier-instructors (*soldats-instituteurs*) (Le Glay 1921: 13; cf. Colonna 1975).[4] Alongside a number of village parochial schools established by army chaplains and members of the *Pères Blancs* Jesuit order, Prime Minister Ferry created in 1881 eight schools in Kabylia according to the secular, national education standards he had proposed for the metropole two years earlier and that he would apply more generally two years later throughout Algeria and France (Lorcin 1995: 190). Using the latest cartographic techniques, maps in greater and greater detail were drawn of the regions of Algeria and were incorporated into maps of the French Hexagon hung on Algerian schoolroom walls. The academic year followed the same rhythms and breaks as schools in Paris, without regard to the agrarian cycles or Islamic festivities. Secular textbooks imported from Paris declared that the students' history began with "our ancestors, the Gauls" (Citron 1994). In this respect, the famous "civilizing mission" (*mission civilisatrice*)—the self-aggrandizing ideological form that was employed by colonial ideologues to justify imperial expansion—had less to do with the "white man's burden" to ensure a universal human progress from savagery to civilization as it did with an imperative to secularize or disenchant the territory and chronology under French control, to integrate these spaces and times into a centralized, national structure.[5]

The Arab Threat

The constitution of the French imperium in the late nineteenth century involved more than the integration of peripheral populations through the simple erasure of autonomous regions of social, political, and economic (read cultural) difference. Rather, the colonial endeavor often involved the ironic reification of these categories of difference themselves. In spite of claims made by certain scholars and contemporary Berber activists (cf. Gellner 1972; Camps 1984), the Arab-Berber divide in North Africa is not a primordial survival that has been maintained in relatively unchanged form from time immemorial to the present. Nor, as has been asserted by Algerian state ideologues (cf. Kaddache 1973; Merad 1967), is it a pure invention of French colonists, the elimination of which is the condition of possibility for Algerian national unity. Berberophone groups in Algeria are certainly embedded in identifiable, if always already hybridized, social formations and cultural logics that in any given instance and to one degree or another differ from the various concatenations of social formations and cultural logics found elsewhere in the region. However, as a matrix of *objectified* differences and discursive schemas inscribed in ethnoracial terms—as an object of cultural intimacy and structural nostalgia (Herzfeld 1997)—the Arab-Berber divide is a patently modern form that has been repeatedly created and recreated from the early descriptions of fourteenth-century scholar Ibn Khaldun, through the colonial period, to the Algerian nationalist movement, and finally into the present struggles of the Berber cultural movement.[6]

In particular, the techniques of enumeration and categorization (primarily mapping, cadastral surveys, ethnographic and linguistic studies) employed to consolidate rule and centralize authority throughout the French empire contributed to the production of hierarchical schemas along which various populations encountered in Algeria were slotted. Building on the philosophical models posed by mid-century social evolutionists like Herbert Spencer and racial theorists like Arthur de Gobineau that had gained a central place in important Parisian research institutions (the École Polytechnique in particular), military geographers, linguists, and ethnologists catalogued the racial traits, language forms, sociopolitical traditions, and religious rites

they observed among the conquered peoples along a continuum of progress
from savagery to civilization (Lorcin 1995).[7] While colonial policy sought
to transform such "natural," incompatible differences into the mere folkloric appendages of a modern society, the continual use of hierarchical cultural schemas for governing purposes (particularly for the formation alliances
and divide-and-conquer tactics) resulted in the unforeseen generalization
and reification of such subnational categories as essential means of group
identification—most significantly, the formulation of what would become
known as the "Kabyle Myth."[8]

Tocqueville in Algeria

The intimate connection between ethnological knowledge production and
colonial conquest derives in no small part from the interventions of Alexis
de Tocqueville. Having visited the new colony of Algeria in May–June 1841
and again in October–December 1846, Tocqueville became an ardent supporter of the colonial project, publishing a series of pointed letters and longer
academic works and serving on a number of colonial commissions while a
member of the French Chamber of Deputies between 1842 and 1849 (Richter 1963; Todorov 1991). While initially defending France's "right of war"
(*droit de la guerre*) to "ravage" the country in order to defeat Abd al-Qadir's
revolt, he later excoriated the French military for "having made Muslim
society much more miserable, disorderly, ignorant, and barbarous than it
was before meeting [the French]" (1841: 78; 1847: 170). He argued that
military domination, based on the conquest and enslavement of the populace, must eventually give way to a civilian colonization, based on the reproduction of centralized, republican political models of France, both for
practical as well as ethical reasons (1841: 64, 114–119; 1847: 179).

   In order to achieve this "new society," however, a more detailed knowledge of the country's indigenous inhabitants was required. Tocqueville lauded
the army for its "intelligence" and "brilliant courage," for its "patient and
tranquil energy" which subjugated Algeria's population and opened up new
avenues to understand them: "Victory has allowed us to penetrate their
techniques, their ideas, their beliefs, and has finally delivered the secret to
governing them. . . . Today we can say that the indigenous society is no
longer veiled for us (*n'a plus pour nous de voile*)" (1847: 152). This sexual-
ized link between colonial knowledge and power in the "penetration" and
"un-veiling" of Algerian society through its women would be continually
re-enacted throughout the colonial period: in the Orientalist paintings of
Eugène Delacroix of voluptuous private scenes of "Algerois Women in Their
Apartment"; in the profusion of colonial postcards of veiled, semi-veiled,
and even bare-breasted Algerian women (Alloula 1986; Borgé and Viasnoff
1995; Clancy-Smith 1996); and even in the anti-colonial critiques of Frantz
Fanon's revolutionary "Algeria Unveiled" essay (1965).[9] Not merely a sexual

act, the ethnological unveiling of indigenous society as described and pre-scribed by Tocqueville consisted of a rape, a ravaging of the native's culture as well as its land: "We can only study the barbaric peoples with guns in hand" (1847: 152). As such, it would not only be revealed, it would be taken away. "We know the history of the different tribes almost as well as they; we *possess* the exact biographies of all the influential families" (1847: 153). And once taken, it could be replaced. Not only, through the establish-ment of native intermediaries and the *bureaux arabes,* could the Algerian people be "put under surveillance" and their "actions controlled," but, ac-cording to Tocqueville, they could also be made to integrate the "French maxims" of "individual property and industry" (1847: 166–172). The *mis-sion civilisatrice* conceived by Tocqueville, then, amounts largely to a vio-lent cultural rape.

However, as Tocqueville reminded his French parliamentary interlocu-tors, this civilizing project, while not as impossible as others had claimed, nonetheless needed to overcome several obstacles. The first of these con-cerned the nomadic character of the Arab and Bedouin tribes, their lack of spatial fixity, and hence their resistance to surveillance and civilization. Analyzing Abd al-Qadir's revolt, Tocqueville underlined the leader's main-tenance of the existing social structure: "He knows very well that the no-madic life of tribes is his surest defense against us. His subjects will become ours the day they fasten themselves to the soil" (1841: 80). In this respect, Tocqueville recommended "re-anchoring the tribes in their territories" rather than "transporting them elsewhere" and thus underwriting their anterior nomadic tendencies (1847: 174–175). Secondly, the natives' religiosity, and moreover their "fanaticism," likewise posed an obstacle to their potential assimilation. In particular, Tocqueville noted the role of "fanatical beggars, belonging to secret associations, a type of irregular and ignorant clergy" in the recent armed resistance and insurrections organized along the lines of a "holy war" (1847: 173). Rather than being completely savage, Islam rep-resented a "backwards and imperfect civilization," or rather a "half-civili-zation" caught in a "feudal" or "aristocratic" past (1841: 72–74; 1847: 169). The French needed to overcome this evolutionary *blocus* and bring "Africa" into the historical path of "the movement of the civilized world" (1841: 61).

However, in Tocqueville's analysis, not all of Algeria's indigenous popu-lations (or "races") were alike in presenting these obstacles. If the colonial relations with the Arabs centered on those political and religious questions just posed, relations with the Kabyles (or "Cabyles" in Tocqueville's tran-scription) needed to be pursued in terms of "civil and commercial equity" (1837: 47). Tocqueville maintained that, as opposed to the Arabs, the Kabyles appeared anchored in their mountainous refuges, fixed to the material pos-sessions and profits which came from working the land. If Arab tribes claimed territory according to the loose arrangements of communal *arch,* maintained through historical ties and agreements, Kabyle families retained holdings as individualized *melk,* closely resembling European systems of private property (Tocqueville 1837: 46; cf. MacMaster 1993: 26). Further, unlike Arabs, Kabyles seemed to Tocqueville "less faithful" religiously, unwilling to suppress individual liberties in the interest of the group or community: "For the Cabyles, the individual is almost everything, society almost nothing." Even in the midst of the armed religious insurrection, Kabyle villagers continued to "frequent our markets and come rent us their services" (1837: 46). Given these cultural resemblances and "frequent, peaceful relations," Tocqueville concluded that however impenetrable their territory may be, the Kabyles would likely assimilate to French "mores and ideas" due to the "almost invincible attraction that brings savages towards civilized men" (1837: 47). In the end, the Kabyle became, in Tocqueville's account, the ideal target of the French cultural, if not territorial, rape: "[While] the Cabyle's country may be closed to us, the Cabyle's soul is open and it is not impossible for us to penetrate it" (1837: 46).

The Arab Obstacle: Nomadism and Islamism

Through these writings, Tocqueville succeeded in outlining the major avenues for the production of the "Kabyle Myth." Following Tocqueville's injunction to "know thine enemy," the French Ministry of War initiated in 1837 a vast "scientific exploration" enterprise under the direction of the State-Major Colonel Bory de Saint-Vincent and manned by a "scientific commission" consisting of a group of trained and amateur historians, sociologists, and linguists in the employ of the colonial army (G. Mercier 1954). While the commission in its official capacity was short-lived (1840–42), its members would eventually publish thirty-nine independent works based on the research completed under its aegis, many of which—including Ernest Carette's *Etudes sur la Kabylie proprement dite* (1848) and later L. Hanoteau and A. Letourneux's *La Kabylie et les coutumes kabyles* (1871)—would become the key ethnographic texts underlying the "Kabyle Myth" (Lorcin 1995; Goodman 2002: 88–91). Moreover, the commission's immediate findings would provide the necessary reconnaissance information for the later full-scale invasion of Kabylia (1850–57, in spite of Tocqueville's objections), just as its final published works—specifically Hanoteau and Letourneux's study of Kabyle legal codes (*qanoun*)—would later facilitate the establishment of a centralized administration there (Favret 1968: 19; Lorcin 1995: 41–52). Colonization and military manuals incorporated "basic facts on the Algerian mentality" (irrationality, impulsiveness, fatalism, thievery, vindictiveness, susceptibility), and suggested corresponding actions which one should take: "do not admit him into your house," "use simple words that he can understand," "know to flatter him on occasion," etc. (Anon. 1881: 17–23; *El Moudjahid* 15/1/59: 132–155). Through these arrangements, then,

Tocqueville's discursive link between colonial knowledge and power was written into colonial policy.

In particular, Tocqueville's identification of nomadism and fanaticism as the prime characteristics of Arab society and obstacles to the colonial *mission civilisatrice* would find itself replicated over the next hundred years in various guises as part of the "foundational myths" of the French colonial presence in Algeria (Guilhaume 1992). The sedentary/nomad dichotomy provided a frame for the colonial reinterpretation of world history that drew in large part on Ibn Khaldun's analysis of the cyclical rise and fall of nomadic and city-based empires (Issawi 1987). In the case of Algeria, this historical opposition was encapsulated in the colonial scholarship in geographic tropes, as, in the words of one elementary school textbook, an "incessant battle between the natural forces of the Mediterranean and those of the Sahara, the conflict between sedentaries and nomads, between men of the sea and men of the desert" (Fontaine 1957: 22). In the words of Emile Masqueray, the pre-eminent scholar of Kabyle segmentary organization whose work would have a profound influence on Emile Durkheim, "one must always have this opposition [between sedentary and nomadic] in mind when explaining contemporary Algeria" (1886: 16; cf. Colonna 1983).

While, in point of fact, the Algerian Sahara was occupied throughout the colonial period by both Arabophones and Berberophones, it was the former who were consistently linked to the nomadic lifestyle. On the one hand, their nomadic wanderings posed a security threat to the colonial forces, who had difficulty keeping track of potential sources of resistance. Military leaders like General Bugeaud addressed this problem through policies of forcible sedentarization and the creation of model villages. On the other hand, the Arabs' supposedly continual spatial movement implied the cultural and political characteristics of instability and disorganization, qualities understood as inherently opposed to modern civilization (Guilhaume 1992: 88; Lorcin 1995: 37–40). Indeed, colonial scholars understood the tribal organization of the Arabs as representing, according to developmental models being developed by Herbert Spencer and Lewis Henry Morgan, an earlier order of social evolution; the Arab "is an essential nomad who, besides, has not passed the stage (*stade*) of the clan in his evolution" (Gautier 1931: 19). Moreover, as a premodern nomad, the Arab had failed to modify the land itself, to plant crops and produce his livelihood. His lack of agriculture was thus equated with his lack of culture.

> The Arab is the most incapable of farmers: he is only good at wasting and destroying the natural richness of the Tell, earth *par excellence*. . . . and this is an inseparable result of the patriarchal regime of barbarism in which he delights. . . . What did we find when our soldiers arrived to punish the pirates? Invading scrub brush and palm trees, and all the earth once again needing to be cleared [for planting]; and if today there exist real cultivated fields, it is to the colonizer whom Algeria owes thanks. (Pomel 1871: 18)

By reinforcing the image of a precolonial desert land, French colonists created the myth that it was *deserted*. In working the land, in making it fruitful and productive, they could justify their occupation of it (Guilhaume 1992: 232–236). As such, within the primordial war of sedentaries against nomads, colonization became the only and legitimate means of reopening the country to evolution, progress, and history in general.

The second obstacle to colonial assimilation outlined by Tocqueville and appropriated by military scholars concerned the reduction of Arab civilization to Islam, and the perceived incompatibility of the latter with French (Christian) modernity. Such a concern belied fears of Islam as a unifying political force during nineteenth-century anti-colonial revolts, a fear that was re-energized during the twentieth century by the nascent Arab nationalist movements across North Africa and Egypt (Lucas and Vatin 1975: 34). In colonial discourse, Islam served as the primary trope for explaining two opposed characteristics of the observed Arab personality: on the one hand, their bellicose, hostile nature, attributable to their religious fanaticism; and on the other hand, their inveterate laziness, resulting from their reverent fatalism. Islam (or "Mahometism," as it was derogated), in this respect, provided the necessary complement to the Arabs' premodern nomadism: "Mahometism appears specially adapted to societies whose social evolution arrested in the phase of barbarous patriarchy . . . a theocratic status of which absolutism is the pivot and fatalism the measure" (Pomel 1871: 5–6). In the first place, French observers argued that the Arab's absolutism placed him in a "permanent state of war with the infidel, a duty of eternal war which cannot be suspended" (Servier 1923: 345–346). "Holy war is the aim of all the wishes, all the efforts of the Arab" (Anon. 1873: 49). Islam served as the main explanatory factor for the horrors of war (beheadings, tortures, mutilations) witnessed by the French expeditionary forces during their conquest of Algeria, horrors attributable to the "vindictive and cruel character" of Arabs "who know no other law than that of the strongest" (Hamelin 1833: 7). Studies conducted by military ethnographers paid particular attention to those Algerian religious organizations, like the marabouts and the Sufi brotherhoods (*khouan,* according to colonial transcription), that wielded mystical authority and were capable of organizing believers into potential violence (cf. De Neveu 1846; Rinn 1884).

In the second place, scholars focused on a contradictory aspect of Islam—fatalism, the absolute reliance on Allah to determine one's future. They viewed it as the root cause of a long series of vices: ". . . laziness, dissimulation, dishonesty, suspicion, unpredictability, love of voluptuousness, luxury and feasting . . ." (Van Vollenhoven 1903: 169), decrying the Muslim Arab as a professional "sun-drinker" (*buveur de soleil*) (Docteur X 1891: 55). This reverent laziness was understood to reciprocally weaken the Muslim's intellect, impeding all social progress toward modernity.

Intellectually, the Muslim is . . . a paralytic. His brain, subjugated for centuries to the stark discipline of Islam, is closed to everything not predicted, pronounced, specified by religious law. He is therefore systematically hostile to any novelty, to any modification, to any innovation. . . . Such a conception [of fatalism] prohibits all progress, and, in fact, immobility is the essential character of any Muslim society. (Servier 1923: 346–347)

Moreover, French administrators perceived this essential religiosity of Arabs as an inherent stumbling block to their administrative or legal incorporation into the French nation. "In the Mahometian civilization, religion and law are too intimately confused for the juridical condition of Muslims to be identical to that of Frenchmen or Europeans" (Larcher 1903: 16). Colonial naturalization laws followed a similar logic in denying Muslim Algerians (and not Jewish Algerians) French citizenship unless they renounced their religious "personal status." When in 1891 the Third Republic considered eliminating this last impediment and naturalizing all Algerians, a violent debate broke out within the Parliament. One senator, M. Sabatier, opposed the reform on the grounds that it would implicitly condone "Coranic" civil and familial practices, from feudal land tenure to polygamy, which "escape French laws, not to mention French morality" (cited in Borgé and Viasnoff 1995: 18).

What was at issue, then, was not the individual's right of accession to French citizenship, but rather the feared legitimation of a religious doctrine that through its fanaticism and fatalism would respectively undermine French state security and Christian morality. Beyond a "constant system of surveillance," the best way to reduce the authority of religious leaders who "exploit the ignorance of the people" was through the instruction of Muslim children in French language and ideas. "Instruction destroys prejudices, prevents the unreflected adoption of others' ideas . . . it will eliminate the multitude of absurd beliefs which the Arab people accept because they do not have the means to dispute them" (De Neveu 1846: 13).

In this respect, the civilizing mission went hand in hand with an "educating mission" and a "Christianizing mission." Such a connection was explicitly made by Charles de Foucauld, explorer and colonial missionary in the Moroccan and Algerian Sahara who spent fifty years proselytizing and educating the Touaregs. "We, French, have two duties in Africa. The first is the administration and civilization of our northwest African empire. . . . In civilizing it, we lift its inhabitants morally and intellectually. . . . The second [duty] is the evangelization of our colonies" (Bazin n.d.: 408). Many soldier-colonizers further viewed themselves as doctors, bringing a sick Algeria back to spiritual, intellectual, and economic health. "When one encounters a sick person on the road, one brings him to the hospital and heals him without asking his opinion. . . . The human duty is to help every individual, to lend him aid and assistance. . . . Barbaric peoples are invalids; civilized peoples are doctors" (Servier 1913: 203).

While there were certainly critics of the *mission civilisatrice* within the French academy and government (cf. Marchal 1901), the colonial administration generally employed such medical imagery as moral justification for their violent conquest, their rape of Algerian land and culture. Such a justification assumed an "intemporal myth" by which Arab-*cum*-Muslim civilization was equated with a barbarous and oppressive past which the French forces had an ethical duty to eliminate in order to raise Algeria (and its impoverished people) to the present of modernity and the future of civilized nation-states (Guilhaume 1992: 196–198; Addi 1996). Without the French administrators' constant vigilance, Algeria would unfailingly return to its barbaric, Islamic past, and the primordial bonds that were seen as constituting Algeria's precolonial unity would recalcify in no doubt violent fashion.

The Kabyle Myth

In the primordial battle between sedentaries and nomads, Christians and Muslims, the Mediterranean and the Sahara, the French administration sought an ally to aid them in their colonial labors and to justify their civilizing mission. Following Tocqueville's lead, they identified a number of ethnic, racial, and religious divisions within Algeria's indigenous population: Turks, Moors (city-dwellers of Andalusian origin), Kougoulis (miscegenated Turks and Arabs), Bedouins (Arab desert nomads), Arabs, Jews, and Berbers (among which the Kabyles were numbered). Located in close proximity to Algiers, but relatively isolated in steep mountain passes, Kabylia's endogamous, patrilineally related villages attracted military ethnologists and archaeologists in their search for pristine, unadulterated forms of North African culture. This desire was heightened by the increasingly close contacts between colonists and Kabyle villagers seeking work in the city or on the surrounding colonial plantations after the 1871 land expropriations. Within a few short decades, a network of research centers, archives, and journals devoted to the scientific study of Berber language and culture had sprung up in both the Maghreb and France.

The Space of Culture

Researchers of Kabyle society sought to map out the exact contours of the Berber presence within the colony, pursuing extended research in the Aurès mountains, the Djurdjura range, the Mzab, and the southern Sahara. Alongside laying out the geographical boundaries of present-day Algeria, French administrators subdivided Kabylia into "Greater Kabylia" and "Lesser Kabylia" along the Soummam Valley. "The French [created] the term 'Kabylia', just as they had created the term 'Algeria'; they even multiplied it into Kabylias" (Morizot 1985: 18–19). In a sense, by establishing such a homeland, and dividing it from Arab lands (despite its proximity to the capital of Algiers), French administrators sought to further reify the Kabyles as an entity that was mutually exclusive from and directly opposed to the Arabs.

In the second place, ethnological and linguistic studies attributed a cultural particularity to the Berbers' spatial identity. This identity was largely defined in terms of the oppositions—between sedentary and nomad, Christianity and Islam—outlined above. If the Arabs were seen as nomadically wandering the land, using it but not adding to it, the Kabyles were understood as the prototypical sedentaries, holed up in their mountain refuges, the architecture and village layout of which became the object of scrutiny. Military ethnographers detailed the various spaces of Kabyle livelihood, devoting particular attention to the mixed-use house (*axxam*) and village assembly area (*tajmaât*) (Daumas 1855; Hanoteau and Letourneux 1871). Moreover, as sedentaries, the Kabyles were projected as consummate peasants, faithfully tilling the soil. "[The Kabyles] own land whenever possible. They hold in high respect all property and although there are often no markings each property owner always knows the exact limits of what belongs to him" (Wysner 1945: 136). Scholars described the Berbers as frugal by nature, endowed with a "commercial instinct" which clearly demarcated them from the frivolous Arabs and made them appear similar to the European colonizers (Demontès 1922: 9). These "puritan businessmen" (Chevrillon 1927: 84) "work a great amount in every season; laziness is shameful in their eyes," in contrast to the Arabs, who "hate work" (Daumas 1855: 178; Daumas and Fabar 1847 (I): 21). Unlike the immobile, changeable but lazy Arabs, the Kabyles were seen as "patient, energetic, sober, intelligent, hard-working, strongly attached to their land" (Garrot 1910: 1046). Finally, in contrast to the Arabs, they "know the value of money" and "contrary to the Muslim law, loan it out with interest, very great interest" (Daumas and Fabar 1847 (I): 38).

If the Kabyles resembled the French in their sedentary economic practices, they also did so in terms of their religiosity. Less fanatically attached to Islam, the Kabyles "have accepted the Koran but they have not embraced it" (Daumas and Fabar 1847 (I): 77). From their worship of saints and reliance on heteroprax marabouts, to their failure to observe daily prayers, Ramadan fasts, and prohibitions on alcohol and pork, "the Kabyle people are far from the religious ideas of the Arab people" (Daumas and Fabar 1847 (II): 55). Moreover, their lack of religiosity was symbolized by women. Ethnographic evidence was mobilized to claim that Berber culture was originally matriarchal, and that the Islamic invasions of the seventh and eleventh centuries deposited only a thin layer of patriarchy on its surface. According to the scholars, the Kabyles continued to hold their women in high respect; Kabyle women were masters of the household, went in public unveiled, and generally "have a greater liberty than Arab women; they count more in society" (Daumas and Fabar 1847 (I): 40; Hamelin 1833: 15). The divorced or repudiated woman, instead of being made a slave in her father's house, enjoyed all of her liberties (Daumas and Fabar 1847 (I): 34; Pomel 1871: 56–57). Moreover, the Kabyles, colonial scholars emphasized, did not practice the polygamy that their religion allowed them, "contenting themselves generally to a single wife" (Garrot 1910: 1047). In the end, then, the Kabyles seemed to approach French Christian morals in their practices, proving that their Islamization had always been merely superficial.

> Beneath the Muslim peel, one finds a Christian seed. We recognize now that the Kabyle people, partly autochthonous, partly German in origin, previously entirely Christian, did not completely transform itself with its new religion. . . . [The Kabyle] re-dressed himself in a *burnous,* but he kept underneath his anterior social form, and it is not only with his facial tattoos that he displays before us, unbeknownst to him, the symbol of the Cross. (Daumas and Fabar 1847 (I): 77)

In parallel fashion, the Kabyles' political structure, not determined by Islamic absolutism, belied a proximity to postrevolutionary French ideals of "liberty, equality, fraternity." Colonial scholars characterized the Berbers as honorable warriors, fiercely defending their mountain refuges against all invaders (Phoenicians, Romans, Arabs, French). Unlike Arabs, Kabyle fighters displayed intelligence, courage, and honesty—rarely stealing and never cutting the heads off their enemies (Daumas and Fabar 1847 (I): 35; Pomel 1871: 59). Whereas the Arab accepted the tutelage of Islamic caliphs, the "fiercely independent" Berber, according to the reports, abhorred the very idea of central authority and was prepared to defend his absolute liberty to the death (Guernier 1950: 171–172). Their natural "anarchy" was seen to represent an underlying democracy, symbolized by the village assembly (*tajmaât*) and its elected officials. "In this republic, the dominating spirit is that of republican equality" (Guernier 1950: 172; cf. Masqueray 1886; Rambaud 1892). Rather than assimilating the *shari'a* (Qur'anic law) into civic life, the assembly rendered judgment on the basis of customary *qanoun* (cf. Hanoteau and Letourneux 1871; Pomel 1871). These laws not only regulated individual contracts and feuds, but also determined the bases for social solidarity, defining the individual's duties to the community in terms of collective labor (*tiwizi*) and taxes. As such,

> [The Kabyle's] political and social constitution is equally well different from that of the Arab people, and it must have been vigorously anchored in the mores and needs of the race for it to resist against the dissolving action of Islamism whose political regime presents an absolute contrast. In effect, instead of a despotic patriarchy which annihilates individual liberty, we find a democratic organization which is its antipode. (Pomel 1871: 56)

In the end, Kabylia represented for these scholars a "savage Switzerland" composed of federations of independent tribes/cantons (Daumas and Fabar 1847 (I): 419).

In this way, colonial scholars drew on economic, religious, and political comparisons to argue that the Kabyles were the exact cultural opposites of the Arabs. Rather than a single people united by a single religion, the Algerian Muslims were deemed to constitute in fact two peoples divided by a primordial hate. "Everywhere these two peoples live in contact, and everywhere an impassable gulf separates them; they only agree on one point: the Kabyle detests the Arab and the Arab detests the Kabyle. Such a vivacious antipathy can only be attributed to a traditional resentment, perpetuated from age to age between a conquering and a vanquished race" (Daumas and Fabar 1847 (I): 75). The same primordial struggle between the French colonizer and the Arab, between Christian and Muslim civilizations, between the Mediterranean sedentary and the Saharan nomad, then, was mapped directly onto the Berber-Arab ethnic dichotomy.

As such, the Kabyles were constituted as the natural ally of the French colonizers and were hence singled out as the privileged targets of the *mission civilisatrice*. "If the utopia of assimilation is realizable between the European and the native . . . it is therefore the Kabyle race which will be solely capable of it" (Pomel 1871: 60). With Islam constituting for the Kabyles a "superficial varnish, a simple stamp," their transformation into colonial subjects would be comparatively unencumbered. "This feeble religious, and uniquely religious, imprint frees other domains and opens up for us a much greater field and possibilities for action and education than on the plain" (Anon. 1924: 216). Moreover, with their sedentary history of working the land, their thrifty, proto-capitalist spirit, and their willingness to migrate in search of work, it was believed that, with a little training, the Kabyles "will easily assimilate to our ideas, to our labor methods" (Demontès 1930: 360). Indeed, the Kabyles' very lack of social and economic evolution was considered a boon for their colonial development under the tutelage of French educators.

> The young Kabyles will very quickly become good laborers (*bons ouvriers*), even quicker than Europeans, for their primitive natures are the most receptive; they have a great vacuum to fill; they absorb knowledge almost without effort, unconsciously, as a dry sponge absorbs water. It is a virgin land where fecundity arrives almost spontaneously. They assimilate languages, arts, formulas with a marvelous promptness. (Rambaud 1892: 324)

In this way, the Kabyle Myth served to underwrite a two-headed rape of Algeria's resources and cultures, simultaneously underwriting both the practical mission of conquest and colonization and the ethical mission of civilization.

The Historical Record: Times and Others

In order to support the narrative of a future of progress and civilization, scholars employed a historiographic approach, plotting the spatial and cultural alliances and oppositions detailed in the present back over time (cf. Fabian 1983). Drawing on linguistic, archaeological, and physiological comparisons, a series of conflicting hypotheses concerning the ancient origin of Berber tribes were developed and argued in colonial journals like the *Revue Africaine, Revue du Monde Musulman,* and the *Revue des Deux Mondes.* Some contributors, following Ibn Khaldun, attributed a Semitic origin to Berber tribes as descendants of the Canaanites chased out of the Holy Land by the early Israelites (Mercier 1871; Odinot 1924; Tauxier 1862–1863). These military ethnologists regarded the observed sedentary position of the Berber tribes as a recent innovation, viewing them as naturally nomadic. "They still have the blood in their veins of the movement that motivated the migrations of their ancestors" (Odinot 1924: 140). Indeed, the entire history of North Africa could be read, according to one theory, as a succession of invasions by migrant peoples, as a perpetual movement from Orient to Occident stretching up until the sixteenth century (Tauxier 1862: 444). While Berber-speaking populations during the colonial period differentiated themselves from their Arabophone neighbors, there remained a cultural and linguistic Semitic kinship traceable across time and space. "If one observes the everyday life of the Berbers, one will see that their fibbery, their duplicity, their love for lies are comparable to the most puerile defects of their Arab brothers and their cousins, the Jews" (Odinot 1924: 148). In this respect, there remained for both Berbers and Arabs an unsurpassable gulf to European civilization, a gulf measurable in terms of a distant temporal and spatial origin evidenced by currently observable cultural traits.

Against these theories of cultural distance, other colonial observers insisted on the hybrid character of Berber tribes, as simultaneously belonging to the Orient and Occident. Whether as sedentaries or nomads, as relatively recent arrivals or virtual autochthones, the Berbers, according to such theorists, had integrated cultural features from Asia, Africa, and Europe (Mercier 1871; Rinn 1889). Linguistically, the Berber language was classified as Hamito-Semitic, with an estimated one-third of its vocabulary deriving from Arabic and the rest from East African (Hamitic) tongues. Physically, Berber-speaking populations exhibited somatic features identified with a variety of geographic regions, from the dark skin of Africa to the high cheekbones of Asia to the green eyes of northern Europe. Moreover, according to these scholars, each successive invasion of the North African region had laid a sediment of cultural heritage absorbed and preserved in the social memory and everyday practice of the contemporary Berber peoples (Rinn 1889: 189). In this respect, the Berbers were identified, in their cultural, linguistic, and physiognomic hybridity, as the exemplars and vessels of a particular North African history and identity, one in which Europeans and Arabs had played only a marginal role.

Parallel to this particularistic reading of North African history, a Eurocentric narrative developed, one which insisted that the Berbers belonged directly to one or more European races (Brémond 1942; Guernier 1950; Maunier 1922). Drawing on a range of archaeological and physical anthropological evidence, these scholars traced the Berbers to ancient European tribal migrations from across the Mediterranean. As early as 1792, scholars had hypothesized a Vandal origin to North African tribes, and this hypothesis was given renewed weight by the discoveries of Celtic-like steles near Constantine by the archaeologist Louis Féraud in 1863 (Ferrié and Boëtsch 1992b: 190).

Indeed, the attribution of kinship with indigenous European peoples, whether Basques and Catalans on the one hand or Gaels and Celts on the other, was more generally accompanied by heuristic attempts to understand the Arab/Berber divide via comparisons with other ethnic and linguistic divisions extant in Europe. Ernest Carette, for one, attempted to relate the ethnic divisions in Algeria to the medieval French regional-linguistic opposition between the northern *langue d'oïl* and the southern *langue d'oc* (Carette 1848: 60–70). While Carette associated Kabyle culture with the spirit of the northern *langue d'oïl*, subsequent ethnological studies concluded the contrary (cf. Busset et al. 1929). Lucien Bertholon argued both sides of the controversy, alternately identifying blond-haired "native European Berbers" (*Berbères de souche européenne*) with Celts, Ligurians, Danubians, and Aegeans (1898). In spite of these differences, many scholars would end up agreeing with the subtitle of Général Edouard Brémond's 1942 book, that "Barbary is a European Country." In that work, Brémond identified the Berbers as having maintained many of the traditions (from clothing to architecture to funerary rites) at the origin of those extant in modern Provence or Auvergne, concluding definitively that "[t]here is absolutely no doubt that the [Berber] populations of North Africa were originally Mediterranean or Nordic European and have not since been modified" (1942: 114). Or, as Eugène Guernier later opined, "The Berbers are part of the rational West in formal opposition to the Arabs, who are above all of the imaginative Orient" (1950: 173).

However, if the Berbers shared a racial and cultural kinship with the conquering French, their development, as Carette implied with his comparison with medieval France, had stagnated several centuries prior (Lorcin 1995: 43–45). Louis Milliot described the Berbers' socioeconomic institutions as "rude and primitive," resembling those of medieval France of the tenth century (1932: 129). Brémond concluded his study similarly: "If the Maghreb received nothing from Arabia, little from the Sudan, and almost everything from the Mediterranean, it has also many traits in common with our Middle

Ages, traits which we have since forgotten" (1942: 362). As such, the Berbers, for colonial scholars, rather than primitive savages in need of salvation, represented an earlier period of Europe's own past, a past which could be resurrected and then modernized once the bark of Arab and Islamic civilization had been stripped away.

As such, the colonial debates over the origins of the colony's natives established a set of ethnic categories and oppositions which equated observable cultural phenomena with a variety of distant pasts. Such conflicting comparisons mark the structural ambivalence of a colonial project with both scientific and military goals, operating under a joint imperative to map out and classify ethnological differences and simultaneously assimilate such difference into the knowable and practicable. In assimilating Berber and Arab tribes to a uniform Semitic origin, colonial scholars portrayed colonialism as an inherent spatial conflict between East and West, between Islam and Christianity. Contrastingly, the association of Berbers with Europe's past underwrote the ambivalent assimilationist strategies of the colonial project, with the Berbers singled out as the privileged targets of the *mission civilisatrice*. In either case, the Berbers' cultural antiquity represented a threat to the spatiotemporal unity of the empire, a threat of anteriority that had to be overcome lest it lead to sectarian tribalism. The ambivalent approaches to such difference—its isolation or assimilation—depended on whether the Berbers' relation to Islam, a religion approached as incommensurate with French norms, was constituted as central or merely superficial.

France's *Mare Nostrum*

The elaboration and spatiotemporal mapping of Kabyle ethnic particularity in French colonial scholarship dovetailed and interacted with two parallel ideological processes. The first concerned the centralization of French hegemony in the metropole in the context of great regional linguistic heterogeneity. The colony provided a site of experimentation with the norms and institutions of modernity (e.g., urban planning and education), which could later be reapplied to the metropole (Colonna 1975; Rabinow 1989; Wright 1997). The *mission civilisatrice* thus concerned not only the indigenous populations of Algeria, but also the peripheral populations of metropolitan France. Secondly, the designation of the Kabyles as the prime targets of social and cultural incorporation corresponded to explicit attempts to ideologically realign the French nation with its own classical past via the Mediterranean. In identifying proto-democratic social structures and material culture parallels among the Berbers, colonial scholars posited a circum-Mediterranean cultural unity that not only justified the colonial endeavor, but also recast French civilization as the natural inheritor of the Roman Empire. These two processes—of French metropolitan centralization and imperial expansion—belie a structural ambivalence within colonial French cultural policy which simultaneously, as Michael Dietler (1994) has demonstrated, sought to derive its legitimacy from both its Latin heritage and its Gaulish ancestry.

Regionalism and French Centralization

The recurrent colonial reference to ethnic divisions in France in the colonial debates over Berber origins indicates a late-nineteenth-century obsession with integrating peripheral metropolitan populations into the national project of the Third Republic. While French history textbooks written during this period (and often still in use today in one form or another) attributed French ethnic origins to "our ancestors, the Gauls" and treated the French nation as a *fait accompli* with the 1789 French Revolution, scholarly debates over these origins and unity continued apace throughout this period.[10] As Eugen Weber (1976) has poignantly argued, the process of the nationalization of France actually continued well into the twentieth century, with cultural and political power only gradually being taken away from local clergy and notables by state-appointed and elected schoolteachers and prefects.

Of particular importance in this gradual construction of the French nation was the place of local languages in the national education system. In many cases, especially in Brittany, this question of linguistic homogenization was tied directly to that of secularization. There, the four administrative districts (*départements*) established after the 1789 French Revolution were mapped directly onto the former province's four historical Catholic dioceses or bishoprics, which themselves corresponded to four linguistic areas where different dialects of Breton were spoken (Ford 1991). After Napoleon's 1801 concordat with the Catholic Church, as reiterated as late as 1850 in the Loi Falloux, clergy members gained a greater say in school administration and everyday teaching. Schools became primarily establishments for children to learn religious catechism, and, given the ambiguity of the legislation, this teaching was administered in the respective Breton dialect (McDonald 1989: 37). In this way, the reproduction of Breton cultural belonging was largely mediated by the church through the school system.

It was exactly these religious means of ethnolinguistic identity production which the Ferry laws of the early 1880s sought to eliminate. These laws made all elementary schooling compulsory and secular, removing all influence of the clergy from the school system. Further, they unequivocally established French as the only acceptable language within the schools. As such, these centralization measures sought to further entrench the national presence in the peripheral French regions. By regaining control of the national education system, the Third Republic hoped to reinstill a threatened sense of national unity and allegiance and, in so doing, forestall social movements in the name of infranational identity. Besides the Paris Commune and the

Kabyle revolt, the years 1870–71 had seen the growth of separatist movements in the southeastern Occitan-speaking region, such as the *Ligue du Midi*. By the late 1930s, the Third Republic had created explicit legislation outlawing these movements as threats to the national territorial integrity. In this way, there exists a clear correlation between the efforts at national integration within the metropole and those employed within the colonies (particularly Algeria), a continuity which has not been lost on contemporary regional activists in France who have repeatedly decried the French nation-state as engaging in a protracted policy of "internal colonialism" (*colonialisme intérieur*) (cf. Sibé 1988).

Nonetheless, as in Algeria, such practical measures often enabled the elaboration rather than the erasure of ethnic and linguistic categories of belonging. As in Kabylia, nineteenth-century ethnologists and linguists were attracted to rural, peripheral areas like Finistère (Brittany) and Auvergne (Occitania), where supposedly pristine cultures, unsullied by modernity and industrialization, could be observed. These Third Republic scholars published ethnographies (esp. Chevallier 1934), collected traditional songs and dances (Quellien 1889), and compiled dictionaries. These endeavors contributed largely to the outlining of essential cultural characteristics shared by the inhabitants of a given region and the attribution of such differences to natural racial categories or "genuses" (*génie d'oc* vs. *génie d'oïl* for instance). Moreover, such folkloristic accounts were readily consumed by a late-nineteenth-century Parisian elite in the midst of a romantic artistic revolution in which an Occitan/Provençal literary renaissance, and particularly the poems of Frédéric Mistral, flourished. A parallel rediscovery of Celtic identity occurred during this same period, with the figure of Vercingetorix, the Gaul chieftain who surrendered to Julius Caesar, being resurrected and assimilated into the doxic foundational myths of the French nation, particularly as a symbol of national revenge after the 1870 defeat to the Prussians (Dietler 1994: 588–589). This romantic celebration of cultural difference should not be seen as contrary to French modernization, but rather as assimilation's determined opposite, part of the "ambivalence of modernity" (Bauman 1991), part of a structural nostalgia for a time before the state (Herzfeld 1997). Moreover, as in the Kabyle case, the perpetuation of a discourse of ethnic difference would later be mobilized within the regionalist movements themselves.

The Colonial Construction of the "Mediterranean"

The second discursive formation into which the elaboration of Kabyle ethnic particularity fed was the articulation of a trans-Mediterranean unity, originally conceived by the Roman legions, reanimated by the French colonial forces, and reappropriated in the contemporary cultural politics of Algerians in France.[11] Two separate but interrelated tropes underlie such articulations—the Mediterranean as source and the Mediterranean as crossroads—each of which was largely elaborated during the period of French colonial expansion in Algeria. In the first place, the construction of the Mediterranean category in colonial scholarship was linked to narratives of loss and recovery. This was based on a historical understanding of the region as the cradle (*berceau*) of human civilization. Colonial scholars read the history of the Mediterranean as an Augustinian "Fall" from this primeval unity to a state of cultural, religious, and ecological disorder, with Islam displacing and subjugating Christianity.

In this sense, many observers viewed the colonial conquest of the western Mediterranean as a new Crusade, as yet another opportunity to restore Christianity to its birthplace. More specifically, they understood the colonization as finishing the work of the Castillian *reconquista* of Muslim-controlled Andalusia and reuniting both shores of the Mediterranean. "In the sixteenth century, the reconquest of Spain by the Christians, the installation of Turkish piratery on the Algerian coast, caused the isolation of Algeria from Europe. This tie was not reestablished until the arrival of the French in 1830" (Di Lucio et al. 1938: 9). Following this religious trajectory, Christian missionary work served a concomitant role in the colonial project, with French Jesuit and other proselytizing groups establishing churches, monasteries, and educational facilities throughout the Middle East and North Africa. The *Pères Blanches,* for instance, not only provided exemplary schooling to local villages, but also compiled local cultural and linguistic data which would contribute to the elaboration of Kabylia as a target of assimilation and Mediterranean kinship. As such, the French colonial empire was interpreted as messianic in nature, as the restorer of a Mediterranean paradise lost.

Alongside the vision of the Mediterranean as a cultural source since decayed lay a parallel image of the Mediterranean as a crossroads (*carrefour*), a site *par excellence* of cross-cultural communication. While the first image was based on a historical notion of a primeval cultural homogeny, the second emphasized a heterogeneity over the *longue durée,* with diversity and internal hybridity seen as giving the region its strength. In large part, this latter notion derived from the development of the human sciences since the sixteenth century, and specifically the elaboration of geographic and climatological theories of human behavior. Already, Enlightenment philosophers like Rousseau, Diderot, and Montesquieu had resorted to a "geographic spirit" (*esprit géographique*) to explain human diversity across Europe (Ruel 1991: 8). Johann Herder took this logic a step further, developing a classificatory system of culture (*Kultur*) as related to warmer or colder climes (1968 [1792]). The Mediterranean, in this classification, took on a particular role, as an identifiable and unified geographic and climatic region situated between the temperate zone of Europe and the tropics of Africa. For instance, the colonial geographer Emile-Félix Gautier argued that the North African

Djurdjura, Atlas, and Rif mountain ranges constituted an integral part of the Alpine system, outlining the contours of the sunken continent of "Tyrrhénide" (1922: 7–8). More generally, the Mediterranean was seen to serve as a mediating agent (*agent médiateur*) between the two, giving Europe access to Africa's warm breezes (cf. Reclus 1876).

From this geographic and climatological conception of the Mediterranean developed a cultural understanding of its inhabitants as likewise midway between Europe and Africa, between the Orient and the Occident (Ruel 1991: 8–9; Shavit 1994: 320). The colonial geographer Elisée Reclus made the connection forthright, describing the Mediterranean as a "junction between the three continental masses of Europe, Asia, and Africa, between the Aryans, Semites, and Berbers" (1876: 33). In large part, this discursive movement from geography to human behavior contributed to the outlining of a *homo mediterraneus* racial type displaying a mixture or "melting pot" of physiognomic and cultural features from the continental regions surrounding it (Bodley 1926: 37; Shavit 1994). The ideal form of this type was the *homme frontière*, the border-crossing figure of an Ibn Khaldun or a Leon Africanus who, like the ancient Phoenicians, traveled across the region, diffusing cultural knowledge throughout. In Fernand Braudel's later wording, the sea served as a "transport surface" (*surface de transport*) for these inveterate navigators, and the region as a whole existed as a "system of circulation," a veritable "space-in-movement" (*espace-mouvement*) (1977: 57, 77).

This construction of the Mediterranean as a primordial site of cultural exchange and miscegenation similarly underwrote arguments for colonial expansion into the region. The 1830 attack on Algiers sought to reopen trans-Mediterranean trade routes blocked by the dey's pirates. More generally, the colonial mission sought to restore the proto-capitalist circulation of people and commodities blocked by the political divisions and taxations within the Ottoman Empire. Throughout the nineteenth century, the French military actively disaggregated isolated villages and urban neighborhoods throughout Algeria, underwriting the mass movement of native laborers within the colonies and to the metropole. Alongside the diffusion of French language and cultural knowledge through the colonial school system, this circulation of labor thus inscribed itself within a colonial construction of a *longue durée* of Mediterranean cross-cultural communication.

Alongside the use of these parallel images of the Mediterranean (as source and crossroads) as a justification for colonial intervention operated a third historical antecedent—that of the Roman Empire. While the Napoleonic and various Crusader empires had been short-lived, the Roman legions were presented as having successfully unified the entire Mediterranean basin (considered its *mare nostrum*) for more than three centuries, bathing it in the font of scientific advancement and a universal legal framework. In North Africa, according to colonial historiography, they had further enriched the land—settling the nomadic peoples, building great cities, establishing irrigation canals and aqueducts, and generally transforming the desert into the "bread-basket of Rome" (Fontaine 1957: 23). However, the rise of Islam in the region was seen as having destroyed this progress, leading to the degradation of the famous canals and the return of the region's inhabitants to a state of cultural and physical "insalubrity" (Anon. 1836: 2–4).

The French colonial state, in politically reuniting North Africa with Europe and refertilizing the soil on their plantations, could claim itself as the rightful guardian of the Latin *mare nostrum*. Colonial institutions dressed themselves in the clothes of their classical antecedents and explicitly presented themselves as the heirs and restorers of rational civilization, of a new "Pax Romana," to a region which had since fallen into barbary (Guilhaume 1992: 199; Lorcin 1995: 20). As René Maunier concluded in his study of the French colonial presence, "We have thus many proofs that the Mediterranean has remained even today the Greco-Roman sea, and that the flame of classical civilizations has not been extinguished. It is up to our country to maintain [the flame] on Algerian soil; it is up to France to use her force to confirm the grandeur of Rome, as she has perpetuated its wisdom through her genius" (1922: 107).

Designating the Native: Berbers and Latins

Moreover, in order to understand the natives they encountered, French military ethnographers returned consistently to Roman texts, particularly to Sallust's *War of Jugurtha* and Tacitus's *The Germania*. Citing these texts, colonial writers like Emile Masqueray (1886), René Maunier (1922), Ernest Mercier (1871), and Général Edouard Brémond (1942) argued that the Berber-speaking inhabitants of Kabylia had a particular affinity with the Roman Empire. Général Brémond, for instance, signaled the centrality of Berber rulers to the Roman Empire, both in providing emperors, popes, generals, and theologians (including Saint Augustine), as well as Rome's most feared enemies (particularly the North African chieftain Jugurtha, who battled Rome in the Punic Wars). However, in spite of the political enmity between Berbers and Romans, the Berbers were understood as nonetheless respecting and borrowing from their conqueror. "If Rome was for the Berber the detested occupier, she represented for him an ideal, a wisdom made from peace, order, and unity" (Guernier 1952: 195). "In fact," Brémond added, "the Berbers were able to contribute (*garnir*) to Rome and make it better than it had ever been" (1942: 160).

Furthermore, in spite of the fall of the Roman Empire and the Islamic invasions, colonial scholars viewed the Berbers as having maintained this Latin genius in their lack of religiosity and their "democratic" social organization. They made frequent comparisons between the *tajmaât* and the Roman Senate, as well as between the *qanoun* and the Roman *interdicta* (cf. Garrot 1910: 649; Masqueray 1886: 50, 56; Maunier 1922: 106). Lucien Bertholon, in an article entitled "A Comparative Sociology between the Homerian Acheans and Contemporary Kabyles" (1913), argued that Aegean civilization had diffused across the Mediterranean and had been incorporated into modern Kabyle institutions and cultural traits. René Maunier likewise devoted his course in Algerian sociology at the University of Algiers to demonstrating the "perennial character of classical civilization" among the Berbers (1922: 106). Finally, Emile Masqueray viewed his study of Berber settlements as "the surest means to understand the primitive institutions of classical states and to rectify or confirm that which ancient and modern historians have said" (1886: 222). In this respect, the Algerian Berbers came to represent for French scholars a vehicle with which to reconnect to their own classical past, to recenter French national-colonial identity around the Latin Mediterranean south instead of the Germanic north (Ferrié and Boëtsch 1992b: 193). Moreover, embodying the paradise lost of a Latin Africa or unified Mediterranean, the Berbers' persistence served to legitimize the French conquest—as a liberation of France's classical ancestry from the clutches of Islamic barbarism.

Moreover, the Berbers represented for the colonizer not only the privileged inheritors of Latin civilization, but also the true *homo mediterraneus*. Many scholars classified the Berbers as the original inhabitants of North Africa, who had preserved more than any other people their Mediterranean identity (cf. Brémond 1942; Mercier 1871). Other scholars argued that they constituted the prime example of an *homme frontière*, embodying the cultural heterogeneity that marked the "genius" of the region (Mercier 1871; Odinot 1924; Rinn 1889; Tauxier 1862–1863). Tracing their origins from the simultaneous movements of peoples from the European West and the Asian East, the Berbers accordingly represented the perfect middlemen between the Orient and the Occident, Europe and Africa, just as the Mediterranean Sea itself did climatologically speaking. Indeed, the Berbers were often represented as the consummate peddlers, moving from town to town throughout the region trading goods or offering their services (cf. Daumas and Fabar 1847 (I): 26; Wysner 1945).[12] The contemporary Berber cultural movement has mobilized these stereotypes of racial and cultural hybridity to make claims for their assumed role as the privileged mediators in the contemporary cultural politics of the Mediterranean region.

A New Latin Race?

The colonial discourse of Mediterranean culture, in both its originary and crossroads personas as well as in its Latin heritage, was not limited to the Berber people alone. Rather, in paradoxical fashion, colonists simultaneously constructed a similar ethnic category for the particular mixture of European peoples which had come to settle in Algeria by the early twentieth century. With settlers arriving from Spain, Italy, and Malta as well as France, colonial Algeria constituted a veritable "melting pot of the Mediterranean" in which, through intermarriage and miscegenation, a "new white race"(or Cagayous) was being created (Lorcin 1995: 196–197).[13]

> A new people is being created on the sunny shores of the Mediterranean, and one witnesses its formation every day. A very mixed people, formed from the most diverse ethnic elements—French, Spanish, Italian, Maltese, German—but a people which will soon have its own individuality and unity; for, under the powerful effects of this soil and this African sun and in the presence of races opposed to the European by their mores and religion, the oppositions, regardless of how alive they were at first, erase themselves and the divergences disappear. (Demontès 1906: 8)

Spurred by the writings of the academician Louis Bertrand, a "Latin Africa" (or *Algérianiste*) movement arose which viewed the Algerian "crucible" as the privileged site for the development of a new Rome to heal Europe's recent decadence (Bertrand 1921). The "Eternal Mediterranean" of Roman grandeur, according to Bertrand, persisted under the African sun, "piercing through the trompe-l'oeil of modern Islamic décor," and provided the means for "France, fatigued by centuries of civilization, [to] rejuvenate through contact with this apparent vigorous barbary" (1930 [1889]: 8–13). While the Berbers may have preserved a certain degree of Rome's heritage, they did so in a "bastardized" form, diluting it with African and Islamic traditions (Bertrand 1921: 33). The southern European settler, unencumbered by these outside influences, better preserved the true Latino-Mediterranean civilization and virile traits which could lead to human progress, instead of posing, as Islam did, a barrier to it.

Bertrand and his followers disseminated the notion of a Latin-Mediterranean race throughout colonial North Africa and France primarily in the form of novels and personal memoirs published in reviews and serials throughout the 1920s and 1930s (Lorcin 1995: 207–208; Ruel 1991: 13). These fictional and autobiographical accounts celebrated the vitality of the Latin settler who, in being "rebarbarized" through his contact with the native, provided the key for "national regeneration" (Lorcin 1995: 204; cf. Bertrand 1930 [1889]). However, the movement, with its fascist intonations, committed political suicide in the late 1930s and was replaced by the more inclusive "eternalist" vision of the Mediterranean of the *Ecole d'Alger* (Haddour 1993). Spurred by the left-leaning fiction of Gabriel Audisio and Albert Camus, this school emphasized that the "Mediterranean" existed as more than a body of water linking different port cities, but as a liquid "continent," an integrated "country" (*pays*) and even a "homeland" (*patrie*) (Audisio 1935).

These literary debates spread beyond the immediate consuming public in the region. As Patricia Lorcin (1995: 209) has discussed, the elaboration of a Latin-Mediterranean race found its supporters in European ethnological circles, displacing the privileged position the Berbers had occupied in racial geographies and taxonomies of North Africa. Braudel himself began his doctoral studies in the 1920s, at the exact moment in which the racial and historical dimensions of Mediterranean unity were being fiercely debated. In his subsequent works, he would side clearly with the *Ecole d'Alger*'s vision of the "Eternal Mediterranean," maintaining its insistence on the region as an integrated geographic and historical system. Furthermore, within the framework of colonialism, this latter Mediterranean universalism, while tempering the jingoistic French triumphalism overlaying colonial practice at the time (Basfao and Henry 1991: 45), nonetheless continued to underwrite associationalist policies which failed to reconcile with the burgeoning nationalist movement (Lorcin 1995: 211; Haddour 1993). This celebratory tenor and savior role attributed by Bertrand to the new, miscegenated Latin-Mediterranean race echoed in the more radical wartime defenses of the colony and the violent opposition of certain settlers to the French government's decision to negotiate with the Muslim parties and eventually withdraw from Algeria.

In this way, the Mediterranean category provided the simultaneous means for France to justify its colonization of Algeria, and for the Algerian colony to then specify itself within the French empire. For, if the Berbers, as the retainers of a lost Roman legacy, could ideologically be vivisected from the Arabo-Islamic indigenous mass and made the natural allies (if not historical cousins) of the invading French, then a rebarbarized, miscegenated Cagayous race could likewise be removed from the larger imperial entity, thus further underwriting the opposition between colony and metropole. "Algeria made itself, one can say, against the will of the French government, thanks to the valiant French soldier, to the intelligence and tenacity of several colonizers, and aided by the conquering push of Latin immigrants" (Bertrand 1934: 45).

In this sense, questions of colonization inscribed themselves in an ongoing process of French national elaboration. However, as the debates over Berber ethnogenesis make clear, this process of national construction, while seemingly dependent on the assimilation of primordial cultural and linguistic differences, actually deployed elaborated versions of them in its nostalgic myths of legitimacy, and thus indirectly underwrote future regionalisms and ethnic nationalisms. Although Algeria never had a specific "Berber policy" as in Morocco,[14] Kabylia arguably received disproportionate attention in terms of the execution of national legislation, with many of its particular cultural-legal forms practically tolerated (Ageron 1960; 1991: 72–73).

The ambivalent implementation of the Kabyle Myth had a dual effect. First, it opened up wide avenues for emigration to France. Often expropriated from their family landholdings by colonial land laws and exposed to French language and culture in school, Kabyle men became prime targets for government and private recruiters to man the French war machine (as soldiers or factory workers) during the two world wars (Khellil 1979: 72–77). Although this migratory flux was to spread gradually to Arab Algeria as well, on the eve of the Algerian war more than 60 percent of Algerian immigrants in France still came from the Kabyle provinces, and nearly one-quarter of all Kabyle families had at least one member working in France (Khellil 1994: 14). Second, such colonial attention underwrote the later development of a Berber cultural movement in the days following independence. Often adopting the rhetoric of the Kabyle Myth, Berber cultural and political associations continued to employ anti-assimilationist claims of being simultaneously primordial (ante-Arab) and European (or at least as a synthesis of East and West, a bridge across the Mediterranean) in their appeals to European governments for economic and political support. Likewise, their stipulated ancestral association with indigenous French minorities (Auvergnats, Basques, Celts) has provided groundwork for their current association with regional cultural movements from these regions.

Decolonization and National Identity

The Algerian war constituted a significant transformation in the internal organization of both the French and Algerian nation-states. Commencing before the dust had settled from Dien Bien Phu, the 1954–62 war was not just about the national liberation of Algeria, but it was truly played out and understood as a civil war *within* France.[15] In a few short years, nearly four-fifths of France's territory was torn away, and the entire state apparatus of the Fourth Republic had been toppled, replaced (by a returned Charles de Gaulle), and then almost toppled again in an aborted coup d'état by an ultra-conservative faction of France's own military, the Organization of the Secret Army (OAS). Under the direction of de Gaulle, France turned its political orientation 180 degrees to the north, to the construction of an integrated and unified Europe, the groundwork of which had been recently laid in the 1958 Treaty of Rome (Fabre 1992). Pulling out of NATO and supporting Francophone secessionist movements in Quebec, France embarked on a postcolonial national trajectory as an independent player in the bipolar geopolitical system. In this regards, decolonization created not just one new nation, but two.

The Berber in Algerian Nationalism

From the perspective of Algeria, the colonial elaboration of an Arab/Berber dichotomy would have a profound impact on the sociocultural modalities of the Algerian nationalist movement and the nascent Algerian state.[16] In the 1920s and 1930s, the various rival tendencies represented within the broader Algerian nationalist movement—from the constitutional reform initiatives of Ferhat Abbas's Democratic Union for the Algerian Manifesto (UDMA) to the Islamic reformism of 'Abd al-Hamid ben Badis's Association of Algerian Muslim *'Ulama* (AUMA) to the radical separatist nationalism of Messali Hadj's Algerian People's Party (PPA) and Movement for the Triumph of Democratic Liberties (MTLD)—each in its own way explicitly sought to overcome the supposed ethnic divides between the various peoples of Algeria. In the first place, the AUMA drew its ideological inspiration from the larger *salafi* reformist movement of Muslim modernist intellectuals that sought a return to the supposedly pure Islam of the "pious ancestors" (*al-salaf al-sâlih*) (Haddab 1984; Merad 1967). In this pursuit, Algerian nationalist theorists—including Tawfiq al-Madani, Malek Bennabi, Mohammed Lacheraf—forged a counter-history to that written by the French colonizers, seeking to inscribe an Algerian national spirit into the precolonial past (McDougall 2003; Touati 1997). These writers, closely following the arguments of Ibn Khaldun and echoing the ethnogenetic theories of Tauxier and Odinot, held that the current Berber peoples were descended from a Semitic tribe that had migrated to North Africa from ancient Canaan hundreds of years before the emergence of Islam (El Tayeb 1987: 5). Reversing the Kabyle Myth while borrowing directly from it, they presented Berbers and Arabs as essentially unified groups whose co-existence in North Africa since the seventh century constituted the basis for the future Algerian nation.

Tawfiq al-Madani, a *salafi* scholar and *'ulama* figure in the nationalist movement, presented a particularly poignant version of this ethnonational narrative in a series of historiographic works originally published in the 1920s and 1930s. Invoking scientific truth, he directly attacked French colonial scholars' misrepresentation of the historical reality of the Berbers' true origins, claiming that they

> committed a horrendous outrage against history and . . . wishing to serve political schemes, have attacked and effaced historical facts; they have said that the Berbers are of Germanic or of Latin origin, that they migrated to Africa from Europe. Those who make such statements have no aim but to influence the Berbers, to distance all that is Asian from them and to convince them that they are of European origin; that they must return to Europe and to all that is European. (al-Madani 1963 [1932]: 97, quoted in McDougall 2003: 73)

Having berated colonial scholarship for its divide-and-rule politics, he nonetheless appropriated both its positivist methods and imagery, portraying the Berbers, with language drawn straight from the Kabyle Myth, as frugal laborers and noble warriors with a fearless love of freedom (al-Madani 1963 [1932]: 99–100). While staunchly resisting all foreign invaders, the Berbers were progressively civilized by the Phoenicians and finally the Arabs, with whom they shared an essential Eastern spiritual kinship, who brought them the true light of civilization in the form of Islam.

> Arabs and Berbers [. . .] became one nation, without the Berbers having greatly changed their ancient customs or the Arabs adopting those of the Berbers—they were brought together by their unity of religion, of morality and of interests. [. . .] The two peoples were of one inclination and one sentiment, and they shared a love of honor and glory, a passion for freedom, and the custom of greatly honoring guests. This commonality of inclination and morality broke through the barriers which the Romans, Vandals and Byzantines were unable to pierce. The Berbers became the strongest auxiliaries of the army of Islam. (al-Madani 1986 [1927]: 161, quoted in McDougall 2003: 79)

Writers like al-Madani thus constructed the Berbers as a prenational "national signifier," as the products of a centuries-old *mission civilisatrice* from the East that exactly reversed what the French portrayed themselves as accomplishing (McDougall 2003: 77). In so doing, they assimilated them into the "authentic" Algerian nation that was, at its essence, Arab and Islamic (Merad 1967: 93). Adopting the slogan "Islam is my religion; Algeria is my nation; and Arabic is my language," the AUMA foresaw the construction of a "new Algerian man," erased of superficial ethnic distinctions and purged of the urban cultural decadence and rural economic poverty imposed by colonialism. As it was adopted into the broader nationalist movement and the postcolonial state's ideology, this vision of the racially fused "new man" was promulgated as tantamount to a "decolonization of the mind" (*décolonisation des esprits*), thus seamlessly merging *salafi* reformism with the avowed socialism of the revolutionary National Liberation Front (FLN) (cf. Bennabi 1948; Benyahia 1970; Ibrahimi 1973).

In the meantime, Berber Algerians were not silent objects of the national conflict. From the very beginning, Kabyles were prominent in the nationalist parties, particularly in the movements of Messali and Abbas (who himself was Kabyle), marching side by side in protest with their "Arab brothers" both in Algeria and in France, where Kabyle emigrants dominated the nationalist scene. In France, thirty-five of the sixty-four founding members of the PPA were of Kabyle origin, including Amar Imache, second in command under Messali (Direche-Slimani 1992: 118). Kabylia was likewise the center of revolutionary activism, with the first congress of the FLN held in the Soummam Valley near Akbou in August 1956 and presided over by Kabyle leader Abane Ramdane. Revolutionary songs were composed in Berber, calling upon Kabyle villagers to "Rise up, Berber son!" (*Kker a mmi-s umazigh*) (Chaker 1985: 218). Indeed, the centrality of Kabylia to the nationalist movement was much noted by the colonial administration, who treated the region as a hotbed of anti-colonial activity and eventually targeted it during the war with a "scorched earth" policy, burning down villages to weed out nationalist fighters and relocating displaced villagers to government resettlement camps (Bourdieu and Sayad 1964; Quandt 1972).

Such joint participation did not, however, imply ideological unity. Opposing the *'ulama*'s univocal construction of an Arabo-Islamic Algeria, certain Berber activists within the nationalist movement underwrote a second discursive framework—an "Algerian Algeria" (*Algérie algérienne*)—that articulated a secular and multicultural vision for the future nation-state. The most extreme of these groups, led by Ali Yahia Rachid, even called for a rejection of any inclusion of Algeria in the larger Arab world, on the basis that Algeria was rightfully Berber in nature (Harbi 1980: 33). Beginning in 1949, such supporters of a multiethnic Algeria were successively excluded from the nationalist movement in a general purge that has become known as the movement's "Berberist crisis" (*crise berbériste*) (Carlier 1984). Kabyle Francophone authors like Mouloud Mammeri and Mouloud Feraoun were condemned for their anachronistic "regionalism," for trying "to please the colonialist press" at the expense of the nationalist movement (Lacheraf 1953; Sahli 1953). In subsequent years, other Kabyle revolutionary leaders, including Ramdane and later Krim Belkacem (one of the founders of the FLN), were assassinated for openly departing from the FLN's program (Stora 1991: 156–171).

These tensions between visions of an *Algérie algérienne* and an *Algérie arabo-musulmane* resurfaced after independence in 1962, as the FLN solidified its material and ideological authority. The Algiers Charter, adopted in April 1964 as Algeria's de facto constitution, declared Algeria to be an "Arab-Muslim country" and decried regionalist identities as "feudal survivals" and "obstacles to national integration." Perceiving this direction in the ruling FLN ideology, the Kabyle war hero Hocine Aït Ahmed founded the first rival political party in independent Algeria, the Socialist Forces Front (FFS), in September 1963 and subsequently led a ten-month guerrilla insurrection throughout Kabylia against the Algerian national army and what he decried as the "ethnic fascism" of President Ahmed Ben Bella. While the revolt failed to gain widespread support, the FFS remained a strong oppositional (though unarmed) force to the Algerian regime in both Kabylia and France even after Aït Ahmed's arrest and flight to Europe in 1965.

After 1973, the regime of Colonel Houari Boumedienne further demonized Berber identity as simultaneously backwards as part of the ante-Islamic age of ignorance (*jahiliyya*) and colonialist as having been privileged (if not invented) by the French. He pushed forward a program of Arabization of the Algerian media and educational system, importing teachers from Egypt to oversee the implementation of Arabic-only classrooms through the high school level (Grandguillaume 1983). Simultaneously, the government progressively eliminated university courses in Berber linguistics, in place since the colonial period, and established a disproportionate number of Islamic institutes in Berberophone areas.[17]

Vehemently opposing these measures and drawing on the earlier history of Kabyle emigrant activism in the nationalist movement, a group of Paris-based scholars (including Mouloud Mammeri), artists (including singer Taos Amrouche), and FFS activists (including Bessaoud Mohand Arab) founded the Berber Academy for Cultural Exchange and Research (later renamed in 1969 as *Agraw Imazighen*) in March 1967. While originally dedicated to the "universal" and "harmonious cooperation between all humanity," the *Agraw*'s goals became increasingly irredentist—"to introduce the larger public to the history and civilisation of Berbers, including the promotion of the language and culture" as stated in the second article of its 1969 statutes. Adopting the appellation *Imazighen* ("free men") and drawing on the imagery of Berber historical figures of resistance, members of the Academy worked to standardize Berber (Tamazight) and develop a neo-Tifinagh orthographic script.

This intellectual slant of Kabyle expatriate activism was underlined in the 1973 formation of the Berber Study Group at the Université de Paris-VIII-Vincennes. Dedicated to teaching Berber language and culture, it received national and international recognition, garnering the participation of many sympathetic, non-Kabyle scholars including such eminent names as Pierre Bourdieu and Ernest Gellner. In 1978, it formed the *Ateliers Imedyazen,* a publication cooperative in Paris, to diffuse such intellectual debates to a more popular level. Over the course of the next several years, the cooperative published works on linguistics, theater, poetry, and other literature, including translations into Tamazight (of Brecht, among others), grammar manuals, *dossiers de presse* that followed events in Algeria, and political communiqués, including the 1979 FFS party platform. These publications were further paralleled by the growth of a Kabyle recording industry in France, and particularly the invention of the "New Kabyle Song" (*neo-chanson kabyle*) by recording artists including Lounis Aït-Menguellet, Idir, Ferhat M'henni, and Lounès Matoub. Drawing on the earlier sung poetry of Taos Amrouche and the musical commentary on exile (*lghorba*) by Slimane Azem, these singer-songwriters produced "revolutionary songs of struggle" and eventually came to play direct political roles in the struggle for Berber linguistic rights (Mahfoufi 1994). Given this development of emigrant cultural production, as Salem Chaker has remarked, "it would not be an exaggeration to say that thousands of young Kabyles have learned to read and write in their language from those works published in France" (1985: 222).

Since the 1980s, these cultural productions have been underwritten by the formation of hundreds of Berber cultural associations, several Berbero-centric political parties, and a transnational World Amazigh Congress operating across an imagined Berber native space (*Tamazgha*), but largely based in France. Relying on the robust symbolism of the *tajmaât*, the *axxam*, and the "spirit of independence" of the "eternal Jugurtha," these groups have underlined the multicultural identity of Algeria as Arab, Berber, Muslim,

Flyer announcing a spectacle of Kabyle political folk music in Saint-Ouen (Paris) to commemorate the nineteenth anniversary of the 1980 "Berber Spring." Flyer is in the shape and color scheme of an Amazigh flag, with the Berber Z in the foreground. Characters under the headlines are in Tifinagh.

African, and Mediterranean, and vehemently opposed any "Middle Eastern or Afghan identity" proffered by Algerian state ideology.[18] Moreover, they have deployed physical anthropological evidence to claim that the Berbers' ancestors were the original Proto-Mediterraneans dating from 7000 B.C. (cf. Camps 1984). In a 1996 public lecture at the Tamazgha Berber cultural association in Paris, Kabyle historian Jean Dumaurier even claimed that the first Berber was Lucy herself, and then proceeded to present a Berberocentric rendition of human history as the progressive unfolding of the "Berber soul" (*âme berbère*). In this way, the repression of Berberity (*berbérité*) in Algeria and its simultaneous rehabilitation in France served to reinforce an Arab/ Berber opposition that in many ways echoed the colonial Kabyle Myth (Maddy-Weitzman 2001; Silverstein 2003).

French Regionalism

The Algerian conflict had simultaneous and similar repercussions for regionalist movements in France. Already in 1920, as the Algerian nationalist movement was emerging from within the Algerian immigrant community in France, the early Breton separatist movement, *Breiz Atao* (Brittany Forever), expressed overt support for liberation movements of indigenous peoples within the French colonies—with particular emphasis on Algeria —viewing their struggles as unified under the anti-colonial banner. However, by the 1930s, its leaders began to embrace the rising National Socialist party in Germany, and their visions of autonomy became increasingly racialist, imagining an exclusive Celtic state free from Arab "contamination" (McDonald 1989: 122–123).

Such racial essentialism has been the exception rather than the norm in the great political diversity that characterizes regionalist movements in France. Many regional movements have adopted overtly Marxist rhetoric in their discursive critiques of the French nation-state's internal colonialism (cf. Marti 1975; Sibé 1988). The Algerian war of national liberation in particular served as a crystallizing moment for many Occitan and Breton militants in the radicalization of their political beliefs, taking on for themselves the image of the Algerian peasant-revolutionary (cf. Marti 1975: 70). On the eve of the Algerian victory and the fall of the Fourth Republic, a large number of regional nationalist organizations were founded throughout France, from the Movement for the Organization of Brittany to the Occitan Committee for Study and Action to the Corsican Committee for Independence, all following the example of the FLN and anticipating a possible power vacuum in Paris.

These developments further gained institutional support from the Fourth Republic's tentative decentralization policies. With the 1951 Loi Deixonne, it offered de facto official recognition of minorities in France, allowing both the teaching of regional dialects as part of a university degree curriculum and the use of these languages in French language instruction. While certain organic intellectuals within the movements, like the Occitan scholar Robert Lafont, did recognize that significant differences separated the plight of a colonized Muslim Algerian and a Breton Frenchman—namely that the latter enjoyed full political and civil rights (Lafont 1967: 141)—decolonization nonetheless became the general lens through which ethnic movements in France interpreted their struggle and refined their methods, eventually drawing directly on the FLN's successful use of public strikes, demonstrations, and even urban bombings.

In this way, the anti-colonial nationalisms in both Algeria and France provoked debates over the place of ethnolinguistic heterogeneity within the nation-state on both sides of the Mediterranean. As in Algeria, the French Fifth Republic searched for motifs through which to present its postimperial identity. De Gaulle's overt turn to Europe, his support for the European Coal and Steel Community and later the Common Market, and his renewed alliance with Germany constituted one set of recenterings, against which his support of the Quebec liberation movement can be seen as militating. Such ambivalence between regional integration and national determination can likewise be seen in his wavering support for the Loi Deixonne and the teaching of regional dialects in the national education system. As during the colonial period, the nation-state and its infranational formations of ethnoracial and linguistic difference continued after decolonization to be reciprocally and nostalgically constructed as salient and affective categories of belonging.

National Difference

The French nation-state has thus proved to be fundamentally ambivalent in its management of ethnoracial and linguistic difference, as it has simultaneously avowed and disavowed—produced and erased—subnational categories of identity. The joint participation of state actors and subaltern leaders in the elaboration of ethnic stereotypes and myths throughout the colonial and decolonizing periods undermines continued assumptions of primordiality extant in the discourse of certain essentializing nationalist and culturalist ideologues, as well as in naïve constructivist approaches to the nation-state and its discontents. While constructivists have continued to treat race and ethnicity as the "genuine" building blocks of "imagined" or "invented" nations (cf. Gellner 1983; Hobsbawm 1990), cultural activists today employ these same assumptions of primordiality to justify their own claims of originality and signal the oppression which they have experienced at the hands of nation-states.

Within the Berber cultural movement in Algeria and France, various engaged activists and intellectuals continue to make a concerted effort to portray Berberity as the true, originary identity of Algeria, the Maghreb, and the southern Mediterranean as a whole. Engaged in a play of cultural intimacy, they nostalgically highlight tangible symbolic diacritics of Berber particularity—such as the *tajmaât* and the *axxam*—in their cultural productions and political discourse. They frequently cite the writings of early Roman geographers (especially Sallust and Procop) and underline colonial linguistic theories to demonstrate that Berber language and culture are autochthonous features of North Africa. They decry the Algerian state's adoption of the *salafi* reformist efforts to project a transhistorical Algerian nation united in Arab culture and Islam (Merad 1967; McDougall 2003) as Arabo-Islamic (or even "Arabo-Ba'athist") imperialism, as a denial of the Algerian people's essential Berber identity. They view the disunity of Algeria, embodied most poignantly in the civil war that claimed upwards of 100,000 lives between 1992 and 2002, as resulting from an "identity crisis" that has left the Algerian people utterly disoriented in an increasingly globalizing world, willing to grasp at the first strong organizing principle to arise—in this case Islamic fundamentalism. They thus propose a return to Algeria's true identity—Berberity—as the requisite solution to the crisis.

Breton and Occitan cultural activists have likewise engaged in structural nostalgia for a time before the nation-state, mobilizing claims to primordiality and levying harsh criticism against the centralist government for suppressing their regional heritage (*patrimoine*). Drawing on historical arguments regarding the French language as a postrevolutionary Parisian imposition on the French countryside by the state's centralization policies and national education practices (cf. Weber 1976: 67–94, 303–338), they have demanded multicultural and multilingual education on the basis of their respective pre-French Celtic and Latinate character. Such militants view the economic exploitation and ecological decimations of their regions since World War II as consonant with 200 years of cultural and linguistic homogenization (Beer 1980; Touraine et al. 1981). As in the case of the Berber cultural movement in Algeria, the revitalization of primordial ethnic and linguistic identities in France would serve, according to Occitan and Breton militants, as a means to counter global challenges to the integrity of national models; that if the French state only embraced its regional cultures, it could maintain its cultural individuality in the face of German and American imperialism.

Moreover, there exists a close relation between such cultural production and changing modes of political contestation. Most significantly for the contemporary period, there has occurred a series of shifts in the imagination of internal and external boundaries, as the contours of the French political imaginary alternately expand and contract to encompass a colonial empire or a unified Europe. Both the Algerian immigrant community and regional groups alike have outlined new possibilities for the enactment of civil society. From street demonstrations to electioneering to jointly petitioning the Council of Europe or the European Union, French citizens of "minority" linguistic or ethnic origin have been able to articulate an identity politics that reaches beyond the confines of assimilation to French republican norms. While this transnationalization has on occasion abetted the growth of religious or ethnic extremisms, it has more often than not led to policy changes that support migrant and minority cultural and political expression under a discourse of universal human rights (Soysal 1994). Above all, such ambivalence over the espousal and denial of subnational difference within the postcolonial metropole points to the perduring character of coloniality within postcoloniality (Comaroff and Comaroff 1997).

3 /

Spatializing Practices: Migration, Domesticity, Urban Planning

Mounir lives alone in a cramped one-bedroom apartment in a public housing project (*cité*) in the northwest Parisian working-class suburb of Argenteuil. A Kabyle emigrant, Mounir was born in a small village near Bejaïa in 1966. Shortly after he turned twenty-four, Mounir came to France to study linguistics. Quickly he found himself caught between his postgraduate studies and a variety of part-time jobs in Paris. Three nights a week, he works behind the front desk of a Parisian hotel owned by his maternal uncle, who came to France after the war in Algeria to join his father, Abdullah. Abdullah himself came to France in 1927 at the age of seventeen to work in a factory, returning seasonally to Kabylia to his wife and five children. After serving in the military in the north of France during World War II (and being taken prisoner by the Germans), Abdullah eventually earned enough money to open a variety of businesses in Algeria and France—including an olive oil plant, a merguez sausage factory, and a hotel—run by his children and their families. Following his grandfather Abdullah's example, Mounir has remitted thousands of francs to his remaining family in Kabylia for investment in an *épicerie* (food market) and mini-bus taxi service. In addition to his work, Mounir has become increasingly involved in Berber cultural activism, as a local organizer for the immigration wing of one of the major Kabyle political parties, as a radio announcer for a Kabyle-language program on the North African–oriented Beur FM, and as a teacher of Tamazight to second-generation Kabyle children in a variety of Berber cultural associations in Paris and its suburbs.

Given the distance between his home and Paris, and the lack of *métro* (subway) service to Argenteuil, Mounir's activism and work keep him away from his apartment most days and many nights. Indeed, he often finds himself staying overnight at his uncle's hotel even on his nights off, particularly when his studies or association activities have caused him to miss his last train home, or when he has an early meeting or seminar the next morning and cannot stomach an hour-long commute each way. Beyond the transportation difficulties, Mounir is generally unhappy with life in the *cité*. The main supermarket at the center of the housing project was burned down by local youths during battles with the police in 1990, and nothing has taken its place. The turnover rate for the few small shops that continue to operate is great, and their prices are often substantially higher than what can be found in Paris. In addition, Mounir, although not a small man, feels unsafe when walking around the complex, particularly at night. His apartment has been broken into on two occasions, and his mail repeatedly stolen from the box located in the entrance to his building. He believes that local teenagers were the culprits and further resents their raucous behavior that often keeps him up at night. Nonetheless, he ultimately holds the state responsible, blaming its failed education and urbanization programs for producing a rebellious generation that cannot find its place in either contemporary French society or in the social worlds of their (French or immigrant) parents. In an effort to address this problem, Mounir founded a local Berber cultural association that, through classes in Berber language and culture, hopes to acquaint neighborhood youths with the culture of their parents.

When I first visited Mounir's apartment in January 1996, I was immediately struck by a series of contrasts. A large computer desk piled high with books and notes and a desktop PC Mounir had assembled with the aid of a friend dominated one end of the main room. This dormitory-like atmosphere sat uneasily with the generic form of the public housing space clearly designed for a small family. More strikingly, the apartment's otherwise drab and deteriorating walls and carpeting were vibrantly decorated with sheepskins, a working loom, a large Kabyle robe (*abernus*) woven by Mounir's mother, and even a clay hand mill (*tasirt*) that still received occasional use; the accoutrements were imported directly from Kabylia to fill every remaining square meter of the apartment, giving the apartment the appearance of a Kabyle *axxam*. The pièce de résistance, lovingly displayed in the center of the main room's table, was a cruet of olive oil drawn directly from the village press his grandfather had built and his mother still runs, carefully hand-carried past French customs in plastic water bottles.

One of the central targets of French colonial ethnological discourse and contemporary nostalgia by Berber activists is the Kabyle house, or *axxam*. In the colonial context, the *axxam* was projected as a space of cultural exteriority that functioned simultaneously as an object of assimilation practices and a foil to French conceptions of order, civilization, and modernity. In the postcolonial context, debates about the assimilability of Muslim indigenous subjects have been replaced by a discourse concerning the integration (or lack thereof) of Muslim immigrants and their progeny as productive subjects of the nation-state. Such state-directed integration efforts have often taken the form of urbanization and urban reform policies that have targeted the ultra-modern housing projects (*cités*) built across the French urban periphery, and particularly in the northern suburbs (*banlieues*) of Paris, that today suffer from high rates of unemployment, physical dilapidation, and crime. Through these integration discourses and measures, the *cités* and their residents have become endowed with a similar representation of otherness as the impenetrable Kabyle village, as signifiers for that which is not, or at best is problematically, French.

This historical shift from colony to postcolony, from *axxam* to *cité*, as the site of national anxiety, reflects a dialectic of centralization and peripheralization, of circulation and containment, by which categories of city and suburb, metropole and periphery, become structurally valorized. The establishment and development of the modern French nation-state has been historically predicated on internal and external mobility, on the increasing capacities for rapid communication (in the form of roads, railroads, and telephony) between center and periphery, between colony and metropole (Mattelart 1996; Weber 1976). The seasonal movement of North African laborers to France in particular facilitated the rapid modernization of the country following the two world wars, replacing the labor of the generations lost (Noiriel 1988; Talha 1989). Since the economic downturn of 1973, however, those who rebuilt France have been increasingly represented in right-wing discourse as an unwanted burden who take "French" jobs, or at least their welfare benefits. *Cités* originally constructed to socialize immigrant factory workers and facilitate their movement between home and work now function as sites of spatial isolation, economic exclusion, and social containment, reinforcing physical and mental boundaries between city and suburb, French and immigrant. Within this context, Algerian immigrants and their children have engaged in what Michel de Certeau (1984: 96) has called "spatializing practices," constructing alternate social totalities and subjectivities on the embers of built and dilapidated urban forms, endowing them with frameworks of value and hierarchy not necessarily isomorphic with those projected by assimilation and integration projects of the French nation-state.

What is of central concern here are the processes by which states and their immigrant subjects collude and compete in the production and consumption of locality. Scholars have emphasized the role of the colonial state—

through the decisions of government officials, architects, and scientists—in the discursive ordering of space and the regulation of the colonized body (cf. Mitchell 1988; Rabinow 1989; Wright 1991), and such microphysics of power, while transformed, perdure in the postcolonial metropolitan context as well. It is in this setting that situated actors' spatializing practices operate, producing locality (Appadurai 1996). At the same time, the techniques and practices which serve to order metropolitan place and produce the bounded locality of the *cité* constantly confront the operations of capital that, through the medium of new technologies of communication and transportation, embody an imperative to eliminate borders and produce a global, smooth space of circulation and exchange. This "compression" of space (Harvey 1989) dialectically contradicts the defining, identifying features of the *cités* and enables flexible models of cultural and political belonging that allow migrant subjects, as Mounir's apartment exemplifies, quite literally to inhabit multiple spaces between Algeria and France simultaneously. Rather than resulting in a transnational homogeneity, such transformations have actually increased the "haunted" or "enchanted" nature of village or *cités* (de Certeau 1984: 108, 201).

In this sense, spatial cosmologies within a given locality—e.g., the *axxam*, Paris, the *banlieue rouge* (Paris's formerly communist northern suburbs), the *cité des 4000* of La Courneuve—are necessarily plural, the result of multiple operations of power and subversion, of creation, appropriation, and consumption. Ambivalent state concerns of stability and order (and their corresponding techniques of mapping, enumeration, and containment) and mobility and integration (with the development of urban transportation networks) find themselves replicated in the practices of actors at every structural level, from government agencies to neighborhood associations to households. It is in the interaction of these groups that spatial divides and subjectivities are established and subverted, that the global is localized and the local becomes global.

Kabyle Domesticity and Nostalgia

The Kabyle house, or *axxam*, functions as a particularly salient site for the enactment of spatializing practices, the production of spatial subjectivity, and the nostalgic construction of synecdoches of cultural difference. Within both French colonial sociology and contemporary anthropological theory, the *axxam* has occupied a privileged position as a touchstone of Algerian cultural distance (i.e., exteriority) as mediated by particular relations of domestic distinction (i.e., interiority). While described in detail by early colonial military ethnographers (cf. Daumas 1855; Hanoteau and Letourneux 1871), the *axxam* is today most closely associated with the structural analysis of sociologist Pierre Bourdieu, whose work has been repeatedly appropriated by contemporary authors for the general elaboration of a non-Western model for the organization of social space (cf. Mitchell 1988). In this respect, his analysis merits critical attention as a refractive lens through which to view processes of colonial objectification and nostalgia.

In Bourdieu's analysis, the *axxam* (or *akham* in his transliteration) is a fully structured space that both reflects and structures—and thus infinitely reproduces—Kabyle habitus: the system of "structured structures predisposed to function as structuring structures" of Kabyle social life (Bourdieu 1977: 72). It maps in inverted fashion the fundamental structural oppositions within Kabyle society as a whole: male/female, high/low, dry/wet, day/night, light/dark, human/animal, honor/shame (*nnif/horma*), fertilizing/fertilized (1979: 140). As such, the Kabyle house, as a site of inverted privacy, simultaneously opposes the public and natural world and embodies its basic values and hierarchies. The placement of its objects and the use of its spaces hence reflect a particular habitus and reproduce its constitutive elements for its inhabitants. While for a Kabyle inhabitant the line between public and private, between individual and societal space, is clearly demarcated by a series of thresholds separating the village (*taddart*) from the countryside, the patrilineal agglomeration (*adrum*) from the *taddart*, and the *axxam* from the *adrum*, Bourdieu's analysis understands these divisions and inversions as participating in a unitary symbolic order and thus exhibiting an overarching continuity. In this sense, the practices constituting the *axxam* are seen to maintain a relation of synecdoche with Kabyle society as a whole, and are directly rooted in the social and natural landscape on which it is built. As Kabyle sociologist Mohand Khellil has since echoed: "The house serves as the centerpiece of all social organization" (1984: 36).

As the natural center of the spatial configurations and differentiations extant within Kabylia, the Kabyle house functions, within Bourdieu's framework, as a prime generative mechanism for social subjectivity and hierarchy. Internally, binary oppositions of generation and gender (e.g., male/female, parent/child) are seen to be spatially organized in interior living, working, and sleeping arrangements. He cites proverbs that associate men with the *axxam*'s master beam, and women with the central pillar and/or foundation, and sees in the physical intersection of these features a metaphor for sexual reproduction. These domestic spatial divisions moreover structure life-cycle rituals. Marriage enjoins the literal and symbolic making of a house (*adyeg akham*). After the initial wedding celebration, for instance, the bride (*tislit*) participates in a three-day ritual period of liminal separation and feminine visitation that takes place on the mezzanine (*takhana*) floor midway between the animal (*adaynin*) and human (*agouns*) sections of the house. Likewise, birth rites are similarly structured domestically, with the infant's umbilical cord buried in the confines of the *axxam*, along the walls associated with each gender.

Bourdieu's structural analysis of the *axxam* of course raises a number of questions, especially for its presumption of an iron cage of social reproduction (cf. Comaroff 1985: 5; Eickelman 1977: 40). More importantly, it situates itself as an example of structural nostalgia for an institution in the process of disappearance. With emigration to cities in Algeria and France, the population of Kabyle villages had dwindled dramatically by the late 1950s. Those new houses that were built were generally constructed by emigrants out of imported materials and followed "European" architectural styles. On the one hand, such construction signaled a "myth of return" upheld by emigrants—an attempt to maintain concrete connections with the villages they had left, in preparation for an anticipated repatriation (cf. Sayad 1999; Zehraoui 1994). On the other hand, these new, modern-style homes functioned as potent forms of symbolic capital that symbolize the success of the emigrants to their natal communities. In either case, what is clear is that Bourdieu's details of the *axxam* were derived primarily from interviews with Kabyles living in a very different social and architectural setting than the one described in the essay. Indeed, the bulk of his research was conducted in the modern housing blocks built by the French administration for Algerian workers in and around Algiers (Çelik 1997) or in the wartime resettlement camps for Kabyle villagers displaced from their homes. His account is thus largely a post facto reconstruction of a social institution that, given the context of his field research during the Algerian war of national liberation, he could not observe directly and about which his informants could primarily speak of in a language of loss. In this respect, the nostalgia for the integrity of the Kabyle house and village life derives both from Bourdieu and his informants' self-essentializing presentation of a "static image of an unspoiled and irrecoverable past" (Herzfeld 1997: 109).

Likewise, Bourdieu's focus on the *axxam* as a space of structural stability that mirrors and reproduces Kabyle culture writ large contrasts directly with his relative neglect for other unifying social institutions, most notably the mosque. In this respect, as Abdellah Hammoudi (2000) has suggested, Bourdieu's analysis follows closely upon the earlier colonial discourse that imputed a cultural divide between Kabyles and Arabs on the basis of their religiosity and tended to view the mosque as an imposed institution. Such a focus further dovetails with the privileged status accorded the domestic dwelling by contemporary Berber cultural activists like Mounir, who nostalgically view the *axxam* as the prime site for intergenerational cultural transmission and thus see its disappearance as a prime factor in the breakdown of Kabyle cultural strength and unity. According to expatriate Kabyle anthropologist El-Hadi Iguedelane, the "*axxam* is the reflection of an ancient culture, a unique situation where all life functions occur in harmony. . . . With the appearance of the 'modern' house, [the Kabyles] witness . . . the disintegration of their culture" (1996: 100).

Spatial Uprooting

The representation of Kabyle domestic space as a coherent center of non-Western social structure relates as well to larger narratives of loss and continuity that interpolate migration and modernization. Rather than located solely within emigrant nostalgic discourse, these narratives derive from a colonial anxiety over rural and urban enclaves as spaces for the reproduction of insular, primordial identities incompatible with a modernity of civic-based nation-states. Within both the colony and the metropole, the state administration developed plans to break down these enclaved structures and replace them with regularized, "modern" spatial forms designed to encourage migration, promote circulation, and eventually assimilate local populations to national norms. These measures were justified primarily through tropes of state and individual security, as the enclaved spaces were viewed as centers of both potential revolt and the spread of epidemics (Mitchell 1988: 34–94; Rabinow 1989; Çelik 1997). Both the nineteenth-century reconstruction of Paris and the reorganization of villages in colonial Kabylia explicitly responded to revolts understood as enabled by the sociospatial structures of the two countries.

At the same time, alongside the imperative to break down established collectivities, Parisian and colonial planners acted along a parallel though contradictory impetus to create new forms of sociality, to re-place those displaced populations. For displacement and uprootedness, like communal emplacement, were also seen as a prime factor of chaos and disorder. Before it became the pre-eminent trope of migration and refugee studies (Malkki 1992),[1] "uprooting" (*déracinement*) functioned in nineteenth-century French rightist discourse as an index of the upheavals provoked by a centralizing, revolutionary modernity gone awry. In his 1897 novel *Les déracinés* ("The Uprooted"), Maurice Barrès excoriated the French national education system for "uprooting" children from the soil and social group, thus bringing about the moral degeneration of the countryside. This notion of uprooting became a central pillar of the regional nationalism of Charles Maurras's colonialist *Action Française* movement that voiced extremist articulations of an *Algérie française*, a French Algeria (Apter 1999: 35; Ford 1991: 21–23). Both social enclaving and displacement were thus understood as threats to colonial state stability. Human mobility had to be encouraged and limited at the same time.

In this respect, the colonial state sought to control the indigenous populations that its security measures had displaced. On the one hand, French industrial, agricultural, and mining concerns established the mechanisms of circulation—including recruitment centers, transport companies, etc.—to bring Kabyle men to metropolitan centers in North Africa and France on short-term (six months to one year) contracts. During World War I, the

French War Ministry centralized these migration services under the Service for the Organization of Colonial Laborers, designed to provide more efficiently the heightened wartime need for foreign labor in the metropole (Talha 1989: 65). After the war, these services—including the regulation of migrant life in the metropole—were taken over by the General Immigration Society, and later, after the Second World War, by the National Immigration Office (ONI).

On the other hand, the re-placement of Kabyle populations expropriated after the 1871 rebellion occurred through the establishment of modular government villages that embodied a growing concern for surveillance and hygiene (Çelik 1997: 123–129; Mitchell 1989: 45–48). These model villages were not built around lineage distinctions of moiety (*ssef*) and patriliny (*adrum*) typical in the Kabyle *taddart*, being arranged instead according to regulated, uniform patterns. Military architects placed homes in parallel rows with exterior rather than interior courtyards. With an eye to modular flexibility, larger families could be accommodated by opening up partitions between walls, rather than attaching a new structure (and thus creating lineal enclaves). Further, distances between domestic structures, fields, and water sources increased, necessarily changing the social functions of these sites. No *tajmaât* as such existed for a village assembly, thus altering agnatic relations of authority and equality. Likewise, as the village was walled, attaining the water source necessitated passing through areas populated by people outside one's extended family, thus limiting its access by women to particular hours of the day when men were in the fields. Finally, the homes themselves did not follow the same pattern as the *axxam*, with no place for livestock or grain storage, no mezzanine *takhana*, and no relations of cardinal inversion as described retrospectively by Bourdieu. Stables and storerooms were placed with the guardrooms in the external village walls, enframing the homes instead of providing an integrality to intra- and extra-domestic tasks.

These modular villages provided the model for the resettlement camps (*villages de regroupement*) established by the French military during the war of national liberation (Bourdieu and Sayad 1964; Çelik 1997: 124–129). Bourdieu and his Kabyle colleague Abdelmalek Sayad criticized the displacement of Kabyle villagers and the transformation of their domestic space as a veritable crisis of agricultural practice, an "uprooting": "The peasant can only but live rooted in the land on which he was born and to which his habits and memories attach themselves. Uprooted, there is a good chance he will die as a peasant, in that the passion which makes him a peasant dies within him" (Bourdieu and Sayad 1964: 115). According to Bourdieu, the destruction of the agrarian cycles and social practices of *tiwizi* shattered the misrecognition that "veiled the relationship between labor and labor's product" and underwrote the good-faith economy. The resulting social situation was one of "complete disaggregation" and "high instability" (1963b: 264) in which the Kabyle peasant "painfully experiences the cold and brutal impersonality of work relations (*rapports du travail*)" (1963b: 280). Through such "disenchantment of a natural world" (1977: 176) in which the Kabyle peasant lived, Kabyle habitus itself was destroyed in the resettlement camps. "It was as if the colonizers had instinctively discovered the anthropological law which states that the structure of habitat is the symbolic projection of the most fundamental structures of a culture; to reorganize it is to provoke a general transformation of the whole cultural system itself" (Bourdieu and Sayad 1964: 26).

Kabyle scholars, following Bourdieu and Sayad's lead, have described postcolonial Algerian agricultural and urban policies through the same lens of uprooting. In the period immediately after Algerian independence, the governments of the victorious FLN actively sought to forge a unified national entity that transcended and overcame local cultural distinctions and divergences. In addition to the promulgation of a singular national identity around an "Arabo-Islamist" ideology borrowed from the *salafi* reformers, the FLN also established a four-year plan to create 333 Socialist Agricultural Villages (SVA) with the goal of disenclaving Kabyle villages and integrating their inhabitants to civic national norms (Benmatti 1982: 157). Iguedelane (1996) has studied one such SVA, simply known as "La Cité," built to relocate inhabitants of the village of Tizouyar in the Bejaïa province. Like the resettlement camp, the modular houses of La Cité were constructed with imported materials along parallel contours, with no respect for the internal organizing principles of the *axxam* or *adrum* as described by Bourdieu. Following Bourdieu and Sayad, Iguedelane views this spatial transformation as a process of destructuration, as a "breakdown [*bouleversement*] of social and familial organization" (1996: 72). In this respect his study can be viewed as another instance of structural nostalgia that parallels that of Bourdieu and his informants.

When Iguedelane's ethnography is read against the grain, what proves fascinating about La Cité is the continuity, not the rupture, of Tizouyar modes of social organization even in the new space. In spite of the opportunities for upward mobility engendered by the new possibilities, if not necessities, of labor migration, established patrilines maintained a relative stability of social position, as more wealthy families were better positioned to take advantage of the economic opportunities. Likewise, while no *tajmaât*— the male political space *par excellence*—was built in La Cité, the new institutions established, particularly the *café arabe* or the residence of the village head (*ccix*), came to serve as sites for informal village assemblies.

Moreover, while the parallel arrangement of the new houses inscribed a logic of breaking down the insular nature of the patrilineal *adrum*, lineage still continued to determine the order of residence. In the case of La Cité, two sets of parallel houses were constructed on either side of the national highway that bifurcated the village. The relocated families grouped themselves according to *ssef* in inversed spatial order from their original location in Tizouyar, with the road between the two halves replicating the line of division formerly represented by the shared spaces of the mosque, the *tajmaât*, and the cemetery (Iguedelane 1996). In addition, while the houses of La Cité were not built according to the model of the *axxam* as described by Bourdieu, their inhabitants, like Mounir in the ethnographic narrative that began this chapter, imported features from their previous residences. Although there was no distinction between *agouns* and *adaynin*, with the rooms being broken down instead into living room, bedroom, kitchen, etc., the residents filled the new spaces with storage jars (*ikoufen*), bridal chests, and sheepskins found normally in an *axxam*. Even architectural features associated with Europe, like the kitchen window or the electric range, were denoted with terms borrowed from the idealized *axxam*: the *taq takhana* (exhaust vent in the ceiling of the *adaynin*) and the *kanoun* respectively. Finally, the residents of La Cité continued to participate in the everyday social life of Tizouyar, from attending village assemblies, to participating in *tiwizi* collective labor, to generally being governed by the customary oral laws (*qanoun*) (Iguedelane 1996: 94, 99). In other words, the building of La Cité did not inherently imply the replacement of Kabyle habitus by European modes of sociospatial organization, but instead indicated a transformation characterized as much by continuity as by rupture. Rather than viewing changes in the structure of the *axxam* as a synecdoche for the uprooting and destruction of an integral Kabyle culture, one should approach such transformations as yet another moment of historical change for a social form and structure that is always already hybridized and subject to a multiplicity of external influences and internal differentiations.

From *Bidonville* to *Banlieue*

Processes of spatial transformation and nostalgic appropriation continued outside of Kabylia as well. If the destruction of Kabyle villages as insular entities responded primarily to nineteenth-century insurrections and the martial imperatives to maintain colonial state security, these procedures served as an example for parallel processes within the metropole. A burgeoning number of scholars, with immense historical acuity, have demonstrated how "specific intellectuals" operating in positions of authority within France's North African holdings, like Robert de Souza and Maréchal Lyautey, viewed the colonies as "offering the greatest field for experimentation and embodying hope for planning" that could then be applied within the metropole itself (Rabinow 1989: 273, 289; cf. Çelik 1997; Wright 1997). Primary among the concerns of these planners was the fostering of circulation via the destruction of isolated neighborhoods and the construction of roads and thoroughfares.

In addition to the expropriation of Kabyle villagers from their *taddart,* colonial construction originally resulted in the massive destruction of entire neighborhoods in North African cities and their replacement with administrative buildings, hospitals, and new residences (Çelik 1997). From 1912 to 1914, Lyautey regularized these measures for Morocco as a whole. First, he divided the protectorate's major urban areas by functionality—with Rabat as the administrative capital, Casablanca as the commercial and financial center, and Fez as the cultural core—and connected them with modern roads and train tracks. Secondly, he divided each city into two separate zones, native and European, by leaving the pre-existing *medina* largely intact, building new quarters adjacent to it, and separating the two by a "sanitary corridor" (*cordon sanitaire*) of monuments and parks (cf. Abu-Lughod 1980). Finally, he decreed a unitary building and hygiene code to cover both areas and worked with local authorities to maintain the standards and inspect individual neighborhoods and residences (Rabinow 1989: 288–296). In this way, Lyautey was able to simultaneously promote the containment requisite for efficient surveillance and foster the circulation necessary for a functional economy and a hygienic society, all without completely destroying senses of communal solidarity and alienating the governed populations.[2]

Parisian Transformations

Paris likewise followed a similar series of spatial developments and reconstructions in the nineteenth and early twentieth centuries. Land enclosures and the migration and proletarianization of rural inhabitants from the northern provinces, Brittany, and Auvergne underwrote the Industrial Revolution and contributed to the growth of large areas of impoverishment in the heart of the capital. The Parisian region (Île-de-France) had approximately 1.35 million inhabitants at the beginning of the nineteenth century, a figure which represented less than 5 percent of the total population of the country. By 1880, this figure had increased to six million, or 14.5 percent of France as a whole. According to censuses taken during the last half of the nineteenth century, more than half the population of the *département* of the Seine (including Paris and the abutting *arrondissements* of Saint-Denis and Sceaux) was born in the provinces (Soulignac 1993: 26–29).

Paris in particular experienced rapid demographic changes. From a population of 580,000 at the beginning of the century, it grew to more than two million by 1870. Ill-equipped to deal with such a sudden influx of migrants, Paris suffered from extremely congested roads and markets, poor sanitation, a limited supply of potable water, and the spread of disease (three epidemics of cholera between 1847 and 1849) through its teeming poorer neighborhoods (Rabinow 1989: 73–74). These conditions contributed to the instability of regimes, as destitute populations could easily barricade off entire neighborhoods (*faubourgs*) from which they could launch offensives

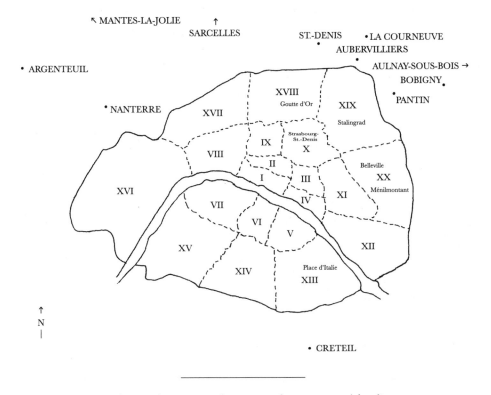

↖ MANTES-LA-JOLIE

↑ SARCELLES

ST.-DENIS

• LA COURNEUVE

AUBERVILLIERS

• ARGENTEUIL

AULNAY-SOUS-BOIS →

BOBIGNY•

• NANTERRE

PANTIN

XVIII

Goutte d'Or

XIX

Stalingrad

XVII

Strasbourg-
St.-Denis

IX

VIII

X

II

Belleville

I

III

XX

Ménilmontant

XVI

VII

IV

XI

VI

V

XV

XII

XIV

Place d'Italie

XIII

↑
N
|

• CRETEIL

Map of Paris showing northern *arrondissements* and *banlieues.*

against government forces. In response to these threats of revolt and disease, reformers at the École Polytechnique developed a series of plans to reconstruct Paris, proposing the destruction of congested *faubourgs,* the opening up of wide avenues, and the construction of a rail and canal system.

Baron Hausmann, appointed by Louis Napoleon as prefect of the Seine between 1853 and 1870, adopted these ideas for the reconstruction of Paris proper. Over the course of his tenure, he directed the construction of more than eighty-five miles of new streets (including the Champs-Élysées and the extra-wide *grands boulevards* across the northern half of Paris) and more than 2,000 hectares of parks (including the Bois de Boulogne, the Bois de Vincennes, and the Parcs Monceau, Montsouris, and Buttes-Chaumont). These transformations were enabled by a burgeoning legal structure. The law of 25 December 1852, for instance, granted the government the right to expropriate the land necessary for major public works (*grands travaux*) by executive order alone. Such measures allowed for the 1860 annexation of twenty-four independent communes lying within the city's defensive ramparts, and the resulting expansion of the number of *arrondissements* of Paris from twelve to twenty.

This process of expropriation and expansion had followed different courses in different districts throughout the city. In the central and western districts, city forces simply evicted the poor as insalubrious structures were remodeled into six-story apartment buildings. In the peripheral, eastern areas, however, the military isolated and enclosed the poorer quarters, building strategic inroads for efficient surveillance and the quelling of potential discontent. These areas were particularly struck by high levels of overpopulation, unemployment, and poverty, with a mortality rate nearly twice that of the central districts (Soulignac 1993: 52–53). The result of these procedures was the further segregation of Paris into compartments resembling Lyautey's Rabat in reverse: a newer quarter for the (indigenous) bourgeoisie and an increasingly decrepit one for the (increasingly immigrant) working class.

Increasing concerns over the spread of disease and rampant mortality among the proletariat led Louis-Napoleon to promote experiments in housing. Inspired by the utopian ideas of Fourier and Jeremy Bentham, the architect Gabriel Veugny constructed the Cité Napoleon on the rue Rochechouart in the peripheral northern eighteenth *arrondissement*. Similar to the model government village (or the later La Cité) in Kabylia, the Cité Napoleon was established according to norms of modularity, openness, and orderliness. The housing project provided eighty-six two-room apartments with kitchens arranged along galleries on three floors surrounding an open courtyard. In addition, a number of services, from laundry to baths to elementary schools to a medical center, were provided within the closed grounds. Moreover, the Cité was ruled by a code of regulations containing 100 articles covering proper sanitary use of the facilities and establishing a strict curfew. Louis-Napoleon originally planned to construct like structures in every district of Paris; however, while the average rent was kept as low as 180 francs per year—the average worker earned 4.50 francs per diem—very few workers opted to live in what international workers' organizations denounced as "barracks." In the end, the project was abandoned and the built structures were later transformed into bourgeois residences (HLM Aujourd'hui 1989; Rabinow 1989: 85; Soulignac 1993: 56). Nonetheless, the model of the Cité Napoleon would re-emerge in the 1950s and 1960s in various forms as suburban "dormitory projects" (*cité-dortoirs*).

With the immediate failure of the Cité Napoleon project, urban planners opted for the expulsion rather than the accommodation of urban laborers. After Hausmann's reconstructions, land speculation spiraled out of control, substantially raising the average cost of housing throughout the city. In ten years, between 1850 and 1860, the monthly rent in Paris increased 75 percent, from an average of 120 francs to 210 francs (Soulignac 1993: 53). The housing shortage continued to increase after the fall of Louis-

Napoleon's Second Empire as refugees from the provinces of Alsace and Lorraine, now occupied by the Prussians, fled to Paris. In addition, economic depressions in 1870 and 1890 forced peasants off their lands, from which many migrated to Paris in search of work in the burgeoning heavy industry (Bastié 1964: 177).

As the majority of these factories were established on the northern edge of the city, or in abutting suburbs where rents were lower, potential workers tended to migrate more and more to areas outside of Paris's walls (Bastié 1963: 137–160).[3] In this regard, the suburbs experienced a vertiginous increase in population, with a growth rate of 7 percent per annum between 1840 and 1920, or twice that of Île-de-France as a whole. In the same period, the population of France remained virtually stable, with only a 0.2 percent annual increase (Soulignac 1993: 26).

The particular history of the *banlieues* varies from suburb to suburb.[4] Some—such as Saint-Denis, Sceaux, and Mantes—had been regional centers of commerce since medieval times; others—including Pantin, Aulnay-sous-Bois, and Creil—came to prominence with the late-nineteenth-century construction of new transportation networks; and still others—including Sarcelles and Bobigny—were created as experiments in working-class housing. However, in general, the majority of suburban areas that would become bastions of factory labor by World War I began their growth in the 1830s as sites for bourgeois pavilions benefiting from high land values: e.g., Bondy, Romainville, Saint-Cloud, Saint-Maur, Argenteuil, and Suresnes (Rabinow 1989: 253; Soulignac 1993: 51). With the construction of railroad lines throughout the nineteenth century,[5] these upper-class residences were located increasingly farther away from the city, while the inner suburbs became largely proletarian. Moreover, nearly 42,000 men and women lived in a series of shantytowns (*bidonvilles*) in a 400-hectare area known as the "Zone" located just outside Paris's ramparts, the name of which is preserved even today in *banlieue* youths' reference to themselves as "zonards" (Soulignac 1993: 55). The Zone lasted until the 1930s, when urban planners leveled it for the construction of the *Périphérique* ring highway and a network of parks and sports complexes. As in Lyautey's Rabat, even this new Zone served as a de facto *cordon sanitaire* separating the bourgeois city from the proletarian suburbs.

Immigrant Trajectories

The arrival of the first waves of Kabyle migrant workers in France corresponded largely with these transformations of Paris. From firsthand narratives, published novels and memoirs, and interviews with their descendants, the spatial trajectories they generally followed become clear. Upon arrival, employers generally provided them with housing in dormitories on the grounds of the factory or mine in which they worked. These dormitories were of a highly transient nature, put up quickly and experiencing a rapid turnover of lodgers as the workers were on short-term contracts. They often lacked running water and proper sanitary facilities, and, as their upkeep was purely at the discretion of the employers, they were not subject to public hygiene inspections. However, not all employers were equally unscrupulous. In the late 1880s, drawing on British precedent, the industrialist Menier created an entire village for the workers of his foundry in Noisiel. Consisting of a group of rental houses, two hotel-restaurants, a food cooperative, day-care facilities, and an elementary school, the village offered a self-sustained community for a reasonable rate (a maximum of 150 francs per year). Moreover, a rent allocation was provided for workers at a variable rate as part of their salary, presaging national social welfare reforms enacted sixty years later (Soulignac 1993: 56).

The Noisiel village aside, most Algerian men arriving in France were forced into the same exorbitant housing market as the average Parisian worker. They often relied on cousins or village contacts already arrived who generally resided in a series of transient hotels (hôtels de passage) that had sprung up in the working-class neighborhoods in and around Paris. To save money to send back to their families in Algeria, they, like Mounir's grandfather, would share rooms, sometimes taking turns sleeping in a single bed if they had complementary shifts. Moreover, as these hotels provided a minimum of water and cooking facilities, whole Kabyle villages would be virtually reconstructed over communal plates of couscous. In addition, local cafés, more and more being run by semi-permanent immigrants, became centers for the transfer of information and village news between recent arrivals and those installed in France, as well as sites for informal village assemblies.

In this respect, the migration of single men from Algeria to the metropole from the late nineteenth century through the Second World War, while an accumulation of individual short-term stays, actually contributed to the constitution of relatively cohesive Kabyle residential areas in the peripheral regions of Paris and the close suburbs of Saint-Denis, Aubervilliers, and Gennevilliers. The establishment of such "urban villages," to borrow Herbert Gans's apt term, attracted the attention of established historians and sociologists of the Middle East and North Africa. In 1921, Louis Massignon (1930) conducted a study of Kabyle immigrant residential centers in Paris proper, identifying particular enclaves of 6,000–8,000 residents each in the northeast (especially La Villette), the southwest (around the avenue du Maine), and the southeast (near the Place d'Italie) of Paris. According to Massignon's surveys, these men worked primarily in automobile and machinery industries located in the northern suburbs of Billancourt, Levallois, Clichy, Saint-Ouen, and Aubervilliers. From 1950 to 1953, Robert Montagne edited an expansive ten-volume government study of Muslim workers in the metropole, concluding that these residential groups were "the reflection of the social and geographical structures of the region of origin which guards the workers against the solitude, unemployment and other crises which led them to exile originally" (AOM 762; cited in Direche-Slimani 1992: 54).

Vestiges of these centers of migration still remain to this day in spite of massive out-migration to the suburbs in the 1960s, continuing to haunt the Parisian landscape overlaid with multiple sets of immigrant trajectories. The thirteenth *arrondissement* around the Place d'Italie, for instance, has all but lost its former Algerian character, with only the nearby Mosque of Paris and Muslim Institute (built in 1926) remaining in what is otherwise Paris's second Chinatown. Likewise, the Goutte d'Or in the northern eighteenth *arrondissement* still has its internationally famous, Moroccan-owned Tati discount department store and Medina Hammam bathhouse, but its inner streets are now lined with sub–Saharan African import-export businesses, groceries, and music stores. Belleville's mosques, synagogues, Sephardic delis, and Hallal butchers in the northeastern twentieth *arrondissement* still attract large crowds, but most new restaurants and groceries opening up in the area reflect the growing Chinese, Vietnamese, and Cambodian populations. Finally, the Strasbourg–Saint-Denis area in the north-central tenth *arrondissement* maintains a North African presence in the zone just south of the Gare de l'Est and Gare du Nord train stations, but today the couscous restaurants must share the region with Ashkenazi Jewish kosher caterers and bakeries along the rue Richier, African hair salons and music studios along the boulevard de Strasbourg, Tamil and Pakistani curry shops and video rental places along the rue du Faubourg Saint-Denis, and Turkish-Kurdish tea rooms and immigrant aid societies on rue des Petits-Écuries and rue d'Enghein. These small, relatively well delineated regions of Paris thus find themselves today crosshatched with multiple immigrant constituencies, garnering their neighborhood identity more from this multiethnic character than from a particular region of immigrant origin.

Likewise, the spatial delineations of neighborhoods altered with the growth of extended Algerian family structures in France. During the Algerian war of liberation, many wives and children of immigrants joined their husbands working in France both to escape the violence of the war and to avoid the increasing difficulties in regular travel of men back to Algeria. While these families ended up residing in a variety of different contexts, many of them settled initially in a number of large shantytowns (*bidonvilles*) that had developed throughout France after World War II. Inhabited both by the refugee and displaced populations produced by the war, as well as by the local destitute populations which had previously lived in the Zone, these shantytowns were constructed on abandoned and destroyed sites around the urban metropolises of France. The largest were located in the Paris suburbs of Champigny, Nanterre, and Saint-Denis, as well as outside of the southern port city of Marseille. By the late 1960s, the *bidonville* at Champigny alone housed around 14,000 people (Bouderon and de Perette 1988: 289). Photographs and souvenirs collected by and from former residents of these areas attest to the complex organization of the shantytowns according to kinship or area of origin, with individual camps demarcating Portuguese from Spanish from Algerians. Located at a distance from urban centers, the shantytowns had their own local services, including grocery stores, butchers, and repair shops. Residents aided each other in accomplishing daily tasks, from carrying water to cooking to the amelioration of living quarters to filling out paperwork for their residence and work permits. Such communal solidarity, in spite of the harsh daily conditions, has since become the object of nostalgia for many former residents, a nostalgia captured in picture books, films, and autobiographical novels (cf. Begag 1986; Lallaoui 1993).[6]

Public Housing and the Civilizing Mission

The destruction of shantytowns and the relocation of their residents occurred gradually over a period stretching into the mid-1970s. With a logic similar to that of its wartime relocation policies in Kabylia, the French government initiated a series of urban reform measures to undermine the FLN's network in France—spatialized by the FLN as the *wilaya* VII of organizing and operations (Haroun 1992)—by destroying the spatial cohesiveness of the immigrant neighborhoods.[7] In 1956, it constituted a semi-autonomous National Corporation for the Construction of Housing for Algerian Workers (SONACOTRA) with the explicit objective of resettling Algerian residents of the Nanterre *bidonville* that had functioned as an important center for FLN recruitment. Likewise, the 1958 creation of the spatial category of Urban Priority Zones (ZUP) targeted urban renewal in areas of heavy Algerian populations—including the suburban municipalities of Saint-Denis, Champigny, Aubervilliers—in large part to rupture proto-ethnic solidarities considered potentially outside of the law. The first step in this process of relocation was to build prefabricated camps and foyers (*cités de transit*) in the vicinity of the bulldozed shantytowns in order to lodge the families while more permanent structures were being constructed in the municipalities. In the case of the Franc-Moisin *bidonville* of Saint-Denis, which housed upwards of 4,000 people by the mid-1960s, residents were moved between 1968 and 1970 to three *cités de transit* that provided centralized running water, public bathrooms, and shared cooking facilities, before being relocated into twenty different public housing projects built by 1975 (Bouderon and de Perette 1988: 291–292).

The history of replacement of the *bidonvilles* with more permanent structures parallels the increasing intervention of the French state in the provision of public housing and the control of urban development since the late nineteenth century. The ideology behind this concern for urban renewal incorporated socialist discourses of land management and hygiene, in addition to state security. As early as 1889, under pressure from international trade unions and in the midst of political upheaval, the French state created a semi-public corporation for low-cost housing (HBM) that would be directly responsible for the construction of affordable workers housing throughout France.[8] In 1894, the National Assembly voted into effect the Siegfried Law, which released large sums from the national treasury for the support of HBM construction companies, thus formalizing the state's role in the accommodation of its urban populace. However, until World War I, HBM companies succeeded in building only a handful of buildings (particularly in the near-northern suburbs of Saint-Denis and Aubervilliers) accommodating only about 2,000 inhabitants (Soulignac 1993: 57–58). Like the Cité Napoleon, these projects were ill-conceived and poorly regarded. In the meantime, expropriations of poorer populations from Paris, due to a soaring housing market, continued apace, leading to situations of overcrowding within the northern *banlieues* increasingly exacerbated by an influx of refugee populations fleeing the war-torn northern provinces of France. To counter these conditions, Parisian factory workers founded the Federal Union of Renters from France and the Colonies that organized protests against evictions and insalubrious conditions. By 1921, membership in the union reached 300,000 throughout the country, or 1 percent of the entire nation's population (Soulignac 1993: 60).

Responding to this pressure, the government, largely under the administration of Louis Blanc's socialist Popular Front, initiated a series of plans to construct "garden cities" (*cités-jardins*), self-contained and self-sustaining workers' communities in the districts around Paris. The chief architect of these plans was Henri Sellier, who directed the construction of fifteen garden cities from 1914 to 1939 (Soulignac 1993: 60–62). Using arguments well-rehearsed in the colonies, Sellier averred that social disorders (poverty, disease, crime) derived primarily from a breakdown of "traditional" norms of sociability brought about by the displacement of rural and village populations to the city. To combat these disorders, he sought to create a new urban "civil society" rooted in a complex social division of labor. Based on the models of Robert Owen and Saint-Simon, this re-education would be achieved through the regulation and centralization of social and administrative services, through the construction of uniform housing projects that would incorporate all aspects of work and leisure—from factories to housing to playing fields to hospitals—into a single site (Burlen 1987: 99–103).[9] On a 1925 public poster advertising his project, Sellier juxtaposed social justice and economic advancement, promising that "while pursuing . . . vigorous effort in hygiene, education, and social protection *in favor of the working class,* from which we emerge, we will devote our attention to the *economic prosperity of our beautiful City . . .* to assure . . . the *maximum of well-being and liberty*" (HLM Aujourd'hui 1989, emphasis in text).

Such an ambivalent civilizing discourse that tried to promote industrial development while assuring social equity and justice failed to garner the necessary financial support. In all, only about 100 *cités-jardins* of varying sizes were built nationwide, totaling merely 20,000 living quarters. Add to that another 60,000 lodgings appropriated by the HBM administration from the rampant building spree of the interwar years (Soulignac 1993: 65), and still the improvements did not reach even a third of the demand. Further, these construction projects were seriously impeded by the economic crisis of the 1930s, as well as by the Second World War and subsequent reconstruction efforts that diverted public and private funds to the military and industrial sectors. In the end, by the eve of the Algerian war, the housing crisis had exacerbated dramatically, leaving the *bidonvilles* as Paris's primary housing option for the marginal classes.

The mid-1950s through the mid-1970s brought a boom in construction, providing employment for immigrant laborers as well as an impetus for state reinvestment in public housing for these new workers. In this period, more than one million accommodations were constructed in Île-de-France, with the most intense growth occurring between 1965 and 1970. Such a growth in public housing was in large part a response to the sudden housing needs of French citizens of the former Algerian colony who were, in the nationalist discourse of the period, "repatriated" to the metropole at the close of the war.[10] For instance, the north-suburban Parisian major public housing complex, Sarcelles, was built specifically to provide housing required for displaced *pied noirs,* Algerian Jews, and Muslims who contributed to the French war effort (*harkis*). This surge in public housing construction concerned wholly the suburbs, as Paris actually experienced a decrease in the number of accommodations over the same period. While the majority of the new accommodations were built by mixed public-private companies (with partial state funding in exchange for an equivalent percentage of low-rent apartments), 30 percent were built directly by the new administration for low-cost housing (HLM).

Following the guidelines of the 1958 ZUP legislation, the state invested primarily in major public housing complexes (*grands ensembles*), incorporating large apartment buildings, schools, recreational facilities, and commercial centers. Motivated more by the grandiose ultra-modernism of Le Corbusier than the more subtle utopian visions of Sellier, the ZUPs required a minimum of 500 residences per site, though more often the projects built in the mid-1960s well exceeded this minimum. One site in La Courneuve is known simply today as *les 4000* for the number of apartments included in its four 400-meter-long, eighteen-story towers. Other *cités* in Aulnay-sous-Bois/Sevran and Créteil reached as high as 18,500 and 16,000 lodgings respectively (Soulignac 1993: 68). While many of these complexes have been partially dismantled in favor of more decentralized structures, the largest ZUP in France today, Val-Fourré in the Parisian outer suburb of Mantes-la-Jolie, still houses more than 25,000 people.

A *cité* in Aubervilliers. Photograph by author.

Today, in spite of the deceleration in housing construction and the parallel disengagement of the state, the HLM system of public housing in France remains a major feature of the French urban landscape. Currently, 600 different organizations operate more than three million HLM lodgings. Of these, the state runs 30 percent directly; 25 percent are operated by the municipalities in which the lodgings are found; and the rest are under the control of semi-public HLM corporations (Daoud 1993e: 78–79). Critics of the system I spoke to, including former employees of HLM companies, argued that it is unnecessarily complex and inefficient. Beginning in 1958, employers were required to contribute 1 percent of the total of their employees' salaries each year to the office for public housing (OPHLM) for the construction and maintenance of public housing. The OPHLM then redistributed a percentage of this sum to individual HLM companies responsible for the construction and management of those housing projects not run directly by the state, but for whose day-to-day operations the companies had to rely on the municipality in which the projects were located. These HLM operators then leased or sold the individual apartments to employers who subsequently sublet them to their employees. The housing contracts thus included three separate but equally important parties—the employer, the HLM company, and the state—each of whom was required to verify the status and approve the demand of the individual for an apartment.[11]

Critics have blamed this management morass for both the dilapidation of the *grands ensembles* and the further alienation of residents from the buildings and grounds which they inhabit. Structures rapidly built during the 1960s out of concrete and prefabricated building materials, beyond their architectural monotony and visual drabness, have failed to weather the thirty years of heavy usage and rapid tenant turnover which has transpired. Hundreds of buildings have been demolished, and an estimated 80 percent of the rest suffer from water damage, insulation problems, broken elevators, or worse (Daoud 1993e: 77). Not only have these not been replaced with new structures, but there have actually been more than 300,000 more apartments phased out than built since 1989. The result has been a situation of increasing overcrowding and squatting, as well as a growing homeless population in urban France, estimated to be as numerous as 400,000 (Daoud 1993e: 78).

Moreover, beyond dilapidation and overcrowding, suburban housing projects have become sites of economic stagnation. Since the 1973 oil embargo, urban France has experienced a significant deindustrialization, with Paris's northern suburbs being particularly affected. The number of industrial jobs has diminished by 50 percent since 1954, with the vast majority of jobs currently being offered in the tertiary (service) sector and requiring a certain level of formal education. Nationwide, youth unemployment has reached figures as high as 20 percent, or twice that of the national average. In the ZUPs (amounting to more than 500 housing projects across the country), the figures are even higher, with unemployment among young residents on average above 30 percent and as high as 85 percent (Daoud 1993b: 75).[12] It is little wonder, then, that the shopping centers built at the center of housing projects like Mounir's in Argenteuil have largely been abandoned and that the turnover rate for those shops still open is incredibly high.

These housing projects were the eventual site of settlement for the majority of Algerian immigrant families who came to France in the 1960s.[13] In many cases, they viewed this relocation as a vast social and economic improvement, as the housing projects had been originally built and publicized by the government as a haven for the lower middle class outside the bustle of big-city life. Moreover, as the parents generally still aspired to return to Algeria for a prosperous retirement, many were disinclined to become homeowners in France. However, with the deterioration of the economies in both Algeria and France, this hope has increasingly proven to be a myth, with Algerian families moving more and more into privately owned houses and apartments. In fact, in a statistically representative survey of 1.43 million North Africans conducted in 1982, only one-quarter indicated their continued residence in an HLM project. While it is true that in the most precarious *cités,* foreign nationals in general tend to be up to seven times more numerous than French citizens, the latter still represent the majority of the inhabitants of HLMs globally. Even in the northern *banlieue rouge* ("working-class suburbs")[14] of Paris—e.g., Saint-Denis, Aubervilliers, Levallois-Perret, Nanterre, Champigny—that have a long history of immigrant residence, the overall immigrant population does not exceed 40 percent of the total, with only a third of these being of Algerian origin (Daoud 1993e: 80).

Nonetheless, the representation of the *cités* of Paris and Lyon by the national media has largely focused on their immigrant (and particularly Algerian and Muslim) character, particularly in the context of confrontations between multiracial youth and police throughout the 1980s and 1990s. A racial calculus, mobilized both by xenophobic political movements and the French public more broadly, has increasingly linked a given municipality's socioeconomic misery to the relative presence of North Africans, and its commercial boons to the relative number of East Asians. This has led to unofficial quotas being installed in the public housing system. Housing contracts not only ask for one's juridical citizenship (*nationalité*), but also require one's place of birth in order to differentiate between "native" and "naturalized" citizens. According to an interviewee who worked for an HLM company, certain towns, like Asnières-Gennevilliers, refuse to accept additional non-Asian immigrants in their housing projects. Further, his company at the time kept its own ethnoracial statistics and set ethnoracial limits for its buildings so that when a certain percentage was surpassed, the application would be refused.

In this way, a state housing system, built as part of a larger integrating (if not civilizing) mission, has become a site for economic exclusion and racism (cf. Dubet and Lapeyronnie 1992). Once a testament to ultra-modernism, the *banlieue* housing projects are now increasingly portrayed as sites for the reproduction of primordial, anti-modern tribalism. For the municipalities in question, the housing projects have become pariahs, co-existing with difficulty in the *banlieues* alongside the grassy pavilions inhabited by an older, middle-class populace that itself co-exists across the *cordon sanitaire* of the *Périphérique* ring road with a generally bourgeois Paris proper. Recent state measures have further increased these economic and racial divisions. In 1986, the mayor of Paris, Jacques Chirac, artificially elevated property values in Paris in an attempt to push poorer residents out of the city (De Rudder 1990). Although the market has been on a downswing since, with record low demands and the flight of the *nouveau-riche* to the suburbs, the city has refused to devalue the property. Instead, in 1996 the Tiberi administration instituted a loan program by which young couples (whose total age did not surpass sixty-five) could borrow up to 100,000 francs ($20,000) at no interest, and another 100,000 francs at 1 percent interest, if the funds were used for the purchase of a home in Paris. By November 1996, working-class quarters, like the Strasbourg–Saint-Denis area discussed above, were undergoing massive transformations, with former rentals and office space being resold as condominiums. These measures have only exacerbated a situation of sociospatial division between city and suburb, and within each suburb between pavilion and *cité*—marking the latter, like the Kabyle *axxam,* as a space of cultural exteriority. In the process, these measures have reified a set of spatial subjectivities that mark different qualities of French national belonging.

Banlieue Verte, Banlieue Rouge, Banlieue Grise

In order to illustrate the processes of spatial integration and exclusion that have contributed to the representation of exo-Parisian *cités* as culturally marginal and the production of Algerian immigrants and their children as racialized and spatialized "others," I will focus on two suburban cases, Pantin and Mantes-la-Jolie, in both of which I spent extensive time in 1996. The two present complementary and yet contrasting pictures of internal socioeconomic and ethnoracial dynamics. While Pantin historically was a center of industry intimately dependent on the neighboring metropole, Mantes-la-Jolie had for centuries a separate village identity that rested uneasily with encroaching factories and commercial developments. In spite of this difference, however, both communes have been significantly transformed by the wave of public housing construction of the 1960s and the incorporation of immigrant workers and their families into their populations. Today, both municipalities function according to an unwritten détente between the two sides of their personalities: the grassy, pavilion *banlieue verte* and the *banlieue grise* of HLM parks. Nonetheless, this co-existence continues to be fraught with tension and, occasionally, violent conflict.

Pantin: Feeling at Home in a Banlieue Rouge

Pantin, a communist municipality of 60,000 people, borders Paris to the northeast and occupies a liminal position in the Seine–Saint-Denis *département* between the working-class suburbs of Aubervilliers, Drancy, and Bobigny to the north and the more middle-class communes of Les Lilas, Romainville, and Pré-Saint-Gervais to the south. Pantin itself is divided along a southwest-to-northeast axis by the Canal de l'Ourcq waterway, which, via the Canal Saint-Martin, joins the Seine directly to the Marne at Meaux. Built in the mid-nineteenth century, the Canal de l'Ourcq provided a direct means for raw materials from the mines of northeastern France to be transported to Paris and exchanged for finished products. Pantin owes its spectacular growth over the turn of the twentieth century (from barely 4,000 in 1851 to more than 20,000 in 1901) to the emergence of a sizable cement and textile industry enabled by this waterway. While today the canal is primarily used by Parisians jogging and cycling along the picturesque trails built along its banks, barges nonetheless continue to traverse its length, anchoring alongside the remaining factories that have not yet been transformed into warehouses or shopping malls.

Moreover, the Canal de l'Ourcq serves another function today: as the de facto sociospatial border dividing Pantin into two separate but interdependent entities, Quatre-Chemins to the north and Le Petit Pantin to the south. On the one hand, Quatre-Chemins ("Four Routes"), bordering Aubervilliers and Drancy, is largely industrial, with a number of factories, warehouses, and a network of train tracks deriving from the Gare de l'Est in Paris. It shares with its abutting suburban neighbors to the northwest a similar demography, as it, like Aubervilliers and Saint-Denis, served as a prime location where factory workers and immigrant labor historically found cheap housing outside of the metropolis. On the other hand, Le Petit Pantin ("Little Pantin"), while not wholly without factories and warehouses, has more of a village character, consisting primarily of single-family pavilions, grassy parks, and a sixteenth-century church. Unlike Quatre-Chemins, its residents represented an older generation of settled workers, and it was not until recently a site of immigration.

This Janus-faced character of Pantin found itself exacerbated by the wave of public housing construction in the 1960s and 1970s. While, according to district statistics, only 10–20 percent of Pantin's total residences are state-subsidized, there were nonetheless a number of housing projects and immigrant foyers built in the municipality during this period. The housing administration situated the majority of these in Quatre-Chemins, where land owned by the national railroad company (SNCF) could be easily transferred to OPHLM hands. Further, those projects built in Le Petit Pantin were located either along the canal dividing the two town moieties, or along Avenue Jean Lolive (National Route 4) which runs parallel to and 100 meters from the canal, thus placing them for all practical purposes within the imagined borders of Quatre-Chemins (which for some Le Petit Pantin residents begins with the Avenue Jean Lolive and not the canal). These decisions resulted in the further division of the two halves along ethnic and racial lines, as the representation of Quatre-Chemins as immigrant found itself reinforced by the presence of the HLM structures.

In this way, then, contemporary Pantin has a strikingly similar structure to the Kabyle *taddart,* with its division into two *ssefs* constituted along historical if not genealogical lines. As in the *taddart,* where the common spaces of the cemetery, mosque, and *tajmaât* supplemented topographic features in marking the social and physical boundary between the two village halves, so too in Pantin are the municipal structures distributed accordingly, with the town hall, the police commissariat, the health center, and the social security office located along the "natural" border of the canal. Similarly, as each Kabyle *ssef* maintains a certain degree of independence through separate spaces of socialization of fountains and cafés, so too has the communist government of Pantin endowed each town half with separate elementary schools, sports facilities, cinemas, and daily markets.

However, separate, in the case of Pantin, does not always imply equal. Sports facilities in Quatre-Chemins are inconveniently located and do not include a modern stadium like that in Le Petit Pantin. The cinema in Quatre-Chemins plays primarily high-profile American action films dubbed into French, while the movie house in Le Petit Pantin shows a wide range of European and American films in their original version, and often includes discussions and debates after the screenings. In fact, spaces of cultural production in general—from picture galleries to *ateliers* to a statue park—are located in Le Petit Pantin. Further, while the two halves each have daily markets, the market in Le Petit Pantin offers fresh produce, cheeses, and meats sold by farmers in the shadow of the historic church; the Quatre-Chemins market, in contrast, features local residents selling Arab music cassettes, plastic toys, and African-style clothes and jewelry along a busy street. Finally, when the municipality portrays itself to the larger French public, it consistently centers its tourism efforts on the side of Le Petit Pantin. Of the four subway stops built in Pantin during the 1930s and 1980s extensions, three are located in Le Petit Pantin while only one is located in Quatre-Chemins. Likewise, during the annual running of the *Foulées de Pantin* ("Strides of Pantin"), when the commune invites local, national, and international competitors to tour Pantin's streets in an official semi-marathon, the course never crosses Avenue Jean Lolive, thus remaining firmly embedded in Le Petit Pantin.

In spite of this abetting of sociospatial divisions within Pantin through the provision of municipal services, the patent inequality of the distribution has created contradictions that have led to the direct competition of groups from the two halves for the same resources. During my nine-month residence in Pantin, I pursued my daily exercise routine in a municipal weight room. The gym normally was located squarely in Le Petit Pantin, in the Charles Auray stadium, and drew its clientele primarily from either the immediate area or the surrounding *banlieues vertes* of Les Lilas and Romainville. However, during my stay in Pantin, the commune was in the process of renovating the stadium, so in the interim the gym had been temporarily moved to a new location a block away from the canal, in the rooms of a former health center. AIDS- and hepatitis-awareness posters dotted the walls between hastily attached pictures of Arnold Schwarzenegger and diagrams of various exercises, haunting the gym's healthy workout ethic. No effort was made to remove these health posters or the old biological hazard signs, or even to repair the broken window and cracked walls, as the city had informed the gym's management that the stadium's renovation would be finished within a few months. Given this avowedly short-term duration, and in spite of the squalor and deficiencies (e.g., the lack of changing facilities or drinking fountains), members chose to continue their adherence to the gym instead of joining one of the other similarly priced weightlifting facilities offered in the neighboring suburbs.

As such, for the first month, the facility operated very much as it had previously, if slightly more improvised. The managers set a workout schedule, but, in recompense for the shabby conditions, allowed members to use the gym whenever they chose; the front door was secured solely with a punch-key lock and members were each entrusted with the combination. However, as the months passed and the stadium's repairs lingered—due in large part to the series of strikes from November 1995 to February 1996 by French public workers—the demography and practices of the gym altered. The old health center was not only located within a block of Quatre-Chemins, but had also been built virtually on the grounds of one of Le Petit Pantin's few housing projects, and its former patients had been primarily local residents of these areas. As such, local youth, mostly of North African and Antillean descent, soon discovered the gym, viewed it as part of their neighborhood, and began using it regularly as a complement to their kickboxing and basketball practice. Initially, beginning in February 1996, the volunteer manager of the gym, Philippe, a city employee and trade unionist, welcomed these young members even though officially one could join the gym only at the beginning of the academic year (October–November), either prorating or eschewing their membership fees. For Philippe, this decision resulted from a willingness to maintain good social relations with local residents in light of the temporary nature of the gym's location. As he told me later, "Most others would have simply refused, but, as long as they seemed mature (*sérieux*), I didn't see any reason why not."

This attitude would soon change. As the gym became better known in the area, more and more local young men began using its equipment after hours, having learned the code from friends (or friends of friends) who had been officially enrolled. On several instances, Philippe, having neatly arranged the gym when he had closed up the previous evening, opened the gym the following day to find weights scattered across the floor and the benches in a general state of upheaval. In response, he installed a key lock in the front door and informed those younger members from the *cité* that they were responsible for cleaning up after themselves, and that their use of the gym "was a privilege, not a right." Unfortunately, these measures proved ineffective, as non-members (as well as members disgruntled by the new policies) continued to enter after hours through a partially boarded-up window. Moreover, the following week Philippe discovered several weights and bars to be missing and that a portable radio belonging to the gym had been smashed. Philippe grew increasingly disgruntled, placing the whole blame directly on "those Blacks and Arabs" whom he had recently admitted.

One Saturday afternoon not long thereafter, Philippe arrived at the end of the workout session to lock up. Noticing that the weights had not yet been properly arranged and that a group of local youths were still there, he flew into a fit of rage and began hurling weights and benches in their direction, yelling, "This is how you clean up after yourselves?! I can play that game too!" After calming down, he fumed to me, "They treat this place like it's their house (*chez eux*). Maybe that's okay where they come from, but not here. I'm not a racist, but those youth, those Blacks and North Africans, always mess things up for us. They force me to act like this . . ." In the following days I had a chance to talk to several of those he had blamed, who, in point of fact, were among the most regular, competent, and "serious" members of the gym—much more so than Philippe himself, who recently had only been coming to the gym to lock up or to sit in the back room and drink whiskey. One local teenager, Ahmed, whose parents immigrated from Kabylia after the Algerian revolution, interpreted the incident to me as follows: "I don't know what came over him. He went crazy! We have been good about putting away the weights we use. Why doesn't he yell at others? He's completely racist. We have as much right to be here as he does. We live here [in the neighborhood]." Within two months, the weightlifting gym had moved back to the stadium, and Ahmed and his friends began to use a different municipal gym, on the Quatre-Chemins side of the canal.

The incident described above should not be understood simply through the lens of race relations, as a testament to the irreconcilability of ethnic differences. Rather, the incident resulted directly from and contributed to the production of and resistance to physical and imaginary borders that have created the two sociospatial entities known as Le Petit Pantin and Quatre-Chemins and their respective residents as differentially national subjects. In designating these spatial divisions and underwriting their separation, the (unequal) distribution of municipal services, viewed from the top as an element of social justice, has contributed to the reification of social categories of belonging as seen from below. The dispute was over who was really "at home" (*chez soi*) in a liminal space as represented by the state but over which two differently imagined groups had equal claim—one, through temporal means, as long-standing gym members; the other, through spatial means, as proximate residents.[15] In the end, both groups successfully asserted their claims, for Ahmed and his friends proved they could not be evicted from a space which they occupied as their own, but in which they could never be allowed to feel "at home."

Mantes-la-Jolie: Modernity Awry

The spatializing practices of suburban residents, who seek to forge relations of domesticity within the sociospatial divisions established by French urban planning policies, thus directly engage a discourse of cultural exteriority through which the *cités* are represented. These practices are further evidenced in the case of Mantes-la-Jolie, where residents confront and reconstruct daily a set of social segmentations that reinforce the divide between city and suburb, between Parisian and *banlieusard* (suburbanite). Approximately the same size as Pantin, Mantes-la-Jolie is located about fifty kilometers northwest of Paris in the *département* of Yvelines. Like Pantin, the municipality is divided into two separate but unequal parts: the quaint medieval village of Mantes with its windy streets and its fourteenth-century cathedral built along the banks of the Seine; and the immense ZUP of Val-Fourré, a concrete agglomeration of twenty-plus-story towers and more squat but longer apartment blocks. Designed in the early 1960s to house residents of an overcrowded, partially devastated postwar Mantes, Val-Fourré was advertised by the OPHLM as an ultra-modern haven for the lower middle class (*cadres moyens*) and state functionaries who wished to escape the cramped living quarters of the metropolis.

By the time the construction was completed in 1977, however, the goals and local demography had altered significantly. In the postwar economic boom, the Seine valley had undergone a rapid industrialization, with Renault and Talbot opening large factories in nearby Poissy and Flins. Needing to house those Maghrebi and African immigrants recruited overseas, area companies began investing in the Val-Fourré housing project that, under the control of the municipality, had incurred a substantial budgetary deficit. By 1977, the automobile industry had acquired one-quarter of the apartments, and company buses shuttled workers twice daily to and from the housing project. By the 1990s, Val-Fourré housed more than 25,000 people, half of whom were of immigrant origin (primarily Moroccan, Portuguese, and Senegalese), in eight distinct *cités*. The 200-hectare complex, built on the site of a former airport, includes eleven schools, sports facilities (including a skating rink), a cultural center, and an outdoor shopping mall (Boubeker and Daoud 1993: 22–23).

As in Pantin, the socioeconomic and cultural rift between Mantes and Val-Fourré is substantiated by both physical and imagined boundaries. The housing project is situated a full three kilometers away from downtown Mantes and is completely surrounded by a peripheral boulevard. Public buses run infrequently between the two, and the walk takes nearly forty minutes. In the original planning, such transit was considered virtually unnecessary, as the ZUP was designed to be largely self-sustaining, with its own schools, shops, entertainment centers, multidenominational church, and mosque. Mantes's cafés and shops cater to its middle-class residents or richer tourists, and their owners generally look upon Val-Fourréiens with suspicion. The one nightclub in Mantes, according to young adults with whom I spoke, does not admit dark-skinned revelers. Equally incredibly, one Kabyle resident of the *cité*, Akli, estimated that at most 5 percent of the youth from Val-Fourré had ever entered the Mantes cathedral, a site visited by thousands of tourists each year.

This planned autonomy has become increasingly unstable since the early

1990s. Industrial cutbacks and the closing of several of the local factories have contributed to high unemployment levels, especially for young males of immigrant origin. The apartment courtyards and shopping malls are filled with *hitistes* (literally "wall-hangers" in Algerian Arabic), young men who are mostly unemployed or otherwise engaged in local drug or gray-market (*trabendo*) industries. Confrontations between these youth and police have multiplied, culminating in the 1991 death of Aïssa Ihich at the hands of law enforcement agents and the subsequent riot that led to the death of another youth and a police officer. At the time of my research, the Leclerc supermarket, as well as more than half the other shops in the commercial center, remained boarded up, and no effort had been made to repair the damage inflicted on the cultural center or gymnasium by rioters.

Given this lack of services, residents I encountered had formulated two responses, both of which amount to the constitution of a parallel economy that, while allowing for quotidian survival, reproduced their structural marginalization from the national (moral) economy. Val-Fourréiens held a daily market on the site of the defunct shopping mall, with merchants re-selling produce, foodstuffs, and clothes purchased in bulk at the hypermarkets in and around Paris. Neighborhood cultural associations filled in for the poor learning conditions in the local schools with after-school tutoring and preparation classes for the baccalaureate national high school exam. Certain local entrepreneurs further developed an informal taxi system to shuttle Val-Fourré residents to and from Mantes and surrounding points, thus taking the place of the factory shuttles that had become defunct. Regular lines of commuters waited for such taxis at the entrance of the complex to catch a ride into the city or to the train station.

For, like other distant Parisian suburbs, the only efficient public transportation network connecting Mantes-la-Jolie to the outside world is an SNCF national train line, constructed between 1843 and 1851, that spreads radially from Paris's Gare Saint-Lazare station. Given its centralized form, the rail network makes commutes that appear short on paper into a trying experience. Merad, a Kabyle activist, splits his time between associations in Val-Fourré, where he resides, and the relatively nearby urban development of Cergy-Pontoise. Twice a week he thus takes a fifty-minute train ride to Paris, changes trains, and then comes back another forty minutes in nearly the same direction to get to Cergy, from which he then has to catch a bus to the association. For those working in more distant suburbs, the commute can reach up to four hours a day in public transportation.

These structures of economic degradation, police confrontation, and transportation difficulties have redrawn the lines of division in Mantes-la-Jolie. Within Val-Fourré itself, each of the eight individual *cités* (Écrivains, Aviateurs, Peintres, etc.) has developed its own separate identity, often expressed in racialized terms and reinforced by particular administrative features of schools and social centers located in different areas. Residents use the dialectical Arabic term *gaouri*—literally meaning either "peasant" or, paradoxically, "neighbor," but often used in Algeria to signify a *Français*—to designate outsiders, a category that includes not only those from Mantes and beyond, but also those from a different *cité* within Val-Fourré (Daoud 1993c: 26). While walking around Val-Fourré one afternoon, Merad pointed out a group of *hitistes* in the Écrivains section, speculating that they were likely drug dealers. "Really?" I inquired. "Do you know them?" "No," he replied. "I'm from Explorateurs, so I don't actually know this area very well." This segmentation of the ZUP is further overlain with a patchwork of gangs (*bandes*) of young residents who mark their *cité* territory with graffiti tags and control the local drug markets. As in other ZUPs across France, these spatializing practices can occasionally lead to border disputes and violence, conflicts that the media has often interpreted as social unrest or anti-police "riots" (*émeutes*).[16]

Furthermore, following a segmentary logic akin to the fission and fusion of Kabyle patrilines, these sociospatial groups forge ties of solidarity in opposition to more distant *gaouris*. In close proximity to Val-Fourré, but in a different municipality, lies another ZUP, La Noé of Chanteloup-les-Vignes. As in Pantin, conflicts between residents of these two ZUPs have centered on municipal structures, particularly concerning access to the skating rink, a structure that La Noé is lacking. In at least one case, the conflict has resulted in a violent encounter between residents of the two areas outside the rink (Daoud 1993c: 27). This rivalry has led to the production of racialized stereotypes and unflattering nicknames that residents of each ZUP hurl at each other. For instance, La Noé residents have deformed Val-Fourré (literally "fleecy valley") into Mal-Bourré ("badly drunk") and generally refer to Mantes-la-Jolie ("beautiful Mantes") as Mantes-la-Folie ("crazy Mantes"). Cédric, a nine-year-old Antillean whom Merad and I met in the Mantes train station, expressed his own interpretation of the difference between Val-Fourré and his native La Noé: "Me, I don't live in Val-Fourré because I'm not bad. You [pointing to Merad] look like [*avoir la tête de*] a Val-Fourréien. Me, I'm mixed (*métis*); I'm from La Noé."

These oppositions notwithstanding, residents of both Val-Fourré and La Noé find themselves on similar ground as *zupiens* (ZUP inhabitants) in relation to village or town residents, and, more generally, as *banlieusards* in relation to Parisians. Since the mid-1980s, the national media have largely represented the *cités* as spaces of crime and violence, further reinforcing the negative stereotyping and defensive spatializing practices Parisians employ to differentiate their own sociospatiality from their neighbors to the north. My Parisian friends commonly blamed northern *banlieusards*—particularly from the *département* of Seine–Saint-Denis, whom they consistently racialized as being immigrants—for bringing violence and insecurity to Parisian streets and *métros*. One friend even claimed that Paris's traffic and parking problems were primarily the result of cars driven in from Seine–Saint-Denis, a provenance clearly marked by the last two numbers of 93 on the license plates. Given its history of confrontations between police and local youth, Val-Fourré has been particularly affected by such negative representations that have led to a further restriction of employment opportunities of its residents. Several residents I talked with recounted stories of job applications being rejected when the potential employer discovered the applicant's residence. Akli, who believes he was refused an accounting position during the final interview for exactly this reason, now uses his sister's address in Paris for all employment-related correspondence.

In this sense, in spite of the internal divisions between Écrivains and Explorateurs, between Val-Fourré and La Noé, or even between Quatre-Chemins and Le Petit Pantin, the *banlieue* as a whole exists in segmentary opposition to the Parisian center, as a space of cultural exteriority that functions reciprocally to redefine a certain French metropolitan identity. While constructed as ultra-modern vanguard spaces in the postcolonial mission to integrate (read civilize) working-class and immigrant residents into productive and commensurable national subjects, the *cités* have today become, for many critics, tangible signs of the state's failure to solve the immigration "problem." In this sociological representation, the internal sociospatial segmentation of places like Pantin and Mantes-la-Jolie appears to index the intransigence of primordial cultural differences, a perduring tribalism that threatens to tear the French nation-state asunder. If the *axxam,* in colonial discourse, reflected the Kabyles' cultural immutability, it is the postcolonial *cité* that today has been racialized as an immigrant enclave on the cultural margins of the metropole. If colonial officials projected the destruction of the *axxam* as the condition of possibility for the productivity and security of the Algerian colony, urban planners today view the renovation, if not the razing, of the *cités* as the primary means to alleviate social exclusion and resuture the national political and moral economies.

Civility and Disorder

The ethnographic examples of Pantin and Mantes-la-Jolie at first blush testify to a national state that has largely abandoned its suburban housing projects to the vagaries of neo-liberalism, approaching them as failed experiments to be policed and contained. While the national government has indeed since the mid-1970s abdicated much of the day-to-day responsibility for these housing projects to individual municipalities and private HLM companies, it nonetheless continues to operate 30 percent of the more than three million public lodgings. Moreover, from as early as 1977, it has developed social programs for the renovation of the more dilapidated quarters and the better integration of their residents into the social and economic life of French urbanity. This has involved the investment of billions of francs in the ZUPs and other quarters deemed particularly "precarious" (*sensible*) or "problematic" (*difficile*), with, for example, 200 million francs invested in Chanteloup-les-Vignes alone during the 1980s (Daoud 1993e: 78). In the process, the state has established direct ties with local grassroots cultural and economic associations, treating them as cultural mediators between immigrant or excluded populations and the French republic.

On the one hand, this continued state involvement in public housing has followed the logic of Sellier's utopian modernism, aiming to promote social prosperity through a highly regulated living environment. On the other hand, the attempt to maintain control of the urban landscape—which the state views as threatened by chaotic real estate development, the perseverance of shanties and squatters, and the appropriation of the ZUP economies by local gangs or religious organizations—derives from exigencies of state security. If the original construction of public housing responded to the simultaneous impetus of labor socialism and military concerns accompanying the Algerian war, the urban renovation and rehabilitation efforts since 1980 have followed a similar double logic, simultaneously attempting to forge a new urban civil society while paying close heed to questions of state security.

Most often, these actions have responded to particular events that have drawn national attention to the gross socioeconomic disparity between the private-sector housing and the public housing projects. For example, after the 1981 "rodeos" in Lyon's working-class suburbs of Vaulx-en-Velin, Villeurbanne, and Vénissieux—in which local youths stole more than 200 cars, engaged police in chases, and then burned the cars—the socialist government initiated a National Commission for Neighborhood Social Development (CNDSQ) that declared twenty-two neighborhoods to be "sensitive zones" (*blocs sensibles*) and invested sixty billion francs over the next ten years in the destruction of decrepit buildings and the rehabilitation of more than 100,000 apartments. Again, in 1990, after a series of violent battles between police forces and young residents of Mantes-la-Jolie, Argenteuil, and Vaulx-en-Velin, the government invested another 100 million francs for the revitalization of sixty particularly impoverished and dilapidated neighborhoods (Daoud 1993a: 136–139).

The perceived link between violence and the *cités* reached new heights in the mid-1990s. Suburban areas deemed particularly "hot" (*chaud*) became a media obsession, with article after article, news program after news program, detailing the "hatred" (*la haine*) felt by young residents of the *banlieues* toward police or governmental authorities. Minor incidents involving police and youthful offenders in "difficult quarters" (*quartiers difficiles*) received front-page headlines repeatedly throughout the summer and fall months of 1995. One *Libération* (30 October 1995: 3) article written during this period provided the curious reader with a detailed statistical breakdown of the 152 armed incidents perpetrated in the French suburbs during the first eight months of the year: eleven "drive by shootings" [*sic*], fourteen punitive expeditions, thirteen gang battles, etc. A series of films produced during this period—including *La Haine* (dir. Matthieu Kassovitz, 1995), *Raï* (dir. Thomas Gilou, 1995), *États des Lieux* (dir. Jean-François Richet, 1997), and *Ma 6-T va Crack-er* (dir. Jean-François Richet, 1997)—presented the *cités* as ticking time bombs, with each of the films ending with scenes of violence. In fact, several such films—including *La Haine* and the earlier *Cheb* (dir. Rachid Bouchareb, 1991)—incorporated television footage of actual riots into the opening credits sequence, thus seamlessly melding a fictional narrative into a journalistic reality familiar to audiences. While produced with the intent of exposing the *banlieue* "problems" to a larger public, these portrayals have indirectly contributed to the production of a scopic regime fetishizing dark-skinned immigrant bodies in masses wielding weapons of destruction.

This racial imagery of violence was further complicated by the addition of another category of difference: religion. Scholars and journalists targeted the suburbs as veritable *banlieues de l'Islam* ("Islamic suburbs") (Kepel 1991), as the prime site of the implantation of France's second-largest faith. Of particular concern was the arrival of North African "fundamentalist" or "integralist" (*intégriste*) movements into France, their incorporation into the *cités* with subterranean prayer rooms in the basements of HLM structures, and their recruitment of impoverished youth to become soldiers for global *jihad* (cf. Pujadas and Salam 1995). Police certified these fears with the shooting of Khaled Kelkal, a Beur from Vaulx-en-Velin accused of playing a role in the summer 1995 bombings attributed to the Algerian Armed Islamic Group (GIA). The spatioeconomic distance marked by the post-industrial landscape of the *banlieue* was thus reinforced with the cultural distance of a reified Islam.

In response to this elaborated threat, beginning in November 1995 and continuing through June of the following year, Prime Minister Alain Juppé unveiled a "Marshall Plan for the *banlieues*" (including the National Urban Integration Plan and the Urban-Revival Pact) promised by President Jacques Chirac during his April 1995 election campaign. Targeting *quartiers difficiles,* including the Val-Fourré of Mantes-la-Jolie and the Val-d'Argent of Argenteuil—areas that had witnessed both anti-police demonstrations and the rise of Islamic associations in the early 1990s—the plan envisioned the creation of twenty "duty-free zones" (*zones franches*) in which local businesses and industries would be exempt from paying most taxes. Moreover, the plan delimited 546 "precarious urban zones" (*zones urbains sensibles*)[17] in which local associations, acting as mediators between the state and the *zupiens,* would receive subsidies to hire young residents to work in internships. As such, like the original Marshall Plan initiated by the American government in postwar Europe, Juppé's plan sought to reintegrate France's peripheries into the national economy and away from the gray-market system that supposedly contributed to the growth of Islamist groups.

As in previous urban planning projects in both France and Algeria, the Juppé "Marshall Plan" displayed an ambivalence of purpose, counter-poising needs for the surveillance and isolation of these *zones sensibles* with the imperative to foster the circulation of capital. In addition to establishing the free-trade zones, the plan responded to demands for the further policing of the designated neighborhoods. Following the Vigipirate emergency security plan enacted in the wake of the 1995 bombings, the Juppé plan provided funding for the further surveillance of the *cités,* with police conducting round-ups (*rafles*) of suspected Islamists and deporting undocumented immigrants on "charter" flights. The plan, brokered by an interministerial delegation uniting the interior and justice ministers, received direct encouragement by the national police labor union, which complained of the growth of "non-legal zones [*zones de non-droit*] in which the law of the Republic is totally absent" (*Le Monde* 7 September 1995), of a veritable Wild West in the *banlieues* in which, according to the interior minister, an "Intifada" was imminent (*L'Express* 9 November 1995). In February 1999, responding to a report that juvenile delinquency had increased over the previous year, socialist Prime Minister Lionel Jospin topped his conservative counterpart and proposed a new plan to bring 13,000 riot police and 17,000 military gendarmes to patrol these same public housing projects. In 2003, Interior Minister Nicolas Sarkozy further increased these numbers as part of his larger war on terror, responding to the increased public concern over "security" that followed the 11 September attacks in the United States. In this respect, the *banlieues,* constructed under an ideology of modernization, are today portrayed by the state not only as spaces of economic marginalization and cultural distance, but also of anti-civility and disorder—as spaces of potential hostility to the French state.

Transportation Violence

An important site in the ambivalent production of the *banlieues* as spaces of order and disorder, tribalism and modernity, is the transportation industry.[18] Public transportation both delineates racialized compartments and violates them, enables mobility and delimits the possible avenues through which such movement can occur. For if the development of rail-road lines throughout the nineteenth century and their electrification after 1929 facilitated the integration and growth of urban peripheries, the current public transportation system has paradoxically maintained their social distance and exclusion. By the year 2015, given current rates of population growth, travel between non-contiguous suburbs will likely represent more than three-quarters of the total daily commutes in Île-de-France (Soulignac 1993: 129). However, according to a 1990 INSEE report, nearly 60 percent of these suburban municipalities lack their own train station (Daoud 1993e: 77).

The lack of regular train service in the *banlieues* contrasts distinctly with the well-developed transportation network in Paris proper. For its approximately seventy-five square kilometers, Paris is endowed with more than 240 *métro* stops on fifteen lines and an additional twelve light rail (RER) stops on four lines, or more than three stations per square kilometer, with this density increasing as one moves toward the center of the city. Moreover, this grid is overlain with nearly 100 bus lines, servicing those rare trajectories not directly connected by a single subway line. In my experience, it generally takes no more than forty-five minutes door-to-door between any two spots within the city limits, a time estimate confirmed by standard Parisian folk wisdom. While the *métro* and RER lines extend into the proximate suburbs, they represent only about 120 stops for several thousand communes in Île-de-France, with the further suburbs served, if at all, by local SNCF trains emerging from Paris's six stations. Radially laid out, the RER and SNCF lines connect the suburbs directly to Paris, leaving only bus service and one tramway to link suburb to suburb.

Aware of this inequality between metropole and periphery, the transportation administration of Île-de-France developed a comprehensive project in 1992 designed to standardize and integrate transportation in the region. The plan, beyond calling for the construction of more expressways, had two aims: to extend current RER service to increased numbers of suburbs and to facilitate exchanges between different forms of pre-existing public transportation. The plan foresaw two new RER lines and an extension of existing ones to accommodate the larger *grands ensembles* of Mantes-la-Jolie, Cergy-Pontoise, Boissy, and Meaux. Additionally, the Parisian transportation administration (RATP) began construction of two automatic *métro* lines that would link the various SNCF stations in Paris and thus provide easier transfers between different means of transportation. To facilitate these new interchanges, the two transportation companies (SNCF and RATP) have standardized their ticketing procedures, allowing for a single ticket to be used within any of the five concentric zones for which it has been purchased. In other words, the plan envisioned a unified space of commensurable destinations while simultaneously maintaining the centrality of Paris as a hub of circulation.

In addition to these centralizing tendencies, the 1992 plan called for a longer-term project to build a comprehensive intersuburban light rail system with 170 kilometers of track and 170 stations, many of which would connect extant SNCF lines (Soulignac 1993: 129). However, the construction of this network has been repeatedly delayed. In fact, if anything, recent government actions have impeded rather than promoted circulation to and from the *banlieues*. For while, from Lyautey to Sellier to the *banlieue* Marshall Plans, circulation has long been considered in urban planning measures to be an integral aspect of national integration and economic progress, it has also been viewed as a site of potential disorder. In the late 1980s, the directors of the SNCF began publicly complaining that they had "lost control" of their suburban transportation network. According to railway division commissioner Guy Puchon, in addition to increasing "problems" of vandalism, graffiti, and muggings, "we found we had become unwilling participants in the drug scene. Our trains were transporting poor suburban youth to the city after school to make drug deals" (Rivière-Platt 1993: 26). In 1989, the SNCF, with direct support from local and national governments, initiated a comprehensive "security plan" that earmarked more than 600 million francs over the next three years for a policy of "rapid intervention and increased surveillance" along the suburban network. This plan included hiring 600 new security agents and assigning another 380 policemen to patrol the suburban lines. In addition, the SNCF installed video cameras in all of its suburban train stations (Rivière-Platt 1993: 26).

Nonetheless, the representation of the suburban transportation network as a space of disorder has continued apace. Following the subway bombings in the Saint-Michel and Port-Royal RER stations in 1995 and 1996, the system garnered renewed public attention as a target of terrorism. The state's response, in the form of the Vigipirate emergency security plan, has concentrated directly on the suburban lines, as the assumption was that these attacks resulted from the ability of suburban youth to enter Paris undetected from the *cités* in La Courneuve and Aulnay-sous-Bois further down the line. In addition to hiring additional private security agents, the Vigipirate plan assigned roving patrols of heavily armed riot police and military gendarmes to every SNCF and RER station in Paris. Furthermore, police were assigned to RATP controllers in order to analyze the security risk of those individuals caught without tickets. In 1996, RATP and SNCF agents were directly empowered to detain suspects.

Policy procedures reinforce the representation of uncontrolled circulation between the urban peripheries and center as a source of potential disorder. This link is underlined by popular attitudes that racialize suburban spaces and violence, that represent *banlieusards* as a culturally distinct species prone to uncivilized, violent behavior. In order to illustrate the performativity of these representations, I recount a series of discussions I had about a violent incident to which I was unfortunately a party.

Late one Friday evening in the spring of 1996, I was returning to my home in Pantin. As this was the last *métro* for the night, the car in which I was traveling was sparsely populated, and became even emptier as the train moved further along its trajectory to the outskirts of Paris. Following the *hexis* of *métro* riding, I had my eyes fixed on the newspaper I was reading, with my backpack full of archival notes pressed between my legs. Indeed, it was not until I glimpsed a figure moving toward me that I realized that the *métro* car, which had just crossed the border into Pantin, had nearly entirely emptied, leaving only myself and a group of five young men seated a few benches behind me. As he approached, the young man, dressed in the *look*

Beur (a baseball cap, name-brand sports vest, jeans, and gym shoes associated with the North African *banlieue* youth), formed his hand in the shape of a gun and pointed it at my head. Misrecognizing his action as humor or as some form of address associating weaponry and masculinity, I performed the same gesture, directing my own handgun at him. Only when he reached for my bag and I began to feel the blows from his companions striking the back of my head did I realize that his gesture was neither a joke nor an ironic greeting, but a clear sign and opening act of aggression. In the minute-long melee that ensued, during which I futilely attempted to maintain a grasp on my notebooks, suffering countless blows for my efforts, not a word passed between myself and my attackers. Finally, the train entered the next station, and the group forcefully ejected me onto the platform, minus one backpack. As the train pulled away, the young man who had begun the attack and I replayed the opening gambit, once again directing handgun signs at each other.

In the weeks following the subway confrontation, informants presented me with a number of different possible interpretations as to what had transpired. For many of my Parisian friends, the attack was simply inevitable; indeed, they had previously expressed concern for my safety living in the *banlieues* in general and Seine–Saint-Denis in particular. The event likewise had a ring of normalcy for the security forces who happened to be waiting at the following station and to whom I reported the incident five minutes after it occurred: "They were Black and Arab, right? Damn! We just saw them five minutes ago. I knew we should have stopped them!" With local police backup, they began a search of nearby housing projects on the border of Pantin and Bobigny, but, not finding the culprits, came to the conclusion that the attackers must have come from one of the other *cités* further in Bobigny.

Many local residents of Pantin concurred with the police's assessment, viewing the attack as an aberration in Pantin. For them, Pantin, in spite of its many public housing projects, was still a "safe" place, unlike the more distant, well-known *quartiers chauds* of Bobigny or Aulnay farther down the *métro* line. The incident further seemed an aberration to them because, according to my Franco-Moroccan friend Mohammed, the mixture of Blacks and Beurs in the group seemed to them to violate the rules by which *bandes* were formed—this even though Mohammed, whose own Moroccan immigrant father had married a French woman, had close friends that crossed racialized lines. The general belief among Pantinois was that I had simply been unlucky (*mal tombé*), as violent incidents such as the one I experienced were not part of *la vie pantinoise*. I was, of course, personally inclined toward this line of reasoning, as I had lived in Pantin for more than six months at that point and found it difficult to accept that my attackers could have been members of a community into which I felt integrated.

Regardless of the exact provenance of my attackers, what the discussions following the mugging indicated was a tendency to link race, space, and violence to the transportation network. One Pantinois friend used my story as a renewed excuse to drive wherever he went, even when traveling to locations on a direct *métro* line from his residence. Philippe, the manager of the weight room, succinctly expressed the sentiment: "This never used to happen here. The problems started when they extended the *métro* lines to Bobigny." Such a statement dovetails with the SNCF and RATP's assessment of transportation security as inherently endangered by *banlieue* violence.

This image of the *métro* runs counter to *banlieusards'* own experience of the transportation system as a space of harassment, racism, and alienation. Since the installation of the Vigipirate plan, police have stopped nearly three million North African–looking *banlieusards* in stations and on trains, demanded their residence papers, and even arrested them if such papers were not in order. I witnessed a number of such interpellations. In one instance, I was walking through a subway hall with an African immigrant and Fethi, a Franco-Kabyle friend from the Parisian suburbs. When we encountered the security detail, the African man stopped dead and took an alternate route. Giving him only a sidelong glance and me no notice at all, the security agents stopped Fethi and demanded his papers. Although he was a legitimate French citizen (born in France to Algerian parents born in Algeria under French rule), he had yet to update his national identity card to his recent move to Châtillon, and hence there was a discrepancy with his *métro* pass. On that basis, the security guards detained him for thirty minutes before writing him an injunction requiring him to present an updated version of his national identity card to the local police station within two weeks. In later conversations with Fethi and other Kabyle friends, we discussed local strategies used to sidestep these confrontations, from using alternate routes, to avoiding certain stations at certain times, to using mocked-up train passes. One friend asserted that by eschewing the *look Beur* and always carrying a briefcase—i.e., by never *appearing* to be a *banlieusard*—he had succeeded in never being stopped. What such experiences indicate is the intimate connection between categories of race and transportation in the constitution of the *banlieues* as spaces of violence.

These associations are underlined by immigrant narratives that center on the confusion of the newly arrived migrant when confronted with the confusion of the transportation system (cf. Boudjedra 1975). Often the incidents are of a relatively minor, everyday character—from misreading the subway plan to misusing the tickets to being robbed of one's suitcase. One Kabyle friend was detained by police within an hour of his arrival from Algeria, as he had bought the wrong RER ticket for his train trip from the airport into the city. Although he was soon released with merely a fine, these incidents can also turn violent. In July 1983, nine-year-old Tawfik Ouanes was shot and killed by a subway security officer in La Courneuve in an incident that would become a central rallying point for immigrant activism. Likewise, in a novel based on the 14 November 1983 murder of Algerian tourist Habib Grimzi on a train from Bordeaux to Marseille, Ahmed Kalaouz (1986) portrays the kilometer-by-kilometer escalation of violence, at the conclusion of which Grimzi is thrown to his death by four off-duty French legionnaires. In a very visceral sense, technologies of circulation and communication can thus also serve as tools of embodied exclusion.

Within this violent context in which sociospatial subjectivities are constituted and racialized, *banlieue* residents have appropriated various aspects of the transportation system as their own, engaging in spatializing practices that de Certeau has generally termed "poaching" (1984: xii). In individual artistic expressions, they have inscribed train cars and stations with graffiti, from elaborate pictorial displays to personalized tags. These renditions serve not only as acts of intragroup bravado among age or artistic peers, but also as a means by which suburban groups reclaim municipal institutions located on a territory constituted as their own. Likewise, certain *banlieue* residents use the transportation network as a site for economic gain—as an entrepreneurial space—in terms of gray-market vending, panhandling, or even drug sales. One talks of "doing a *métro*" (*se faire un métro*) to indicate a type of petty theft involving using the sudden crowds of the subway as interference in a pickpocketing scheme. The same practice, as Mehdi Charef (1983: 103–108) has shown in novelized form, can also utilize racialized notions of criminality when multiracial pickpocketing groups use a clean Beur member as a fall guy (cf. Rosello 1998).

Nonetheless, it is important not to overemphasize the illegal use of the *métro* and thus underwrite a set of racialist discourses about *banlieue* criminality. Indeed, the more everyday, tactical form of symbolic violence against the public transportation authority is an elaborate system of fare dodging, from jumping gates to distracting ticket takers to forging monthly passes. To combat this tendency, the RATP has developed ever more complicated and intricate ticket systems. However, the more enterprising *bricoleurs* have always found ways around such technological innovations. Yunis, the Kabyle immigrant living in Saint-Denis who had trained as an engineer in the Algerian navy, used his technical knowledge to adapt a tape recorder to duplicate the magnetic strip on monthly *métro* passes. Rather than profiting from this innovation, he donated these forged passes to suburban friends unable to afford the official, escalating prices. When I asked him about his motivation, he recounted the following story:

> You see, Paul, one afternoon a couple of years ago I was taking the *métro* when a group of RATP ticket controllers entered the train. My ticket was in order, so I wasn't worried, but when they reached the older woman sitting across from me, there was clearly a problem. She was from Algeria, and her French wasn't very good, so I offered to translate. It turns out that she had just bought a monthly pass, but hadn't realized that she had

to provide a photograph and write the ticket number on the card. I tried to explain to the agent that it was an honest mistake, that she had just arrived in town to visit her older brother's family and hadn't understood the correct procedures, but he refused to budge, claiming that "ignorance was no excuse." From that moment, I decided never again to pay for a single ticket.

Through practices such as Yunis's, *banlieue* residents have mobilized within the racialized disorder of the suburban transportation network and have developed their own "illegitimate" tactics of respatialization (de Certeau 1984: 96) in their embodied attempts to take possession of spaces defined violently.

Walking in the Suburbs

These respatializing practices infuse contemporary (sub)urban transformations across France and Algeria, even beyond the transportation network, incorporating forms of nostalgia and cultural objectification into the urban space. In the first place, forms of Kabyle village sociality have been reborn in the heart of French urbanism, magnified in part by the recent arrival of Kabyle political refugees fleeing the current Algerian civil war. In the outdoor public squares on the edges of neighborhoods with prominent Kabyle populations like Belleville and Ménilmontant, crowds of older men generally from the same village congregate daily and engage in vigorous debate over issues of local and international politics. Kabyle men have likewise established more formal village assemblies in Parisian and suburban cafés owned by former residents of their village. In their monthly meetings, they make decisions on infrastructural improvements to their natal areas, arrange for the repatriation of their members' corpses, and collect funds to sponsor the migration of family members or otherwise help a member in need. More recently, the migrant *tajmaâts* have reconstituted themselves as official associations benefiting from French public funding and separate locales. These assemblies operate in parallel with informal *tajmaâts* that have continued to function in Kabylia in spite of the Algerian state's centralization and Arabization policies. Like the *tajmaâts* in Kabylia, the Parisian village assemblies have become increasingly politicized in the wake of the Algerian civil war and the growth of rival Kabyle political parties that operate transnationally. As in Kabylia, these associations have a tendency to fission along familial and political lines.

Furthermore, domestic arrangements of Kabyles in France continue to provide a space for the constitution and performance of subjectivity, in spite of an explicit awareness of the loss of the *axxam* as a structuring space of social reproduction and contestation. As Joëlle Bahloul (1992) has demonstrated, domestic architecture serves as a privileged locus for the maintenance and transmission of social memory and nostalgia in Algerian diasporic settings. Berber cultural associations in and around Paris have consciously incorporated domestic imagery into their after-school instruction for children of Kabyle migrants in Berber history, language, art, theater, and dance. *National Geographic*–style photos of villages and houses festoon the walls of the associations' headquarters and are featured prominently in the slide shows that almost always accompany seasonal holiday celebrations. One of the main textbooks employed in Tamazight language classes sets its lessons in a mythical village, Tizi-Wwuccen (Mountain Pass of the Jackal), with each chapter taking place in a different setting: the *axxam,* the fountain, the fields, the *tajmaât,* etc. In the process, an objectified version of Kabyle culture is nostalgically presented to the younger generation, one that is rooted in a particular set of spatial features.

Such nostalgic spatializing practices are reinforced in individual households. If individual Kabyle emigrants have exported European symbolic forms of value to their natal villages in the form of new home construction, they have likewise imported various aspects of village domestic architecture into their living spaces in France. Since at least the 1910s, they have generally filled their French domiciles—even when such accommodation amounted to temporary shanties, immigrant foyers, or employer-provided housing—with oriental rugs and brass tea sets brought over from Algeria or purchased in the multiple North African shops (*épiceries*) that dot the Parisian landscape. Today a number of members of the younger generation have translated this into a veritable fetish of the physical accoutrements of the *axxam.* The transformations of Mounir's HLM apartment in Argenteuil were mirrored in a number of apartments I visited. For instance, my friend Sonya, born in France to parents born in Kabylia, lives in a functionary apartment provided by the primary school in which she teaches in Aulnay-sous-Bois. When I visited her in 1995, the apartment was filled with a number of items reflecting Algerian culture, including a water pipe, a brass teapot, and even a ceramic representation of a mosque. Moreover, the walls of the apartment were covered with photographs and paintings depicting stereotypical Kabyle village scenes: women collecting water at the fountain, men harvesting the fields, etc.

One Kabyle architect friend, Hend, a devotee of Bourdieu who had just begun a university degree in ethnology, had explicitly attempted to transform his Parisian home into a miniature *axxam.* On one of the walls of his thirty-square-meter studio apartment, he had built a small, lofted *takhana* (mezzanine) on which he displayed scale models of various types of *ikoufen* (storage jars). Next to the *takhana* sat a full-size *achemoukh* (water jug), underlining the iconic representation of the miniatures. He completed the spatial overdetermination by featuring on his coffee table a large-format picture book of old photos of "traditional" Kabyle houses, simply titled *Axxam* (Abouda 1985). While this initially struck me as an extreme case, I

BONNE ET HEUREUSE ANNÉE
ASEGG͞ÁS AMEGGAZ
1996

A Berber New Year's card distributed by
the Association de Culture Berbère,
displaying a nostalgic image of a Berber
woman at the domestic *kanoun*.

Berber nightclub in Paris. Windows are decorated with images of
Kabyle villages and storage jars (*ikoufen*). Photograph by author.

found myself stepping into a very similar space when I revisited Mounir in
1999. In the three years that had passed, Mounir had married Karima, a
woman born in France to Kabyle parents, who was on maternity leave from
her job as an accountant for a small company in Paris, as she had recently
given birth to a son, Amar. Together they had purchased a two-bedroom
townhouse in a neighboring commune, far away from the din and violence
that Mounir had feared in the *cité*. When I arrived, I found them hard at
work renovating the entire apartment, re-covering the floors and walls with
tiles and storage jars Mounir had collected on his last trip to Kabylia to
present Amar to his family. While seemingly superficial changes, these efforts highlight the tactics of spatial appropriation that migrant subjects like
Sonya, Hend, and Mounir deploy to create domesticity in an ultra-modern
context.

A second type of spatial sociality which has developed among France's
immigrant subjects defies the work of cultural nostalgia and explicitly forges
a multiethnic unity within the working-class neighborhoods of the Goutte
d'Or, Belleville, and Ménilmontant through annual rituals and institutions.
The yearly Goutte d'Or Festival, for instance, consists of a carnival-type

July 1995 street parade in northern Paris celebrating the
annual Goutte d'Or Festival. Photograph by author.

parade of costumed children who follow behind a flatbed truck of musicians playing popular tunes to which the children sing boisterously. Celebrating the multicultural vitality of the neighborhood, the children wield
giant marionettes depicting characters from multiple (Antillean, Arab,
French) folktales. The procession winds through the streets of the Goutte
d'Or in northern Paris, mapping out its boundaries for participants and
spectators. Such concrete efforts at sociospatial solidarity are likewise manifested by neighborhood associations and enterprises that maintain social
centers where local residents are provided with evening classes, artistic work-
shops, and after-school tutoring sessions. Monthly publications, like Ménilmontant's "Le Ménilmuche," further keep residents informed of upcoming
events, relevant news items, and weekly changes within the neighborhoods.

On a larger scale, various groups have appropriated the multiple levels
of administrative identity imposed by state and municipal structures, and
even have revalued their negative representations. Residents of north-suburban Sarcelles, de Certeau notes, have adopted the national image of their
banlieue—as a "total failure" of urban planning—as a symbol of social
prestige (1984: 220). Indeed, the appropriation of self-designations like
zupien, zonard, and *banlieusard* by residents of *cités* reflects a willingness to

transform negative characteristics into positive attributes of social differentiation. In this respect, French rap groups have engaged in particularly elaborated forms of what Robin D. G. Kelley (1996: 136), in discussing U.S. hiphop, has called "ghettocentricity," underlining local ties over national ones and organizing themselves around "posses" of fellow residents of their natal housing projects, who often serve the groups as managers, promoters, security guards, and backup singers. They invoke locality in tags, album titles, credits, and song lyrics that reference their particular *banlieue* belonging. For example, Suprême NTM constantly "shouts out" to its native Saint-Denis, or the larger *département* of Seine–Saint-Denis—and its shorthand postal code 93—in song (e.g., "Seine–Saint-Denis Style" [1998]) as well as in the name of their posse and tag: *93 NTM*. For Ministère Amer, the constant reference is Sarcelles, or *95200* (the name of its 1994 album); for Alliance Ethnik, it is Creil (e.g. "Creil City" [1999]). This respatialization of the *cité* as the center of the rap musicians' cognitive maps reaches its logical extension in a statement of political purpose in the songs of one avowedly Marxist group, Assassin: "My only nation is my posse. . . . The flag of unity is planted in the 18th [*arrondissement* from which the group hails]" ("Kique ta merde" [Kick Your Shit] [1993]).[19]

In this way, Algerian immigrants and other *cité* residents on the French urban periphery have created their own structures of civility, their own sociospatial subjectivities, within and through the state technologies employed to integrate them economically while excluding them socially. This has been largely enabled by the ambivalences that inhere in the French state's production of (sub)urban space; namely, while urban planning measures have sought to break down putatively tribalized enclaves (the *axxam*, the *bidonville*) in order to integrate them into national and global economies and social orders, they have simultaneously sought to maintain certain socioeconomic and cultural divisions, to separate indigenous quarters from colonial European cities, postcolonial metropolises from postindustrial *banlieues*. These ambivalent imperatives have led to a singular contradiction: that the ultra-modern built spaces of the suburban *cités* are now constituted through reconstruction programs and media representations as sites of ethnic tribalism, dysfunction, and disorder. The social life of *banlieusards* both reproduces and resists, competes with and colludes with, such policies and representations. They engage in a variety of spatializing practices that reinscribe domesticity into the urban built environment and nostalgically reconstitute objectified cultural forms for a younger generation born and raised in the diaspora. In this respect, the production of space and spatial subjectivity remains a dialectical and dialogic process in which Muslim immigrant actors, the French state, and transnational cultural movements are all engaged.

4 /

Islam, Bodily Practice, and Social Reproduction

Fethi was born in Dieppe to Kabylia-born parents. His father came to the northern port city in 1946 at the age of fifteen to join his own father and work in the family store. Fethi's grandfather originally came to Dieppe as a young man at the end of the First World War to work in the shipbuilding yards, but soon had earned enough money to open a small store catering to Kabyle emigrants. Both father and grandfather returned to Algeria in 1960, Fethi's father to fight in the war of liberation, Fethi's grandfather to retire definitively. At the close of the war, Fethi's father married one of his cousins (on his mother's side) in the village in which they both were born. After giving birth to two children, they emigrated to Bordeaux to live with the parents of Fethi's mother, where they remained until 1968. It was then that they moved to Dieppe and Fethi was born a year later.

Fethi grew up with his two older sisters in Dieppe, away from any North African neighborhoods. As young children, they attended a Catholic primary school, thus replicating their parents' own education in the *Pères Blancs* missions in Kabylia. Fethi grew up without many Algerian or Kabyle friends, and almost none shared his life history. However, his family maintained close ties with their relatives in Kabylia. When Fethi was growing up, they spent every month of May in his parents' natal village. Assuming the family would eventually resettle there, the parents built a large family home in the village, and additionally bought an apartment in nearby Tizi-Ouzou. They sent Fethi's two sisters to Algeria for their secondary education and encouraged them to marry young men from Kabylia. In 1988, after Fethi passed his baccalaureate high school exam, the parents sold all their possessions in France and moved to Algeria. Fethi enrolled in university law courses in Algiers, but his parents soon realized that their children "could not support life in Algeria" with the increasing violence and instability the country was facing. They returned with all three children to Dieppe where they, for the first time, purchased a house in France. Fethi completed degrees in law and business before taking jobs in insurance in Dieppe and then Paris where he is an insurance sales manager.

Given these life experiences in France and Algeria, Fethi describes himself as having "one foot in the couscous, one foot in the *choucroute* (sauerkraut)"; for him this means being equally at home in two distinct cultures. Although he has not been back to Algeria since the beginning of the civil war in 1992, he actively consumes Algerian books and newspapers and has even started attending events and Tamazight courses at Berber cultural associations in Paris in order to become closer to the Kabyle community there. When I first met him in 1996, he had recently become engaged to a young Franco-Kabyle woman, a match he considered important because of cultural and religious compatibilities. Indeed, since his year living in Algiers, Fethi has become increasingly religious, praying five times a day, fasting during the month of Ramadan, and abstaining from alcohol and pork. While his family as a whole supports his religious practice, his father—the most culturally "traditional" of the family but the only one who does not fast during Ramadan—"did everything in his powers to prevent me from becoming religious," fearing that Fethi would become a radical "Islamist." According to Fethi, his father's fears were less about religion per se than about the dangers that marking oneself as different might pose for citizenship and belonging in France. However, for Fethi religion constitutes essentially a means to connect with his parents' North African heritage and does not represent for him a political act; he rarely prays at mosques largely out of prudence, as he sees these spaces as highly surveilled and potentially dangerous.

Moreover, religion fits seamlessly into Fethi's larger sense of bodily discipline. Fethi lives alone in a spartan two-bedroom apartment owned by his company that lacks the Kabyle accoutrements of many of his contemporaries. He has converted the apartment's broom closet into an office with a small desk and reading lamp, and in what little time is left over in the day he is taking correspondence courses in English to help him in business. As importantly, Fethi's discipline extends to sports practice. As a young man, he was very athletic, particularly in judo, in which he achieved a black belt. To this day, Fethi continues to practice and compete, working out every day at a club just a few blocks from his home and agency in the southern Parisian *banlieue* of Châtillon. For him, sports practice, like praying, provides the same kind of release from the daily grind that he used to find in smoking or drinking. Such an association of sport and religion is even inscribed in his domestic space. The apartment's second bedroom is occupied by a set of weights on one wall, a *qiblat* (plaque indicating the direction of Mecca) on the other wall, and a large mat on the floor on which he works out or prays, depending on the time of the day.

The postcolonial production of Algerian subjectivity in France extends beyond the construction, regulation, and renovation of the built environment in which immigrants live and move. The spatializing practices that structure daily life in the *cités* are mirrored and supplemented by a larger set of embodied techniques—most notably religion and sports play—that have been at the crux of the larger media and governmental debate over immigrant integration. Engaging in a metonymic logic through which the body is understood to stand for the transcendental individual subject and the subject for the society as a whole, the French state and immigrant actors have competed and colluded for the control of immigrant bodily practice in order to ensure the social reproduction of local and national forms of identity and belonging.

In the ambivalent mission to integrate (read civilize) the Algerian immigrant's racialized body into the unmarked national body politic, the French state has positioned the embodied practices of religion—particularly Islamic prayer and veiling—and sports—principally football (what is referred to in the U.S. as "soccer")—as in distinct tension. The colonial reification of Islam as a fanatical and fatalistic belief system that poses an inherent obstacle to indigenous assimilation finds its historical continuity in the postcolonial elaboration of Islam as incommensurable with the French norms of state secularism (*laïcité*). If ideologists for the republic, like Fethi's father, blame Islamic practices of headscarving, mosque building, female seclusion, and the public slaughter of lambs during the festival of Aïd for exacerbating immigrant sociospatial exclusion, they point to the successes of immigrant athletes—and particularly the victorious, multiracial 1998 World Cup football team—as the hallmark of an inclusive New France. These conflicts over the legitimacy and pragmatics of sports vs. religion simultaneously involve localizable debates concerning school uniforms and mosque building, as well as the more disparate interests and aesthetics of multinational corporations and transnational religious and ethnic movements that seek to convert Muslim immigrant bodies into consumers or militants respectively. In the end, these two aspects—local state-immigrant relations and global markets—are inseparable, as they mutually inform each other and together contribute to the production of categories of immigrant subjectivity in the gendered public spheres of the stadium and the studium, in the realms of sports and education.

The efforts of various French state and transnational actors to construct binary oppositions between Islam and *laïcité* through the medium of sports have had unintended consequences. In the state's underwriting of sports play as a panacea for the *cités,* the possibility emerges for immigrant actors to utilize athletic funding and institutions for the constitution of various heteroprax religious Islamic practices and organizations. Rather than being erased in the social reproduction of the French nation, categories of religious belonging can find themselves reinforced through sports play itself. In other words, France's new Muslim citizens, like Fethi, have been able to negotiate an urbane multicultural identity through the seamless, creative incorporation of sports *and* religious practice in their everyday lives.

The link between sports play, religious identity, and social reproduction—whether viewed through the lens of Durkheimian rituals of collective effervescence (Durkheim 1915) in which primary cultural categories are represented and transmitted through sports (cf. Loy and Kenyon 1969), or as part of an instrumental "civilizing process" (Elias 1939) initiated by the state toward its internal and external subjects (cf. Dunning and Rojek 1992)—has been well-demonstrated in both colonial and postcolonial settings. In the colonial context in particular, British and French government officials and educators encouraged sports practice to train colonial subjects to European values of fair play and sportsmanship, and otherwise defuse anti-colonial violence through its symbolic enactment on the playing field (cf. MacClancy 1996). Alongside schools, the French administration in colonial Algeria established athletic clubs like the Sporting Youth of Kabylia (JSK) in an effort to break apart the supposedly primordial tribal and Islamic social totalities and affiliations that marked the region. Reciprocally in the metropole, Third Republic ideologists linked sports discipline to national moral strength and incorporated athletic practice into the developing institutions of compulsory military service and mandatory school attendance (Arnaud 1997). In this respect, contemporary metropolitan efforts at integration through sports represents a perduring feature of coloniality in the postcolonial period.

Sports play and spectatorship, beyond its instrumentalization in state power and cultural hegemony, also holds subversive implications and effects, serving as a center for subaltern political expression. The inchoate subjective passions generated by sports play and support defy their mere functionality within a state-directed social system. Indeed, the practice of sports, the fervor surrounding them, and particularly their colonization by the state often underwrite the very ethnic, racial, and religious bodies that sport, if purely instrumentalist, would eliminate. After the Second World War, Algerian football clubs like the JSK became key sites of anti-colonial demonstrations and violence (Hare 2003: 138). After independence, the Algerian state attempted to nationalize the clubs, Arabizing the JSK's name to *Jam'iyya Sari' al-Kawakib* ("The Star Runners") to eliminate the reference to Kabylia and later renaming it Electronic Tizi-Ouzou (JET) in order to highlight the nationalized electric company located in the city of Tizi-Ouzou. In spite of these state efforts, the JSK remained a site for the rallying of Amazigh consciousness, as supporters have deformed the various acronyms to *Je Suis Kabyle* ("I am Kabyle") and *Jugurthe Existe Toujours* ("Jugurtha still lives"), and singer-activists have written praise songs to the club (Silverstein 2002c). In this respect, beyond the well-studied processes of "appropriation" or "hijacking" that make cricket Indian (Appadurai 1996) or transform football into a Zimbabwean game (Stuart 1996), sports operate within a moral universe of differently motivated identity formations that often exist in mutual opposition. In France, the state and various immigrant groups have each attempted to control the means of production of immigrant subjectivity through the control of Muslim religious expression *and* the promotion of athletic practice.

Moreover, the dialectic of religious and sports practices in the constitution and reproduction of social subjectivity extends beyond the nation-state. Sports play, spectatorship, and sponsorship exist within global economies of commodities and signs in which multinational corporations like Nike and Adidas compete for consumers of sporting identities (Appadurai 1996). Such corporations mobilize local and national loyalties in the sale of their products, and in so doing often find themselves colluding with states in the game of the production of national subjectivity. While such aligning of national and transnational interests is largely fleeting, it nonetheless points to a set of larger structures through which France's new Muslim citizens negotiate sociality and belonging in the *cités*.

Football, Corporate Sponsorship, and the New France

Two moments in recent French sporting history particularly highlight this intersection of bodily practice, religious identity, national reproduction, and transnational capital in the constitution of Algerian immigrant subjectivity in France: first, the 1994–1996 rise of the Paris Saint-Germain (PSG) football club to national and international prominence; and second, the fairy-tale victory of the French national team in the 1998 World Cup and the advent of Zinedine Zidane as an icon of a new multiracial France. During the spring months of 1995, a series of advertisements plastered the Parisian metropolitan subway walls. Although created by the American sportswear company Nike, the advertisements barely featured the shoes that were explicitly being sold, and in fact only indicated their corporate sponsorship through a "swoosh" (the Nike emblem) in the bottom right-hand corner. Instead, they focused on the PSG, who were at the time the highest-ranked French club and hopefuls to win the ongoing European Champions League tournament. The posters showed blurred images of PSG players engaged in various athletic feats, from bicycle-kicking a goal to diving for a fingertip save, with a series of slogans written over them.

The first poster's slogan stated, "There is not but one God; there are eleven." There are eleven players on a football side, and the starting eleven for the PSG, if we are to believe Nike, had achieved a mythic, if not deified, stature. The second advertisement, appearing several weeks after the first, continued in a similar vein: "No law prohibits you from wearing a PSG jersey to school." In fact, sports jackets and jerseys emblazoned with team logos had become the fashion among Parisian children. The third poster followed in the tradition of its two predecessors, though the message was more grandiose: "In 2041, your grandchildren will ask you if you really saw the PSG during their reign of glory." Again, the advertisement reiterated the heroism of the current PSG team and demarcated the historicity of that moment.

Football has had a long history in France, and it remains by far the most practiced sport, with a large percentage of young males competing on school or club teams.[1] For many sociologists and media commentators, football has come to symbolize France's national ideological triad of "liberty, equality, fraternity." On the one hand, the advertisements' slogans index the fraternal, teamwork aspect of football, highlighting "the PSG" as a team entity rather than any given player. On the other hand, football's emphasis on individual feats of excellence, as celebrated in the Nike advertisements' abstract images of football prowess, dovetails with the meritocratic ideology behind the French educational and occupational systems. Football thus appears as the ultimate democratic game in which skill trumps background: as a "temple of virulent individualism" that "carries with it egalitarian values" (Joffrin 1998). Indeed, the PSG was highly multiracial in composition, having recruited top players from throughout Europe, Latin America, and Africa.

The Nike advertisements thus evoked a universalist conception of the French nation in their evocation of consumers of the Nike-sponsored PSG as belonging to an imagined community constituted through football celebration. As the PSG—France's sole representative in the Champions League tournament—became transformed into a token for Paris if not for France as a whole, consumers of PSG matches and the surrounding paraphernalia joined in a solidarity that stretched beyond the immediate mechanical ties of race, class, gender, and ethnicity to that of metropolitan, if not national, subjectivity. In this respect, as Appadurai has discussed with regards to Indian cricketers, the emblem of national subjectivity became "inscribed, as practice, on the . . . body" (1996: 112).

Nonetheless, Nike's interests transcend those of the French state. The posters sold the *Nike-sponsored* PSG, allying the PSG jersey to its other emblazoned sportswear products worldwide. In the advertisements, the PSG joined the Nike team of sports personalities from across athletic genres in a single global aesthetic. As a sponsored team, the PSG in effect came to represent Nike and its image in competition with other teams sponsored by rival companies and representing rival aesthetics. Through the play of representations that united the PSG to Paris to the French nation, Nike, an American-based transnational corporation, ironically presented itself as a sponsor not only for the PSG, but for French universalism writ large. Under the image of the swoosh, the PSG brought a global market of football talent into a metropolitan space of unity and competition that served as an emblem for a new postcolonial France. In this way, the posters participated in a larger structure of late capitalism, in which multinational corporations employ an older logic of national patriotism to mobilize consumer loyalties across territorial boundaries.

To Be Like Zizou: The Iconography of Zinedine Zidane

At no time were these dialectics of global capital and national identity in football sponsorship made more explicit than during the 1998 World Cup held in France. As in 1995, Paris became the terrain for debates over the character of French republican subjectivity in and through sports play. To a great extent, the football competition in the stadiums was replayed in the advertising spaces of subway posters and television time slots, with Nike, Adidas, Puma, le Coq Sportif, and several other major sportswear manufacturers competing for national and international consumers. Both Nike and Adidas colonized the physical landscape of Paris, establishing "football parks" in La Défense and Trocadéro respectively, replete with big-screen televisions and appearances by players and celebrities. Abandoning its 1995 strategy of abstract representations of individual athletic feats, Nike embarked on a new publicity campaign, *La République populaire* (The People's Republic), with constructivist posters and imperative slogans such as "Youth of the world, football is calling, join in" and "Play, train, improve" that anti-racist groups decried as evoking the propaganda of Stalinist Russia, Fascist Italy, and Vichy France (Amalou 1998a).[2] Nike and Adidas were further accused of unduly influencing the player selection on the national teams they sponsored, exerting pressure on coaches to privilege players already under contract with the given brand.

Such controversies only underlined the circulation of discourses of race, ethnicity, and national identity within the larger context of transnational capital accumulation. Taking a diametrically opposite tack from Nike's arguably racist campaign, Adidas, the official sponsor of the French national side, went out of its way to emphasize a "mixture of French-French and of hybridities" in its publicity spots (Amalou 1998b). Commercials profiled French players of North African, African, and Antillean immigrant ancestry alongside white players. These spots largely contributed to the growing media celebration of the French national team as the hallmark of a multiracial and multiethnic "New France," or even "World France" (*la France Mondiale*) (cf. Castro 1998; Joffrin 1998). Journalists, politicians, and scholars alike celebrated the 12 July championship as a victory of the "French melting-pot" (*le creuset français*) (Tribalat 1998), a success for the French "model of integration," and a defeat for the xenophobia of the Front National (Desporetes 1998). The carnivalesque atmosphere of the Champs-Élysées, with more than a million spectators of diverse backgrounds cheering the team onto victory, was even hailed as France's "new Bastille" (Farbiaz 1998) two days before the anniversary of the original one's taking, with the new multiracial tricolor, "*black-blanc-beur*" ("Black, White, Arab"), hoisted alongside the older "*bleu-blanc-rouge*" ("Blue, White, Red") of the national flag and team jersey (Lipietz 1998).

And the icon of this revolution was the team's midfielder Zinedine Zidane, hero of the championship match with two header goals against a supposedly unstoppable Brazilian side. Dubbed "the flagbearer of a plural France" by the spokesman for MRAP, this Marseille-born twenty-six-year-old of Kabyle parents became quickly viewed as the "emblem of a success-ful integration," with immigration political advisor Sami Naïr even going so far as to claim that "his loping gait (*déhancements*) accomplished more than ten or fifteen years of integration policy" (Dély 1998). Chants of "*Zizou*" (Zidane's nickname) filled the stadium and streets of France, with echoes reaching across the French and Algerian diasporas. The Champs-Élysées celebration occurred under his image, projected onto the façade of the Arc de Triomphe. Footage of him kissing the World Cup trophy and crying while singing the Marseillaise sealed him permanently as a *French* national hero.

An unlikely hero perhaps—soft-spoken, introverted, slightly ungainly in appearance—Zidane's rise to French superstardom was spectacular. His balding profile soon adorned billboards and television commercials in France for products as diverse as cologne and supermarkets. While a reluctant mi-nority role model, he used the platform of his success to express solidarity with those suffering in Algeria's ongoing civil war, and he even dedicated the World Cup victory to "the thousands of Algerians of my generation who emigrated to Europe, but who never abandoned their culture." More-over, he publicly declared the widespread support for the multiracial na-tional team as a "victory of wisdom" over intolerance and xenophobia (Zidane 1998). At the same time, he by no means took up the banner of the "New France." Rather, he indefatigably localized his identity to Marseille, citing his experiences growing up and his ongoing ties in the *cité* of La Castellane (Vinocur 1999), thus bypassing larger questions of ethnic or na-tional belonging.

As a result, Zidane has repeatedly disappointed Algerian interest groups who have attempted to appropriate him for their social movements. While they have used his prominence in support of European legislation for the officialization of Tamazight as a minority language of France, many diaspora Kabyle cultural activists I spoke with regretted that he has not made strong statements in favor of Berber linguistic and cultural rights. Likewise, Algerians in general interpreted his marrying a Spanish woman and naming his sons Enzo and Luca as a regrettable act of self-distancing from his cultural heritage. They bemoaned the short-term nature of the Zidane moment, decrying his status as that of another "virtual Arab" (*arbi mzowar*) deployed by the French state to vindicate a model of integration that they view as culturally violent. Responding to this violence, Algerians in France have become progressively disenchanted with *Les Bleus* since 1998, to the point of hissing during the playing of the French national anthem and invading the pitch while waving Algerian flags during a France-Algeria friendly match in Saint-Denis in October 2001 (Hare 2003: 137).

In many ways the Zidane moment does indicate a perduring colonial racial logic by which certain *évolués* (including intellectuals, musicians, and athletes) are held forth as products of a successful *mission civilisatrice* in order to justify the larger imperial presence.[3] As in Roland Barthes's famous discussion of the image of the black legionnaire saluting the French flag, Zidane becomes a mythic sign for the grandeur of the postcolonial New France and a confirmation and naturalization of its ethical inviolability (1972: 116–128). As a postcolonial *évolué*, Zidane thus escapes the ire of exclusionist politics. White bar patrons in Paris during the World Cup cheered on the national team in one breath and exchanged racist slurs about an Algerian passerby in the next, apparently without noting the contradiction (Rosenzweig 1998). In spite of the supposed defeat handed to racism and intolerance by the World Cup victory (cf. *Libération* 14 July 1998), the Front National and its breakaway National Movement continued to gain electoral support for a largely xenophobic platform, garnering 9 percent of the national vote in the June 1999 European Parliamentary elections, and 16 percent in the first round of the 2002 presidential elections. The militarization of the *banlieues* has continued apace particularly since 11 September 2001, and the World Cup itself was preceded by a series of police roundups of hundreds of suspected Islamist terrorists in the name of state security. In other words, the celebratory discourse of multiculturalism in the wake of the World Cup victory exists in tandem with a nationalist discourse that deems certain types of cultural and religious difference as incompatible or dangerous to the French nation.

Islam and Public Life: Ambivalences and Transformations

In French integration discourse, sports multiculturalism thus finds its ideological counter in Islamic practices, the political or integral character of the latter being considered anathema to the process of incorporation of young immigrants into the New France. This negative juxtaposition of sports and religion is evidenced in the 1995 Nike-PSG campaign. The first slogan, "There is not but one God; there are eleven," was a clear play on monotheistic doctrine in general, and the Muslim witnessing of faith (*shehada*) in particular: "There is but one God and Mohammed is his prophet." The *shehada,* in its oral repetitions, is a central feature of everyday Islamic practice, uniting Muslims globally. Nike's version of the *shehada* consisted not only in a revision of the phrase's basic structure, but a delegitimation of religious values in favor of secular sports ones.

Nike's juxtaposition of religious and exercise practice in favor of the latter finds its critical reflection in the 1995 graphic novel *Jambon-Beur,* created by the Franco-Algerian (Beur) cartoonist Farid Boudjellal. On facing pages, Boudjellal shows his protagonist Charlotte-Badia, a young girl of a Beur father and a white French mother, respectively visiting her paternal and maternal grandmothers. On the first page, she joins her paternal grandmother in one of her daily prayers, mimicking her motions that accompany the chanted Qur'anic verses projected from her cassette deck. On the facing page, she imitates the same motions of her maternal grandmother, this time to a French exercise tape. Boudjellal has drawn each corresponding panel identically, with the only significant difference being the words emerging from the stereo and the script in which they are written. Interspersed with the panels are a series of questions which Charlotte-Badia asks herself: "Why does mommy's mommy pray only once per day?" "Why does daddy's mommy wash herself before and mommy's mommy after?" (Boudjellal 1995: 20–21).

If, for Charlotte-Badia, the parallelism of practices of Islam and sports generated confusion, in public spaces the juxtaposition created tension. The Nike advertisement and the World Cup victory coincided with the growing representation of integral Islam in state and media discourse as anti-consumerist, anti-national, and increasingly a threat to state security and public life *tout court.* By the early 1990s, Islam had become the second religion of France, unseating Protestantism and leaving Judaism far behind. This development was linked both to the continued influx of Muslim workers and refugees from sub-Saharan Africa, Bosnia, and central Asia, and to the increased missionary work by Muslim organizations within France's working-class neighborhoods. More importantly, the intensification of the Algerian civil war and the daily news coverage of Islamist violence on both sides of the Mediterranean contributed to an amalgamation of mental categories of Islam and terrorism by the general French public.[4] This "Islamalgam"— as it was referred to by the media—was exacerbated by the 1995 Vigipirate anti-terrorist measures that singled out "Arabs" as potential threats to state security. In this respect, by the mid-1990s, Islam had become a contested feature in French public life.

The contentious relationship between Islam and the French state represents a relatively recent development. While alarmist writers today insistently point to a primordial clash of civilizations that has continuously opposed Western and Islamic belief systems in France since Charles Martel's famous defeat of Saracen forces at Poitiers in A.D. 732, mosque and state in France have in fact not always been opposed. In particular, the history of metropolitan mosque construction indicates the various transformations of the public life of Islam in France, with the building of the colonial-era Grand Mosque in Paris contrasting directly with more recent ventures. Beginning in 1849, French colonial officials and North African indigenous leaders recommended that the French state construct a mosque in Paris as a symbol of the empire's commitment to its Muslim subjects. The mosque was finally approved in 1921 as part of a larger compensation package to honor the 26,000 Algerian colonial subjects who had given their lives in World War I. Moreover, it was believed that such a mosque would assure the future loyalty of the southern colonies. In the words of deciding councilman Barthélemy Rocalglia, "It is by such means that France can secure the love of all its indigenous subjects who, one day, will not hesitate to sacrifice their lives for the defense of such a beautiful fatherland" (cited in Kepel 1991: 69–70). Conforming to the 1905 law on *laïcité*, the mosque, located within a short walk of the Sorbonne and the Senate, exists primarily as a diplomatic and cultural institution rather than a place of religious worship.

The history of the Ad-Da'wa Mosque stands in stark contrast. Located in the working-class Stalingrad neighborhood of northeastern Paris, the mosque was established in 1969 by a Muslim cultural association in a condemned building, but was subsequently relocated to a church crypt and then an abandoned garment warehouse. Since 1985, the warehouse Ad-Da'wa Mosque has become one of the prime places of worship in Paris, attracting up to 5,000 visitors a day during the holy month of Ramadan. Mosque officials submitted applications in 1994 for a permit to construct a 2,200-square-foot building that would accommodate 3,600 worshipers. The municipality denied the permit out of security fears and worries over traffic congestion. In the meantime, the Front National appropriated the proposed mosque as a rallying point to redirect its anti-immigrant platform. On several occasions throughout 1996, hundreds of protesters appealed to residents of the quarter to stand up against the project that they claimed would "make the installation of immigrant populations definitive" and lead to the "Islamization" and "Lebanonization" of the racially and religiously diverse neighborhood (*Libération* 18 March 1996: 16). While most scholars and political parties distanced themselves from the Front National's positions, the Ad-Da'wa Mosque remained in public scrutiny. Its rector, Larbit Kechat, was at the time of the demonstrations living under a year-long house arrest for his reputed ties to outlawed Algerian Islamist political groups, although the mosque publicly eschewed all direct political affiliation. In this sense, the French state, guided by its ideology of *laïcité,* took an active role in mediating the plurality of religious communities, both supporting and ob-structing religious institutions as necessary to maintain national unity and underwrite particular notions of French identity.

A second site for the negotiation of the public character of Islam in France has been suburban factories. In the 1950s, the Renault and Citroën automobile companies, located in the northern *banlieues* of Paris, with overt support from the Gaullist government established prayer rooms in a num-ber of their factories for their North African employees. On the one hand, the companies viewed this policy change as another means to divide immi-grant workers and labor unions. On the other hand, as with the construc-tion of the Grand Mosque, the state's implicit support of Islam amounted to a paternalistic strategy to gain subject loyalty and defuse potential immi-grant labor unrest. By the 1970s, however, given the increasing spatial sta-bility of North African immigrants in France, Muslim workers became more and more unionized both in immigrant syndicates and in the national labor confederations. These unions organized strikes in both the automobile fac-tories and SONACOTRA foyers, demanding, *inter alia,* the construction of additional prayer rooms (Cesari 1994: 175). While by no means supported by every Muslim resident or factory worker, the protests nonetheless had the effect of appropriating secular private and public spaces for religious practice. Islam proved to be a rallying point around which immigrant workers of different national and ethnic backgrounds could organize themselves, rather than simply a tool wielded by the state to hold subaltern laborers in check.

Suburbs of Jihad

The victory of the strikers fueled the fire of a burgeoning alarmism within official and popular France that feared that the metropole was being colo-nized by (Muslim) immigrant subjects. By the mid-1980s, this alarmism increasingly focused on the purported Islamization of children of immigrants born in France. The election of Mitterrand and his legalization of immi-grant associations paved the way for the development of a diverse and thriv-ing Islamic civil society in France. From the approximately 150 such groups that had been established in France prior to 1981, more than 600 associa-tions existed at least on paper by 1985 (Kepel 1991: 229–242). Associa-tions varied greatly in size, adherents' nationality, and purpose: from the overtly militant, inspired by Islamic resistance movements in the Middle East and North Africa, to the more mainstream associations supported by governments abroad. Initially poorly organized, short-lived, and sometimes marginalized even among most French Muslims, these Muslim associations originally received relatively little attention from the French media.

Several developments occurring in the late 1980s and early 1990s altered this marginalized status and made these groups the target of generalized fears over the cultural breakup of France. During this period, Islamic associations had become the main sites for local organization and grassroots development in the French *cités,* offering unemployed men and women jobs working in mosques or selling wares in local markets, and even organizing summer camps in the provinces for *banlieue* youth. They developed informal prayer rooms in the basements of public housing buildings, often outside the purview of established state or religious authorities, drawing attendance away from the more easily surveilled mosques. In the wake of travel restrictions to Algeria and the departure of most foreign journalists from that war-torn country, these groups, alongside nascent Berber associations, functioned as a primary instrument through which news from Algeria circulated to and from France. The number of young men and women who joined these groups is unclear and varies greatly from one housing development to another. Nonetheless, for researchers, journalists, and security officials concerned with the future of the *cités,* Islamic associations appeared to offer local Muslim youth a seductive alternative to a life potentially characterized by drugs, delinquency, and prison (cf. Guéant 1995). In fact, for the political scientist Séverine Labat, membership in these groups constituted an "alternate form of integration" for excluded populations of the *cités* (interview in *Le Monde* 13 October 1995).

Concerns over Islamic associations in the *banlieues* dovetailed with French news coverage of the Algerian civil war that primarily focused on violent acts of Islamist terrorists and on the potential for such violence to spill over into France. Two events in particular, both occurring well before the 11 September 2001 attacks, consolidated national attention around this possible connection between marginalized *banlieusards* and international political Islam. The first involved the 1994 sentencing to death in Morocco of Stéphane Aït-Idir and Redouane Hammadi, two young Beurs from the Parisian suburb of La Courneuve, for their involvement in an armed attack on a Marrakech tourist hotel attributed to Islamist insurgents. The second involved the summer 1995 bombings in Paris and Lyon attributed to the GIA in which two Beurs from the Lyonnais *banlieue* of Vaulx-en-Velin— Khaled Kelkal and Karim Moussa—were accused of participation. These two events, taken together, appeared to confirm the existence of an international terrorist network that supposedly linked Algiers to Cologne to Sarajevo to Kabul via France's immigrant suburbs (cf. *Le Figaro* 16 August 1995). Young Beur "delinquents" were, according to these reports, recruited through Islamic associations, indoctrinated in "Islamist summer camps," and then shipped off to Bosnia or Afghanistan or Algeria proper to fulfill their destiny of "*jihad*" (cf. Pujadas and Salam 1995: 107–137).

One of the constants of the alarmist accounts from the mid-1990s, with a few notable exceptions, was the portrayal of *banlieue* Islam as a mass movement that operates through processes akin to Durkheimian collective effervescence, whereby the individual believer loses his identity to the group (cf. Altschull 1995; Pujadas and Salam 1995).[5] These portrayals of the observed "re-Islamization" of Muslims in France generally relied on a functionalist, if not mechanistic, explanatory device: unemployment, poor education, and exclusion/racism force young men into a life of drugs and petty theft from which they are recruited by Islamist militants with political agendas. News reports of this persuasion underlined the collective effervescence function of *banlieue* Islam through the repeated use of mass images of crowds and group prayers. Whether in the form of gatherings to hear the Friday sermon with banners flying and Qur'ans held high (cf. Boudjedra 1992) or street scenes of many people simultaneously kneeling in prayer (cf. *Libération* 29 June 1995: 3; *Le Figaro* 16 August 1995: 7), these pictures focused on the uniform and public character of Islam rather than on its internal diversity and its emphasis on the personal relationship between the believer and God. In addition, by indicating the French location of these scenes either through captions or the inclusion of significant details—including notable landmarks, street signs, automobile license plates—the pictures explicitly sought to shock the reader by defamiliarizing France. Lurking behind this portrayal was an implied threat, namely, that these collective, uniform, repeated bodily practices of prayer could develop into a mass uprising, a fear underlined by the presence of riot police in many of the images. Through these technical means, the writers and editors transformed Muslim prayer and its accompanying statement of faith—"There is but one god, God"— into a transgressive peril to the public order. In this way, media discourse in the mid-1990s largely contributed to the production of a reified image of Muslim religious difference as unassimilable to French secular standards.

In totalizing Islam into a single, fundamentalist frame, the alarmist discourse ignored and, in the post–11 September world, continues to ignore the fact that neo-orthodox Islamist movements—with radical political and conservative social agendas—are decidedly modern. While employing "traditional" Islamic critical practices of moral advice (*nasiha*) and proselytization (*ad-da'wa*) in an attempt to create a cohesive Franco-Muslim community, French Muslim leaders have historically deployed the state's legal system, labor organization, and association structures to assert their right to live in a culturally distinct manner with their own religious institutions and everyday practices of prayer and *halal* dietary regimes (cf. Asad 1993: 272). Likewise, these groups employ a decidedly modern discourse that borrows directly from the same tropes of universalism and particularism as the French state.

As such, the growth of Islamic associations in France is to a great extent a byproduct of a history of French state intervention designed alternately to appropriate Islam to unite colonial subjects under the aegis of a paternalistic empire and to disunite proletarian workers in other times of internal class conflict. Given this history, it is little wonder that a category of Muslim religious difference should provide an effective script for many North African immigrants to express and protest ongoing socioeconomic hierarchies and inequalities in the *cités*. In the context of the Algerian civil war, such religious identities have become increasingly politicized and threaten to outline independent corporate bodies that call into question "the inevitability of the absolute nation-state—of its demands to exclusive loyalty and its totalizing cultural projects" (Asad 1993: 266). As in governmental and media discourse, these newly politicized religious groups rely on a metonymic operation by which the body as mobilized in prayer stands for the transcendental Muslim subject which itself comes to represent the potential for a new social order, a Muslim France. As such, the French state and its politically motivated Islamic other find themselves in direct competition on the same discursive playing field.

Integration through Sports

In response to this threat over the loss of control of immigrant bodies and subjectivities, the French state has attempted to remaster immigrant bodily practice through the medium of sports (cf. Chantelat et al. 1996: 117–150). In the early 1990s, the government, agreeing with the alarmist reports that the summer 1995 bombings in Paris and Lyon represented but the tip of a larger separatist iceberg, began to take proactive measures to halt the perceived rise of radical Islam in France. On the one hand, as would occur again before the 1998 World Cup and in the wake of 11 September and the arrest of the French-Moroccan Zacarias Moussaoui as "the twentieth hijacker," French police and intelligence agencies increased surveillance measures within immigrant neighborhoods and conducted multiple roundups of suspected terrorists, breaking into prayer rooms and association locales. Under the aegis of the Vigipirate national security plan, these checks served both to incarcerate those believed to belong to blacklisted Islamic associations and to discover illegal immigrants and deport them.[6] Most importantly, this French war on terror reasserted direct bodily control by the state over residents of the so-called *banlieues de l'Islam* (Kepel 1991).

On the other hand, the second set of proactive measures involved the establishment of more and more intrusive quasi–Marshall Plan policies for the revitalization of those neighborhoods in which Islamic associations were attracting membership. One of the consistent features of the variety of revitalization projects for the *cités* has been the construction of social centers and sports facilities. Housing projects designed by chief architect Roland Castro under the "Banlieues 89" urban revitalization plan have included central areas featuring football fields and basketball courts, as well as indoor gymnasiums replete with boxing rings. Moreover, sports figured highly in the twenty measures proposed by Prime Minister Michel Rocard in 1990 in response to the *émeutes* in the working-class suburbs of Vaulx-en-Velin and Mantes-la-Jolie. In September 1992, the Ministry of Urbanization, headed by entrepreneur and then-owner of the Olympique Marseille football club, Bernard Tapie, launched a Youth and Sports program that invested forty million francs over the next several years in the construction of 1,000 sports installations and 100 fields in 120 different municipalities.

One Youth and Sports activity was the Summer Prevention operation, which in 1992 alone sponsored more than 1,500 *banlieue* youth to go on weekend excursions and summer camps (Daoud 1993d: 141; Sakouhi 1996: 82–83). The camps' explicit goal was not only to prevent violence, delinquency, and drug abuse, but also to defuse the sectarianism supposedly promoted in the parallel Islamic summer camps that were increasingly being presented by the media as *jihad* training bases. This emphasis on sports as a "privileged remedy for contemporary social dysfunction" (Sakouhi 1996: 81) derived from the vaunted capacities of athletics to retrain Muslim bodies away from religious practices. In other words, the urban renovation of the *cités* sought in large part to transform young Muslim *banlieusards* into the moral subjects—as defined by a secular attitude, a sense of fair play, and a strong work ethic—that their fathers, as factory workers, had been.

Moreover, *cité* sports programs have received direct support from the transnational world of professional athletics. French sports stars of immigrant background like the tennis player Yannick Noah, the light-heavyweight boxer Anaclet Wamba, and the world kickboxing champion Khalid el-Khandali—Zidane's predecessors as icons of integration—have participated directly in the various programs. The PSG offered thousands of free tickets for its games at the Parc des Princes to young *cité* residents as part of the Youth and Sports operation. In a similar fashion, large multinational sportswear companies like Nike, Reebok, Adidas, and Puma have played a role in suburban renewal projects. Nike and Reebok sponsored playground basketball tournaments and slam-dunk competitions in 1995 and 1996, while Adidas and Puma, with further support from Coca-Cola and Orangina as well as the French Soccer Federation, initiated football challenge matches for *banlieue* youth during the same period (*Le Monde* 14 April 1995: 16; Sakouhi 1996: 93). The Nike company's support for the PSG thus fits into this situational alliance between the French state and multinational capital in the production of commensurate consumers of sports and national identity.

"Ghetto Sports"?

Top-down sports development sought to reimpose state national and corporate structures onto seemingly uncontrollable immigrant neighborhoods marked by a potentially separatist Islamic religious alterity. These integration efforts have often had unanticipated consequences. In many cases, the sports programs, rather than reproducing *habitus,* have actually become sites for cultural innovation. Moreover, they have been the cause of youth resentment, if not of the very violence they explicitly sought to defuse. When I asked Lounis, a Kabyle friend living in north-suburban Saint-Ouen, about local state funding for football clubs, he decried the effort as "yet another example of integration by sports and music" that stripped immigrants of their culture. The local *cité* teenagers who used the Pantin weight room had a similar disdain for municipal sports structures, considering Philippe basically a "spy" and expressing little sadness over the vandalism that had occurred.

In general, residents of the *banlieues* are painfully aware of the intimate connection between suburban renewal and policing procedures. Since the late 1980s, violent struggles with security forces have often destroyed sports facilities along with schools and police commissariats. Rather than acts of juvenile delinquency or mass hysteria, the conflicts have in fact been relatively well organized displays of resistance targeting the particular state structures imposed upon the neighborhoods. In Vaulx-en-Velin in 1991 and again in Bron in 1994, residents destroyed the sports edifices—a climbing wall and a gymnasium respectively—that had been just previously built as part of a larger government initiative. The emerging *banlieue* cinema has replayed these tensions between sports integration and conflict. In *Raï* (dir. Thomas Gilou, 1996), the object of contention is the swimming pool in which the Beur protagonist Djamel works that gets destroyed in a climactic youth-police battle following the police killing of Djamel's brother. In *La Haine* (dir. Matthieu Kassovitz, 1995), a boxing gym is burned down in the opening scene of the film. When the local boxer-protagonist Hubert is later approached by a police officer and offered support to rebuild the gym, Hubert responds dourly, "What's the point? Kids today are more interested in hitting the police."

Nonetheless, the *banlieue* sports scene thrives in spite of these conflicts. While youth in Pantin were critical of the municipality and its agents, they still used the weight room. Likewise, the football fields and basketball courts that dot the *banlieue* landscape, though suffering from palpable disrepair, are filled with aspiring Zinedine Zidanes and Michael Jordans as well as the many others with less lofty ambitions. However, this sports play should not imply an equivalence between the football practiced in the *cité* and the game played at the Parc des Princes or at the Stade de France. Rather, young residents have appropriated *banlieue* public spaces for their own games based on their own revised sets of rules; they have in effect privatized them and created what critics of government sports projects have bewailed as "ghetto sports" (cf. Sakouhi 1996: 92–95). In a manner similar to the street ball played in the U.S. and watched by the many *banlieue* youth who are active consumers of American basketball magazines, a single playing field or court can equip multiple games occurring simultaneously, with book bags and jackets used to demarcate the goals or boundary lines. Sometimes even younger siblings will be recruited into football matches quite literally to "play the goalpost." Likewise, the enforcement of formal structures of the games like offsides rulings and traveling penalties varies with the number of participants and how seriously they take the outcome. Far from constituting an unruly chaos, such practices reveal an internal organization and permissive creativity that are flexible to the field and player constraints and simultaneously allow for self-organized challenge matches and tournaments. Indeed, these *cité* settings are increasingly seen—like the courts of American street ball or the fields of La Castellaine where Zidane got his start (Vinocur 1999)—as productive of the next generation of superstars, who are forced to learn the speed, deft control, and fancy passing that are not only locally fetishized but are an absolute necessity "in order to keep hold of the ball in the middle of a swarm" (Charef 1983a: 114).

More importantly, the appropriation—or privatization—of public sports spaces in the *cités* involves the demarcation of categories of belonging and local identity. Much like the weight room in Pantin or the skating rink in Val-Fourré, residents of a given area often protect a local athletic facility from the use and abuse of outsiders. In my experience, Parisian *banlieue* residents create bonds of solidarity not only through their domestic proximity, but also through their access to particular spaces.[7] They likewise combine participation in sports programs with the expression of ethnic and religious identities. Beginning at a relatively young age, children group themselves into teams according to background and challenge coresidents of different origins to matches on these bases. Berber and Islamic associations have followed in this practice and incorporated football and judo teams into their activities, in part to attract younger members, in part to foster loyalty to a political or religious cause via the medium of sports. Some Islamic associations have gone as far as investing in local sports facilities in order to increase membership, often taking over financially where government programs leave off.[8] In direct opposition, the Paris-based Berber Culture Association founded a club football team, FC Berbère, to promote *berberité* as an alternate form of identity for Beur youth subjected to what it perceived as an Islamization of the French *cités*.

If North African parents in France have not fully supported their children's participation in organized sports, they often provide economic reasons rather than religious ones, questioning their children's priorities. Nonetheless, many children of Algerian origin—and particularly Beur men like Fethi—are initiated to sporting activity in French grammar schools and enamored by heroic images of North African Muslim athletes on the international scene. As a result, they continue to pursue some form of sports outside of the educational establishment and are encouraged to do so by local association leaders. Like Fethi, they seamlessly incorporate sports play into their everyday lives as marked Muslim citizens of France, seeing no necessary conflict between their athletic practices and their embodied exercising of their religious or ethnic identity.[9] In this way, the incompatibility of sports and religion posed within official discourses of integration proves unfounded in practice. The measures adopted by government programs to control the reproduction of national subjectivity through the control of immigrant bodily practices thus find themselves co-opted for the production of what are often represented as transgressive categories of belonging. While certainly not producing the Intifada imagined by alarmist discourse, such transformations have nonetheless facilitated the Muslim PSG supporter to continue in the belief in "but one god, God."

The Studium: The Headscarf Affair, Education, and Social Reproduction

In addition to the stadium, a second crucial site in the conflict between the French state and immigrant institutions over the control of immigrant subjectivity and bodily practice is the studium, the public school. Beginning in the late 1980s, an animated public debate took place concerning the legitimacy of religious adornment in national educational institutions, a legitimacy that the second Nike advertisement—declaring "No law prevents you from wearing a PSG jersey to school"—played directly upon. The state's discourse on integration not only concerned the imagined, masculinized subjects of the "terrorist" and the "footballer," but also centered on young women as agents of social reproduction and pillars of cultural continuity. In particular, national debates accompanying what became known as "the headscarf affair" (*l'affaire du foulard islamique*) indexed mounting fears over the uncontrollable growth of Islamic identities incommensurate with other ethnic and religious categories of difference in France. Moreover, the debates point to young women as the crucial site for the transmission of this religious incommensurability.[10]

On 18 September 1989, Ernest Chenière, principal of the Gabriel Havez grammar school in the far northern Parisian suburb of Creil, expelled three young girls (aged thirteen to fourteen) of North African parentage for refusing to remove their headscarves in class. On 4 October, the national socialist newspaper *Libération* picked up the story, and within three days the fate of Fatima, Leïla, and Samira became the focus of national attention. On 10 October, through the mediation of a local Tunisian cultural association, the parties reached a compromise that the girls would be free to wear their scarves in the halls, but not in the classrooms themselves. By 20 October, however, two new cases had arisen in the southern cities of Marseille and Avignon, and, in addition, the three Creil girls found themselves once again excluded from class for wearing their scarves in violation of the compromise.

Amid a flurry of news reports, interviews, debates, and proclamations from all sides of the political, religious, academic, and association spectrum, the National Assembly convened its 25 October nationally televised meeting to determine how to address these issues, returning to them again on 8 November. Over the course of these debates, the socialist minister of education, Lionel Jospin, in the face of severe criticism from the conservative Gaullist contingent, affirmed his simultaneous commitment to a secular school system and to absolute equality in education. Following a 1937 circular prohibiting proclamations that might jeopardize the religious neutrality of the educational institution, he asked that children "not come to school with any sign affirming a religious distinction or difference," but stated that this in itself could not be grounds for expulsion (*Journal Officiel* 25 October 1989: 4114). He then requested a special high court to examine the question constitutionally, and on 27 November, the high court concluded that wearing a Muslim headscarf was not in principle incompatible with a secular educational system, and that the expulsion of such a student would only be justified if the headscarf presented a "risk of a threat to the establishment's order or to the normal functioning of teaching" or, in other words, if it,

> in its ostentatious or political (*revendicatif*) character, constitutes an act of pressure, of provocation, of proselytism or of propaganda challenging the dignity or liberty of the student or other members of the educational community, compromising their health or security, or perturbing the progress of the teaching and the educative role of the teachers. (*Extrait du registre des délibérations de l'Assemblée Générale* 346.893: 5)

Jospin reiterated these conclusions in his 12 December circular to school directors and staff of the Ministry of Education, thus officially, if tentatively, equating headscarves with Christian crosses or Jewish *kippas* that enjoyed a legitimate presence in the classroom. In effectively declaring these signs to be in and of themselves personal signs, he was able to uphold the normative values of universal education and *laïcité* while maintaining good relations with Muslim associations and institutions. Further, in underlining these normative values, he reiterated the project of the national education system as the preparation of children for "their responsibilities as citizens" (quoted in *Hommes et Migrations* 1990: 112).

The vagueness and subjectivity of the category of "ostentatious or political character" inspired continued debate and left school directors great room for interpretation and maneuver, thus setting the stage for a series of mini-affairs that have arisen in every year subsequent to the decision. On 2 November 1992, the high court overturned the 1990 expulsion of three headscarved girls from the southern Parisian *banlieue* of Montfermeil and reaffirmed its 1989 ruling. Again, in March 1994 it reinstated two other young girls of Turkish parents in Angers. In both cases, the court did not give positive support for the wearing of headscarves in classes, but rather

negatively sanctioned the particular school officials for making policy decisions that did not correspond to the 1989 circular.

In the meantime, however, a strong opposition to the perceived laxity
of the headscarf legislation had developed.[11] On 20 September 1994, the
newly appointed minister of education, François Bayrou, addressed a circular to school principals that reiterated the distinction between "discreet signs"
of personal conviction that would be tolerated, and "ostentatious signs"
that "in themselves are elements of proselytism" and would therefore be
prohibited (Burdy and Marcou 1995: 310). While he did not specify precisely which articles of bodily adornment belonged in which category,[12] his
references to the recent "multiplication of ostentatious signs" clearly indicated that headscarves would be prohibited. In any event, no newspaper or
school official was duped by his ambiguous statement, and over the course
of the 1994–1995 school year, more than 150 young women were legally
expelled from public schools.

Bayrou's circular differed from Jospin's in one significant way. Whereas
Jospin justified his pronouncements in the name of the constitution of the
Fifth Republic, ratified international conventions, and the "fundamental
principles recognized by the laws of the Republic"—including liberty, equality, pluralism, neutrality, and, of course, *laïcité*—Bayrou introduced a new
entity: the nation. As stated in his circular, "The nation is not only a collection of citizens possessing individual rights. It is a community of destiny."
In employing this formulation, Bayrou followed a line of conservative thought
from Maurice Barrès and Charles Maurras that understood the French nation as united through an inalienable, enracinated cultural and historical
continuity. In an October 1996 interview, Bayrou elaborated on this understanding of the French nation as having a historical and moral weight, as
being a shared "idea" transmitted to each succeeding generation: "We must
tell our children that they are not living in a world that began today. What
is at stake is the idea of the French nation itself" (*Le Monde* 15 October
1996: 16). For Bayrou, Muslim headscarves counter this idea of unified
nationhood for, as (foreign) ostentatious and proselytizing symbols, as heterogeneous bodily presentations, they sow the seeds of sectarianism and
prescribe conflicting communities of loyalty.

> The French idea of the nation and the Republic is, by nature, respectful of
> all convictions, particularly religious and political conviction and cultural
> traditions. But it excludes the splintering of the nation into separate com-
> munities, each indifferent of the other, only obeying their own rules and
> laws, engaged in a simple co-existence. (quoted in Burdy and Marcou
> 1995: 310)

Bayrou, in excluding the headscarf, like Jospin in tolerating it, claimed to
defend a particular vision of the French nation-state and assure its future
social reproduction.

A sticking point in these debates has been the close relationship between sports and education in the reproduction of the nation. While the high court overturned cases where schoolgirls have been expelled for wearing their headscarves to gym classes, it has consistently upheld expulsions that followed from students having refused on religious grounds to participate in physical education altogether. In his original statement before the National Assembly, Jospin specified that a refusal to participate in sports education would be legitimate grounds for expulsion: "I stipulate that children and their families must respect the school program. . . . No child of any family can decide to go or not to go to physical education, biology, fine arts or history. Adherence is mandatory, and any violation will justify exclusion from the school" (*Journal Officiel* 25 October 1989: 4115). He later reaffirmed this intent in an October 1993 ministerial circular, predicating that "only medical reasons . . . can legitimate a dispensation from physical education classes. No other departure is admissible." In other words, while the socialist government showed a willingness to tolerate the headscarf as a sign of Muslim difference commensurable with embodied symbols of other faiths, it drew the line at the integrality of sports to the national curriculum. As such, the French state continued to view sports practice as a sacred site for social integration and the reproduction of equivalent and productive citizens.

Gender, National Reproduction, and the Sacralization of the State

It is not accidental that the polemic over the reproduction of the French nation focused on young women. Women have historically served as potent symbols for "the continuity and immutability of the nation" (Mosse 1985: 18). Nationalist ideologues and reformers have idealized women as bastions of public order and moral respectability, in direct contrast to men, who have represented progress and civilization; women stand in for the stasis of the cultural nation as opposed to the dynamics of the political state (Auslander 2000; Chatterjee 1995). However, as the domestic agents of social reproduction, women are potentially a threat to national order. "As the embodiment of conflicting forces that simultaneously compose and disrupt the nation, women are the guarantors of national identity . . . as *symbols that successfully contain the conflicts of the new historical situation*. At the same time, women are the supreme threat to national identity insofar as *its* endemic instability can be assigned to *them*" (Woodhull 1993: 11; emphasis in text). In this respect, the display of Islamic belonging in the French public sphere by young women—the putative symbols of the future of the New France—symbolized a potential threat to the moral order.

At first blush, it might appear ironic that the practice of Islam could be perceived as threatening to a nation-state seemingly bereft of religion, with a largely non-practicing Catholic majority and an officially secular public sphere. However, French *laïcité* does not imply the absence of the sacred in public life, but rather, as Etienne Balibar has argued, the "sacralization of the state" (1991: 94). Following Durkheim's theory of religion as the pre-eminent mode of social organization (Durkheim 1915: 22), Mona Ozouf has demonstrated how postrevolutionary attacks on the influence of the Catholic Church resulted not in the secularization of French society, but rather in the "transference of sacrality" from Catholicism to a new "civic" religion. Through the medium of republican festivals social categories of time and space, previously imbued with Catholic significance, were reformulated to align with revolutionary historical events and the open, public squares of municipalities rather than parishes (Ozouf 1988: 282).

In addition to festivals, the growth of the national education system in the Third Republic (1871–1940), as Eugen Weber has argued, succeeded in gradually diminishing the powers of local clergy and church notables and reinforcing the French state's monopoly of the public sphere, as well as its increased presence in the everyday lives of its citizens. In this sense, rather than seeing the French nation as a *fait accompli* in 1789, it is important to recognize that this sacralization of the state continued well into the twentieth century, turning peasants only recently into "Frenchmen" (Weber 1976). With the Ferry reforms of the 1880s, the French state endowed the schools as particular sites for the transmission of national unity through the teaching of a common language, a common history, and a common geography. It further divested itself of religious functions—including the appointments of clergy, construction of churches—and legislated the religious and political neutrality of the education system with the 1905 *laïcité* law. Through these reforms, the school became the symbol *par excellence* of the secular state and the civic nation.

In this way, French *laïcité* operates much like a religion, with the nation operating as the moral symbol of collective solidarity. It is not because the church and state in France are separated that public expressions of Islam remain a sticking point for French republican ideology. Rather, it is because they are functionally one and the same; the state is, for all practical purposes, the church of republican France. As gay rights activist Guy Hocquenguem argued: "'France' is to the French what Allah is to Muslims, indescribable, non-representable, since it is itself the foundation of all representation" (1979: 22). In other words, the basis for the perceived conflict does not reside in two fundamentally different and hence mutually incompatible organizations of national *qua* religious belonging, but rather in their structural similarity. As Edward Said has argued elsewhere, what underlies the "threat" of Islamic civilization is not its great cultural distance, but its competitive proximity (1981: 5).

Given the structural similarity between the French state and Islam, and the cardinal importance of the republican school system to the French state's myth of legitimacy, it is little wonder that the various headscarf affairs since 1989 have garnered heightened national media attention.[13] One particularly poignant image emerging from the 1989 affair featured Fatima and Leïla sitting studiously at a table, writing in their exercise books. Appearing originally in the Catholic magazine *Le Point* (16 October 1989: 22–23) and later in cropped form in the liberal weekly *Le Nouvel Observateur* (12–18 October 1989: 15), the photo appears at first glance to have been taken in a classroom, as there are several blackboards and a variety of books in the background. However, in reality, as we learn from a small-point caption in *Le Nouvel Observateur,* the scene occurred in their parents' home. The striking feature of the image, in clear focus behind the girls' covered heads, are the blackboards, embossed with the recognizable "ABC" in the corner, but completely covered with Arabic script and surrounded by presumably religious books embossed with Arabic calligraphy. More than any statement, this image, repeatedly brandished across the media, encapsulated the perceived subversion of secular education, the appropriation of the tools of the education system—blackboards, exercise books, ballpoint pens—seemingly for the purpose of religious indoctrination. It constituted the negative inverse of Barthes's black soldier saluting the tricolor or of Zidane singing the Marseillaise; it mythically naturalized not the continuity and moral inviolability of the sacralized French nation, but its fragility if not imminent rupture.

What made the introduction of Islam into the school system particularly problematic for ideologists of the French republic was the perceived incommensurability and incompatibility—rather than structural similarity—of Islam and French *laïcité*. In particular, media pundits, particularly those harking from the conservative end of the political spectrum, harped on a presumed absence of a separation between religious and civil society in Muslim theological and political theory (*Le Point* 16 October 1989; *Politis* 26 October–1 November 1989; *La Croix* 4 November 1989). As one oft-quoted scholar of Islam averred, "Islam in France finds itself impregnated by religious convictions, and the dimension of faith is inseparable from political reflection" (Lamand 1986: 30, quoted in *Le Point* 16 October 1989). According to this logic, Leïla and Fatima were not simply young girls learning to read the Qur'an; they were de facto political agents infiltrating the foreign politico-religious doctrine of their father into the very heart of French public life—the school system.

In an attempt to check the spread of this presumably always already politicized Islamic practice, the French state has progressively attempted to outline a secular brand of French Islam and sell it to the French Muslim community as a whole. In the wake of the 1989 affair, Interior Minister Pierre Joxe created the Working Council on Islam in France, a commission of six imams, in an effort to "republicanize" Islam into a secular religion (Cesari 1994: 143–158). Joxe's successor, Charles Pasqua, continued this process, publicly advocating an "Islam for France" endowed with representative institutions holding public powers (Maréchal 1994). Working with the Algerian rector of the Grand Mosque of Paris, Dalil Boubakeur, Pasqua established the Advisory Council of French Muslims to fix the dates of Islamic rituals and regulate their public practice. The thirty-seven articles of the resultant Charter of the Muslim Faith in France (Boubakeur 1995) declared the "emergence of a French Islam and its normal insertion into the national community on an equal basis with other religions" (Article 24) that "strives for the development of an expression of *laïcité* that will bring religions and the State into a state of harmony" (Article 32).

> Recognizing that *laïcité* implies the religious neutrality of the State, French Muslims, loyal to the most authentic Muslim tradition, disassociate themselves from all extremisms and witness their attachment to the State which, in accordance with the law, assures the freedom of belief, guarantees the freedom of religion, and treats all religions as equals. (Article 27)

However, Pasqua and Boubakeur's efforts were opposed by the two major Islamic umbrella organizations in France: the National Federation of French Muslims (FNMF) with close ties to Morocco, and the Union of Islamic Organizations in France (UOIF) with supposed historical links to the radical Egyptian Muslim Brotherhood. Resentful of the Grand Mosque's influence and in an attempt to out-secularize their rivals, they created their own High Council of French Muslims in order to overcome institutional divisions and "assemble all democratic Muslims in defense of the principles of *laïcité*" (*Libération* 18 December 1995). Given this multiplication of institutions speaking in the name of French Muslims, the process of national Islamic organization was stillborn.

After 11 September, the new law-and-order interior minister, Nicolas Sarkozy, breathed new life into the officialization of Islam in France, creating a French Council of the Muslim Faith (CFCM) as part of his larger war on terror that also included sweeps of radical Islamist groups and the reinforcement of *cité* policing. In a January 2003 radio interview, he justified this decision, claiming, "It's a chance to create an official Islam of France and a way to fight the Islam of cellars and garages (*l'Islam des caves*)—an underground, clandestine Islam that feeds fundamentalism and extremism" (quoted in *New York Times* 15 January 2003: A4). In citing an *Islam des caves* and opposing it to an "Islam of the mosques," Sarkozy implicitly linked the unofficial Islamic organization in the *cités* to global Islamist terrorism pre-eminently represented at that time through images of al-Qaeda holed up in the caves of Afghanistan. While the CFCM was an elected body chosen by French Muslims and supported by an estimated 80 percent of mosques, Sarkozy worked to guarantee its secularist tendency, preassigning its initial presidency to Boubakeur of the Grand Mosque. When the 14 April 2003 elections results gave majority representation to the FNMF and UOIF over the Grand Mosque (which won only six of the forty available seats), Sarkozy threatened to expel any imam whose views ran counter to *laïcité*.

In a speech a few days later, Sarkozy further encouraged members of the UOIF to "take the hand offered to them by the Republic" and to respect the authority of French secular laws. While he was silent on the issue of headscarves in schools, he strongly backed a 1999 ruling that banned headscarves from national identity card photographs.

An Ambiguous Sign

Politically poignant as an image of otherness, the headscarf has thus remained a salient trope in larger anxieties over the growth of Islamism on French soil that have underlain official attempts to co-opt Islam into *laïcité*. In its reporting on the various affairs, the media has augmented the visibility of the headscarf, semantically transforming the object in question from a *foulard* (headscarf) to a *hijab* (a cover, wrap, or drape) to a *voile* (veil) to a *chador* (Iranian-style full-body covering). With each transformation, the piece of fabric looked more and more sinister, more and more like, in the words of the former French ambassador to UNESCO Gisèle Halimi, "the flag of fundamentalism" (*Le Monde* 30 November 1989). As a focus of obsessive anxiety, the headscarf is connected to larger, historical processes of fantasy and desire. In his study of French colonial postcards, Malek Alloula argues that veiled women stood as "mobile extensions of an imaginary harem whose inviolability haunts the photographer-voyeur" (Alloula 1986: 13). In the postcolonial context, headscarved schoolgirls similarly operate as unobtainable objects of desire in the fantasy of national integration.[14]

In point of fact, headscarf wearing among French Muslims is statistically rare, and even rarer among those of Algerian origin (cf. Gaspard and Khosrokhavar 1995). Given the political battles over the organization of an official French Islam, it is not surprising that French Muslim groups have historically been highly divided over the legitimacy of the headscarf in France. For instance, in the wake of the 1989 exclusions, two Muslim cultural associations, the Voice of Islam and the Islamic Association in France, organized demonstrations in Paris to show their support for the girls in question, with more than one thousand headscarved women marching from the multiracial neighborhood of Barbès to the central Place de la République. However, the Grand Mosque and the FNMF not only refused to participate in the events, but organized a well-attended counter-protest.

Likewise, two of the largest anti-racist organizations in France, SOS-Racisme and France-Plus, came out on opposite sides of how to respond to the 1989 affair, with the Muslim president of France-Plus, Areski Dahmani, opting for a strict secularist line, while the Christian president of its rival, Harlem Désir, expressed outrage over the expulsions.[15] Indeed, many of the strongest proponents of anti-headscarf legislation—including Ernest Chenière, the Creil principal (and later member of Parliament) whose decision touched off the initial controversy—were themselves of recent immigrant origin. Kofi Yamgnane, then the socialist minister of integration (himself a naturalized Togoan immigrant), publicly stated his own conservative departure from the 1989 high court decision: "Islam . . . must accept the Republican pact. That is to say, accept the separation of Church and State, renounce polygamy and the wearing of headscarves in school." Otherwise, he claimed, Muslim immigrants should "stay at home" (*Le Monde* 10 October 1991: 9).

Likewise, one of the strongest sources of criticism for the headscarf has actually emerged from educated North African women, many of whom have fought against the headscarf in North Africa as a tool of patriarchal domination and a sign of social conservatism (cf. Lazreg 1994: 166–222; Mernissi 1987). In my discussions with Kabyle activists in Paris, many young women harshly criticized their peers for adopting the headscarf as a sign of protest. For these women, the expelled young girls were operating under a false consciousness through their tacit support of an Islamist political position, and thus merited their expulsion from school. Sonya, the Franco-Kabyle schoolteacher in Aulnay-sous-Bois, who abstains from alcohol and pork and who fasts during Ramadan, told me that she could not understand her headscarved students, seeing in it a conscious rejection of integration. "If you don't want to live here, go home. If I felt so out of place in France, I wouldn't stay." In a similar vein, Khalida Messaoudi, an outspoken Kabyle feminist who fled Algeria after receiving death threats from the GIA, decried the "veil" as a "uniform marking the segregation of women and their lifelong status as minors." Famously comparing headscarves to Jewish yellow stars, she warned that France, in accepting the headscarf, was debarking on the same slippery slope to Islamic totalitarianism that she had witnessed in Algeria (*Le Figaro* 29–30 October 1994: 27; cf. Messaoudi 1995). In a view that dovetailed with an implicit assumption in the French media (cf. Altschull 1995), headscarved girls like Leïla and Fatima were portrayed as the innocent victims of the political manipulations of their fathers.

Reactions by Muslim women in France have gone beyond this critical, if not alarmist tone; many, as sociological surveys indicate, have been incredibly supportive of their peers' decisions (Cesari 1994; Gaspard and Khosrokhavar 1995). The issue of veiling has long split the feminist movement in Muslim countries, as feminists have hesitantly recognized that adopting such sartorial practices has endowed women, particularly during periods of intensified colonial surveillance, with an ability to circulate freely within masculinized public spaces. The general repugnance for the veil expressed by European feminists has often provoked their Muslim counterparts to take a more open, culturally defensive position (Abu-Lughod 1998). These positions reject a universal understanding of the meaning and politics of headscarving. Along these lines, Frantz Fanon, in his remarkable essay on the changing, historical dynamic of veiling practices during the Algerian war of liberation, has shown how orthoprax Islamic dress can hold multiple political significations, both as a reactionary means to control women as bearers of both shame and tradition, and as a revolutionary device through which anti-colonial battles can be fought (Fanon 1965).

An understanding of the polysemy of the headscarf as a symbol and medium for the expression of identity finds its way into the work of Franco-Algerian women like Hanifa Cherifi, who are called upon by the French state to mediate between schoolgirls, parents, and school officials in cases of headscarf-related expulsions. Cherifi, a self-defined secular Muslim in the employ of the state, acknowledges the legitimacy of the headscarf while simultaneously recommending it be abandoned for pragmatic reasons: "it's all right [for a girl] to fight for ideals, but she should not put her schooling at risk" (*Asian Wall Street Journal* 27–29 June 2003: A5). This process of negotiation was portrayed in the 1996 television movie *Sa vie à elle,* in which screenwriter Zaïda Ghorab-Volta explored the decisions of a young French Muslim woman, Yaqine, to wear a headscarf, and then finally, under pressure from teachers and parents, to remove it. For Ghorab-Volta, the goal was neither to demonize the headscarf nor to support it. "The point was not to be for or against the veil. There are no answers, only questions" (*Libération* 19 April 1996).

The headscarf in postcolonial France thus has operated simultaneously as a sign of female subjugation to male desire generally, or to a conservative Islamist social agenda particularly; *and* liberation from the male gaze and (post)colonial domination. In this respect, it has been understandably greeted with ambivalent sentiments of hope, confusion, fear, and outrage. As a metonymic symbol, the responses its wearers received have encapsulated the copresent discourses of anticipation and anxiety central to the integration of immigrant groups in France. As an object of legislative debate, it has epitomized the contradictions of rights and restrictions within French *laïcité.* However, in spite of these ambiguities and multiple connotations, for many politicians, from Bayrou to Raffarin, the headscarf remained necessarily an ostentatious sign of a politicized religion, a religion incompatible with secular education and the French nation as a whole.

The opposition of Islam to education set the context for the Nike-PSG advertisement campaign in 1995. The second slogan—"No law prohibits you from wearing a PSG jersey in school"—clearly referenced the Bayrou circular institutionalized the previous summer, as well as the government's consistent support for physical education as a fundamental aspect of republican education and integration. However, the advertisement blurs gender lines, for the target consumers of PSG jerseys were most likely young men, not the schoolgirls whose headscarves were the object of contention. The clothes associated with male Muslim believers have not provoked the same alarmist reaction as the headscarf. Stereotypical adornment—including *caftans* (long white robes), sandals, and white knitted skullcaps—has been primarily limited to elder *barbus* (bearded ones). Portrayed by the media as fundamentalist "preachers of *jihad*," these men have been subject to police roundups, identity checks, and general suspicion. And yet, due to their structural locations of gender and age and their distance from the sensitive education sector, they have not posed an equivalent challenge to the processes of social reproduction and national destiny as headscarved girls.

Ironically, the sartorial style of preference for young male North African *banlieusards* in the mid-1990s was exactly that which the Nike advertisements explicitly sought to promote: sportswear in general, from outerwear to baseball caps to sneakers (*les baskets*). This "Beur look" borrowed from mainstream consumerism and a generalized global youth culture, allying its wearers with contemporary American inner-city gangsters and marking their separation from (if not outright "hate" for) a republican system that they have systematically condemned—in speeches, graffiti, and rap lyrics—as repressive and racist. In spite of its performed aggressiveness, such a style bore an intimate structural relationship with the interests of capital and the French nation-state in the promotion of sports. The "Beur look" thus represented a double bricolage, an appropriation of hip-hop culture appropriating the styles of mainstream sports activity.

In this way, young Muslim males consumed the Nike advertisements through the mediation of an appropriated hip-hop style and in reference to a particular history of confrontations with a juridical and administrative system pre-eminently concerned with the enactment of headscarf legislation, the militarization of the *banlieues,* and the creation of an official French Islam. *Cité* residents have not only appropriated and transformed government-sponsored sports programs, but they have also co-opted the corollary sportswear apparel. Understanding this appropriation as a potential threat to the visibility of Muslim difference, a 1995 special edition of *L'Événement du Jeudi* warned, in typically alarmist fashion, that the next "soldiers of Islam" may no longer be wearing the now forbidden headscarves, but rather may be dressed in the very PSG jerseys "no law prohibits" (21–27 September 1995: 6–7).

Islam in France/Islam of France

Debates over the legitimacy of particularized social practices in France—including but not limited to public prayer and Islamic adornment—have centered on the production of Franco-Algerian religious subjectivities and their integration into a national community of destiny. Rather than erasing religious difference, as instrumentalist theories of schooling and sports practice suggest (cf. Dunning and Rojek 1992), the events surrounding the various headscarf affairs, the roundups of suspected Islamist terrorists, and the officialization of French Islam indicate the production of two particular images of immigrant (religious) identity, a production over which the French state and Muslim associations have both collided and colluded. On the one hand, in reference to the Algerian civil war and the 11 September attacks, the government and media have bolstered the image of an internal Islamist terrorist threat. This Islam, viewed as the logical outcome of the delinquency, petty crime, and drugs of the *cités,* has been largely attributed by journalists and social scientists to a culture of immigrant poverty. Its followers, manipulated by international forces and trained in the eminently violent *jihad,* have been presented, in this construction, as mere automatons, deriving their identity solely from the logic of sectarianism. Government officials and media pundits have reified this version of political Islam as incommensurable with French *laïcité* and hence a threat to state stability. Sports programs, in their explicit combating of communitarian identity, have fed into this process of reification.

On the other hand, the discourse on state secularism and education has constructed a second Islam: a republican and capitalist Islam in which believers-*cum*-consumers express their faith in the privacy of their homes or in state-sanctioned mosques. Government and mosque officials like Sarkozy and Boubakeur have presented this official French Islam as unthreatening, with its adherents as fully participating citizens in public French life. They have foreseen such an Islam as mindful of the laws of the French republic and rejecting all forms of sectarianism. The particularities of such an Islam would not provoke concern, for they are assimilable and commensurate with all other forms of difference in France—religious, ethnic, cultural, or philosophical. Practitioners of such an Islam, would, like Fethi, work by day, practice judo at night, pray regularly, and vote in municipal elections every two years. Unlike Fethi, their religious beliefs would be directed wholly to life in France and not to Kabyle or Algerian identities located elsewhere.

Both the "fanatical Islam" and the "secularist Islam" surely find their exemplars in France, though never as purely as government policy seems to suggest. By no means Islamists, French Muslims like Fethi and Sonya incorporate Islamic practices into their daily lives as French *and* North African subjects. Political Islam and secularist Islam represent two ideal types, somewhere between which everyday French Muslim practice operates in many diverse forms (Cesari 1994; Wieviorka 2002). Nonetheless, both discursive poles have underwritten state policy and provided the building blocks on which different kinds of immigrant subjectivity are constructed. Indeed, legislation and policy have continually opposed religious and sports bodily practice and, in doing so, have outlined different forms of national belonging. For, as the third Nike advertisement—"In 2041, your grandchildren will ask you if you really saw the PSG during their reign of glory"—implied, national unity depends on a shared historical memory, a memory itself constituted in common bodily practices and localizable within a territorially bounded space. In the effort to ensure such national reproduction, policy decisions and enforced bodily disciplines have ironically provided the groundwork for the imagination and practice of alternate subnational and transnational belongings.

5 /

The Generation of Generations:
Beur Identity and Political Agency

Sonya was twenty-five when she met Kamel, five years her senior, in the northern Paris suburb of Villetaneuse. She was finishing a degree in education at the university; he was studying sociology. Her Kabyle parents didn't approve of this relationship—they dismissed Kamel, who was born in western Algeria and raised in France, as an "Arab" and not suitable son-in-law material. But Sonya is independent and determined to have a different life than that of her mother and maternal aunt, and today the couple live together, in spite of parental objections, in Sonya's state employee apartment in Aulnay-sous-Bois.

Sonya was born in Paris to parents born in the late 1940s to patrilineally related families of notable lineage of the same Kabyle village near Bejaïa. At the start of the war in Algeria, in the familiar pattern of *lghorba* (exile), members of both families came to Aubervilliers to join their husbands and fathers, who had been there since the mid-1930s working in the north-suburban factories. Although both sets of Sonya's grandparents would return to Algeria after the war ended, Sonya's parents would come back to France together after their marriage in 1966 and settle in a private apartment in a recently built *cité* in Saint-Denis, where Sonya was born shortly later. Educated for the most part in France, Sonya's father worked as a designer in a sports equipment factory, eventually opened his own small sportswear production business, and moved his family into a single-family pavilion in Aubervilliers. Sonya grew up with her younger brother and sister in the northern suburbs of Paris, and feels very attached to her *département* of Seine–Saint-Denis, or what she refers to simply as "93."

At the same time, Sonya feels largely "at ease" in Kabylia. She spent her summer vacations with her father, mother, and three siblings in her family's village in Kabylia until 1993, when the civil war in Algeria made these visits too dangerous. During the last visit, she stayed in the village for an extra two weeks by herself, but while she felt completely "at home" (*chez moi*), she did not want to stay any longer. Her two brothers felt the same way, for while their paternal grandfather very much wanted them to do their military service in Algeria, they insisted on doing it in France. On this issue, they had support from their parents, who taught them that it was important, as second-generation immigrants, to be integrated in France. Likewise, Sonya's parents never put pressure on her to conform to Muslim orthopraxy, though Sonya abstains from alcohol and pork out of respect for their cultural and religious values. However, her parents did oversee her sexual life and expressed a strong desire that she marry another Kabyle. Absolutely not wanting to follow the example of her mother or her mother's sister, who is only two years older than Sonya—married at fourteen and fifteen years old respectively to men from their village—Sonya spent five years from the age of sixteen convincing her parents to let her live by herself. They have never fully accepted her independence nor her exogamously dating an "Arab," which they view as almost as bad as her dating a "Frenchman." Even today, when her grandparents return for a visit from their retirement in Algeria, she returns to her parents' house and "plays the good daughter."

As teenagers in the early 1980s, both Sonya and Kamel, like many of their peers, became involved in the multicultural and anti-racist movements that swept France. For his part, Kamel became very active in the burgeoning milieu of Beur associations, participated in the 1983 March for Equality and Against Racism (widely known as the *Marche des Beurs*), and eventually took part in the organizing committee of the 1985 March for Civic Rights. His decision to take an active role in community development sprang from two directions: first, his discovery as a late teenager of the richness of his Arab heritage that had been obfuscated in school; and second, his every-day experiences of racism growing up as a young Algerian in France. Kamel was born in western Algeria, but came to France with his parents when he was a baby just after the war. In one instance that he recounted, "I was playing with my brother and a friend in the courtyard of his *cité*. A guy came and accused us of having broken a window. He threatened us with his attack dog. My father arrived, and the guy began to fight with him until the cops came and took the guy away. The crowd that had gathered got mad, saying that it was 'only an Arab.'" Kamel quit the association scene after the 1985 march and decided at that point to return to Algeria. However, he never left France, and today he is beginning the administrative process of naturalizing himself as a citizen.

Sonya participated in the 1983 march with the Villetaneuse

branch of SOS-Racisme, although she herself had never personally experienced any instances of racism. Rather, she marched in order to express herself as "an individual who pays her taxes and holds within her Maghrebi culture." Considering her participation as one and the same as her domestic struggles for sexual freedom, Sonya organized with her classmates a series of high school expositions on "problems of identity" and on being a "Beurette" in France. Sonya has brought this engagement into her career choice, having trained to work as a primary school teacher in *quartiers difficiles*. After her first posting in a *cité* in Tremblay, she now teaches in *les 3000* of Aulnay-sous-Bois, one of the most marginalized of all the *grands ensembles*. Moreover, when I met her in 1996 she had just begun to take Tamazight classes at the Berber Culture Association (ACB) in Ménilmontant. She hoped the civil war in Algeria would soon end so that she could see her family in Kabylia again.

The imagination and practice of belonging in immigrant France is mediated by forms of generational identity and political engagement. Complex and often tendentious relations between different ages of Algerian emigrants, or between parents and children within a single immigrant household, mark daily life in the *cités*. With the coming of political age of the "second generation" (or Beurs) in the early 1980s, the French state and immigrant actors alike emphasized cultural conflict and struggle as the pre-eminent characteristic of relations between parents and children (cf. Abou-Sada and Millet 1986; Aïssou 1987; CCI 1984; Jazouli 1986). Presenting themselves as occupying an intermediary position between North Africa and France, the Beurs were ambivalently embraced and feared by French state officials as either icons of a new multiracial France or, alternatively, as the carriers of potentially incommensurable ethnic and religious identities. As the objects of state anxieties about the future cultural cohesiveness of the French nation-state, second-generation Algerian immigrants have likewise become the privileged targets of integration policies.

Beur subjectivity in France has transcended state discourse and manipulation, forming the basis for immigrant collective action that has transcended the generational divide. Cultural and religious transmission between genealogically related or fictive parents and children has continued apace in the context of the *cités* rather than being simply replaced by state socializing institutions of the school, the factory, and the sports program. As such, modernization models that presume a discontinuity or rupture between generations of immigrants fail to account for either the daily lived reality or the transpolitical mobilization of multigenerational Algerian subjects in France. However, in spite of such continuities, social reproduction in the *cités* continues to be an object of struggle for Franco-Algerians, with children of immigrants resisting, and at times even reversing, processes of intergenerational transmission. In such cases, the second generation acts not only as the cultural mediators between Algeria and France, but also as the agents of social memory, of the nostalgic objectification and re-presentation of different Algerian Kabyle or Muslim cultural forms.

The generation of generations is an important anthropological problem not only for the study of Algeria in France, but for the understanding of cultural transmission and transformation more generally. Relations between generations determine how cultural forms of value and authority are produced and reproduced in societies over time, as well as how internal social registers of commonality and difference are inscribed and challenged. Theories of socialization and migration, from German sociology (cf. Mannheim 1952) to American immigration studies (cf. Kriegel 1978) to French practice theory (cf. Sayad 1977, 1994b), have focused on intergenerational exchanges and ruptures as the motor of social production and reproduction. While these theories often presume a teleology of historical progress and immigrant integration, they nonetheless underline how generational identities make their way into everyday social life as objects of political struggle. In Algerian France, immigrant subjects of various ages reproduce and contest generational belonging and practices, and in so doing call into question a larger French national politics of difference.

Emigration and Generational Conflict

Algerian generational subjectivity in France has been repeatedly formed and reformed across the history of emigration to France. The first Algerian emigrants to France in the late nineteenth and early twentieth centuries sought to reconstruct village social relations in France and reinscribe a cultural continuity no longer possible in a Kabylia subject to colonial land expropriations. Their experiences in France, however, had a profound impact on the next generation of emigrants, thus furthering the cultural transformation of Kabylia. This generation viewed their mobility as a means to escape the authority of their parents and other village elders. Their children, raised if not born in France around the time of the Algerian war, without the option of a further emigration, formulated their generational subjectivity around political mobilization for immigrant cultural and political rights in France. The failure of these efforts to achieve any concrete results has provoked the subsequent generation born in the *cités* to map their belonging in ethnic or religious terms, transnationally linking their subjectivity with global Berber or Islamic social movements. Given this development, the contemporary immigrant context of the *cités* exists in historical dialectical relationship, rather than absolute rupture, with social life in Algeria.

The first generation of emigrants to France was born in the colonial context of Kabyle social life, marked by the absolute authority of lineage and village elders (*amokran*), whose gerontocracy was reproduced both in the *axxam,* in the fields, and in the village assembly. Elders watched over children from across the village, protected them, and punished them when necessary. Questions of *nnif* (male honor) were tied to the concerns of the lineage as a whole, with attacks addressed by older male agnatic relations as a whole. In addition, generational identity and authority was maintained and reproduced through divisions of labor in the agrarian economy, with fathers and elder sons responsible for planting and harvesting, while younger children took care of the animals and brought them out to pasture. Collective labor (*tiwizi*) in the village accentuated this division, with adult males marking their coming of age with their participation in the construction of houses and the harvesting of olives. Finally, active participation and the eloquence of adult men's speeches in the *tajmaât* constituted an important step in increasing individual and family *nnif*. Through such practices, the older generations constituted their identity within a local hierarchy of authority.

Subsumed to the authority of their elders, the younger generation was often called to act on their behalf, sometimes assuming the responsibility of defending family *nnif* through the regulation of the women's actions or by functioning as the family's agent in the negotiation of marriage contracts or market relations (Bourdieu 1977: 34–35; Khellil 1984: 36–37). They likewise took on such responsibilities when they were selected by village and lineage elders to be the pioneer emigrants to France. Their migration—what they understood as "exile" (*lghorba*)—as brilliantly described by Abdelmalek Sayad (1977, 2000),[1] had the explicit goal of reproducing extant village social life, the material conditions of which had become untenable under colonial land expropriations. With such aims in mind, they were chosen for their "authentic" (*bou niya*) peasant experience, and they organized their work stays in France according to the village social-cum-agrarian calendar, leaving for France after the autumn planting and returning to Kabylia for the summer harvests (Bourdieu 1977: 134, 172; Sayad 1977: 62–63). While in France, these *bou niya* emigrants continued to maintain their physical and cultural separation from the French city dwellers through living communally and reproducing their village social structures within the metropole. Upon their return to the Kabyle village, the young emigrants became the subject of a "process of quasi-ritual 're-integration,'" in which traces of their city life were "exorcised" by their immediately taking on village clothing, visiting extended family members, and tending to the family's fields and animals (Sayad 1977: 63). In this respect, the first age of emigration tended to reproduce the village social order and hierarchies by which the household heads, through the medium of the *tajmaât*, continued to direct the social aspirations of their dependents.

Eventually, the experiences of emigration had their direct effects on the village social order, as the control of the village elders over the *habitus* and social expectations of young migrants was never absolute. The emigrants' remitted income contributed to the monetization of what Bourdieu and Sayad have characterized as the "good-faith economy" of Kabyle villages (Bourdieu 1977: 172–174; 2000; Bourdieu and Sayad 1964). With increasing individual economic aspirations, the second generation of emigrants operated as "de-peasantized peasants" (*paysans dépaysanés*), who emigrated with the goal of escaping rather than reproducing communal obligations (Sayad 1977: 65). Younger and younger in age, emigrants viewed their stay in France as an individual adventure, as a positive change in status that could be extended indefinitely. While the first generation regularly sent all their earnings back to their village, leaving themselves only the minimal amount necessary to maintain their existence in France, the second generation sent regular remittances to cover the immediate expenses of their family members in Algeria, keeping the rest for themselves (Sayad 1977: 67).

Seeking to escape their elders' authority, young Algerian emigrants in France found themselves at the mercy of employers and governmental authorities. Forced to provide constant proof of their legal employment in France, their identity was largely reduced to their pay stubs that became for them de facto passports (Sayad 1977: 70).[2] This protracted economic existence in France further isolated them from village sociality, and their eventual attempts to return to Kabylia and reintegrate themselves in village life tended to fail dramatically. Stigmatized by their clothing and comportment, returned emigrants were treated by villagers as "foreigners," as "guests in their own houses." As such, like the second generation of the early 1980s, this second age felt trapped in a perpetual state of being betwixt and between, doubly alienated in Algeria and France. In the process, however, they succeeded in rupturing, if not reversing, generational hierarchies within the villages, becoming the economic "protectors" of family and village social structure, rather than the dependents of it (Sayad 1977: 74–76).

In this sense, by the end of the colonial period, emigration had become a veritable rite of passage for young Kabyle men of marriageable age, a rite that came to fulfill a similar function as entrance into the village assembly. On the one hand, the experience of *lghorba* granted young migrants a degree of freedom from a family life dominated by their fathers. On the other hand, in spite of the stigmatizing effect, it became the condition of possibility for attaining local status for the emigrant and his larger kin group. In terms of marriage, it enabled the amassing of the necessary bride-wealth (*thoutchith*) and provided the cultural capital of knowledge of French language and culture increasingly valued by potential in-laws (Wysner 1945: 65). For this reason, even if they had not been financially successful in France, they would, if at all possible, return well-dressed, bearing armloads of gifts for all, giving the appearance of prosperity and further perpetuating the myth of France as a land of opportunity. In marrying a woman from a well-respected family, the emigrant amassed social prestige and expanded his family's social network. Although they returned to France after marriage, they hoped to resettle in their villages permanently, marry off their children, and send their sons to France to work. In this way, while emigration provided temporary escape from the authority of elders, it effectively reproduced the gerontocratic system by augmenting the prestige of the elder-dominated household.[3]

Liminality and Violence

Intergenerational cooperation and conflict continued with the growth of multigenerational and multigendered Algerian households in France during and after the Algerian war of national liberation. Kabyle generations in France, as in Kabylia, are generated through processes of dominance and struggle that unite genealogies with territory and history. The gerontocracy of the *tajmaât* has been extended transnationally through the intermediary of neighborhood cafés (*cafés arabes*) that have served as locales for older male residents to make decisions on questions—including funerary arrangements and development projects—that simultaneously affect the immigrant neighborhood and the natal village.

Moreover, this older generation, like Sonya's parents, continues to dominate the immigrant household economy and generally attempts to control the life course of its dependents, including their children's education, cultural/religious practices, and choice of marriage partners. Mahmoud, a fifty-five-year-old Kabyle immigrant who had been in Paris for sixteen years, told me that while he never forced his culture on his three children born in France, he still expects them to behave in a respectful manner. He particularly worried about his thirteen-year-old daughter, who lives alone with her mother (Mahmoud's first wife), fearing that she would grow up with loose sexual mores and even marry a Frenchman. He would like to send her to live with his relatives in Kabylia, but, as he bemoaned, "I feel like I've lost control over her." Indeed, immigrant parents, generally operating with the long-term goal of resettling in Algeria like Fethi's mother and father, often send their children to reside with family in Algeria to pursue family, work, education, or military service—particularly when they see their children as being in some form of trouble at school or with the law, or, in the case of young women, through premarital sexual relations.

At the same time, immigrant parents increasingly defer responsibility to younger generations born in France, with parents making practical use of their children's greater competency in French language and practices learned in school or on the street. As in Kabylia, older male children act as surrogate fathers in surveilling and disciplining younger siblings. They take on a primary role in their siblings' education, as they oversee homework completion and mediate between teachers and parents. Sonya effectively became a teaching assistant for her own younger brother and sister, sometimes even covering up for their poor grades in the face of the potential anger of their parents. Further, children serve as intermediaries between their parents and the French state, acting as interpreters and translators and often taking care of the bureaucratic proceedings necessary for regularizing family members' residence in France. In my many visits to offices of the national immigration authority to regularize my own stay in France, I encountered many older Algerian men and women accompanied by their citizen children, the latter talking on behalf of their parents whenever discussions with officials took place. In this way, children in immigrant France, if generally subsumed to parental authority, have had a degree of generational agency as the primary interlocutors between their families and the larger structures of French society.

Moreover, this structure of generational relations has been expanded across the territory of immigrant neighborhoods and housing projects in France. In the case of the *cités*, residents map domestic kinship terms onto the multifamilial and multiethnic setting in which they live. In a manner reminiscent of Kabyle villages, local elders look after the children and property of their neighbors and participate in forms of *tiwizi* and charity (*sedaqa*) in times of need. For instance, older brothers in the *cités* not only keep an eye on their younger brothers and sisters, but also watch after, lend a hand to, and even punish younger non-relatives in the housing complex in which they live, much like older family members do for the younger children of a Kabyle *adrum*. As Pascal Duret has discussed at length, this tendency has produced the generalized phenomenon of *grands frères* ("elder brothers"), authority figures in the *cités* who "take over (*prendre le relais*) from fathers outside of the family home, in the street" (1996: 33).

To a certain extent, this expanded socioeconomic and moral role of the younger generations within immigrant France has underwritten increased conflict between generations. Young men's and women's quest for freedom from parental oversight in school or on the streets has often been seen by them as a "struggle" (*une lutte*), as part of a future "war between parents and the youth of the *cité*, a war to the death" (Charef 1983a: 26). This is particularly illustrated in the case of young women who run away from home, either to take up residence with sympathetic friends or family, or to try their luck on the street. Sonya's five-year struggle to regulate her own sexual life is recapitulated in the story of Myriem, a twenty-one-year-old runaway (*fugueuse*), who lamented, "It's hard to fight against your father and mother. To explode outdoors and be crushed within! . . . Appeal for one's rights when one doesn't really exist at home. . . . 'They,' you can't make them budge and I don't have any intention of taking a step backwards (*faire marche arrière*)" (cited in Aïchoune 1985: 73). Contrasts between the home and the street, between private Algerian domesticity and public French society, thus underwrite the second generation's sense of existing in a perpetual state of cultural liminality, of being "lost between two cultures, two histories, two languages, two skin colors" (Charef 1983a: 17).

Socioeconomic Modalities: Racist Violence and Political Responses

The second generation's public articulation of cultural liminality, as in Mehdi Charef's novel quoted above, arose from a longer history of immigrant struggle and activism that began in the mid-1970s. This activism arose in large part in response to the outbreak of anti-immigrant violence perpetrated by the police forces and the lower-class, European *cité* residents referred to by immigrants as *beaufs* or *beau-frères* ("brothers-in-law"), the French equivalent of "good ol' boys." This racist violence—the history of which can be traced to the *fin-de-siècle* Dreyfus affair and the nativist movements of the 1930s—was cultivated by the burgeoning xenophobic Front National and exacerbated by the economic downturn that followed the 1973 oil embargo.[4] In what the press called the "murderous summer" (*l'été meutrier*) of 1973, more than fifty Algerian male workers were attacked and fifteen killed in separate acts in and around Marseilles. Employing an attack they referred to, using the language of French soldiers during the war in Algeria, as a "rat hunt" (*ratonnade*), a group of *beaufs* would track an Algerian man—whom they derogated as a "rat" (*raton*)—returning from work, corner him, and beat him severely. Often they would destroy his identity papers and *fiches de paie,* thus symbolically, if not practically, revoking his rights of residence in France.

By the early 1980s, the attack ritual had transformed, with the principal prey changing from male immigrant workers to their children. Primarily occurring in the housing projects in the Parisian and Lyonnais *banlieues,* racist violence against the second generation took two main forms. On the one hand, young North African children playing in the courtyard between buildings were shot at by middle-aged, "European" neighbors from their apartment windows using .22-caliber rifles, primarily employed for hunting. In the month of July 1983 alone, at least seven incidents of this kind occurred in Paris-area *cités,* including the injuring of two young North Africans in La Courneuve, the killing of fifteen-year-old Kamel in Tourcoing, the injuring of twelve-year-old Badiane Massamba in Aulnay-sous-Bois, and the killing of nine-year-old Salah Djennane and the injuring of two others in Saint-Denis (Aïchoune 1985: 141–143). The image of the .22-caliber rifle—serving as a token for the attack as a whole—became a recurrent trope in second-generation activist writing and political mobilization that would respond to this anti-immigrant racism (cf. Charef 1983a).[5]

On the other hand, anti-immigrant attacks during the early 1980s followed a second model, that of the unnecessary use of force by the police and security officers against young North African *banlieue* residents. The attackers were primarily private guards and security forces assigned to supermarkets and train stations located in the *cités,* spaces representing the state and hence subject to residents' respatializing practices of shoplifting and graffiti. In the spring of 1980, three young North Africans were shot and killed by police in the Parisian *banlieues.* In the *été meutrier* of 1983, attacks against second-generation immigrants included the killing of nineteen-year-old Moussa Merzogh in the Parisian suburb of Livry-Gargan by a Radar supermarket security officer, the shooting of twenty-year-old Toumi Djaidja in the Lyonnais *banlieue* of Vénissieux by a police officer, the killing of nine-year-old Tawfik Ouanes by a subway security officer in La Courneuve, the serious injury of twenty-four-year-old Kader Layachi in Tourcoing by an off-duty police officer, and the killing of nineteen-year-old Djamel Itim and twenty-three-year-old Djamel Kherko in Montreuil by a former security officer. As in the case of the .22-caliber-rifle attackers, the perpetrators often succeeded in pleading guilty to lesser sentences or being acquitted on the basis of "legitimate defense" (Aïchoune 1985: 141–143).

As a result of such seemingly legitimated violence, second-generation Algerian youth came to understand the law enforcement and legal systems as prime forces of racism and inequality, and began in the 1980s to mobilize collectively against them. The first manifestation of North African immigrant youth political agency borrowed the English name Rock Against Police (RAP) and organized free concerts to increase public awareness of racism after the 1980 shootings. The second concert, held on 15 May 1981, took place in the *cité* of Couzy in the Parisian suburb of Vitry, on the exact site where one of these victims, the young Kader Lareiche, had been killed by a night watchman three months earlier (Aïchoune 1985: 127–128; Jazouli 1992: 28). Likewise, the first grassroots organization of young North African women in France was formed in March 1981 in the Busserine quarter of Marseille where two youths, Lahouari Ben Mohammed and Zahir Boudjlal, had been just previously killed. The association was founded by the sister of Zahir and had the explicit goal of documenting racist assassinations. In a similar fashion, the anti-racist Association Gutenberg of Nanterre was founded in November 1982 following the .22-caliber-rifle assassination of a local community youth organizer, Abdnebi Guemiah (Boubeker and Abdallah 1993: 65).

Finally, the October–November 1983 March for Equality and Against Racism, in which hundreds of thousands of Beur youth participated in a two-month march from Marseille to the Place de la République in Paris to raise public awareness of racist violence and immigrant rights, responded directly to the violent summer of 1983. The event was organized by Les Minguettes (Lyon)-based Association SOS Avenir Minguettes, whose twenty-year-old president, Toumi Djaidja, had been seriously wounded several months earlier while attempting to intervene between several policemen who had unleashed their dogs on a group of young residents of the *cité*. Marchers displayed banners commemorating the young men and women killed during the summer and were greeted along the way with local memorials for residents assassinated during the previous year (Jazouli 1992: 60). In this way, the initial cohesion of North African immigrant youth as a political generation corresponded to assassinations of *banlieue* youth who were seen by community organizers as "brothers" (*frères*), whether actual, as in the case of Zahir Boudjlal, or fictive (Bouamama et al. 1994: 50). Moreover, the actions taken contributed to the elaboration of these youth as a generation-as-victim of racist violence and structural inequality. Under this persona, the second generation's actions amounted to demands for equal inclusion in French political and civil societies.

This collective action simultaneously outlined a parallel subject position for young North African *banlieusards* in France: that of generation-as-avenger. This political identity resulted not from a logic of political inclusion, but from one of exclusion and rejection. While the 1983 march operated under the tutelage of the Protestant minister Christian Delorme and drew its avowed historical inspiration from Martin Luther King's non-violent demonstrations, it received severe criticism from marginalized immigrant youth throughout France, who saw its approach as ineffectual. In many cases, the assassination of a young *cité* resident precipitated local practices of retribution and feud and demanded a "bloodwealth" (*prix de sang*) to be paid (Bouamama et al. 1994: 51). However, as the actual attacker, under police custody if not a police officer himself, was not directly available for punishment by the victim's immediate kin, the local community as a whole took action, directing their rage at the police forces as a whole as well as at the symbols of their economic exclusion in the *cités*. For instance, in the summer of 1981, following a police raid in the Cité de la Cayolle in Marseille in which a number of women, children, and elderly residents were injured, resident youths firebombed the shopping centers and police commissariats in neighboring housing projects.

Also in 1981, when a hunger strike by immigrant youth in Lyon failed to overturn deportation legislation,[6] and when a young woman from neighboring Saint-Dizier was deported to Algeria, Les Minguettes exploded in a series of violent confrontations between young residents and the police. In an estimated 250 separate incidents, groups of mostly North African youths stole expensive cars, engaged police in a chase, and then abandoned and burned the cars. According to one resident, Djamel, these "rodeos" were a means to regain control over lives subsumed under seemingly wanton police authority. "It was from the moment of police provocations that the youth began to become aggressive, because they didn't understand the police's aggressions towards them. The rodeos were to respond to everything they had undergone, they and their parents. . . . The rage they had in themselves was directed at the cars" (cited in Jazouli 1992: 21–22). One of the earliest organizations of *cité* youth, Zaâma d'banlieue, was founded to negotiate the closure of these violent confrontations. Farida, one of the group's founders, described this trajectory:

> The rodeos and their fallout posed serious problems. . . . There were [those] who saw in them a legitimate and spontaneous expression of the violence of the *banlieue* youth, a violence which it was necessary to channel and structure. But the majority of them didn't want there to be a repetition of this type of action, because we knew that it would have negative repercussions (*retomber sur la gueule*) for those who were the worst off. It was necessary to find the means for the youth to organize themselves, for them to become conscious that the stakes went beyond individual concerns and that, without collective action, we couldn't get out of the mess (*la galère*). Concretely, our activities at that moment targeted essentially the youth of the *cités*. (cited in Jazouli 1992: 25)

In spite of these efforts, two years later, similar confrontations occurred in neighboring Vénissieux, leading to the week-long occupation of the *cité* by a regiment of 4,000 police officers. Likewise, during the same year, young residents of the Monmousseau housing complex of Les Minguettes engaged police in a violent struggle after officers had broken into an apartment suspected of containing stolen goods. The young demonstrators accused the police of not only being racist, but, moreover, of violating their privacy and, above all, of showing a "lack of respect" for their parents (Jazouli 1992: 48). In this designation of the police, and the French government as a whole, as the enemy, second-generation political subjectivity became premised not only on their status as victims, but also on their role as avengers of their "brothers" and defenders of their "parents."

In both taking direct action against the police and negotiating the closure of the resulting violence, young men and women of the *cités* reversed the generational hierarchy of parental authority, just as their parents had done through their emigration with respect to their own parents in Kabylia. Deploying the language game of *verlan* commonly spoken on the *cité* streets, in which a French word is reformed through an inversion of its syllables, they inverted the "Arab" designation given to their parents and called themselves "Beurs."[7] In deploying the vernacular of the *cités,* they indexed their local belonging to a new, multiracial France, in contradistinction to their parents' supposed foreignness. Moreover, in orthographically inverting their parents' ethnonym, they signaled their further separation from the image of their parents, as the passive "Arab" laborers subjected to racist violence and discrimination. In inverting the order of generational responsibility for vengeance and negotiation, they therefore constituted themselves as political subjects distinct from their parents.

The Beur Movement

This process of subject formation through direct political action dovetailed with a series of experiments in multiculturalism that followed Mitterrand's 1981 election to the French presidency on a pro–immigrant rights platform. In the first few years of its tenure, his socialist administration devised a series of decentralization policies that encouraged and supported minority cultures in France. Speaking in Lorient in 1981, Mitterrand defended the "right to difference" as a universal human right (Giordan 1982: 7). This amounted to a redefinition of French national unity according to its multicultural and multilinguistic diversity. In his preface to a programmatic report entitled *La France au pluriel* ("A Plural France"), Mitterrand commented that "we profoundly believe that if France must be united, she must also be rich in her differences. Her unity has enabled our country; respecting her diversity will prevent her undoing. One and diverse, that is France" (Parti Socialiste 1981: 10).

Mitterrand's declarations, while largely campaign rhetoric, did translate into concrete policy. In the first place, following the 1981 uprisings and hunger strikes in Les Minguettes and Vénissieux, Mitterrand abrogated the deportation laws and formally recognized the Beurs as full-fledged citizens. Furthermore, he released funds for a large-scale *banlieue* rehabilitation program and created Educational Priority Zones (ZEP) to promote immigrant student success (Daoud 1993a: 136–137).[8] Under the banner of "popular education," the government created a set of after-school and summer youth programs to subvert youth unrest in the *cités*. These programs additionally brought *cité* youth to weekend camps in the countryside, operated by older *banlieusards* employed on short-term contracts and considered "interlocutors and intermediaries between the [*banlieue*] population and the [prevention] institutions" (Jazouli 1992: 43). Oftentimes, the municipal governments renewed these contracts during the school year, providing older youths with jobs as local "social animators" in various youth centers and sports clubs, with the explicit goal of integrating young Beurs into the social life of suburban France (Merakchi 1985: 55). Indeed, many future Beur political leaders participated at various points in these activities and programs, as they provided training and salaries much needed during periods of unemployment (Bouamama et al. 1994: 54; Jazouli 1992: 96). Finally, citing the success of groups like Zaâma d'banlieue in negotiating the end of the 1981 Lyon riots, the government overturned the 1938 legislation prohibiting immigrant associations[9] and provided funding for these organizations through the Deixonne decentralization program and the Social Action Funds (FAS) established during the Algerian war to earmark government monies for the integration of immigrant workers.

In the wake of these changes, hundreds of second-generation immigrant associations formed throughout France in the early 1980s, focusing on a variety of social and cultural issues, from grassroots urban development (e.g., Association Gutenberg of Nanterre, Vivons Ensemble [Living Together] of Val-Fourré), to anti-racist politics (e.g., SOS-Racisme), to youth politics (Association of the New Immigrant Generation (ANGI) of Aubervilliers), to cultural activism (e.g., Berber Culture Association [ACB] of Ménilmontant). These associations further became sites for Beur cultural production, establishing newspapers (*Sans Frontières* [Without Borders]), publishing houses (Editions Arcantère and Agence Im'media in Paris), radio stations (Radio Gazelle in Marseille and Radio Beur in Paris), alongside a burgeoning complement of Beur novelists, musicians, and actors. These individuals and groups—in coordination with the mass political demonstrations of the 1983 *Marche des Beurs* and its follow-up marches in 1984 and 1985—constituted what would become known throughout France as "the Beur Movement."

In general, the Beur Movement, in its various actions and productions throughout the 1980s, emphasized the "second generation" of North African immigrants as a particular multicultural political subject. In publications like *La Beur Génération* (Aïchoune 1985), Beur activists and writers celebrated the arrival of a new "hybrid" (*métis*) population in France, endowed with their own politicians, academics, and artists. Claiming to occupy, in the words of Beur novelist Leila Sebbar, a subject position "between Algeria and France" (Basfao and Henry 1991: 51), Beur cultural producers sought to represent a generation in all its diversity. Novels written by Beur authors employed dialogical techniques of code switching and heteroglossia to portray Beur cultural in-betweenness. Likewise, Beur musical groups mixed Algerian cha'abi and raï musical styles with Arabic and Kabyle lyrics into Euro-American genres such as rock (e.g., Les Rockin' Babouches), rhythm and blues (e.g., Carte de Séjour), and electronic pop (e.g., Djurdjura).

Beurs thus presented themselves as the ultimate *bricoleurs,* combining multiple codes into their own language and styles particular to the French *cités* of the early 1980s. Cobbling their identity from referents beyond the Mediterranean, some, like Nacer Kettane (1986: 19), president of Radio Beur, saw themselves as the rejects of a globalizing world—"mutants torn from the McDonald's couscous-steak-fries society." Others imagined the Beurs as the vanguard of a particular postcolonial space that linked North Africa and France via the media of American Beat authors and soap operas: "From Santa Barbara to Tamanrasset by way of Dunkerque,[10] Carthage and Marrakech, they will soon be speaking not of Greenwich Village, but of Beur Village, where the Ahmed Ben Kerouacs, Aïcha MacCullers and Abderrahman Burroughs will be sweeping away the fluff [of society] (*balaieront la pâte de guimauve*)" (Ammi 1985: 90). As either the globalized rejects or the avant-garde, the Beurs presented themselves as the generation of the future, of the "year 3000" (Ammi 1985: 90) if not earlier.

In highlighting this multiculturality—in having, as Fethi explained to me, "one foot in the couscous, one foot in the *choucroute*"—Beur authors and activists presented themselves as the ultimate cultural and political mediator between Algeria and France, as a new embodiment of the pan-Mediterranean *homme frontière* of colonial discourse (Silverstein 2002d). Beur leaders attempted to chart a "third route" (*troisième voie*) between the French state's schemas of integration and the attempts by Algerian political parties and social movements to resuture immigrant political life to the other side of the Mediterranean (Bouamama et al. 1994: 99). In this logic of independence, the "new generation" had to separate itself from both French and Algerian political and cultural institutions and establish its own means of intervention. As Saleiha Amara, the president of the ANGI, explained, groups like hers saw their primary goal as preventing the "autonomy" of the demands of immigrant youth from being co-opted by existing political parties or Algerian governmental bodies (Bouamama et al. 1994: 56).

Such a separation, however, was difficult to maintain. In the first place, the autonomy of the Beur associations was challenged by the continued social actions of French and Algerian political parties in the *cités*. Many Beur militants began their activism in the French Communist Party and assorted Trotskyist organizations that had been active in the various housing and factory strikes by immigrant workers during the late 1970s (Jazouli 1992: 27). Kamel, like other Beur activists, regarded these groups with suspicion and retrospectively blamed the death of the Beur Movement as a whole on the undue influence of Marxist organizations: "They had their priorities all wrong. They acted as if they wanted to make a difference when all they really cared about were their political careers." Other Beur activists, however, came to view Marxist ideology as an antidote to the generational parochialism of Beur concerns, as a means to open up the movement to the "universal." One Beur friend, Mustapha, began his political career in the SONACOTRA strikes and went on to found a French wing of the Britain-based Socialist Workers' Party. By 1986, he had grown disenchanted with the Beur Movement, which "was driving a wedge between children of immigrants, their parents, and proletarian struggles more generally." "I built Socialisme Internationale in order to bring together my identity struggles with those of my father in the factories. Socialisme Internationale was a means to fight the growth of ethnic and religious movements in the *cités* that were a capitalist 'lure' (*leurre*) away from the real issues of marginalization."

In addition, the Beur Movement had to struggle against the influence of the Amicale and the National Union of Algerian Youth (UNJA), official representatives of the Algerian government in France, that since the mid-1960s had attempted to unite Algerian immigrants around Algerian nationalist issues through sponsoring cultural events, offering Arabic classes to children of immigrants, and seeking to monopolize services such as the repatriation of corpses to Algeria. Many of the Beur activists' parents encouraged their children to study Arabic and discover their Algerianness through activities sponsored by these groups in hopes of a proximate return to Algeria. While they began learning about their parents' culture through these activities, many Beur militants later rejected the Amicale and the UNJA as irrelevant to their daily lives in France. Moreover, as Beur organizers Saleiha Amara and Rabah Ghomrane have underlined, the bureaucratic organization of these groups and their direction from Algiers continued to marginalize Beur actors, leaving little room for local decision making, for the participant "democracy" that they craved (Bouamama et al. 1994: 53; Jazouli 1992: 32).

Generational Rupture and Reconciliation

If the Beurs, in their self-presentation, embodied the globalized future, they tended to represent their parents as part of a past constrained by impuissant cultural tradition and nationalist politics. Initially, the parents of Beur militants were proud of their children for taking leadership roles within the local community and being rewarded overtly in terms of television coverage and mayoral invitations. They provided logistical support, housed visiting activists, supplied refreshments for activities, and aided associations monetarily when possible. However, this attitude changed when the actions took on a prolonged political character, when they were seen as interfering with professional aspirations and, moreover, endangering their children's chances at acceptance in France and/or Algeria. Ahmed Ghayet summed up the change: "They [parents] experienced a mixture of pride and anxiety. They said to themselves, 'They would do better to study or look for a job. [Their actions] will only cause them trouble. What are they getting themselves into? Oh la la, my son is doing politics'" (Bouamama et al. 1994: 147).

These parental anxieties were multiplied when the child in question was a daughter. In recalling their experiences growing up, Beurettes, while encouraged to succeed at school, often describe being forbidden to participate in the association meetings and other after-school activities open to their brothers. Yasmina, an active member of the Berber culture association, MCB-France, explained to me that she had an oral agreement with her father that once she passed her baccalaureate exam, she would be "emancipated" from his control. However, even after she finished the exam, he still forbade her from joining an association, fearing that such "immigrant politics" would hurt her chances at "integration." As such, taking an active professional or political role constituted a distinct break with family life, one which informed the concerns of many Beurette militants like Yasmina and Sonya.

Conflicts between immigrant daughters and fathers occasionally led to young women fleeing the family home to live with friends or lovers. In certain cases, as the Beurette singer Djura (1991) describes in her autobiography, these escapes could lead to threatened or actual violence inflicted by family members in the name of *nnif*. Given this threat, Beur associations like Zaâma d'banlieue and the ANGI provided temporary housing and counseling to young women who had fled their parental homes and who feared repercussions if discovered. Alongside the image of the *baba cool*—the defiant Beur male of the 1981 "rodeos"—stood that of the female runaway (*la fugueuse*) as a symbol of the Beurs' simultaneous distancing from French and Algerian domestic mores, of their desire to carve their own space for individual expression.

The generational rupture—constituted in Beur discourse as a divide between tradition and postmodernity, between passivity and agency—was directly related to the second generation's limited historical consciousness of the previous political and economic struggles waged by their parents in the Algerian war of liberation and on the *banlieue* factory floor. At the same time, the perceived generational conflict dovetailed with explicit attempts by the socialist government to isolate the Beurs from the larger immigrant community as the privileged targets of social integration. Government research agencies sponsored a number of sociological studies of the particular "problems" of integration of North African immigrant youth (cf. Abou-Sada and Millet 1986; Aïssou 1987; Boulot and Boyzon-Fradet 1988; Gaspard and Servan-Schreiber 1984; Jazouli 1986). Beur associations and cultural productions likewise benefited from strong public funding and were further featured in photographic expositions and live performances at the Georges Pompidou cultural center in Paris in 1983 (CCI 1984).

The manipulation of the rupture between parents and children, this policy of "youthism" (*jeunisme*) (Bouamama et al. 1994: 57–58), amounted, in effect, to an attempt by the French government to symbolically replace the biological father with the universalizing, national father of the state (cf. Rarrbo 1995: 236). In becoming the primary source of financial support and professional aspirations, the state took over many of the roles historically filled by the Beurs' fathers, now portrayed, in both the sociological and the Beurs' own literature, as absent from the home or debilitated culturally and physically. This targeting of Beur youth in integration policy stemmed from a twofold anxiety: first, that the Beurs, in their potential for collective action as illustrated in the 1981 riots, posed a distinct threat to state security; second, that their marginalization could serve to reinforce sectarian forms of religious or ethnic identity and belonging incommensurable with the social reproduction of French national norms. Drawing on the Beurs' own imagery, the socialist government highlighted the Beurs— and particularly Beur public figures like the tennis player Yannick Noah (who wrote the preface for the Pompidou exhibition catalogue) and the singer Rachid Taha of Carte de Séjour—as icons for a multiracial France, much as it would years later with Zidane.

The state support for the Beur Movement as a symbol of a new, plural France was defined under very strict social and cultural parameters. The employment and educational programs initiated by the Mitterrand government served largely, according to former activists like Kamel, to "purchase" potential Beur leaders, to create what would later be decried as "house Beurs" (*Beurs de service*) in order to "avoid the development of collective action" (Bouamama et al. 1994: 81–82). Municipalities actively supported the associations' explicitly "cultural" activities—their concerts and festivals—but simultaneously undercut their attempts at community organization, both by co-opting the associations' leaders and denying future funding and logistical support (Bouamama et al. 1994: 137; Jazouli 1992: 98). According to Saïd Bouamama, president of the Roubaix associations Texture and Mémoire Fertile (Fertile Memory), the socialist government sought to define the limits of Beur multiculturalism. "It was as if they said: 'You have the right to be different insofar as culinary tastes and raï are concerned; but don't you dare try to come speak to us about how to organize your struggles, how to organize your *quartiers,* how to organize your social life'" (Bouamama et al. 1994: 63).

The reduction of Beur hybridity to folkloristic forms, to Fethi's imagery of couscous and *choucroute*, underwrote models of social reproduction that cultural activists like my friend Lounis would later decry as "integration by sports and music." Even the popular Beur marches and demonstrations of 1983–85, in their "youthist" and anti-racist dimensions, received governmental support as they underwrote rather than challenged national civic unity. The Beur demonstrators of the 1984 march, who painted their faces half white and half black in order to portray their liminality, became the overt symbols for the government of a generation in the midst of an imagined transition toward integration. As such, they stood in marked contrast to both the first generation of their fathers locked in the traditions of the past and to the potential next generation of Muslim fundamentalists feared as anathema to the French republic.

In this respect, when Beur leaders broke from the folkloristic mold and participated in the collective actions of their parents, they lost media and government support. Several weeks after the conclusion of the 1983 march, North African autoworkers in the Talbot plant in the Parisian suburb of Poissy staged a sit-in, protesting against discriminatory wages and promotion practices. Radio Beur, demonstrating their solidarity, proclaimed that "we are all the *bougnoules*[11] of Talbot," and a number of Beur militants, including Rachid Azzoug, Kaïssa Titous, and Mehdi Lallaoui, joined the striking workers inside the factory. Whereas the march had been heralded by the ruling Socialist Party, the Talbot strikes were dismissed as "not part of the French reality," and the Beur strikers were decried by their former governmental supporters, including then minister of social affairs Georgina

Dufoix (once considered the "fairy godmother of the Beur Movement"), as "traitors" (Boubeker and Abdallah 1993: 45–46).

As such, actions like the Talbot strikes militated against the "purchase" of the Beur Movement by the socialist government and the imposed models of Beur hybridity that postulated an inherent rupture between Algerian parent and Beur child. Resisting such a rupture, Beur activists in the mid-1980s sought to resurrect memories of their parents' and grandparents' nationalist struggles and labor activism in France. For instance, the 1983 march began its Parisian leg at the Canal Saint-Martin, the site of the 17 October 1961 massacre of Algerian demonstrators by Parisian police, thus commemorating those members of the first generation who died as martyrs. This trajectory of Beur politics, from rupture to reconciliation, constitutes not only a condition of possibility for the production of a Beur generational subjectivity, but also a strategy of intergenerational solidarity with both transtemporal and transspatial dimensions.

Third Generations, Third Space

The Beur generation thus arose through the particular historical context of political succession and opposition of the early 1980s that produced a set of overlapping group identities defined by tropes of victimization and liminality. In contrast, the putative "third generation" of the 1990s and early twenty-first century—or post-Beur generation—refers to three separate but interrelated groups: the genealogical sons and daughters of the second generation whose assimilation had been anticipated in French integration discourse; the age set of younger brothers and sisters of the Beurs, generally known as the "*banlieue* generation"; and the new wave of emigrant students and activists from Algeria fleeing the civil war that began in 1992. It is in the interaction of all three of these groups—as mediated by changing legal, political, and urban institutional structures—that a transpolitics based around ethnic and religious social movements characteristic of the contemporary Franco-Maghrebi scene has been constituted.

From Beur to Beurgeoisie

By the late 1980s, the Beur Movement, in its discourse of hybridity, was in crisis. The majority of associations formed in the wake of Mitterrand's election had disbanded. Militants have retrospectively blamed the failure of these associations on their institutionalization within structures of governance, on their "purchase" by municipalities, national political parties, and Marxist ideologies (Bouamama et al. 1994: 81, 136–137). In particular, anti-racist groups like SOS-Racisme that had gained the socialist government's favor in promulgating civic integration have since been accused by the younger generation of being the "*harkis* of immigration," of selling out the *banlieue* youth for their personal political advancement (Jazouli 1992: 108–109). Meanwhile, dissenters from within the Beur generation have accused successful Beur activists of constituting a cultural and economic "Beurgeoisie," of utilizing the memory of their participation in the Beur Movement to justify their present position as "the only legitimate public interlocutors" between the French state and North African immigrants (Boubeker and Abdallah 1993: 43; cf. Bouamama et al. 1994: 24, 45; Wihtol de Wenden 1990). The Franco-Algerian graphic novelist Farid Boudjellal, who always maintained a certain distance from the mainstream Beur Movement, published a 1996 serial, *Le Beurgeois,* in which he caricatured the *intégration de pognon* ("big-bucks integration") of such Beurs who sought to be "more French than the French."

One particular target of Boudjellal's satire, Nacer Kettane, the former president of Radio Beur and organizer of the 1985 March for Civic Rights, stands as a perfect example of a Beur activist-turned-businessman. Throughout the 1980s, Radio Beur served as the primary venue for the diffusion of North African musical production in France, launching the careers of a number of Beur musical artists and serving as an umbrella organization for more specific community-based radio programs. The station also functioned as a center for the organization of political action, particularly during the Talbot strikes and the various Beur marches and demonstrations from 1983 to 1985. Moreover, the station was a major node in the diffusion of information back and forth across the Mediterranean, particularly during the April 1980 and October 1988 protests in Algeria when, in the face of a dearth of reliable coverage from the mainstream media, the station interrupted its normal programming to provide a news and debate forum for those directly and indirectly affected (Radio Beur 1988). As such, the station was a central institution in the larger Beur Movement.

When Radio Beur lost its operating license in 1992, Kettane reconstituted the association as a professional radio station—financed by corporate advertising instead of dependent on government funding—under the name Beur FM. By March 1996, Kettane had expanded the Paris-based operation to a national level, garnering frequencies in the major urban centers of France and earning the right to broadcast twenty-four hours a day instead of having to allocate six key hours per day of its frequency to other community-based stations. With this move, Beur FM appropriated many of the smaller North African stations, including Radio Berbère and Radio Berbère-Tiddukla, who now were forced to rent air time from it. Kettane publicly stated that this development would serve as a springboard for future expansion—that "from now on we will play in the big leagues (*le grand jeu*)"—including the purchase of four more frequencies over the course of the year and an additional five over the next three years, the launching of a daily newspaper, and

BEUR FM EN FRANCE

PARIS ILE DE FRANCE	106.7 FM
GRENOBLE	97.8 FM
ST ETIENNE	94.3 FM
NIMES-ALES	104.6 FM
TOULOUSE	96.9 FM
AIX-MARSEILLE-ETANG DE BERRE	92.6 FM

BEUR FM EN EUROPE
ET AU MAGHREB

SUR SATELLITE FRANCE TELECOM 2B
CANAL FRANCE 2
SOUS - PORTEUSE 6.85 MHZ

☎ 08 36 68 10 67

Beur FM flyer distributed in March 1996 on the
fifteenth anniversary of the station's founding,
advertising the expansion of its service.

the increase in business turnover from 3.2 million francs in 1995 to 10 million by the year 2000 (Cauhapé 1996: 28).

Kettane has nonetheless tried to maintain his image as an engaged Beur activist. Beur FM has retained its legal status as a "community radio station," exonerating it from the 1994 amendment to the Carignon audiovisual law that required French radio stations to devote 40 percent of their musical program to Francophone productions. While no longer directly organizing political actions, Beur FM has remained one of the primary lines of communication still open between Algerians in France and the residents of war-torn Algeria, diffusing its programs throughout North Africa via the France Telecom 2B satellite. In this manner, Kettane, albeit primarily concerned with expanding the business end of Beur FM, still hoped to forge an "image that would not be a ghetto [*sic*], but rather reflects *our generation*" (Cauhapé 1996: 28, emphasis mine).

As many have rightly pointed out, Kettane's generation no longer reflected the reality of France's *cités* by the mid-1990s (cf. Bouamama et al. 1994; Dubet and Lapeyronnie 1992; Jazouli 1992). For, as Beur activists strayed further and further from the housing projects in which they were born and moved to professional careers in business and academics, the *cités* themselves transformed in their absence. While the physical and economic degradation of the housing projects—including the increase in drug abuse and gang violence—continued apace, very few community development associations arose to take the place of those established during the Beur Movement (Bouamama et al. 1994: 74). Lakhdar and Yasmina Kherfi, two of the founders of the association Vivons Ensemble of the Val-Fourré, expressed dismay that no group continued their renovation and social action projects after their association, at the behest of the municipality, closed its doors in 1987. After four years working on social development projects in New Caledonia, the two returned to find the *cité* completely changed, in particular the attitude of the younger residents. According to Yasmina, "We never had these problems of lack of respect. There was a much stronger solidarity. . . . I find myself completely overtaken by the attitude of the youth." Lakhdar continued, "It's true what Yasmina says, the times have changed. It's like a slap in the face when I see the youth today; I can't manage to understand them" (Boubeker and Abdallah 1993: 60–61).

Former Beur activists like Yasmina and Lakhdar perceive a patent cultural gap between themselves and the younger generation in the *cités*. According to Rachid Taha, while the Beurs were still intimately tied to their parents' history and culture, "Our fifteen- and sixteen-year-old brothers have no points of reference. They only have a French society that in their minds stands for unemployment and prison" (Boubeker and Abdallah 1993: 48; cf. Jazouli 1992: 169). Suffering from historical and cultural "amnesia" (Aïchoune 1991: 21), the *cité* youth of the 1990s seemed bound to repeat the mistakes of their older brothers, promoting an unending "cyclical history" of generations in the *banlieues* (Boubeker and Abdallah 1993: 56). Given these conditions and the general differences in cultural belonging, former Beur activists have generally felt powerless in confronting contemporary social problems and have only further retreated into their professional careers.

Inversely, the *cité* youth of the mid-1990s reproached the Beur Movement's professionalization as causing the generational rupture. According to former Beur organizer Bouziane Delgrange, "The generation which is twenty years old today no longer comes together in movements such as those we developed. . . . They reproach certain among us for having adhered to political parties." Likewise, Ahmed Ghayet believes that "the younger ones, the famous '*banlieue* youth' judge us severely. They call us the 'beurgeoisie'" (cited in Bouamama et al. 1994: 181, 45). When talking with younger Franco-Maghrebis during my field research, I was often told that if I was interested in the Beur Movement, they could introduce me to their older brothers and sisters. Malika, a young woman born in France to parents born in Algeria, once corrected me when I referred to her as a Beurette: "My older brother, now he's a real Beur. He marched with SOS-Racisme and everything. Today he's an engineer." Rather, she and her other North African friends in the *cité* in Aubervilliers where she lived referred to themselves as "Rabeus," syllabically inverting "Beurs" just as their older brothers and sisters had done for their parents' ethnonym, "Arabes."

In addition, this generational rupture was marked by increased political apathy and disenchantment with collective organization as an effective means of social struggle. Younger Rabeus cited the inability of the Beur Movement to prevent ongoing anti-immigrant policies and policing measures as proof that, in the end, "for us, politics is shit" (Aïchoune 1991: 20). Even the Beur Movement's civic discourse of cultural difference and equality—as embodied in the SOS-Racisme slogan of a "right to difference"—found itself co-opted by the Front National that began in the late 1980s to employ essentialized notions of cultural difference to justify a xenophobic politics of cultural separation and exclusion (Balibar and Wallerstein 1991; Gallissot 1985; Gilroy 1990).[12] In response to this new, differentialist racism, SOS-Racisme dropped its earlier motto and declared that immigrants, above all, had a "right to resemblance" (Désir 1987). Faced with this assimilationist double-talk, young *cité* residents in the 1990s have taken two routes in the constitution of their political subjectivity. On the one hand, many have organized themselves informally along spatial lines, forming multiracial crews (*bandes*) identified with particular housing projects rather than forms of cultural identity. On the other hand, many have been attracted to transnational ethnic or religious social movements based in Berberist or Islamist politics that more often than not rejected the premises of integration shared by the Beur Movement and the French state.

The Banlieue *Generation as Threat*

The repeated, violent confrontations between *cité* youth and the police throughout the 1990s must be understood in terms of these two forms of agentive subjectivity taken on by Rabeus. As in the 1981 rodeos, the confrontations largely involved well-delineated groups responding to the killing of one of their "brothers" by representatives of the state. For instance, clashes between youth and riot police (CRS) occurred in November 1990 in the Mas-du-Taureau *cité* of the Lyonnais suburb of Vaulx-en-Velin after the death of twenty-one-year-old resident Thomas Claudio in a motorcycle chase with police; in March 1991 in Sartrouville (Paris) after the assassination of eighteen-year-old Djamel Chettouh by a Euromarché supermarket security guard; and in May 1991 in Val-Fourré after the death of eighteen-year-old Aïssa Ihich, who asphyxiated after being denied his asthma medicine while in police custody. As after the 1981 riots, the government's response to the contestation involved direct intervention into the everyday social life of the *cités* in the form of increased police presence, youth programs, and Marshall Plan–style economic measures.

Through such responses, the French state largely reinforced an image, popularized through the media and in the speeches of conservative political candidates, of a *banlieue* youth increasingly "outside the law." Many sociologists in France, sometimes themselves former Beur activists, described the *banlieue* youth as participating in a "culture of riot" (*culture de l'émeute*) characterized by a generalized historical amnesia and "hate" (*haine*) directed indiscriminately at all symbols of the French state (Aïchoune 1991: 13). If the Beurs, as a hybrid political subjectivity, represented the utopian future of a "plural France" touted by socialist leaders (Boubeker and Abdallah 1993: 43), the youth of the 1990s represented its dystopian mirror image of dangerous "social anomie." In this representation of the *cités,* "community" was viewed as having devolved into "ethnic and territorial gangs" involved in "endemic daily violence" that at best organized itself into a "riot" against the police (Jazouli 1992: 141–142).

The ostensible social chaos of the *cité* youth (dis)organization became a further source of anxiety in that it was seen to leave open a vacuum for the rise of "communitarian" organizations, particularly Islamic "fundamentalist" groups. With the worsening of the Algerian civil war and its crossing of the Mediterranean in the form of political organization and violence, general fears of a *banlieue* "generation-in-revolt" have been translated into particular concerns of North African *cité* youth succumbing to the "temptation of *jihad*" (cf. Pujadas and Salam 1995). The life histories of two individuals in particular symbolized this fear: first, the conversion of Toumi Djaidja, organizer and icon of the 1983 *Marche des Beurs,* to an integralist form of Islam while serving a brief prison sentence; second, the participation of Khaled Kelkal in the 1995 bombings attributed to the Algerian GIA. For French government officials and media pundits, these two trajectories signified the birth of a third generation of immigrants in the 1990s, one founded in the transnational cross-linkages between youth indigenous to the French *banlieues* and those Islamist and Berberist militants who had fled the Algerian civil war to come live in France.

Berber Associationalism and the Banlieue *Youth*

In line with the general change in the generational politics of 1990s immigrant France, the few Beur associations that have maintained their prominence made the transition from the celebration of cultural hybridity to the enactment of transnational engagement. While an association like ANGI continued to survive as a gallery for immigrant artists and a forum for intellectual debate, it had little general influence, even on the neighboring *cités* in Aubervilliers and La Courneuve. The case is very different for the Berber Culture Association (ACB). Founded initially in 1979 by a group of men in their twenties of Kabyle parents, the ACB consisted of a set of ateliers in the local youth center of the Ménilmontant neighborhood in northeastern Paris. Designed to respond to the immediate interests of the large Kabyle populations in the area—providing day care, after-school tutoring, and legal services—the ACB forged close ties with other key Beur associations like ANGI and Radio Beur. However, while founded by Beurs and featuring prominently in the 1983 Pompidou Center exhibit, the ACB never particularly targeted one generation over the next. The president and cofounder of the ACB, Chérif Ben Bouriche—who generally went by Biben and, when I talked with him in October 1996, insisted that I refer to him as such since "everyone knows what I have to say"—portrayed himself as being from "the fourth generation." "My great-grandfather, grandfather, and father all came to France to work at various times. While I was close with people like Saleiha Amara and Nacer Kettane, I refused to lose myself in a Beur Movement I found empty of meaning."

Under Biben's leadership, the ACB strove to reconcile its local community actions with its active support for the nascent Berber Cultural Movement (MCB) in Algeria. On 10 March 1980, the Algerian government banned a lecture by the Kabyle linguist and author Mouloud Mammeri on "Ancient Berber Poetry" to be given at the University of Tizi-Ouzou. This set off a wave of student and worker demonstrations that spread throughout Kabylia, culminating in a 20–24 April general strike and violent confrontations between police and protesters. In these protests—what Berber activists call the "Berber Spring" (*Printemps Berbère* or *Tafsut*), referencing the Prague events of 1968—demonstrators demanded that Berber cultural education be included in the national program established by newly elected Algerian president Chadli Benjedid. The ACB served as a primary center for information and protest. In addition to providing a space for discussion and the exchange of news for Kabyles living in Paris, the ACB helped organize a series of protests in front of the Algerian embassy in Paris calling for the end of police violence, the release of students arrested, and the official recognition of Berber linguistic and cultural rights in Algeria.

In the years that followed, the ACB became the center of the Berber revival in France, following in the footsteps and including many of the original members of the Berber Academy and Berber Study Group of the 1960s and 1970s. In the 1990s, the ACB served as a meeting place for Kabyle scholars, journalists, authors, artists, musicians, and political activists who had fled political persecution and civil war violence in Algeria. Moreover, it served as a staging ground for political action in Algeria, becoming the de facto seat of Said Sadi's Kabylia-based Rally for Culture and Democracy (RCD)

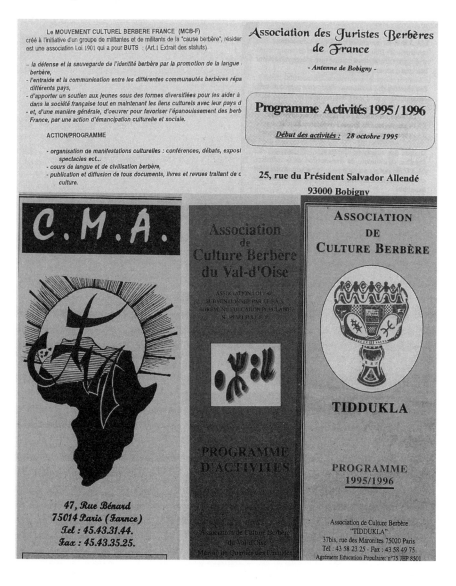

Berber cultural association leaflets.

Public meeting of the FACAF in support of the boycott of the Algerian constitutional referendum, Bourse de Travail, Paris, 9 November 1996. Sign above rostrum declares "Algeria = Tamazight." Under the banner is the Algerian flag. Photograph by author.

political party in France. The ACB helped campaign for the RCD during the November 1995 Algerian presidential elections, hosted Sadi during a May 1996 visit to France, and publicly supported the RCD-led boycott of the November 1996 constitutional referendum. In this way, the ACB maintained its political relevance long after the discrediting of the Beur Movement largely through its explicit transpolitical links with Algeria.

Biben understood the ACB's direct involvement in the Algerian political scene as a continuation of its general engagement in France and particular focus on the everyday needs of young Rabeus in the *cités*. Besides maintaining its community development activities in Ménilmontant, the ACB founded branch associations in the lower-class *banlieues* of Saint-Denis, Créteil, Mantes-la-Jolie, and the Val d'Oise, where a large number of Kabyle families lived. It likewise developed a larger network of Berber associations throughout metropolitan France, the Federation of Amazigh Cultural Associations in France (FACAF), bringing together Franco-Kabyle activists in regular meetings and jointly run public activities. These activities included weekly talks by Berber scholars and artists, political debates, and celebrations of yearly Amazigh festivities. While the weekly talks held in the basement of the association's premises drew a regular crowd of around fifty association members and guests, the larger political events and festivities—including the celebration of Tafsut or the Berber New Year—were held in rented banquet rooms and easily attracted as many as 500 attendees.

These events, even when explicitly celebrations, had a distinctly pedagogical dimension. Commemorations of Tafsut, for example, always involved participants presenting their reminiscences and personal chronologies of the events. The banquet halls contained displays devoted to the documentary record of the demonstrations, as well as memorials to those injured during the events or killed in the various conflicts between Kabyles, Islamists, and government forces that marked the 1990s. The 1995 commemoration was prefaced with a slide show of a recent trip to Kabylia, thus contrasting the ongoing civil war violence with a nostalgic portrayal of village life dutifully recounted for the younger generation in attendance that by and large were born and raised in France. This pedagogical initiative was reinforced through the ACB's publishing of a monthly newsletter and a semi-annual magazine, as well as through its weekly radio program on Beur FM broadcast in both French and Tamazight in order to reach a larger public. In addition to updates on the civil war and Berber activism in Algeria, these media also provided readers with short essays on Berber history, and vocabulary and grammar lessons in Tamazight.

The diffusion of Tamazight is one of the main concerns of the ACB and Berber activism in France more broadly. This effort, while begun by Kabyle intellectuals in France during the 1960s, did not achieve great support from Kabyle emigrants until very recently. According to Biben, Kabyles were originally disinclined to educate their children in Tamazight, as they foresaw a proximate return to Algeria. "When we started offering classes in 1979, we were met with a total refusal of parents to enroll their children. They preferred that their children learn Arabic, what they saw as the national language of Algeria." Noura, a Franco-Kabyle born in the northern suburbs of Paris and member of a FACAF-affiliated association, similarly told me how her father forced her to attend a Qur'anic school as a young girl but "didn't want me to have anything to do with the Berber associations. I wanted to learn Berber, but he preferred I learn classical Arabic." The younger generation, like Noura, saw learning Tamazight as a means to gain an understanding of the culture of the family they visited in Kabylia once a year. Their persistence paid off, and the parents soon realized that attending association functions did not impede their schoolwork or eventual "integration" into France. "My dad is really proud of me now. He even attends our events at the association," Noura continued. Indeed, according to Biben, parents are enrolling their children in Tamazight classes in greater and greater numbers. "Parents push their children to attend. Even children of mixed French and Kabyle marriages are coming to class." Such education received a push from the French state, as Tamazight now functions as the second-most popular "optional language" section of the national high school examination.

The Tamazight classes I attended at the ACB and elsewhere seemed to confirm the assessments of Noura and Biben. Younger children were separated from high schoolers and adults in separate classrooms. The younger children's classes were an extension of the public education they were receiving in state schools, with classes of twenty children and above directed primarily by older Kabyle women, taking place in the late afternoon and on weekends, and thus serving as a de facto day care for working parents. Little distinction was made between language learning, arts and crafts, and basic historical-cultural education; entire classes were often devoted to teaching a Kabyle song or to painting a picture based on a story read in class. By contrast, the smaller preparation classes for the baccalaureate, taught principally by graduate students in linguistics, focused almost entirely on syntax and reading comprehension in Tamazight. Somewhere between the two were the most popular set of classes for older children and adults, themselves primarily spouses or older children of Kabyle emigrants like Sonya and Fethi, who wished to learn more about Kabyle culture and politics more generally. While clearly devoted to acquisition of Kabyle vocabulary and grammar, the expatriate professors were clearly more than happy to respond to the students' desire for a broader cultural-political education. In particular, they employed protest songs by Kabyle activist-musicians like Idir and Djamel Allam to teach new words and phrases of contemporary relevance. The textbooks and written materials provided were likewise in the contexts of village settings or Algerian political events of recent memory. In almost every case, discussions in the classroom segued to larger political conversations between curious students and the professors over coffee or a meal at one of the many Kabyle cafés and restaurants around the ACB in Ménilmontant.

Moreover, the concern with the transmission of Berber culture and language to young Franco-Algerians contributed directly to an overt battle between Islam and "Berberity" (*berbérité*) being waged by cultural associations for the hearts and minds of the *banlieue* generation. In a conference, "Berberity in France," organized by the ACB for the April 1996 commemoration of Tafsut at the Sorbonne, participants sought to respond to the question: "Are there any referents other than Islam for the current generation of Algerians in France?" Under the painted images of exemplars of French scholarship, fifteen university scholars and association representatives presented a set of reports on the state of Berber culture in France to a like-minded audience of more than 200, primarily twenty-something Franco-Maghrebis. Specifically responding to what moderator Hend Sadi referred to as the "problems of the *banlieues*," the presenters testified that Berberity was not only the cultural "soul" of these young Franco-Algerians, but that it was, moreover, open to and consonant with "modernity." In the process, they affirmed their attachment to republican principles of *laïcité* as a bulwark against radical Islam and as a mechanism through which, in the words of the association representative from ACB–Mantes-la-Jolie, "our children can be integrated into French society while maintaining our [cultural] distinctions." Rather than an "assimilation," this imagined integration necessarily involved the retention of a Kabyle historical and cultural consciousness, or, as several presenters claimed, the *banlieues* would fall into a "disorder" that played into the hands of the Islamists.

This sense of an extension of the Algerian civil war to France in terms of a struggle with the Islamists for the future of the *cités* was likewise represented in the larger ACB discourses of the mid-1990s. For instance, in an open letter to candidates in the 1995 French presidential elections, the ACB demanded that the French school system be rid of all Islamist "manipulation" and that only Berberity—referenced as the "eternal Jugurtha" of cultural continuity in struggle—could serve as an effective barrier. In this respect, the generation of the 1990s, the *banlieue* youth, were constituted and valued as a scarce resource within a transnational cultural political economy in which Berberist and Islamist movements were competing. Sharing the government's fear that, in the social marginalization of the *banlieues,* the youth would form a dangerous class of potential Muslim fundamentalists, Berber associations like the ACB positioned themselves as the protectors of the French republic in its secular and implicitly multicultural sense.

Transpolitical Generations

The overt ideological concern with the *banlieue* generation directly affected the interactions between recently emigrated Kabyle activists and the young Franco-Algerians in question. After 1992, a veritable exodus of Kabyle militants to France occurred in response to the heightened violence of the civil war. These included primarily graduate students in their late twenties and early thirties who, like Mounir, were born in Algeria after independence and educated before the FLN regime had fully instituted its Arabization measures. Avowedly more Francophone than Arabophone, these students came of political age in the period between the Berber Spring of 1980 and the later anti-FLN demonstrations of October 1988, during a prolonged breakdown in Algerian national consciousness. Kamel Rarrbo (1995) has demonstrated how the Algerian state, through institutions like the UNJA and the adoption of French models of adolescence, attempted to tailor the Algerian youth into the new bearers of the revolutionary torch. However, in failing to provide either a viable socioeconomic structure or a forum for the freedom of cultural, sexual, and political expression, this strategy produced instead an increasing mass of young, disenfranchised urban men with few professional prospects and few sentiments of personal integration into the national project. Popularly known as *hitistes* ("wall-hangers"), these unemployed twenty-something men had become a distinct source of anxiety for the Chadli Benjedid government of the late 1980s. In calling the army into the streets to repress the October 1988 demonstrations, Chadli further contributed to the elaboration of a generational rupture that opposed Algeria's younger populations to those whom they decried as the "apparatchiks" of the bureaucratic state.

In this sense, there occurred a parallel production of generational identities across the semi-fluid border of the Mediterranean. Generated by intertwined national projects of socialism, decolonization, and integration, the development of parallel, urban "discouraged generations" (to borrow Mounir's apt phrase) in both Algeria and France remained offset only by a short temporal lag. Nonetheless, while bearing a structural similarity to their French counterparts, the Kabyle expatriate students were only marginally able to achieve a sense of solidarity with the *banlieusards* they encountered. Finding a logical home in Berber cultural associations like the ACB, they entered into direct relation with the *banlieue* generation principally as teachers of Tamazight. This pedagogical role placed them in a position as surrogate parents, with the goal of assuring the transmission of a cultural heritage normally accomplished by mothers and fathers, but viewed by the associations as having been irreparably interrupted by the generational rupture fostered during the Beur Movement.

Situated on opposite sides of the pedagogical relationship, expatriate teachers and post-Beur students experienced a certain degree of mutual incomprehension. For many Franco-Algerian students with whom I spoke, the Kabyle expatriates appeared too caught up in the political innuendoes of the Algerian front. They saw the recent emigrants' militancy as exacerbating divisions between the rival Kabyle political parties of the Socialist Forces Front (FFS) and the RCD that had fragmented the MCB and Berber cultural activism more generally. Indeed, independent Berber cultural associations founded over the last several years by Franco-Algerians, including the Parisian suburban groups Association of Berber Students, the Association of Berber Lawyers, and MCB-France, have sought to transcend these rivalries. Fatiha, the president of one such organization that she founded in Nanterre in 1994, described how her association explicitly sought to "break down the elites and political divisions" and be more relevant to its members born uniformly in France. While she had been at various times close to the FFS and then the RCD, in the end she found their engagement too centered on Algeria and not enough on the everyday realities of *banlieue* terrain. Marginalized by the larger RCD- and FFS-affiliated associations who, in Fatiha's words, "have tried to undermine us from the beginning," her association has taken a leadership role in the Paris-based transnational World Berber Congress (CMA) as an independent charter member. Moreover, it has balanced this participation with continued community development activities in Nanterre, where most of its members live and work. Indeed, it shares its premises with several other community organizations and often rents its space to local youth groups regardless of their origins or politics.

If Franco-Maghrebis find their needs underrepresented by the new generation of expatriated Algerian activists, recent Kabyle emigrants have experienced a similar emotive and political distance from the *banlieue* generation. In the first place, while largely supportive of French principles of *laïcité,* they foresee their future within a secular, multicultural Algeria they hope to help forge. Like the first generation of Kabyle emigrants, they view their residence in France as an "exile," and, while not isolating themselves from larger French society, they devote their primary efforts to accumulating monies for the primary purpose of assuring a comfortable life for themselves and their families upon their return. For instance, Mounir, the Kabyle activist from Argenteuil, had by the time I met him in 1996 already sent back enough money to purchase a small store in his native village and a used bus that he planned on operating as a taxi service between Bejaïa and neighboring villages upon his return. Beyond the economic calculus, he viewed his militant activities in France as a political rite of passage that would allow him to advance through the ranks of the RCD, if not the future Algerian state, once a viable democracy had been established. In this sense, he felt socially distant from the *banlieue* generation in France—the *hitistes,* as he called them—whom he blamed for the general insecurity he experienced living in his Argenteuil *cité.* Nonetheless, he cultivated a pedagogical spirit and, in founding a local Berber cultural association, he believed he could make a difference in the daily life of the housing project. While the lack of local support from both residents and the municipality largely "discouraged" him, he developed close ties to his Franco-Kabyle students, and even married one of them, Karima. He hoped eventually to sell his newly purchased suburban townhouse and bring his family back with him to Kabylia once the civil war ended.

As with Mounir and Karima, the interactions of French and Algerian generations across the transnational network could thus transcend the structural and political conflicts. This intergenerational solidarity was reinforced by Kabyle parents who were increasingly drawn into Berber activism through their children's associational engagement. Following their children's lead, they began in the mid-1990s to attend the conferences, performances, and festivities sponsored by the associations and animated by their sons and daughters. The Berber language and history classes I attended often included several older students from the "first generation" seeking to learn the standard written version of a language and history they knew only orally. Moreover, those who attended the festivities and conferences hosted by the associations were generally ebullient, praising their children's actions. One older man attending a conference sponsored by MCB-France in homage to the late Mouloud Mammeri emphasized to me, "What the children (*aqcicen*) are doing is wonderful! People need to know these things. I myself learned so much." As the third generation, in their embrace of their parents' culture as their own, broke down the generational rift promulgated during the Beur Movement of the early 1980s, they reversed generational hierarchies as well, transmitting objectified cultural knowledge back to their parents.

The Fin de Siècle

In this way, the construction of a third-generation political subjectivity among Algerians in France calls into question French state efforts to instrumentalize generational identities as part of its larger integration projects. The fin de siècle, neo-Spenglerian angst of government officials and public intellectuals over the future of the French nation-state was directed at immigrant generations deemed precariously susceptible to sectarian identities imported from across the Mediterranean. In an overt attempt to circumvent this feared eventuality, the socialist government in the early 1980s actively underwrote the production of a new ethnicity—the Beur generation—that, in its cultural hybridity, would become privileged mediators between their parents' generation and a future, plural France.

These efforts failed not simply due to changing political realities—particularly the rise of the Front National in France and political Islam in Algeria—but also because the integration projects, based largely in folklore and sports, were largely out of step with the postindustrial socioeconomic realities of the *banlieues,* with the progressive militarization of the *cités,* and with the general feeling among younger Franco-Maghrebis that their Beur older brothers and sisters had been "purchased" by the state. Stepping into the vacuum left by failed Beur activism, a transnational Berber social movement has sunk roots simultaneously in urban Algeria and suburban France and has constituted new bases for interpersonal solidarity and belonging across time and space. In the process, and in spite of a number of discontinuities, a new generation of political actors has been generated in the transnational space that links a new, multiracial France to a new, post-FLN Algeria.

6 /

Beur Writing and Historical Consciousness

Farid Boudjellal, a graphic novelist who has published more than
fifteen albums in France since 1978, was born in 1953 in Toulon to
Algerian-born parents.[1] His paternal grandmother fled from Armenia
to Algeria during the 1905 genocide in which the rest of her family
perished. While Boudjellal's father was raised as a Christian, he
married a Muslim woman before migrating to southern France.
Boudjellal thus grew up in a mixed religious household in the midst
of the Algerian war of national liberation. Having suffered from
polio as a young child, he was left with a permanent limp that made
him a particular object of derision in that time of already virulent
anti-Algerian attitudes. "I lived through racism. It became a culture
for me," he says. In an effort to escape the Toulon context of xenophobia, he moved to Paris in the early 1980s, where he married a
French woman of Italian heritage and settled in the mixed immigrant
quarter of Belleville where I met him in a café in October 1996.

Boudjellal's works are explicitly autobiographical. Nourredine, his
principal protagonist across several albums, is a young Franco-
Algerian from Toulon. Another character, Mahmoud, suffers like
Boudjellal from a limp resulting from polio. It seems clear that the
context of religious and cultural diversity and racist violence in which
Boudjellal grew up and in which he continues to live have been
explicitly incorporated into his work. Indeed much of the *espoir* in
his other albums derives from the various plays on cultural diversity
through the scenes and the characters. His first work, *Les soirées
d'Abdullah* ("Abdullah's Evenings"), followed the life of an Algerian

immigrant worker who became the victim of a vicious *ratonnade* attack. Finding the product too depressing, he turned to less violent subjects in his next work, *L'Oud,* the first volume of a five-part series that followed the lives of various members of the multigenerational Slimani family. Although the series includes suffering characters— including a *fugueuse* and another daughter who commits suicide after getting pregnant with her French boyfriend—Boudjellal generally saw the albums as having "more hope." Mixed marriages, like that of Boudjellal and his parents, figure prominently in his work, both in the *Oud* series and in his later album, *Jambon-Beur* ("Ham and Beur"), in which nearly every character has parents from different cultural backgrounds. Similarly, several of his albums are explicitly set in the ethnically and religiously diverse Belleville neighborhood in which Boudjellal lives; even a receipt from the café where we met found its way into *Jambon-Beur.* Belleville is particularly apt as a setting for the *Juif-Arabe* ("Jews and Arabs") series in which an orthodox Jewish father and his conservative Muslim counterpart— whose children are scandalously dating—find themselves, in spite of their overt political differences, in a similar predicament as minorities in France. Although both characters are lampooned through the ironic use of racial clichés and stereotypes, Boudjellal received enormous support from the entire Belleville community, with a number of the area's Jewish residents congratulating him on his work.

The autobiographical elements of Boudjellal's oeuvre clearly ally him with the Beur Movement of the 1980s. However, he has remained generally skeptical of the cultural and generational self-consciousness that marks many of his peers' cultural productions and activism as being overly "full of itself." "It was necessary for the period, but today we have to go beyond it." The influences he cites indeed go "well beyond" the Beur scene: American comic strips like *Steve Canyon* and *Peanuts* and the Italian paperbacks on the American Revolution he read as a child. His reading public is likewise very large and diverse, and, according to Boudjellal, Algerians in France have only just discovered his albums. Moreover, in his work since the *Oud* series, he has explicitly reached out beyond specifically Beur concerns to the older and younger generations of immigrants in France. *Jambon-Beur* begins with a brief history of the Algerian war of national liberation as seen from France, and the various French and Algerian characters' conflicting memories of the war create the narrative tension in the album. The work—what Boudjellal described to me as an "album of reconciliation"—fulfilled a feeling that Boudjellal had since 1988 that he "had to do something on Algeria, since my history is the history of the war in Algeria." When I met him in 1996 he had just begun a collaborative project with the author and educator Soraya Nini to create a series of manuals that he hoped would be used in the school system of the *cités* to teach children how to negotiate the multiracial setting in which they live. In this respect,

> Boudjellal sees himself more as a general cultural commentator than a Beur activist: "I'm an artist. What interests me is the diversity around us."

Transformations in Franco-Algerian political subjectivity have been reflected not only in public social activism—including anti-racist demonstrations, the founding of neighborhood associations, and violent confrontations with police forces—but also in the production of literary fantasies and genres that detail possible futures in and out of France. Since 1983, more than seventy semi-autobiographical novels have been written by Franco-Algerian authors.[2] Through a genre known in France as the "Beur novel" (*roman Beur*)—a term that masks a high degree of variation from work to work—writers like Boudjellal have variously and differently avowed their place within French society and in the debates over the multicultural character of the New France. In writing against monocultural representations of the French nation, they have transformed culture into an explicit object of struggle. Their works thus function as situated interventions within a politically charged landscape that is both representative and productive of larger Algerian immigrant social formations in France. In this way, regardless of the quantitative significance or reception of the novels produced, writing has proved to be a centrally important instrument through which Algerians growing up in France construct social and political community and establish for themselves a very real degree of agency in the French public arena.

As cultural products and constitutive elements of a larger sociopolitical formation, Beur texts can be read as "national allegories" (Jameson 1986; cf. Khatibi 1968: 14), works that overtly narrate and represent the public life of the new French nation through the private lives of individual characters. Franco-Algerian narratives draw heavily on the authors' own life histories and blur the genres of novel and autobiography. Intimately tied to the specific social and political situation of the *cités* in the early 1980s, Beur writing represents a foundational social practice in the elaboration of a particular Beur political generation.

In the first place, the writers' emergence as self-proclaimed subjects of politics was directly connected to their access to and estrangement from French public education. While the education system was historically a primary site for the national reproduction of social class and the marginalization of immigrant youth (Aïssou 1987; Boulot and Boyzon-Fradet 1986; Bourdieu and Passeron 1990), it also provided for the formation of a Beur elite whose educational capital opened up avenues of mobility previously unavailable to their migrant fathers, whose social lives were largely determined by industrial labor and continued participation in Algerian village structures.

Beginning in the early 1980s, the French state held up such successful Beur men and women—and particularly writers like Azouz Begag and Leila Sebbar—as privileged cultural mediators, if not spokespeople, for the North African immigrant community as a whole, roles that Beur writers variously accepted and resisted.

Secondly, the entry of Beur authors onto the literary scene in the early 1980s had a distinct political dimension as part of the larger Beur Movement. In addition to opening up avenues for cultural expression in the form of theatrical, musical, and artistic groups, Mitterrand's 1981 repeal of the ban on immigrant associations indirectly provided the institutional and financial backing for aspiring second-generation authors. Supported by the success of media ventures such as Radio Beur and the *Sans Frontières* newspaper and the new public funds now available to him, Hocine Touatbi succeeded in having the first novel written by a Beur author published in that very year. However, it was the 1983 publication, its instant success (25,000 copies sold in the first two years), and subsequent filming of Mehdi Charef's *Le thé au harem d'Archi Ahmed* ("Tea in the Harem of Archi Ahmed") (1983a) that gave future authors the inspiration they needed. When I met Azouz Begag, a Franco-Algerian sociologist and author of two novels and several children's stories, in April 1999, he described how his literary career began the day he read *Le thé au harem*. "It was a thunderbolt for me. I had no idea the son of an immigrant like me could write a novel."

In this respect, the birth of Beur literature mirrors the foundation of a particular second-generation political subjectivity. The eruption of the Beurs onto the national political stage with the 1983 *Marche des Beurs* found itself directly chronicled in Kara Bouzid's *La Marche* (1984), a narrative that is as much a political itinerary of a generation as an autobiography of personal transformation. Other authors followed Bouzid's lead in translating their activism into literary endeavors. Farida Belghoul, a Beurette of Moroccan origin and author of the highly acclaimed *Georgette!* (1986), played a leading role in Convergence 84, the follow-up to the 1983 *Marche des Beurs*. Nacer Kettane, president of Radio Beur and author of *Le sourire de Brahim* ("Brahim's Smile") (1985), likewise was one of the organizers of the 1985 March for Civic Rights. Both novels incorporate such public expressions of Beur anti-racist politics into the text in the personal development of the protagonists.

Beur political activism and writing are thus mutually imbricated and informing practices in the lives of the authors and characters. Beur writing, in and of itself, constitutes a political act in that it narratively reappropriates the Beurs' history and social predicament from the scholarly and governmental discourses that had hitherto spoken for North African immigrants. Opposing themselves to a model of monocultural assimilation, the novels' embrace of various forms of Beur multiculturality highlighted a set of alternative social and political futures for a postcolonial France. In the necessarily repetitive and plural narration of the French nation (Bhabha 1990), Beur novels deploy the lives of the author-protagonists to articulate affirmations of sociopolitical belonging that provide a counterpoint to, if they do not explicitly challenge, the official nationalism and dominant narratives of French imperial and postimperial history. Indeed, the contemporary French nation-state, rather than a teleological outcome of an antediluvian past, is the product of the dialogic movement that brings into conversation the conflicting political subjectivities and historical consciousnesses of its various inhabitants in all their local and global dimensions of belonging. Within this schema, Beur narratives of the 1980s pushed the imagined borders of the French nation in their patent embrace of a multidimensionality of identity that incorporated cultural elements from both sides of the Mediterranean and beyond.

Rather than remaining constant, the embodied social practice of Beur writing has contributed internally to a set of complex historical transformations in the identity politics among Algerians and Franco-Algerians in France. The history of Franco-Algerian literature from 1983 through the present points to a fundamental shift in the historical consciousness of second-generation North African immigrant writers in France. In gradually coming to terms with their parents' original immigration and the colonial experience in the Maghreb, these writers, particularly since the advent of the Algerian civil war in 1992, have narratively realigned their identity politics away from a localized discourse on multicultural hybridity and toward various transpolitical expressions of identity more closely tied to the salient ethnic and religious categories of North Africa. Continuously responsive to the transnational political and discursive environment in which they live and write, they have radically redefined their subject position in postcolonial France, avoiding the discursive traps of both the "right to difference" and the "right to resemblance," of both differentialist neo-racism and cosmopolitan "neo-liberalism." In this respect, Franco-Algerian writing, as a sociopolitical practice, operates within a longer history of North African literature while remaining inextricably tied to the specific French political context from which it emerged.[3] It thus constitutes one of the prime loci for the articulation of immigrant political subjectivity in France.

Migration and Mobility

To a great extent, the Beur novels are structured as traditional migration narratives, as tales of cultural discovery (cf. Hargreaves 1991; 1997). In each text the theme of physical mobility plays a significant, if sometimes only underlying, role. Bouzid's La Marche, in chronicling the political pilgrimage of Beur youth from Marseille to Paris, in many ways explicitly retraces the steps made by first-generation laborers who most often debarked at Marseille on the way to their jobs in the urban centers of Paris or Lyon. Even more explicitly, Akli Tadjer's novel *Les ANI du "Tassili"* ("The ANI of 'Tassili'") (1984), takes place entirely on the Tassili, a well-traveled ferry from Algiers to Marseille, with the protagonist Omar negotiating his relationship with a variety of Algerian and French characters as the ferry negotiates its passage across the Mediterranean. The Tassili thus becomes a key metaphor for Franco-Algerian migration and identity as a whole (Hargreaves 1991: 75).

If, in Tadjer's novel, mobility implies a complex and confusing but eventually successful intercultural dialogue, in Ahmed Kalouaz's *Point kilométrique 190* (1986), it is portrayed as a violent process of exclusion. The subject of this latter work was the actual 14 November 1983 murder of Algerian citizen Habib Grimzi, thrown from a Paris-to-Marseille train by three young men on their way to join the Foreign Legion. The novel, recounted in the first person, traces the route of Grimzi's fateful journey kilometer by kilometer. Mixing the internal reflections of the protagonist with descriptions of the train journey, Kalouaz presents the trip as surreally interminable and the destination as ultimately unreachable. While Grimzi's journey to Algeria represents a reversal of the standard history of migration to France, its violent interruption underlines the continued inextricability of Beur identity and the physical mobility that was its condition of possibility.

The specter of mobility haunts Beur writing even when the narratives are temporally situated in a single, contemporary present and geographically localized in the French *cités*. In these cases, migration continues to frame the text, with a previous journey to France at one end of the narrative, and the possibility of future return to the Maghreb at the other. Boudjellal's *L'Oud* (1983), for example, presents the account of the first generation's immigration in the album's prologue. One of the protagonists, Kader Djaouti, forty-seven years old, is portrayed as having come to France in 1961 as a migrant laborer under almost stereotypical circumstances. Enticed by a friend who claimed that "you will find gold," Kader departs his home town of Ouargla in the Algerian Sahara, leaving behind his veiled wife and two young children. This scene of hopeful departure, replete with classical Orientalist imagery, provides stark relief to the following frame that pictures Kader in a crowded, sordid worker dormitory in France, writing a letter home in broken French, claiming that every day he eats meat while at the same time swearing under his breath for having ever listened to his friend's lies (Boudjellal 1983: 4–5). The rest of the story focuses on the quest of Nourredine, a Beur born in Toulon, to locate his *fugueuse* sister for his parents and purchase an *'ud* for his band so it can play a concert. Neither quest proves successful, as the sister remains out of reach in Paris and the *'ud* is destroyed before the concert's first set ends.

This framing portrayal of the first generation's immigration as a betrayal of friendship perpetrated by Algerians themselves has two narrative and ideological effects. First, it sets up the main subject of the album—Nourredine's family and professional predicament in France—as following seamlessly from the first generation's migration. Second, it returns agency to the immigrants themselves, whose decisions and deceptions underwrite their presence in France. The narratives thus reject sociological theories that hold migrants to be the passive pawns of either push-pull forces or a history of colonial uprooting, pauperization, and proletarianization. In doing so, the novels open up an ideological space for Beur agency in the present and underwrite the production of a variety of possible political futures.

And Return?

The frame of migration is completed in many of the Beur novels through explorations of the possibility of a further migration to North Africa or beyond as materialized in the ongoing but always deferred "myth of return" upheld by the first generation, or in the Beur characters' decisions—voluntary or not—either to strike out on their own or to go live with family in Algeria. In the epilogue to *L'Oud*, Boudjellal returns to the theme of mobility that he broached in the prologue. Nourredine catches a train to Paris in search of his runaway sister, seeking, like Boudjellal himself, to start a new life in the capital. In so doing, he also recapitulates his parents' initial migration to France. Meanwhile, in the next frame, Kader ruminates with a friend over his hopes to reunite his family in some way or another. "I swear to you, Abdulah, if I win the horse race, I will bring my wife and children here, or I myself will leave for there" (1983: 43). The conversation between two friends thus mirrors the scene from the prologue of the album that initially sent Kader into migration. The reader, however, senses that Kader's hopes will be permanently deferred.

The deferral of return migration is a salient feature across many Beur coming-of-age stories. In the first place, the deferral is portrayed as a contradictory feature of the immigrant bargain by which, in order to justify their migration, Algerian parents expect their children to attain the success in France unobtainable to them personally. Within this bargain, education becomes an important means of second-generation social mobility. Azouz Begag's first novel, *Le gone du Chaâba* ("The Kid from Chaâba") (1986), is an autobiographical *Bildungsroman* narrated in the first person that recounts the early years of a Beur—named Azouz like the author—growing up in the shantytowns and *cités* of Lyon. It particularly highlights the role of education in the generational contract by juxtaposing the scholarly success of the narrator-protagonist against the failure of his cousin, Hacène. Azouz and his older sister conspire to allay the wrath of Hacène's father by purposefully mistranslating the final class rankings. Their efforts backfire, however, and Hacène is severely beaten. Azouz's continued high placement, on the other hand, instills in his father a great sense of pride and hope for the future, a justification for all his efforts. "His children will not be unskilled laborers like himself. One day, they will wear the white uniform of a doctor or an engineer and will return to Sétif [a region in eastern Algeria]. Rich, they will build a house. And so what if every day he must work ten hours in order to pay the rent, the electricity, and the water" (Begag 1986: 229). However, as for his own return, the father, Bouzid, shows himself to be less than certain. The last lines of the book present his confrontation with his landlord in which the latter asks facetiously when he plans on leaving France for good. "Oh la la . . . It's Allah who will decide that. Perhaps I'll leave next year, perhaps next month" (Begag 1986: 240).

Secondly, Beur narratives portray the perpetual deferral of remigration as the result of the putative generational rupture between the Beurs and their parents. A common theme in many of the novels is a visit by the Beur protagonists to North Africa in the course of a family vacation or a personal project of self-discovery. Nacer Kettane's *Le sourire de Brahim* (1985) is a political coming-of-age story narrated retrospectively by a Beur character, Brahim, as he tries to negotiate the interculturality and racism of his life growing up in France. Having been born in Algeria and brought to France with his family during the anti-colonial war, Brahim's life serves for Kettane as an allegory not only for the Beur generation but for the young Algerian nation as a whole. After losing his optimism (his "smile") in the aftermath of his older brother's death at the hands of Parisian police during the 17 October 1961 massacre of Algerian demonstrators in Paris, Brahim continued to suffer racism and dislocation growing up in a suburban *cité* and training to be a doctor. Seeking a better life, he decided in his early twenties to leave with his *pied noir* friend Patrick for Algeria, where they hoped to volunteer their medical training to help build a new postcolonial, socialist nation.

Their knowledge of Algeria is derived primarily from the fleeting anecdotes recounted by their parents, but they assumed that it must be more welcoming than the "forbidden zone" of the *banlieues*. "They had left the sun, the freshness, the 'swarming' terraces, the mint tea, for the cold and dry *béton* [concrete]. Patrick and Brahim only knew of Algeria what their parents had told them. For the two of them, it was their country forever" (Kettane 1985: 36). Throughout the novel's first half, Kettane, through Brahim, presents Algeria as beautiful, open, pristine, natural, life-bearing— everything which the Parisian housing projects are not.

> France: "The city looked like a forbidden zone; only the barbed wire was missing, but you could almost imagine it. . . . The buildings were dilapidated to no end. The mailboxes smashed up. . . . The basements threw up their contents. . . . The collective garage had been transformed into an enormous piss hole for dogs and cats." (37–38)

Algeria: "The sky and the mountains seemed to be making love. Nature was awakening. The birds' songs wished him welcome. A rare beauty surrounded him." (106)

The opposition between France and Algeria quickly exploded during Brahim's visit to the latter. Where Brahim expected to discover the solutions to his existential conflicts, he instead found, in his terms, ideological intransigence, religious conservatism, and material backwardness. The country he had envisioned as his own, the people which he had imagined as brothers, proved to be unfamiliar and hostile. Interning as a medical assistant at a regional hospital, Brahim was horrified to see doctors move from one patient to the next without washing their hands. Likewise, he found himself similarly disenchanted by the dogmatism of the ruling FLN party's unpopular plans to collectivize agriculture and rapidly industrialize. In Brahim's words, "Socialism was indeed on the move . . . but in reverse" (101).

Moreover, although he was warmly welcomed in his parents' Kabyle village, he was everywhere else treated as an outsider. The customs official at the border entry assumed that Brahim, being an Algerian citizen, spoke Arabic, and expressed disgust when he discovered that Brahim spoke only French and Kabyle. Through experiences like these, Brahim quickly learned that, for the Algerians he met, "we will always be 'emigrants,' and they make sure you always know [that you] are in their home" (91). In the end, disgusted with the lack of solidarity, Brahim returned to France and tried to resolve his feeling of double homelessness through the forging of a particular Beur subjectivity in his participation in grassroots cultural and political organizations.

The rupture between the first and second generations is further expressed in Beur writing through comparisons between the different religious practices and sociosexual norms prioritized by the Beurs and their parents. Across many of the novels, the lack of formal religious orthopraxy on the part of the autobiographical Beur protagonists creates situations of unease or even conflict. These conflicts range from Brahim's comical attempts to procure a midday meal in Algeria during the fast month of Ramadan, to Nourredine's astonishment when he walks in on his father prostrating in prayer for the return of his *fugueuse* sister (Boudjellal 1983: 32), to the more consequential conflicts between Beurettes and their parents over their freedom to marry whom they wish. Djura's autobiography, *Le voile du silence* ("The Veil of Silence") (1990), is a violent narrative of her quest for sexual autonomy and cultural belonging. After being severely beaten by her father for dating a Frenchman, Djura fled to her natal village in Kabylia and put herself under the protection of her grandmother in order to avoid marrying the cousin chosen by her parents. While she was granted a certain degree of latitude due to her French upbringing, Djura soon realized that she had to comply with her grandmother's strictly observed, gendered bodily practices: from covering her hair to avoiding public contact with men in the village. When she strayed from her grandmother's expectations by flirting with a young French architect residing in Algiers, she met the wrath of her elder brother, who threatened to kill her in order to protect his honor. In flight again, Djura remigrated to Paris, secretly married a Breton, and became pregnant with his child. Somehow, her elder brother tracked her down and one evening attacked her and her husband with a knife. While they both survived the incident and Djura went on to have a successful career as a singer-songwriter of popular Kabyle ballads, the author continues to live in fear of future attacks.

In this sense, mobility in Beurette narratives is largely mediated by violence. Djura dedicated her book to "young women brought up in France, but, having reached the age of marriage, are brought back to the homeland on a pretended vacation, for their parents simply want them to marry the family-chosen man, and who can't return because they have confiscated their papers" (Djura 1990). Such a scenario of forced repatriation is the fundamental source of narrative tension in several Beurette autobiographies (cf. Benaïssa and Ponchelet 1990), and family conflicts during visits to Algeria are likewise a prominent theme in other Beurette narratives (cf. Boukhedenna 1987; Houari 1985). In most cases, the narratives conclude with an ambivalent return of the Beurette protagonists to France that contrasts directly with the infinitely deferred remigration of the first generation in the opposite direction. While the open-ended nature of the latter migration serves to tie the first generation to their self-definition of being in perpetual exile, the Beurette protagonists' actual movement back to France paradoxically underlines their relatively stable, albeit problematic, belonging in France.

Fiction as Historical and Political Narrative

The Beurs' reconstruction of their parents' migratory history thus constitutes a central operation in their consolidation of generational identity and sociopolitical subjectivity. As a narrative, the Beur novel rewrites the immigrant past in order to understand the intercultural present and provide room for future Beur agency in France. As such, Beur writing participates in the same ideological space as nationalist histories that narrate the nation's past in order to represent the current state of affairs as a predetermined, teleological outcome (cf. Renan 1990: 11–12). Despite the best efforts of any single nationalist ideologue, nationalism is neither completely predetermined nor univocal, but rather, like the polyphonic novel described by Bakhtin (1981), contains, in every case, a number of contradictions and conflicting elements which allow for a degree of ambivalence and flexibility, and can even open up a space for resistance.

As narrations of immigration and identity, the Beur novels borrow from and compete with a variety of nationalist and counter-nationalist histories circulating within France during the 1980s. On the one hand, racist accounts, proffered by Le Pen's Front National and other xenophobic political parties, presented immigrant repatriation as not only possible, but absolutely necessary. Their historical narrative presented the past as economic immigration, the future as repatriation, and the present as a necessary evil to be endured with as little contact between French and immigrant populations as possible. Anti-racist discourse, on the other hand, rejected the illusion of mass return but maintained a general presentation that denied immigrant agency. Their narrative consisted of a past as economic immigration, a future as integration, and a present as racism to be overcome.

The Beurs writing in the 1980s and into the 1990s rejected outright these two paternalistic and disempowering historical narratives. Rather, they offered two main alternative narratives that implied different visions of a New France, both of which viewed immigrant history as a central component of the imagined nation. In general, the Beurs understood the past as the agentive immigration of the first generation, the future as Beur empowerment, and the present as struggle. However, the specific manner in which they narrated this sequence varied significantly, in each case responding to the particular xenophobic and anti-racist discourses of nationalism present at the time. From 1983 to 1988, Beur narratives underlined intergenerational conflict in order to highlight a particularist Beur political identity. Later works, by contrast, have attempted a more direct integration of the first generation's history into larger political narratives, siting the Beurs' struggle in a transpolitical context that unites France with North Africa.

Vive la "Beur Culture"!

Early Beur writings centered their narratives not on immigration itself, but rather on the experiences of growing up in the *cités* of suburban France. Often, the story of migration is relegated to a framing device in the prologues (cf. Boudjellal 1983) or to a peripheral set of events told merely in passing about which the protagonists are largely ignorant (cf. Begag 1986; Kettane 1985). Charef's *Le thé au harem d'Archi Ahmed* (1983a) narrates the struggles of the teenage Beur Madjid, his French friend Pat, and their multiracial group of friends trying to get by and plan their futures in the fictional *cité des Fleurs* located somewhere in the *banlieues* of Paris. The novel opens with Madjid repairing his moped in the basement of the public housing building in which his family lives. It continues primarily in that narrative present, with only brief retrospective passages that center on Madjid's and Pat's experiences as younger children. The scene of Madjid's emigration to France from eastern Algeria at the age of seven with his mother to live with his construction worker father in a suburban *bidonville* is only related toward the end of the novel (Charef 1983a: 115–119). Indeed, it is

only at that point that Charef presents the protagonists as residing any-
where but the *cité des Fleurs*. Given this emphasis on the *cité* context of the
Beurs' lives, the early works' historical narratives consist primarily of a past
as France-centered, a future as France-centered, and a present as a struggle
for the negotiation of these temporal experiences in order to define Beur
subjectivity *within* the metropole. In this sense, the negotiation of second-
generation identity *in* France functions as the central narrative problematic
in Beur writing (Hargreaves 1991: 1).

Generational Conflict

An important node in the narrative negotiation of Beur subjectivity is the
theme of generational struggle. In large part, the struggle is underwritten
through the novels' highlighting of the different generational competencies
in French language and social practices. In several of the novels, young Beurs
are required to translate French newspapers, official documents, or the spoken words of government agents to their parents (cf. Begag 1986; Charef
1983a). This cultural distance is magnified by the parents' conscious rejection of French norms. In Kettane's *Le sourire de Brahim* (1985), Brahim's
parents view themselves, despite their residence in France, as engaged in an
ongoing ideological struggle against French colonialism. "In order to preserve their identity, Brahim's parents had withdrawn themselves to their
religion and their language. Especially during the war of Liberation. . . .
Furthermore, not a word of French was allowed spoken at home. That was
the language of the oppressor" (Kettane 1985: 49). In general, Beur novels
portray the first generation as relatively isolated from dominant French cultural and political values and relatively static in their North African ethno-
religious identity. Such a portrayal reifies the narrated cultural distance between the Beurs and their parents.

In contrast, early Beur writing presents the Beurs' own experience of
growing up in France as encompassing a different set of signifiers. Beur
youth are portrayed in their everyday *cité* life, in their interactions with
other *banlieue* age-mates, and especially in their public schooling as inhabiting a different social world from that of their parents. Kettane, for instance, presents Brahim as indelibly oriented toward the world of French
public life. While Kettane's Brahim understood that he was indisputably an
Algerian citizen, "he also knew that once having crossed the threshold of
the family home, the outer world undertook to fill his head with other images. A mixture of people and habits that made him shine with other references. . . . Brahim liked to travel in the imaginary worlds of Rousseau and
Voltaire" (1985: 50). In addition to his attachment to France as mediated
by an intellectual engagement with literature and philosophy, Brahim felt a
further sense of solidarity to his *cité* age-mates via popular culture. "He

sensed his belonging to a group, but without being able to precisely delineate its contours. . . . His friends of the *cité,* workers' children just like himself, had the same problems and the same joys. They listened to the same *yé-yé* [rock] records and hung out in the same place" (1985: 50). Just as ska, reggae, and punk music served as the rallying cries for working-class youth in industrialized Britain, contributing to a subculture which united both native English and Caribbean immigrant children (Hebdige 1979), so too did rock music in the early 1980s serve to unite young men and women of different backgrounds across the French *cités* in contradistinction to the older generation (Hargreaves 1991: 122).

The generational rupture is further illustrated in Beur novels through portrayals of differences in parents' and children's cultural-religious values. Beurette protagonists, as the cases of Djura and Aïcha Benaïssa illustrate, are particularly subject to their fathers' and brothers' violent attempts to control their bodies and sexualities in the name of family *nnif* (Benaïssa and Ponchelet 1990; Djura 1990). The *fugueuse,* in this respect, is a central character across a number of Beur narratives (Boudjellal 1983; Boukhedenna 1987; Houari 1985). For male Beur characters as well, the divergence of religious values across generations is made clear in the early Beur novels. After Azouz's scholarly triumphs in Begag's *Le gone du Chaâba,* his father sits him down and explains that he should thank Allah for his success. "You see, my son . . . God is all around. Allah guides the *mektoub* [destiny] of us all." To this Azouz "slightly smiles," but he rebels more outwardly when his father suggests that he also attend Qur'anic school on the weekend. "Ah no, *Abboué* [Dad], I have already enough school work . . ." (1986: 226).

Language additionally serves as a point of generational contention. Although their maternal language is Arabic or Tamazight, Beur protagonists generally converse, both inside and outside the home, in French. Sometimes, by their French responses, it is clear that they understand only a small percentage of their parents' language (cf. Charef 1983a: 12–13). Moreover, if the characters do speak Arabic or Tamazight at home, their language is portrayed as always already confounded with French phrases and locutions. At the end of *Le gone du Chaâba,* Azouz becomes the favorite student of a *pied noir* high school teacher eager to show off his Arabic. However, it soon becomes clear that the written, classical Arabic known by the teacher has virtually no relationship with the spoken dialect of Azouz's household. In a poignant scene, Azouz fails to recognize the Arabic script for "Allah" written by the teacher on the classroom blackboard. He further shamefully admits the language he speaks at home engages in a number of linguistic crossings between French and Algerian Arabic, with his family using "li zalamite" (Fr. *les allumettes*) for "matches" and "la taumobile" for "automobile" (Begag 1986: 213).

The cultural-linguistic divergence brings Beur characters like Azouz and their parents into open conflict, with occasionally significant results. Before his family relocates to the suburban Lyon *cité*, Azouz lives in the Chaâba *bidonville* within a very insular Algerian immigrant community. At one point during these early years, he puts into practice a civics lesson on hygiene learned in school and leads the police to his uncle's illegal butcher shop (122–127). In so doing, he violates the tenuous solidarity of the community, and, as a result, unwittingly brings about the collapse of the *bidonville*. In other cases, however, the cultural-linguistic confrontation between Beur characters and their parents can be less innocent. In a very piquant mother-son scene in *Le thé au harem d'Archi Ahmed,* Madjid's mother Malika confronts her son, first in broken French, then in Arabic, invoking him to go pick up his father—mentally ill as the result of an earlier work accident—from the local café. Madjid, embarrassed by a father who makes him the butt of his friends' insulting jokes, pretends not to understand his mother's exhortations, claiming, "What are you saying? I don't understand a word." To escape his mother's subsequent chiding and threats to send him back to Algeria to fulfill his military service, Madjid turns up the volume of the English rock group the Sex Pistols (Charef 1983a: 12–13).

Later in the novel, the conflict between parents and children devolves to a veritable "youth-adult mini-war (*guéguerre*)" (26). Tired of the thefts, vandalism, graffiti, and playing of loud music by the unemployed youth of the *cité des Fleurs,* the older inhabitants take matters into their own hands, arm themselves with cattle prods and tear gas, and raid the youths' basement hangout. Through such a scene of protracted intergenerational violence, Beur writers like Charef implicitly rejected the extreme right discourse which sought to equate Beurs and their parents as equally "immigrant." By religiously and linguistically demarcating themselves from their parents, and by demonstrating the very real alliances they had formed with certain dominant "French" values, traditions, and fellow *cité* inhabitants, the Beur authors exploded French nationalist narratives that were based in a strict ethnic and historical distinction between "French" and "immigrant." In effect, their efforts introduced a third term into the nationalist syllogism—"Beur"—a term that referred more to generation and locality than ethnic belonging.

The final, hopeful scene of *Le thé au harem d'Archi Ahmed* poignantly demonstrates this multiethnic subjectivity formed in the working-class housing projects. Madjid, fed up with the cyclical life of crime and boredom of the concrete projects, refuses to flee the police after they stop the stolen car he is riding in with his friends. As the police car carts him off to the station, it is flagged down by his closest buddy (*pote*), the red-headed Pat, who turns himself in as well (183). The scene thus mirrors one that occurred earlier in the novel, when Madjid quits the job he and Pat had obtained in a phonograph assembly factory after Pat is fired. In the uniting spirit of the 1983 March for Equality that occurred within months of the book's publication, Madjid and his multiracial friends provide living illustrations of the anti-racist slogans of multiculturalism that underwrote the Beur Movement of the early 1980s: "Don't Touch My Buddy" (*Touche pas à mon pote*) and "Black, White, Beur" (*Black, blanc, beur*).

Racism and Cultural Violence

The spectrum of multicultural alliances conflicts with other trends in Beur writing of the early and mid-1980s. The Beur characters in these novels were not portrayed as simply assimilating into the French lower class, in spite of the universalist pretensions of French national education and the common socioeconomic plight and cultural style of *cité* youth regardless of race, religion, or ethnicity. In other words, they were not in danger of necessarily becoming the monocultural Georgettes of Farida Belghoul's assimilationist nightmares (1986). In the first place, the rampant racist and xenophobic attitudes and practices poignantly portrayed in the texts violently precluded this simplistic trajectory for the Beur protagonists. Secondly, throughout the works, Beur characters conditionally reaffirmed their North African heritage in response to the state's integration rhetoric, manifesting their own cultural specificity within larger French society.

Across their texts written during this period, Beur authors describe a Beur-French "mini-war" on equal par with the generational one. Instances of racism portrayed in the texts aver a continued colonial predicament within French republicanism. The schoolyard is a particularly salient space where young Beur characters have their first experiences with anti-Algerian racism and colonial nostalgia. In *Georgette!*, the unnamed Beurette protagonist is scolded by her teacher for not having completed her homework. In fact, she had written it in her notebook, but from back to front in the directionality of Arabic script. Searching through the pages, the teacher instead comes across a small pouch containing fragments of Qur'anic writings, a typical gift given by a Moroccan Muslim father to his daughter. The teacher, incensed by the failure of her search, derides the worthlessness of such extracts in comparison to the school exercises, and suggests that the former should be merely tossed out (cf. Hargreaves 1991: 77).

Kettane similarly pinpoints the French national school system as a site of xenophobia, as Brahim, hoping to enter medical school, finds his route blocked by patronizing teachers who relegate their "Arab" students to vocational training. One professor, Monsieur Teigne, states, "I know these little Arabs. They will never be capable of doing the right thing. They're like their parents, good for the assembly line or construction work, it's written in their blood" (1985: 58). Such attitudes are shared, in Kettane's portrayal, by the French media. Commenting on the television representation of Arabs, Brahim and his friends remark, "We shouldn't be surprised that the French mix up everything: Khomeini, Khadaffi, Beurs. For them it's all the same. It's the Crusades all over again" (158).

Moreover, it is on the street, in violent confrontation with the *beaufs*,

that Beur protagonists come to recognize their necessary ethnoracial specificity. In just one of many such scenes in *Le sourire de Brahim,* a group of
white youths from the bourgeois suburbs venture into the *cité* where Brahim lives in order to avenge what they consider to be a "violation" of one of
their sisters by an "Arab" youth. The *beaufs* share in the moral universe of
the larger *banlieue* and regard the union—willing though it was—as a dis-
honor cast upon their family and their "race." In the end, the *beaufs* flee as
the police arrive, but not before "the blood stained the pavement" (39–41).
Unfortunately, the police's intercession does not end the street violence, since
the police, in Kettane's and others' narratives, are as racist as the *beaufs.* As
the police arrive to arrest the Beur participants, an observing Brahim asks,
"How can an Arab be innocent except by being dead?" (41). In a later
scene, after fleeing from a group of *beaufs,* Brahim finds himself again confronted by several police agents looking to short-circuit the justice system.
On the verge of certain death, he is saved by one of the officers' entreaties:
"Don't shoot, Perez, a little 'cleaning' will do" (162).

In this respect, racist violence constitutes a central aspect in the narrative production of Beur subjectivity in the *banlieues.* As Kettane's narrator
muses at the end of the novel, "To the French, we will always be *bougnoules*
and to our 'brothers,' we are little Frenchies" (168). Likewise, when Begag's
Azouz is assigned at school a composition to be written on the subject of his
choice, he realizes immediately that "it was racism that I had to speak about
in my essay" (1986: 222). Even if the Beur characters are willing, or enticed
by schoolteachers, to "become French," their experiences of racism demonstrate the impossibility of such a trajectory. In this way, the Beur characters
suffer from a double rejection from both sides of the Mediterranean. Neither wholly "French" nor "Algerian," the characters remain in the narratives irreconcilably "Beur."

Beur Hybridity: Liminality or Political Persona?

Having suffered from racist rejections, many of the characters in the novels
begin to take a renewed interest in their cultural heritage, mirroring the
Beur Movement's investment in North African cultural associations and
artistic ventures. Brahim, for instance, undergoes a personal transformation after hearing the folkloric ballads of the Algerian singer Taos Amrouche.
Highly impressed by the oral history of Kabylia that he discovers in her
lyrics, he finds his political calling as an organizer of musical spectacles
designed for other Beur youth. In this way, he mirrors the cultural endeavors of Kettane himself, president of Radio Beur and later Beur FM. Other
protagonist-author dyads similarly reflect the engagement of both in various forms of cultural production, notably Nourredine-Boudjellal (1983). In
these works, an aesthetics that traverses the Mediterranean is highlighted as
a significant characteristic of any Beur cultural and political subjectivity.

For the majority of Beur characters, the multiple, antagonistic identity referents—France and Algeria, youth and adult, Islamism and secularism, *beauf* and *banlieusard*—remain in internal, if often vocalized, dialogue. Multivocality—the coexistence of multiple, competing voices in a single text (cf. Bakhtin 1981)—can, in this sense, occur even within the semi-autobiographical genre of the *roman Beur*. In Akli Tadjer's *Les ANI du "Tassili,"* for example, the protagonist Omar comes into personal contact with a wide variety of characters—Islamic fundamentalists, first-generation immigrants, Algerian nationals, *pied noirs*, French social workers, Beurettes—on the ferry from Marseille to Algiers and back. The text progresses through his dialogues with these characters, and it is through his internalization of their voices that the contours of his formative historical and political consciousness are marked. In other narratives, while the dialogic quality may be less explicit, the author, narrator, and protagonist—whether a single individual or multiple characters—equally find themselves bombarded by a number of idioms, references, and examples of direct discourse—including transliterated Arabic and Berber phrases, as well as various slangs and creoles—from parents, comrades, teachers, *beaufs*, and police. Through such competing idioms, Beur characters narrate their pasts and chart their futures. In this way, the novels operate through an implicit heteroglossia that comes to stand for Beur identity as a whole (Hargreaves 1991: 109; Lyons 2001).

In this respect, Beur characters are not simply portrayed as decentered subjects inhabiting a globalized, postmodern world, but rather are narrated as *multicentric*—hybrid products of *both* Algerian and French sensibilities.[4] Many Beur narratives imply that their characters are living in a de facto cultural no-man's-land, as belonging ultimately nowhere in particular (cf. Houari 1985; Sebbar 1982; 1984; Tadjer 1984). Conversely, Kettane's Brahim has a feeling of being at home everywhere, "with the Mediterranean for a flag" (1985: 114), though arguably held in this multiple position as a hostage against his will. Sakinna Boukhedenna engages in a similar multicentric imagery in her autobiographical novel *Journal "Nationalité: immigré(e)"* ("Diary 'Nationality: Immigrant'") (1987), which traces a Beurette's movement from France to Algeria and back in her quest for a coherent religious and cultural identity. Caught in a state of perpetual liminality, the unnamed narrator fantasizes an island situated in the middle of the Mediterranean, halfway between Algiers and Marseille, for Beurettes like her whose passports would read "Nationality: immigrant" (103).

Begag's *Le gone du Chaâba* attests to this multicentric pastiche. To a great extent, the narrative is a postcolonial rewriting of the Kabyle writer Mouloud Feraoun's 1954 autobiographical novel *Le fils du pauvre*. The latter relates the coming of age of the young Menrad Fouroulou—an anagram of the author's name—who, like Begag's Azouz in the French context, rises through colonial Algerian society through his educational success (cf. Achour 1993). Even the titles of the two novels share a structural parallelism, referencing the protagonists as young men (*fils*, *gone*) born in poverty (*pauvre, Chaâba*). The difference, however, is that while the title of Feraoun's novel is fully in French, Begag's, in spite of its setting in France, incorporates multiple registers, with *gone* being Lyonnais slang for "kid," and *Chaâba* an Algerian Arabic term for a shantytown. Azouz is truly the *gone du Chaâba*, a culturally, socially, and economically hybrid subject (cf. Hargreaves 1991: 39). The title's formal bilingualism becomes, in effect, a metonym for the larger operation of *bricolage* through which Beur authors and activists in the 1980s constructed a hybrid subjectivity.

As such, early Beur writing, in both its structure and content, represented an important social practice for the negotiation of cultural specificity in the postcolonial world. Within the general ethnoracial spectrum of *banlieue* France in which all North African immigrant subjects were totalized into "Arabs," the Beurs dissociated themselves equally from singular "French" and "Algerian" identities. Claiming that they resided somewhere between the two categories, Beur authors and activists charted their own multicentric place in French (sub)urban society. In this project of subject formation, the trope of hybridity underwrote Beur self-expressions of identity. As the slogan from the 1984 ("Convergence") march attested: *Mélange, deuxième génération, c'est la meilleure* ("Mixture, second generation, it's the best!"). To this end, autobiographical narratives of personal identity became a poignant means to allegorically express larger visions of a multiracial French nation.

One of the effects of the Beurs' deployment of the standard and recognizable genre of the *Bildungsroman* was the authors' accumulation of symbolic capital that reinforced their status as a "beurgeoisie," as the privileged "cultural mediators" between French and Algerian cultures (Wihtol de Wenden 1990). The novels, while often dedicated to the authors' parents or peers in the *cités,* were generally written for and read by an educated French public far removed from the contexts in which the protagonists lived. Nonetheless, government ministers and journalists touted their writing for its pedagogical function. They viewed the novels' coming-of-age narratives of Beur characters as indicative of potential avenues of immigrant success in French society. The novels thus fit a variety of French integration fantasies as they lionized the self-made Beur as exemplified by the authors themselves. Publishing houses followed suit, with mainstream publishers like Seuil and Stock opening their doors to the autobiographical testimonies of Begag (1986; 1989), Sebbar (1982; 1984), and Tadjer (1985), while less mainstream and arguably more original manuscripts by Boukhedenna (1987) and Kalouaz (1986) were relegated to second-tier, self-financing publishing houses.

The early Beur novels, while certainly personal journeys of cultural discovery and social success, nonetheless envisioned collective political action. To a great extent, Beur narratives represented particular modes of historical consciousness that outlined forms of political subjectivity. By recognizing and expressing an internal, multidimensional, multifaceted self-conception, Beur authors developed an implicit but powerful critique of the totalizing rhetorics of assimilation and exclusion that they confronted in the various xenophobic and anti-racist national narratives circulating in political, educational, and urban planning discourses during the 1980s. Their personalized counter-narratives in the form of coming-of-age stories transformed the private lives of individuals into indexes for future changes in the public life of the French nation (Jameson 1986).

Beur writing thus gave a public voice to Franco-Algerians living in the *cités* of France. By approaching Beur characters as protagonists instead of as criminals or as "problems," the novels presented the Beurs as self-conscious agents of change within the French social imaginary and subjects of their own history. According to Charef, "The best means to affirm oneself is to express oneself, to speak. The media had for a long time denied us the right, letting it be known that a *bougnoule* is incapable of expressing himself and that he only has the right to be silent. . . . [The Beurs] speak, sing, explain their problems and situations, and in such a way a new culture is taking root" (1983b). Beur literature marked the advent of a new immigrant subjectivity, neither purely French nor Algerian, of particular relevance to the 1980s context of assimilation discourse and the burgeoning xenophobia of neo-racism.

In opposing these alternate discourses of Frenchness, Beur writing directly engaged and confronted extant stereotypes.[5] At the end of *Le sourire de Brahim,* Brahim and his Arab friends reject accepted media sound bites about immigrant identity: "'torn between two cultures' . . . They don't understand that we don't have our ass between two chairs and that it's big enough to sit on both" (Kettane 1985: 166). The version of the Beurs' cultural liminality promulgated in French integration discourse viewed Beur culture as a temporary state on the way to their eventual assimilation, or, in the language of Victor Turner (1967), as a period of anti-structure between the structured and determined Algerian and French states. The Beurs' subject position was thus portrayed as unstable, dangerous, potentially corrupting, and marked by crime, delinquency, and failure, as a momentary identity crisis within a larger *rite de passage* to Frenchness. Beur characters' declarations of hybridity and their inalienable "right to difference" thus stood as challenges to these assimilation narratives. Instead of portraying the Beur situation as one of liminal transition, Beur writing presented second-generation immigrant identity as a structured and determinate form. As Kettane promulgated to all who would listen, "Mutants torn from the 'McDonalds couscous-steak-fries society,' we are here, whether you want us or not" (1986: 19).

The limited historical consciousness of the first generation's migratory and cultural history exhibited in early Beur writing thus functions as part of a larger, self-conscious act of generational identity formation. If Beur authors had to distance themselves from assimilation narratives, they also had to differentiate themselves from a marginalized, religiously normative Algerian mode of subjectivity that was being increasingly fetishized by differentialist neo-racist ideologues of the early 1980s. The highlighting of generational conflict in Beur narratives thus played an important role in outlining a Beur political discourse.

Le sourire de Brahim succinctly charts the political trajectory of the constitution of Beur political consciousness. The book opens with the 17 October 1961 demonstration of Algerians in Paris. The resulting massacre by Parisian police, as Kettane recounts, was largely underreported in the French newspapers that limited their coverage of the events to the *faits divers* section. The political frame is completed with the final chapter of the novel that concludes with the arrival of the 1983 *Marche des Beurs* at the Place de la République in Paris. The 1983 march, accomplished without violence, marked the political coming of age of the younger generation. By framing his work with these scenes, Kettane, one of the more didactic of Beur writers, not only created a sense of textual closure, but he also succeeded in highlighting the proximity of political struggles to the act of writing. As one of his characters projects, "As long as we are marginalized from the power and decision-making structures, they will continue their frenzy. . . . We must have deputies, mayors, lawyers, writers, doctors, corporate executives . . . we must make use of our rights so that we will no longer be trampled upon" (Kettane 1985: 169).

Toward a Post-Beur Society

By the late 1980s, the *roman Beur* and its attendant Beur Movement had reached its pinnacle. Not only had the number of novels, autobiographies, theatrical pieces, comic books, screenplays, and other literary works by Beur authors increased manifestly, but a large secondary literature concerning these and other cultural projects had also arisen under the aegis of Beur-organized media establishments (e.g., Agence Im'media) and publishing houses (Editions Arcantère). However, the discourse of multiculturalism embedded in these projects found itself faced in the late 1980s by a neo-racist backlash that naturalized the visions of cultural difference proclaimed by Beur authors and activists and utilized it as a justification for a political ideology of ethnic separatism (cf. Balibar and Wallerstein 1991; Barker 1981; Gilroy 1987). Such neo-racist ideology, in combination with the exacerbation of the civil war in Algeria and the increased political salience of North African Islamist and Berberist movements, had a profound impact on the construction of Beur political subjectivity as expressed in their literary representations. If the Beur novels and autobiographies of the early 1980s rejected universalizing tendencies from both liberal and conservative political fronts and attempted to lay the groundwork for a specifically Beur culture of the *cités*, later Beur writings responded to new ethnic and religious invocations on both sides of the Mediterranean by highlighting a transnational mode of political belonging.

A Fetish of Memory

The particular articulations of such transnational ethnic and religious imaginings in Franco-Algerian cultural productions in the 1990s have been largely mediated by self-conscious transformations in the historical consciousness—or collective memory—of the second generation. Beginning in the mid-1980s and drawing on the earlier theoretical works of Maurice Halbwachs (1980 [1950]), a wealth of anthropological and historical studies emerging in France focused on how individual memories of historical events are socialized and transmitted, preserved and forgotten, ritualized and performed, as part of larger processes of social reproduction (cf. Bahloul 1992; Dakhlia 1990; Nora 1984; Prost 2002). The result has been the creation of a veritable memory industry that has paid particular attention to how particular charnel moments in French history—particularly the Vichy period and the Algerian war—have contributed to the production of French national identity (Prost 2002; Stora 1991; cf. Silverstein 1999).

In particular, collective memory as the key to social reproduction has been linked by French government and academic observers to the process of immigrant integration (cf. Stora 1992; Wieviorka 1993). The resulting studies received direct support from the French state, with Ministers of Integration Charles Bonn and Kofi Yamgnane contributing directly to them (cf. Barou 1993). They sought to determine the extent to which an immigrant generation's knowledge of its migratory past facilitates its insertion into the socioeconomic and political norms of France, or, when taken to its extreme, hinders this process and leads to immigrant ghettoization and exclusion. In this respect, the fetish of collective memory as the measure of integration dovetailed with larger concerns over the cultural breakup of French society and the failure of the republican system to insure the economic well-being of all its denizens and citizens residing in the *cités*.

A focus on collective memory was likewise appropriated by various immigrant groups who by the 1980s had become self-consciously aware that the natural transmission of cultural traits from one generation to the next could not be presumed, and that a conscious group effort was needed to forge immigrant historical consciousness. This recognition led to the creation of a set of cultural productions specifically aimed at portraying North African culture and history to the younger generations born in France (cf. Finifter 1986). While a major topic of memorialization was the migratory and premigratory history of the immigrant first generation (cf. Harzoune and Tatem 1991), the political move of commemoration soon recursively turned in on itself, with the history of the Beur Movement itself becoming a privileged subject of Beur writing (cf. Aïchoune 1985; Bouamama et al. 1994; Boubeker and Abdallah 1993). Indeed, one late Beur association, Mémoire Fertile, founded in the Parisian suburb of Sarcelles in 1987, existed explicitly to maintain a generational memory of the Beur collective action of the early 1980s, believing that retaining such a history of agency was a key factor in the constitution of a "new citizenship." In the end, with the turn toward collective memory, contemporary Franco-Algerian writers and activists have participated in an explicit thematic shift away from the immediacy of the second-generation experience in (sub)urban France to a larger transnational and transgenerational political consciousness.

Transgenerational Historical Consciousness

While Beur novels written during the early or mid-1980s emphasized a direct distancing of the Beurs' experience from that of their parents, later Beur works brought the two generations closer together. Begag's later novels represent a basic version of this schema, proposing in both form and content the impossibility of assimilation and the need for a greater rapprochement between the first and second generations. Begag, in *Le gone du Chaâba*, had been a proponent of classical models of education as the mechanism of immigrant social mobility and integration, with Azouz succeeding in school and hence more generally in Lyon. While his second novel, *Béni ou le Paradis Privé* ("Béni, or the Forbidden Paradise") (1989), appears to tell the same story, it arrives at a far more pessimistic conclusion. Béni, a precocious though slightly ungainly Beur youth, seeks to outdo his French native peers at their Frenchness. He speaks more grammatically than they do—even correcting his teachers' language—plays football more aggressively, and appreciates stereotypical French aesthetics more expressively. He refuses to go by his given name Abdullah, preferring instead the pet name Béni given to him by his father. Meaning simply "my son" in Arabic, Béni also has cognates in French ("anointed") as well as in the English homonym "Benny." However, at the end of the novel, this hypercorrection is brought to an abrupt halt when he is denied entry as an immigrant into the Paradis Privé nightclub, where he had planned to meet his French love interest. Disgusted, he swears off ever having been so deluded. "I said a thousand times 'Fuck your mother!' and all the terrible words that are hidden in the dark recesses of a well-bred child came spewing forth from my mouth. Spitting on their mother, I swore to return the next day and set fire to this shit *Paradis*" (171). However, he never gets the chance for vengeance, as he is hit and killed by a car on leaving the grounds of the club. Thus, like the nightclub, integration proves for the anointed Béni to be a "forbidden paradise," while for the patrons of the establishment, he is yet one more dead immigrant.

The theme of familial rapprochement is more directly broached in Boudjellal's two sequels to *L'Oud*. In *Le Gourbi* ("The Shanty") (1985) and *Ramadân* (1988), Boudjellal continues the storyline of *L'Oud* in dealing with a number of issues central to everyday life in the *cités*: physical dilapidation, drug addiction, delinquency, etc. The primary plot sequence, however, revolves around Nourredine, arriving in Paris in search of his *fugueuse* sister, Nadia. His quest lasts for two years, during which time he experiences a distinctive first-generation-type experience of *lghorba* (exile) in the crowded apartment of his cousins, the Slimanis. Quite by chance, he finally discovers Nadia, pregnant, married to a white Frenchman, and working, appropriately enough, for SOS-Racisme. At the end of *Ramadân*—both the book and the holy month—the two siblings return to Toulon to be reunited with their family for the *'aîd* celebration that concludes the month's fast. Thus, if *L'Oud*, written in 1983, emphasized the centrifugal forces of different social and religious norms that pull generations apart, by 1988 Boudjellal had broached the centripetal cultural and religious ties that bind parents and children.

On the stylistic level as well, the Beur writers by the late 1980s began to emphasize a greater affiliation with their parents' experiences through a departure from the realist mode of the *Bildungsroman* and its basic linear time structure. Charef's 1989 novel *Le harki de Meriem* ("Meriem's Harki") breaks significantly from the coming-of-age genre, experimenting instead with multiple perspectives and alternate temporalities that bring the narrative present of the *cité* in conversation with a set of Algerian pasts of his mother and *harki* father set during the anti-colonial war. Although the novel begins sequentially with the life of the Beur, Sélim, and his eventual murder, the majority of the events described in the novel actually take place before that fateful date. Throughout the novel, the time frame continually shifts, from postwar to prewar and back to postwar again. The last pages of the novel return to the linear time sequence begun in the novel's first pages, though several years later than the initial scenes.

Similarly, the perspective of the narration changes correspondingly, from Sélim to his sister Saliha, who carries his corpse to Algeria for burial, to his father Azzedine, who engages in the French war effort, to his mother Meriem and then finally back to Azzedine as a mourning parent. In this respect, the novel is highly reminiscent of Kateb Yacine's magical realist novel *Nedjma* (1956), both in terms of rhythm and style. Like Charef's later work, Kateb's novel also utilizes shifts in time, locale, and perspective to narrate a story of family and cultural conflict during the waning days of French colonialism in Algeria. While the multiple perspectives in Charef's work revolve around the physical death of Sélim and the parallel symbolic death of Azzedine in his decision to become a *harki,* the lives of the four cousin-narrators in Kateb's novel intersect in the love of Nedjma, the half-French, half-Algerian woman who represents the late colonial hopes, dreams, and contradictions of a multicultural Algeria. To a great extent, Charef's work functions as a postcolonial remake of Kateb's classic, as an equally tragic tale of cultural fusion. Yet it succeeds in bringing characters from multiple immigrant generations together, united in their coming to terms with Azzedine's past and Sélim's death.

War and Remembrance

In this respect, the Algerian war of national liberation is a fundamental *topos* in the transformation of Beur historical consciousness as expressed in literary forms. Following the war, the French and Algerian states fostered an official collective amnesia. On the French side, this amounted to an official non-recognition of the conflict as a "war" and its casualties as victims of national stature, as *anciens combattants* with full veterans' benefits. A series of general amnesties were declared in the years immediately after the war, absolving war criminals from both sides of responsibility for their acts. Books and films treating the subject, while plentiful, failed to arouse public debate, instead focusing in general on the technical and tragic-heroic aspects of the military campaigns (Dine 1994; Donadey 1996). History textbooks dealt with the subject in a brief, cursory manner. Surveys taken among young French citizens who have come of age after the conflict show a profound ignorance not only of the details of the war, but also of their fathers' very participation in it (Coulon 1992).

On the Algerian side, the war was mythified around the now famous rallying cry, "One hero, the people," and employed to forge national consensus around the FLN party as the natural inheritor of revolutionary leadership. In doing so, the state sought to erase the memory of opposing forces and violent conflicts within the revolutionary front (Stora 1995a, 1991; cf. Silverstein 1999). The contemporary Algerian civil war, however, has underwritten a resurgence of war memories into the Algerian and French public spheres. Since 1992, the FLN regime's monopoly of power has broken down under challenges from the Islamist and Berberist fronts, challenges that have taken forms very much akin to the first war. A number of revolutionary actors exiled since independence have returned to national prominence. Likewise, the identifying terms employed by Islamist and Berberist forces harkened back to the vocabulary of *maquis* and *jihad* employed during the anti-colonial war (Stora 1995b). These alternate memories of national struggle conjured up by these resurrections have provided symbolic fodder for Franco-Algerian authors. In their narratives written after 1992, they traced a transnational form of belonging that unites their quotidian lives in urban France with their political, cultural, and historical solidarity with a war-torn Algeria.

To a great extent, Beur authors during the 1980s narrated the 1954–62 war in terms of how it directly affected their lives in France. In the final scene of *Le sourire de Brahim,* marchers in the *Marche des Beurs,* upon their arrival in Paris, stop and lay commemorative wreaths on the spots where Algerian immigrants had been massacred by Parisian police during the 17 October 1961 demonstration portrayed in the novel's first scene. The narrative thus symbolically links the two Parisian demonstrations as bringing together the generations of immigrant parents and children in a common historical struggle for cultural and social equality in France.

The increased violence in Algeria throughout the late 1980s and early 1990s further attracted the attention of Franco-Algerian writers, who increasingly turned to the other side of the Mediterranean as the setting for their works. In large part, they refocused on the older generation's participation in the Algerian war from various Berberist (Imache 1995), feminist (Djura 1993), and *harki* (Charef 1989) perspectives. In particular, Charef's portrayal of Azzedine's decision to enlist in the French forces is particularly poignant as a family tragedy relived by immigrant generations in France. Having joined the French war effort in order to support his extended family during a very difficult economic period, Azzedine's actions are accepted by his mother and brothers only after Sélim's death. Likewise, it is only at this later point that they accept Azzedine's chosen wife, Meriem, a woman already repudiated once for being incapable of bearing children. In fact, after Sélim's death, Meriem returns to the *bled,* to be reunited with those who had previously been so cruel to her. In so doing, she replicates a journey made in the beginning of the novel by Sélim's sister Saliha, a trip that failed in its original intent of burying Sélim, the son of a *harki,* with his ancestors, but that succeeded in establishing a relationship between Saliha and her estranged grandmother. In this sense, if Sélim's death broke up the immediate family in France—with Azzedine remaining in France, Meriem returning to Algeria, and Saliha moving in with her new husband—it re-established ties with the larger family in Algeria, ties that had been broken with Azzedine's forced exile. In broaching these subjects, Charef's narrative likewise foresaw a reconciliation across immigrant generational lines with children being forced to reconcile themselves to their parents' history.

Along similar lines, Rachida Krim has produced a feminist retelling of the war in her 1997 feature film, *Sous les pieds des femmes.* Based in large part on the experiences of Krim's own mother, the film deals with the painful memory of an Algerian woman, Aya, of her participation in the FLN's war effort in France. With a time frame based in the contemporary period, the film recounts the war retrospectively, as Aya, now a grandmother, is confronted with her past in the form of Amin, a former comrade and lover visiting from Algeria. In exploring the ambivalent roles of Muslim women as mothers and activists, the film speaks equally well to a postcolonial present, where Muslim women in France and Algeria are struggling to secure professional careers alongside their domestic responsibilities. Indeed, the catalyst for the recollection, Amin's visit, is itself predicated on the Algerian struggle from which he had fled. As such, the film makes explicit the ties between the two conflicts (cf. Stora 2001: 84–86).

Likewise, a number of Beurette authors have focused directly on the contemporary conflict as a basis for the imagination of transnational solidarity of Muslim women in France, North Africa, and beyond (cf. Bouraoui 1990; Djura 1993; Sebbar 1996). In this vein, Djura directs her second book, *La saison des narcisses* ("The Season of Narcissus") (1993), explicitly toward the creation of a sociopolitical program for women in Islamic societies. Not consisting of a single narrative line, hers is a collection of short life histories chosen to illustrate questions of sexual relations and marriage in Islamic societies. In particular, the work searches for female historical characters who reconcile secularist and pluralist values characteristic of cosmopolitanism with the cultural and religious practices indigenous to North Africa. Instead of rejecting Islam wholesale, Djura discovers in the religion's history heterogeneous stories of debate, heteropraxy, and resistance to patriarchy. The life histories imply that the ideological intransigence that has relegated women to an inferior position in Muslim societies is a contingent and historical development rather than an intrinsic feature of the religion. In the book, Djura explicitly allies herself with a number of women who have succeeded in becoming great leaders in the Islamic world. These heroines range from Sherezade, the protagonist of *A Thousand and One Nights;* to Kahina, the seventh-century Berber chieftain who led her people in battle against the Arab invaders; to Ourida Meddad, martyr in the Algerian war; to her own aunt and surrogate mother Setsi Fatima. The Beurettes' sociosexual struggles in France—as symbolized by Djura's own familial struggles—thus become linked to those of women in general in the Islamic world, and especially to those of her native Kabylia.

Boudjellal brought these two late Beur trajectories of generational reconciliation and cross-border alliances together in his *Juif-Arabe* series of albums. The albums consist of single-page, humorous tableaux depicting the bickering friendship of two fathers, an Algerian Muslim and an orthodox Jew, both residing in Belleville. Their debates and name-calling sessions, in Boudjellal's mocking use of stereotypes and clichés, underline the similarity of their positions as equally subaltern subjects in France. In one exchange the Jewish father declares, "You should recognize the Jewish State of Israel. If [the Jews] weren't there, many would come here and increase the number of immigrants in France." "So what?" the Arab father returns. The first smirks and finishes, "Then Le Pen would be elected" (Boudjellal 1990: 17). The similarity of the two fathers is further exacerbated by the fact that the one's son is dating the other's daughter, an occurrence that draws them even more closely together in opposition to the union. By pre-

The Berber queen Kahina wearing recognizable Berber jewelry, with the Djurdjura mountain range in the background. Poster distributed at the 1996 commemoration of the Berber Spring hosted by MCB-France.

senting such alliances and speaking through the parent first generation, Boudjellal charts new directions toward a transgenerational, transethnic politics based on locality.

In this way, many of the later Beur writings appear to be rejecting earlier, particularist formulations of second-generation identity in favor of modes of political subjectivity that reach out across time and space. In so doing, they have not adopted the slogans of the new anti-racism, which, in response to the neo-racist co-optation of "the right to difference," began in the late 1980s to call for a "right to resemblance" (cf. Désir 1987). Nor have they become proponents of a cosmopolitan universalism that posits the definitive separation of citizenship from nationality, and the individuation of all European subjects as deracinated "new citizens" (cf. Habermas 1992; Kristeva 1993). Rather, Franco-Algerians have emphasized through their recent writings a multicentric form of political subjectivity that reroots the second generation across diasporic, transnational, and, at times, transethnic lines of identity. They thus seem to be fulfilling René Gallissot's keen observation that "identification is becoming transnational, not only because it plays across many nation-states, a fact that had already been evidenced in previous immigrations, but because ethnic reference itself is no longer national in basis" (1992: 127).

To Beur or Not to Beur?

The practice of Beur writing, whether in its earlier portrayals of cultural specificity or in its later claims to transnational allegiance, has become a salient means of articulating political subjectivity in France since the early 1980s. By no means a stable practice, it has operated in dialogue and dialectic with larger transformations in the political discourses concerning immigration and French identity emerging from anti-racist and xenophobic fronts. While dynamically related to such larger ideological shifts, Beur writing has itself internally transformed according to Franco-Algerian authors' and activists' changing historical consciousness of their parents' immigration and their growing awareness of the utility of transgenerational and transnational solidarity for the articulation of an empowering political identity. Clearly, such transformations have not been unproblematic and have not gone uncontested; not every author has accentuated the same issues or done so in the same way. Some, like Azouz Begag and Nacer Kettane, have mobilized Beur motifs of ethnic hybridity for individual social and economic mobility; whereas others, like Sakinna Boukhedenna, have only tacitly allied themselves with such a cultural movement in order to articulate a larger critique of transnational capital and French neo-colonialism. In general, though, Beur writing has critically engaged univocal representations of the French nation. As alternately "national," "intranational," and "transnational allegories," the novels have occupied the same discursive ground and have claimed to speak on the same political plane as the official narratives proffered by Mitterrand, Chirac, Le Pen, and others empowered to speak on behalf of France. While clearly not read by the immigrant generations on whose behalf they speak, the novels have succeeded in articulating political positions for an elite audience and have become indelible aspects of all debates concerning immigration and national identity in France.

Most importantly, Beur writing has constituted an articulation of subjectivity for the Beur authors themselves. Seventy Beur novels do not in and of themselves constitute a significant challenge to the hegemony of the French nation-state as an institutionalized linking of ethnocultural identity and political participation across a bounded territory. Rather, the Beur cultural producers, in writing and drawing, were seeking to find their voice in the French secular modernity of which they remain an integral part. Their writings struggled to make themselves heard over the din of a multitude of other discourses from extremist nationalists and various other minority immigrant and regionalist groups alike, each reinscribing and contesting various features of traditional national hegemonies in Europe. Alternately articulating intranational and transnational ideologies, Beur writing can be read as metonymic of the greater challenges from within and without—from ethnic nationalisms and globalizations—faced by Franco-Algerians and the French nation-state in which they live. Beur writing, regardless of its quantitative significance, has thus served as a robust field in the articulation of Algerian political subjectivity in contemporary Europe.

7 /

Transnational Social Formations
in the New Europe

Born to a Kabyle family living in Algiers, Fatiha came to France for the first time in 1951. She was five years old. Fatiha lived with her father, who owned a café in a Kabyle enclave outside of the southern French city of Nîmes. She returned to Algeria shortly thereafter, but came back to France again two years later with her whole family soon after the beginning of the anti-colonial war. In both France and colonial Algeria, she lived in a primarily French-speaking milieu, was educated in Catholic schools, and was even baptized. "I was basically assimilated," Fatiha told me when I met her in May 1996. Ironically, although Fatiha has legally lived in France for nearly half a century, she has never naturalized herself as a citizen. "Even if you become a citizen, you're not necessarily accepted; you're always a foreigner. What we want is to live as Berbers in a French state, not as French men and women."

At the age of forty-eight, two years before we met, Fatiha had founded a Berber cultural association in the west Parisian suburb of Nanterre. Fatiha's long journey to Berber activism was mediated by Marxist and feminist engagements and followed her movements between France and Algeria. As a teenager during the war, she was active in the FLN's Federation of Algerians in France network. As the war ended, she took part in the creation of Mohamed Boudiaf's opposition party, the Party of the Socialist Revolution. The ruling FLN of President Ahmed Ben Bella declared Boudiaf's party illegal and sent Boudiaf to prison and later to exile in Morocco. A strong proponent of Arab nationalism, Fatiha "did everything I could such that people would treat me as an Arab." In spite of these efforts, her Algerian family scorned her as *française*. Her father was extremely strict with her and her sisters, regulating their comings and goings to the point of violence. As a café owner, he was particularly sensitive to his public persona and the sense of family honor. At the end of the war he married Fatiha to a young Kabyle man from his natal village and sent her at the age of nineteen to live in Algeria, where she split her time between her family's apartment in Algiers and the Kabyle village of her husband's parents. Her first time in Kabylia she was under her in-laws' strict surveillance and was often prevented from leaving home.

Fatiha fought back against her family and her husband. "I revolted. I rejected the idea of being a Kabyle woman. I failed in taking on my Algerian nationality. I wasn't ready to live in a conservative and tribal Kabylia. I had revolutionary ideas." Resisting her family's surveillance, Fatiha became politically active in Algeria. In 1965, she became a member of Hocine Aït Ahmed's Socialist Forces Front (FFS) that was at the time waging a war of opposition in Kabylia against the FLN. "I participated in all of the demonstrations in Algiers and throughout the country." Eventually, however, she became fed up with Algerian opposition political movements, sensing that the leaders, like those of the FLN, were corrupt and self-serving.

In the meantime, she discovered a new pride in her Kabyle cultural heritage. Returning to France in the early 1970s, she enrolled in a degree program in education at the University of Paris VIII-Vincennes, where the Berber Study Group was being formed to preserve and promote Berber language and literature. However, her interest in Kabyle culture, as she recollected it to me, antedated her participation in the group's activities, deriving instead from a chance encounter with a group of Native Americans who were visiting the university in 1972. "I had been traumatized as a child by their portrayal in Westerns and was amazed to meet and talk with them in person." She was struck by the parallels between their situation in the United States and that of Kabyles in Algeria, and in 1975 she went to the United States to see how they lived. She felt an immediate solidarity with their lives and their struggle, discovering in their material culture, rituals, and relationship with their territory as a "providing nature" strengths that could also be found in Kabylia. "It was through this experience that I approached my Berberity."

Fatiha's rapprochement with Berber activism was further invigorated during the April 1980 Berber Spring, when she heard stories of women putting their lives at risk in the student occupation of the university and in confrontations with the police. "Before I had no idea that women in Kabylia had a real strength. It was only after Tafsut that I realized what they could do." After the demonstrations, she increased the frequency of her visits to Kabylia and even constructed a house for her husband and her then four-year-old son in her parents' village. However, she again became disenchanted with Algerian politics, and particularly the partisan tenor that had taken hold over Berberist activism following the establishment of Said Sadi's Rally for Culture and Democracy (RCD) party after the 1988 uprising in Algiers. Nonetheless, she joined the immigration wing of the Berber Cultural Movement (MCB-I) after taking part in a September 1994 demonstration they organized in Paris to call for the freeing of singer-activist Lounès Matoub, who had been kidnapped, presumably by the Armed Islamic Group (GIA).

After Matoub's release, Fatiha continued to work with the MCB-I to raise immigrant awareness of the 1994–95 school boycott in Kabylia, but once again found them too caught up in the FFS/RCD rivalry. Disgusted, she decided to found her own association, bringing together other MCB-I members who were also opposed to the group's internal politics. Her association consists almost entirely of Franco-Kabyles born and/or raised in France and is particularly concerned with the everyday lives and struggles of immigrants. It explicitly seeks to break with both Algerian and immigrant political elites and hopes to help form a new generation of future leaders. Likewise, the association rejects the focus on "citizenship" characteristic of most post-Beur immigrant associations, believing that "it is the tree that hides the forest. The transmission of immigrants' culture is being lost, not the Frenchness (*françité*) that is taught at school." While at first the municipal government of Nanterre feared that Fatiha's association was working "against France," they now support the association's efforts because "they prefer us to the Islamists."

In developing the association's position, Fatiha has formed explicit alliances with Breton and Occitan activists, inviting them to her association's meetings in order to learn from their struggles for cultural and linguistic particularity in the French nation-state. She likewise regards Jewish immigrants as a positive example, admiring the way they constructed a strong community sensibility before socially integrating into France. "We have to develop Kabylia like they did Israel." For, while her association has largely focused on the future of immigrant identity in France, it has explicitly embraced a transnational political perspective that remains focused on the struggle in Algeria. It is an independent member of the World Amazigh Congress (CMA), and, at the time I interviewed her, Fatiha was the only female officer within the Congress. Fatiha closely follows developments in the Algerian civil war, bemoaning the military generals she sees as having hijacked power and kept the country in turmoil. "I want to return to a country free of Islamists who want to kill me. I want to have the freedom of choice to live how I want where I want."

The contestatory narratives of ethnic and political subjectivity outlined in Beur writing have consistently translated into concrete political action framed in transnational terms. In the wake of the Beur Movement, a variety of social movements have been established by Algerian immigrants and their children in contemporary France. These movement have largely drawn on oppositional ideologies in the name of reformist (*salafi*) Islam (i.e., Islamism) and Berber culture (i.e., Berberism) that burgeoned and radicalized over the course of the Algerian civil war. The resulting social movements in France have outlined new spheres for political engagement that have provided Beur actors with effective means of locally contesting state authority. As these Berberist and Islamist transpolitics have developed in both France and Algeria, and as the two contexts are closely tied through the reciprocal flows of people and information across the Mediterranean, there has occurred a veritable transfer of the Algerian civil war onto French soil.

Following the 1992 cancellation of the second round of legislative elections likely to have been won by the Islamic Salvation Front (FIS), the Algerian military government outlawed the Islamist opposition and engaged its numerous armed wings in a bloody conflict that had claimed over 100,000 lives by 2003. The numerous village massacres, political assassinations, car bombings, roadside shootings, and plane hijackings reached their peak in the mid-1990s, shrouding the country in a haze of uncertainty over the true identities and interests of the various forces.[1] In the meantime, various groups in Kabylia centered around the FFS and RCD political parties amplified their call for the official recognition of Berber culture and language. Fighting a two-front discursive, and occasionally violent, war against government and Islamist forces, Berber activists built on the popular awareness generated by the Berber Spring student and worker demonstrations of April 1980, spreading their anti-Arabization messages through the hundreds of village-level cultural associations that had formed after the constitutional reforms of 1989. Sporadically, this Berberist politics translated into violent mass protest, as occurred after the kidnapping in September 1994 and later assassination of Lounès Matoub apparently by the GIA in July 1998, and after the killing of high school student Mohamed (Massinissa) Guermah by a military gendarme in April 2001. These protests further radicalized Kabylia, resulting in the creation of village-level self-defense forces and a transvillage, para-political Coordination of 'Aarchs, Regions, and Communes (CADC) (Maddy-Weitzman 2001; Silverstein 2003).

France has been a particularly important site in the development of Islamist and Berberist sociopolitical movements. After the outlawing of the FIS, Islamist leaders took refuge in France, finding solidarity and support among France's Algerian Muslim population. A number of Islamic associations in and around Marseille, Lyon, and Paris spread various versions of the FIS's *salafi* ideology, proselytizing many younger *cité* residents to an

Islamic orthopraxy that contrasted strongly with the diverse Muslim practices of their parents. While French *cités* by no means became the bastions of Islamist militancy feared by alarmist observers (cf. Pujadas and Salam 1995), some of the violence associated with the government-Islamist conflict in Algeria did spill over into France in the 1994 hijacking of an Algiers-to-Marseille Air France flight, the July 1995 assassination of FIS leader Abdelbaki Sahraoui in Paris, and the summer 1995 bombings in the subways and public markets of Paris and Lyon attributed to the Algerian GIA.

Berberist politics in France have likewise been intimately connected with events occurring in Algeria. Throughout the 1990s, many Algerian Berber activists, artists, and intellectuals took refuge in France, fearing prosecution from the government and death threats from Islamist militias. Drawing on this base of expatriate militants, the RCD and FFS further implanted themselves among Kabyle immigrant populations, where they enjoyed electoral and financial support. Extant Berber cultural associations by and large affiliated themselves with one or another political party and participated in the same games of political rivalry played by their counterparts in Algeria. Crossing partisan lines, Kabyle immigrants and their children engaged in public displays of solidarity with the Kabyle protests of 1994, 1998, and 2001, decrying the Algerian *pouvoir* as an "assassin" of Berber culture in mass demonstrations in Paris and beyond. As in the case of Fatiha, the civil war violence drew increasing numbers of Franco-Kabyles into Berberist politics.

Nonetheless, the sphere of political engagement of Franco-Algerians of various immigrant generations transcended the ideological and violent connections between Algeria and France. The increasingly effective supranational institutions of the New Europe provided the scaffolding for the construction of alternate political communities that transcended ethnic, regional, and national borders. Overt alliances among immigrant and linguistic minority groups across Europe proliferated beginning in the early 1990s, underwriting the creation of transnational social formations around cultural-geographic entities like the Mediterranean and the Pan-Celtic world. On the one hand, this transnationalization of cultural politics across minority groups in Europe greatly benefited from the legal and financial support, and the new possibilities for intra-European mobility, provided by the European Union (EU). On the other hand, European states generally approached these burgeoning political alliances as potential threats. The relaxing of political frontiers between European states required the strengthening of extra-European borders on the periphery, a strengthening that reinforced both state national authority and intrastate ethnic and religious frontiers. Algerian social movements in France thus partake of and underscore what Zygmunt Bauman (1991) has referred to as the "ambivalence of modernity," the fluidity and constant flux between national, infranational, and transnational modalities of political organization in contemporary Europe.

Beur/Berber Imaginings

One set of contemporary transpolitics in France has derived from the reproduction of Algerian political divisions among Franco-Algerian actors. Already in the early 1980s, the near simultaneity of the Berber Spring in Algeria and the Beur Movement in France attested to the intimate connection between social movements in the two countries. Both movements occurred during a period of transition of governmental power and relative liberalization—with the installations of reformist presidents Chadli Benjedid and François Mitterrand—and made similar use of this period of structural weakness to articulate particularistic claims that under previous periods would have been considered prohibitively seditious. Moreover, Beur activists of Kabyle origin often adopted distinctively Berber signs to express this identification as cultural mediators. Their declarations of cultural hybridity largely drew on the Mediterranean imagery of the Kabyle Myth that presented Berbers at the crossroads of European and Maghrebi values. Among the many cultural productions of the Beur Movement, a certain number of theater groups (e.g., Kahina), musical troupes (e.g., Djurdjura), and cultural associations (e.g., the ACB) picked up the baton of Berber activism spurred by the Berber Spring.

The School as Battlefield

In the years that followed, the debate regarding the place of heterodox cultural forms within French and Algerian national ideologies was increasingly politicized. In the mid-1980s, Algeria and France underwent severe economic crises that had their most bitter repercussions for their urban youth and immigrant populations inhabiting the *cités*. The economic downturn of the French *banlieues* was matched by a situation of stagflation in Algeria precipitated by an unprecedented 60 percent drop in prices of petroleum—Algeria's main industry representing 98 percent of total exports—in 1986. Double-digit inflation was accompanied by an estimated 25 percent general unemployment, with figures as high as 60 percent for workers under twenty years of age (Rarrbo 1995: 11, 131; Ruedy 1992: 246). This situation of extreme marginalization contributed to an atmosphere of unrest that produced a number of conflicts opposing French *banlieusards* and Algerian *hitistes* to the respective government forces throughout the late 1980s and early 1990s. In Algeria, these conflicts culminated in the October 1988 demonstrations in Algiers in which as many as 500 young men died.

At the crux of the conflict in both countries was a general dissatisfaction over the role of the state education system as a mechanism of integration and social mobility. Although in form the system was meritocratic, in practice a two-tiered system had developed in both Algeria and France by which extant socioeconomic divisions were reproduced rather than erased. In Algeria, despite successes in the generalization of education since independence, elite Francophone education continued to translate into greater social and economic capital than the proliferating Arabophone school system open to the general public (cf. Rarrbo 1995: 93–126). In France, despite the creation of specially funded educational priority zones in the *cités*, many immigrant and *banlieusard* children were tracked to vocational diplomas rather than to the baccalaureate required for universities.

The response of youth in both countries to this situation of exclusion was twofold: first, a call for pragmatic reforms, increased numbers of teachers, and a democratization of the curriculum; second, a push for the introduction of cultural difference into the national education system. In France, a decade of debates over the introduction of a multicultural curriculum—including calls for the teaching of Arabic, Tamazight, and other immigrant and regional languages—came to a head in the successive headscarf affairs throughout the 1980s and 1990s. Berberist groups in France were particularly outspoken in calling on the republican school system—the "principal instrument of integration and social promotion"—to protect young Franco-Algerians against Islamist "manipulation" by encouraging their *berbérité*, "the most effective rampart against the integralist temptation" and the key to their future "integration" in France.[2]

Moreover, such a solicitation explicitly lent support to a simultaneous social movement in Kabylia that focused directly on the Arabic-based educational system in its struggle for the recognition of Tamazight as an official and national language. A series of student strikes in 1994 culminated in a school boycott for the entire 1994–95 academic year, touching all levels of education from grammar to medical schools. The boycott was extremely well supported in France, with a series of demonstrations in front of the Algerian embassy in Paris—including one organized by Fatiha's association—demanding *Tamazight di likul* ("Tamazight in the schools"). Several of these demonstrations coincided with the April 1995 commemoration of the Berber Spring. The two celebrations I attended that year focused entirely on the school strikes, with banners decorating the spaces inscribed with pro-boycott slogans, Amazigh flags, participants wearing military uniforms signifying a Kabylia at war, and heated debates over the effectiveness of the boycott and the political divisions within the Berber Movement (MCB) that it had made evident. The strike's broad transnational support successfully put pressure on the Algerian government to create a High Amazigh Commission (HCA) to study how to incorporate *amazighité* into national media and educational structures. The strikes—alongside the GIA's simultaneous bomb attacks on schools with mixed-gender classrooms—indicate the centrality of the education system, the nation-state's site of reproduction *par excellence*, as an important battlefield on which contemporary challenges to state national authority in France and Algeria are being conducted.

Transpolitics: Algeria's Crisis, France's Lament

The most direct interface between cultural particularist demands in Algeria and immigrant cultural politics in France occurred in the context of the "second Algerian war." The civil war and its incumbent economic collapse particularly affected Kabylia, which, having neither agricultural nor mineral resources, had been historically dependent on its ability to export manpower to urban centers and abroad—avenues of migration largely closed by contemporary border restrictions. While the civil war did not produce as many casualties in Kabylia as in other provinces, it had visceral effects on the lives of Kabyle men and women. The roads throughout the region were subject to periodic "false roadblocks" by Islamist militias that on occasion resulted in the slaughter of busloads of travelers. Kabyle intellectuals and artists were the targets of death threats and violence, particularly evidenced by the May 1993 assassination of the author and journalist Tahar Djaout, and the September 1994 kidnapping and June 1998 assassination of singer-activist Lounès Matoub. Threatened and actual lethal violence resulted in the flight of many public figures abroad. Prolonged demonstrations in April 1995, July 1998, and April 2001 pitted Kabyle civilians against government forces, demonstrations that in many cases turned violent. This violence resulted in the increased presence of police, gendarme, and military forces in the region, the combined effect of which was to heighten a general sense of insecurity.

Given this violence, civil war politics in Kabylia tended to operate as a dual classification system, following a strict binary logic that alternately opposed Berberists to the state on the one hand and to Islamists on the other. With the founding of the RCD, this binary opposition took on a recursive character, with political life in Kabylia largely dictated by the FFS/RCD split. The FFS consistently espoused a position of reconciliation with the outlawed FIS as the only possible means of resolving the civil war. The party was a cosignatory with the FIS of the Sant'Egidio platform that called for a negotiated, multiparty solution and a civil peace; it boycotted the 1995 presidential elections, and it consistently refused to take part in the various military governments in power since 1992. In contrast, the RCD took part in national elections in 1995 and 1999 and participated in the coalition government under Abdelaziz Bouteflika, who became president in 1999. More significantly, the RCD advocated a hard-line (*éradicateur*) position that rejected any dialogue with Islamist forces. In its literature, it consistently opposed any "Middle Eastern or Afghan identity" for Algeria supposedly proffered by the "peons of the Islamist International," and instead called upon Kabyles to rise up in "resistance" following the "spirit of independence" of the "eternal Jugurtha."[3] Moreover, it brought this discourse to action, supporting the government's formation of self-defense groups—civilian militias armed by the state and charged with protecting local populations from Islamist incursions, universally referred to as "patriots"—in Kabyle villages. While these "patriot" groups may have produced a sense of agency for certain Kabyles, they often resulted in an increase rather than a decrease of violence, as they have been specifically targeted by Islamist militias and have been employed in local operations of vengeance (cf. Garçon 1998).

Beyond these divergences in the enactment of civil war politics, the FFS and the RCD were understood by many Kabyles I interviewed in France to function as rival village clans (*lessfuf*), as embodiments of the ritualized antagonism that is written into Kabyle village social relations and spatial arrangements, and that occasionally results in violent encounters read as wars of *nnif*. More broadly, these *lessfuf* often represented, in the structuralist logic of dual classification systems, two opposed moral universes (Khellil 1984: 33–34). In the case of the *lessfuf* of Kabyle politics, the FFS and RCD were first seen by Kabyle activists with whom I spoke to correspond to two opposed political generations, with the FFS drawing its symbolic capital from the war of national liberation and the RCD attempting to claim a monopoly over those who came of age in the Berber Spring. Furthermore, they were seen as having discrete territorial claims, with the FFS claiming geographical prominence in the eastern province of Bejaïa and the RCD dominating the western *wilaya* of Tizi-Ouzou. Finally, they were seen as corresponding to two distinct classes, with the FFS drawing from the ranks of maraboutic lineages, and the RCD, with its avowed secularist ideology, clearly appealing to the larger population of the laity.

Obviously, these distinctions are ideal-typic and only approximate the complex reality of civil war politics, where brothers and sisters found themselves on opposite sides of the Islamist/Berberist split, not to mention the FFS/RCD one. Nonetheless, these popular perceptions, coupled with the irreconcilable political platforms of the two parties, resulted in the fragmentation of the MCB into factions aligned with each party, making concerted political action difficult. Indeed, although the 1994–95 school boycott did result in the creation of the HCA, it broke down prematurely —without meeting its original objectives of forcing the officialization and nationalization of Tamazight—due to internal strife between the MCB factions. Subsequent popular mobilizations against the state likewise found themselves bifurcated and weakened by the constant doubling of organizational committees, marches, and demands.

In France, the Algerian civil war clearly politicized immigrant cultural activism along lines of binary opposition similar to those in Algeria. In the wake of the failure of the Beur Movement, Islamist and Berberist social movements imported from Algeria offered visions of identity and belonging that, while often posed in strict opposition to one another, shared the common trait of presenting an alternative to official—but, as ever, ambivalent— French policies of integration. Both sought to resuture these children of

immigrants to larger imagined worlds—whether an 'umma or a Tamazgha—
that extended across the Mediterranean and beyond.

Nowhere were these divisions more evident than in the events surrounding the 1995 Algerian presidential elections. Contrasting directly with the
paucity of turnout for the 1991 legislative elections that nearly brought the
FIS to power, 620,000 immigrant voters, or more than a third of the estimated Algerian nationals in France, turned out to vote, with a remarkable
number of the younger generation exercising their double nationality. In
discussions at the polling places, young Franco-Algerians explained to me
that their decision to vote was motivated by two factors: a desire to end the
violence in Algeria and a hope to one day emigrate to a postwar Algeria for
work, as there was "nothing left" for them in France. While 65 percent of
voters in Algeria and France voted for the ruling General Liamine Zeroual,
the remaining 35 percent were split between the Berberist RCD and the
"moderate" Islamist Movement for an Islamic Society.

As immigrant politics became increasingly factionalized between Islamist and Berberist tendencies, so too were French Kabyle politics divided along
RCD/FFS lines. In the 1995 elections, the immigration wings of both parties engaged in heavy electioneering, with the RCD pushing its candidate
Said Sadi, and the FFS joining the FIS and the FLN in publicly calling for a
boycott. Moreover, these political divisions came to map onto Berber cultural associations in France, with the ACB serving as the de facto French
headquarters of the RCD, other groups like Paris-based Tamazgha remaining close to the FFS, and yet others, like MCB-France, remaining purpo-
sively unallied. However, in the wake of the April 2001 clashes in Kabylia,
the non-partisan CADC—what many Berberist activists refer to as the
"Kabyle Parliament"—has taken over much of the FFS's and the RCD's
community organizing in Kabylia and the diaspora. Mirroring its Kabyle
counterpart, a European branch of the CADC has been very active in France
in organizing demonstrations and protests. With these developments, it is
clear that France has become more than ever a central locus of Algerian
civil war politics.

The Mediterranean Dimension

One of the consequences of the movement of political ideologies
between Algeria and France has been the reopening of the Mediterranean as
a space of political identification and maneuver. The myth of the Mediterranean Sea as a crossroads of cultural exchange underwrote justifications for
the colonial conquest of Algeria and the designation of the Kabyles as the
particular target of the civilizing mission. After Algerian independence, the
national myths and geopolitical strategies of both French and Algerian parties rejected such a commonality, retreating to regionalist political identi-

Political declarations and tracts distributed by Berber associations and political movements in Paris.

ties: the burgeoning supranational Europe for France and the nascent pan-Arabist movement for Algeria. However, this denial of Mediterranean identity by both sides at the moment of decolonization did not completely remove the category from the discourse or foreign policy of the countries in question. After Algerian independence, the European Economic Community (EEC) opened trade negotiations with its southern neighbors, which it designated as "*pays tiers méditerranéens*" (PTM), and by 1976 had signed a treaty of cooperation with the Maghreb (Algeria, Morocco, Tunisia) (Naïr 1995). Through the mid-1990s, more than 50 percent of the commerce of PTM countries took place with countries of the EEC or, since 1993, the European Union (EU).[4] Additionally, through loans from the European Investment Bank and the EEC's own budget, the 1976 accord resulted in the granting of more than 500 million euros' worth of loans to Algeria alone from 1978 to 1991 (Khader 1995: 16, 20). While dependent commercially and financially on the European Community as a whole, Algeria retained special ties to France in particular. The 1958 Treaty of Rome that established the EEC officially authorized France, in violation of the standard protocol, to maintain preferential exchange relations with its former colonies and dependents. Although this official status has since been eliminated, agricultural and petroleum products were exempted from free-trade status, resulting in a continuing special economic arrangement between France and North Africa (Khader 1995: 73). In fact, as of 1995, 35 percent of the Maghreb's total exports went to France alone, or well over half of its exports to EEC countries in general. This continued cross-Mediterranean economic dependence was further deepened by migrant remittances (approximately nine billion francs per year during the 1990s [Liauzu 1996: 140]), informal fund-raising of political groups, and continued French government military and financial support for the Algerian regime throughout the civil war.

The privileged ties to Europe were deployed by North African states during the late 1980s and 1990s to distinguish themselves from their Arab neighbors to the east. On the one hand, King Hassan II made claims to Morocco's *méditerranité*, and not to its *arabité*, in his petitions for admission to the EEC and, later, the EU. On the other hand, while the Maghreb Arab Union (UMA) officially maintained an Arabo-Islamic identity, promising in its February 1989 foundational treaty to defend "the spiritual and moral values descending from Islam and the protection of the Arab national authenticity" (Khader 1995: 67), its main goal was to unify the five signatory countries (Algeria, Morocco, Tunisia, Mauritania, Libya) into a joint trading partner with the EEC. As such, the UMA constituted a concerted turn toward the Mediterranean and away from the Middle East, and hence a "means to specify the Maghreb in the Arab World" (Basfao and Henry 1991: 47).

While the Mediterranean, for North African regimes, may have oper-

Le Mare Nostrum restaurant in Rabat, Morocco, invoking
the Mediterranean. Photograph by author.

ated as a synonymous category for modernity and a means to turn its back
on the Orient, for France and other southern European countries, the Mediterranean as a category of identity served to allay fears of an ultra-modern
Europeanism *qua* German imperialism. France's political and economic
overtures to its cross-Mediterranean neighbors since the 1990s were largely
mediated by a structural nostalgia for a "lost Andalusia," for the "cultural
and spiritual heritage" of a cross-cultural "Mediterranean homeland" (Basfao
and Henry 1991: 46; cf. Balta 1992). After 1990, the EEC and its EU successor developed a "Renovated Mediterranean Policy" to establish a part-
nership for the environmental and urban codevelopment of the region. Further, 2010 was set as the date for the creation of a "Euro-Mediterranean
space" of free trade and regional economic and political integration (Naïr
1995). Paralleling these arrangements, France initiated a "Mediterranean
Forum" in 1989 for political and cultural solidarity in the region. Under the
aegis of this latter program, France was able to maintain a privileged relation with its former colonies throughout the 1990s in the form of state
visits, subsidies, and cultural exchanges. While this Euro-Mediterranean
cooperation generally only deepened the economic dependence of the
Maghreb on Europe (Khader 1995: 89; Naïr 1995), it nonetheless provided

a cultural and historical complement to Eurocentric integration schemes envisioned elsewhere.[5]

However, France's renewed attention to the Mediterranean in the postcolonial period belies explicitly pragmatic concerns as well as nostalgic narratives of loss and recovery of a primeval context of cultural exchange and enlightenment. France's relationship with the Maghreb is generally articulated in media and governmental discourse through the trope of state security. In this discourse, the circulation of people, commodities, and ideologies between Algeria and France is constituted as a risk of the spread of poverty, drugs, and terrorism to Europe. Such a conflation is evident in the EU's creation of *forteresse Europe* in which the elimination of internal frontiers is complemented by the strengthening of its external ones. The 1992 Maastricht agreement on European union stipulated that the suppression of border controls between member countries necessitated a joint war against terrorism, drugs, and illegal immigration (Khader 1995: 130).

As such, the Mediterranean, as a culturally laden geographic signifier, has remained a pre-eminent category of foreign policy in the postcolonial period. Continuing to unite Europe and the Maghreb in a state of political and economic dependency, the Mediterranean has retained its ambivalent identity emerging from colonial discourse as both a font of heritage and a promise of modernity. In the immediate postcolonial period, the Maghreb and Europe forged cooperation pacts in an attempt to restore a lost cultural and functional unity. However, given Europe's own concerns with regional integration, these agreements have always been balanced by the flip side of modernity's dogma of free exchange and circulation: surveillance and containment. The Mediterranean, as a transpolitical category, thus points to the perduring colonial character of postcoloniality.

Mediterranean Reappropriation and Political Action

The Mediterranean, beyond a category of foreign policy, has also been appropriated as a marker of cultural and political identity by various subaltern groups in the region, often as a means to contest state national authority. While in France, I witnessed the Mediterranean category mobilized not only by official sources to signify a space of encroaching disorder, but also by immigrant and minority groups—from *pied noirs* to Berber expatriates to second-generation Franco-Algerian citizens—to imagine alternate places of cultural-political belonging. From literary representations of the Mediterranean within Beur novels to working alliances between Berber and Occitan cultural associations in the name of a shared Mediterranean heritage, marginal identity politics in contemporary France has increasingly appropriated the Mediterranean as a locus of transnational identification.

During the colonial period, the delineation of the Mediterranean as a geographic and cultural area contributed to the designation of two alternate, antagonistic groups as the true inheritors and agents of pan-Mediterranean unity: miscegenated European residents of North Africa (Cagayous) and Berbers. In the Cagayous case, the settlers themselves played a direct role in the production of the stereotype of a new, mixed Latin race, rejuvenated by the African sun. In the postcolonial period, *pied noir* writers and scholars have continued to underwrite the myths of a lost Andalusia, either, in the *Algérianiste* tradition of Louis Bertrand, by joining neo-Fascist, xenophobic groups envisioning a new *reconquista,* or, in the memory of Albert Camus and the *École d'Alger,* by founding fraternal organizations of solidarity with postcolonial Algeria. In either case, their interventions amounted to a nostalgic imagination of a Mediterranean community in defiance of present state national borders.

In the Berber case, the appropriation of a Mediterranean identity by the designated natives existed primarily as a postcolonial phenomenon. This effort took two particular forms of political ideology and concrete action, both of which envisioned a Mediterranean identity of one form or another. In the first instance, diasporic Berber associations in France and Spain emphasized Berber culture as the source of Maghrebi identity, however virulently denied by contemporary Arab imperialism. Claiming that Berbers are clearly Mediterraneans but in no part Orientals, associations like Tamazgha (Paris) and MCB-France (Argenteuil) in the mid-1990s sponsored talks by Berberocentric revisionists like Jean Dumaurier, forged working alliances with Occitan, Catalan, and other Mediterranean cultural movements, and organized pan-Berber conferences uniting activists from throughout the region. In August 1997, hundreds of militants gathered at the first Amazigh World Congress (CMA) in the Canary Islands, located symbolically between Europe and Africa at the mouth of the Mediterranean Sea. Further, these groups, in publicly presenting themselves in Europe, explicitly endowed themselves with a Mediterranean identity. Kabyle-owned bookstores with names like *Espace Méditerranéen* dot the Parisian landscape, offering a wide selection of cassettes, videos, CDs, and books on Mediterranean culture. Likewise, Berber groups have petitioned international bodies for cultural recognition in the name of trans-Mediterranean solidarity. In one case, a Granada-based umbrella group, simply named "Mediterranean," succeeded in organizing a special session of the European Parliament on Berber-Amazigh culture held on 11 June 1997. In these ways, the construct of the Mediterranean as a cultural source has been appropriated by Berber groups as a pivotal means for the imagination and foundation of a politically endowed, transnational Berber homeland, or Tamazgha.

Further, the Mediterranean category, in its crossroads image, also functioned in Berberist discourse in the elaboration of a particular political space within extant nation-states themselves. The RCD, while clearly Berberist in its regional representation and imagery, claimed in its 1990s electioneering to stand for Algeria's integral but hybrid identity, as simultaneously Arab,

Berber, Muslim, African, and Mediterranean. More particularly, it sought to stake out a "democratic" middle ground in the Algerian civil war, virulently opposing both Islamist groups and the military government. Likewise, the RCD promoted a mediator image of Berber identity borrowed almost directly from nineteenth-century colonial discourse. In this sense, Berberist groups in France, in a game of structural nostalgia, appropriated the Mediterranean stereotype of Berbers as the natural targets of the colonial *mission civilisatrice* for the postcolonial articulation of claims to cultural authenticity.

Finally, Franco-Algerian militants and writers in France similarly appropriated the hybrid image of Mediterranean culture in the production of their postcolonial categories of political subjectivity. While many Beur activists in the 1980s elaborated a postmodern sense of ethnic identity without a geographical focus except perhaps the multiracial *cité* (cf. Kettane 1986), others have indicated an imaginary location for the site of their mixed Franco-Algerian belonging. In an interview, Leila Sebbar has claimed that she writes from a position between Algeria and France, from the middle of the Mediterranean (Basfao and Henry 1991: 51). Indeed, the passage across the Mediterranean, from France to Algeria and back, constituted a central feature in the majority of Beur novels (cf. Boukhedenna 1987; Kettane 1985; Tadjer 1984). For instance, Sakinna Boukhedenna's imagined "island between Marseille and Algiers" for second-generation subjects like herself (1987: 103) seemed a postcolonial remake of Gabriel Audisio's description of the Mediterranean as a "liquid continent" fifty years prior. As such, the Mediterranean has remained a prime category of transnational or, literally, international belonging for postcolonial migrants and minorities in France and North Africa.

The New Europe

The creation of a transnational space of Franco-Algerian political action extends beyond the Mediterranean region. Post-Beur Franco-Algerian activists have forged working alliances with a number of minority ethnic, linguistic, and immigrant groups throughout France and, more generally, Europe. In the course of my fieldwork, I was often surprised to discover ties between events and incidents explicitly concerned with Algeria and those that were situated within a politics of internal metropolitan diversity. For instance, when discussing the 1995 bombings with friends and acquaintances, three categories of historical memory and reference were mobilized: first, the parallels with the first Algerian war of national liberation, during which the revolutionary FLN utilized guerrilla warfare techniques, including urban bombings; second, the more proximate 1986 set of attacks in Paris by Lebanese militant groups; and finally the 1968 bombing campaign by Breton separatists against government targets in Brittany and Paris.

This last historical connection found reiteration in a second event that I lived through: the winter 1995–96 general strikes by French public workers. For a month, the strikers succeeded in shutting down the French transportation network and postal service in response to the austerity-driven reform of retirement benefits proposed by conservative Prime Minister Alain Juppé. Joining in the many union marches and demonstrations that crisscrossed Paris to accompany the strikes, the Breton nationalist movement used the protest as a forum to denounce recent government decisions of political and linguistic centralization. Graffiti across Paris declared: "Bretagne: French Province, No! European State, Yes!"

Finally, the specter of French regionalism haunted my research again in reference to a third event: the celebrations and debates surrounding the sixteenth anniversary of the Berber Spring in 1996 Paris. If the 1995 celebrations sought to forge a direct link between Tafsut and the ongoing struggles for linguistic recognition in Algeria, the 1996 demonstrations focused more clearly on the French scene. The MCB-France in particular organized a day-long conference-debate on "The Amazigh Question." Alongside testimonies to their cultural trajectories by young Franco-Algerian men and women, Catalan and Occitan militants were also invited to share their struggles for linguistic and cultural recognition in France. The conversations that ensued between participants and audience members were particularly fascinating in terms of their efforts to bridge the differences between the two struggles. Beyond trying to learn from each other's experiences, Berber, Catalan, and Occitan activists presented their movements as all part of a single struggle against the assimilationist ideology of the French nation-state.

In each of the three cases described above, events ostensibly about state security, domestic economic policy, and international politics respectively took on a culturalist mien, being transformed by their participants and observers into an internal French debate concerning the legitimacy of ethnolinguistic differences to the French imaginary—a contemporary *Kulturkampf* in which the French state, regional ethnic and linguistic communities, and postcolonial immigrant groups each have a major stake. The struggle over the cultural makeup or breakup of the New France clearly relates both to internal transformations in the character of French national identity—from an orientation toward empire to one toward Europe—and to the simultaneous development of regionalist challenges to the nation-state in both Algeria and France. The history of the Beur and Berberist movements demonstrates that state discourses and practices of centralization, integration, and control have *produced* rather than erased particular categories of non-national difference which immigrant and ethnic minority groups have appropriated and mobilized for the construction of modes of transpolitical subjectivity. Since the mid-1990s, these movements have increasingly allied their causes with localized Breton and Occitan militant organizations, demanding equal rights of cultural and linguistic expression within France and together petitioning European administrative bodies.[6]

Regionalism and Revolt

Throughout the nineteenth century, French metropolitan elites produced reified categories of intranational ethnic and linguistic particularities—through academic studies, museum exhibits, romantic literary movements, and folklore collections—at the exact same moment they pursued policies of national and colonial centralization (Dietler 1994; Lebovics 1994; Weber 1976). During the late colonial period, indigenous elites in peripheral areas in France appropriated such essentialized identities to articulate various political critiques of Parisian "internal colonialism," thus forging symbolic ties with colonized groups, and particularly Algerians, in search of national liberation. The 1980s brought another period of close proximity between regional and immigrant demands, as Breton and Occitan activists benefited like the Beurs from the tentative government support for multiculturalism and articulation of a "plural France" (Parti Socialiste 1981; Giordan 1982). However, unlike Beur militants, regionalist activists remained sharply critical of the French nation-state even during this period. Instead of participating in the government's integration projects, they instead sought direct ties with other ethnic and linguistic minority populations via Europe's burgeoning supranational institutions.

The approach of regionalist groups to institutions like the European Parliament and the Council of Europe has been historically ambivalent. For regionalist militants ideologically formed in a Marxist tradition, these bodies represented the quintessence of capitalist development as protectors of state economic interests against internal and external competitors. The insertion of the French economy into the Common Market and European Monetary Union had often, in the eyes of many militants, destroyed small businesses and farms, as technocratic decisions made in Brussels were not adapted to local economies such as the wine industry in Occitania (Touraine et al. 1981: 103). However, insofar as Europe functioned as an institutional counter to French nationalism and neo-colonialism, European supranational institutions offered a positive hope for regional development (Alcouffe et al. 1979: 7). In 1974, the European Parliament established the European Fund for Regional Development (FEDER) in order to finance industrial projects within underdeveloped regions. While originally the funds were distributed through a quota system to member states, who then allocated the monies as they saw fit, a series of reforms in 1984–85 allowed for a greater ability of local collectivities to have their dossiers directly examined by the funding bodies. In Brittany alone, more than 1.7 billion francs were received for 500 different projects between 1974 and 1984 (Quémèré 1986: 63).

Paralleling these economic development projects was European institutional support for regional languages and cultures. As early as 1961, the Council of Europe recommended the adoption of a supplementary article to the European Convention on Human Rights stipulating that "Persons belonging to a minority . . . cannot be prohibited their right . . . to have their own cultural life, to use their own language, to open their own schools, and to be educated in the language of their choice" (cited in Giordan 1982: 14). These intentions were reiterated in subsequent years in the Helsinki Accords (1975) and in the initial conference of European cultural ministers in Oslo (1976). Later, in October 1981, in the early days of French socialist experiments in multiculturalism, the European Parliament passed a resolution to establish an EC charter on regional languages and cultures and minority ethnic rights (Giordan 1982: 24). This resulted eventually in the European Charter on Regional or Minority Languages, which the Council of Europe adopted in November 1992. The Charter provided for the official recognition of and financial support for regional and immigrant languages represented on the European territory. In the case of France, this included Arabic and Tamazight, as well as Breton, Occitan, Catalan, Basque, Flemish, and Alsatian. While the French government ratified thirty-nine of the ninety-one resolutions of the Charter in May 1999, the Charter was later rejected wholesale by the Constitutional Council on the basis that it violated France's basic constitutional principle regarding the indivisibility of the French republic.

French regionalist groups responded to these European projects by organizing large conferences throughout France, bringing together a plurality of associations that existed in each of the six major indigenous cultural-linguistic regions of France: Brittany, Occitania, Catalonia, Alsace, Flanders, and Basque country (or Euskadi). In addition, these meetings were supplemented by a series of interregional congresses held throughout France and Europe, uniting various activists from different regional constituencies in an attempt to present their demands in a unified fashion. These congresses drew inspiration from a series of earlier such joint meetings held between Basque and Breton cultural associations during the early 1970s (Sibé 1988: 148). Often, these demonstrations of interregional solidarity were based in the recognition of fictive ties of kinship, as in the case of the pan-Celtic conferences held regularly throughout the 1980s and 1990s between groups from Brittany, Cornwall, Northern Ireland, Scotland, and Wales; or in terms of regionalist movements in Catalonia and Euskadi that traverse official state borders. However, increasingly regionalist groups in Occitania, Brittany, and elsewhere have individually petitioned European institutions like the European Parliament on the basis of European conventions to force individual nation-states to recognize their rights to the public use and instruction of their language and culture. These developments effectively enervated the ability of the French nation-state to regulate fully its own internal diversity and allowed for subnational groups to form lasting transnational connections. As Robert Lafont concluded as early as 1978, "It has now become clear that [Occitania's future] is no longer only a regional affair, or even a French one, but rather one of Europe" (Alcouffe et al. 1979: 199).

Fortress Europe

The socialist government's attempts to reconstruct the French national imaginary along multicultural lines thus contributed paradoxically to the opening up of new avenues of transregional and transnational unity that defied the limits of state national territory. These connections between immigrant and regionalist groups in France increased apace throughout the 1990s. If in the 1980s immigrant and regional groups in France forged connections with spatially distant others defined generally in terms of kinship, by the mid-1990s highly disparate immigrant and regional groups conjoined their activist efforts outside of a discourse of kinship. In large part, this unity has been directly related to a discursive shift in the language of universal rights to a postnational critique of the French nation-state model as the hegemonic sovereign form of belonging and citizenship (cf. Soysal 1994: 156–162).

The resulting shift in activism from a shared model of national civic universalism to one of transnational cultural unity is largely related to the hardening of national borders that accompanied France's post-1995 and post–11 September wars on terror. In the first place, the successive Vigipirate national security plans constituted a retreat from the open borders envisioned in European unification. Moreover, the security measures contradicted and impeded republican ideologies and policies aimed at culturally reproducing the French nation-state in that they exacerbated the further retrenchment of immigrant groups into categories of belonging drawn from abroad. Instead of fostering communal integration or advancing a "new citizenship" (nouvelle citoyenneté) along multicultural lines (cf. Wihtol de Wenden 1988), France's war on terror has led to new exclusions, mapping out internal boundaries of national belonging that effectively opposed those of Muslim faith to a majority defending its cultural values under the umbrella of laïcité. In amalgamating immigration, Islam, and terrorism, the French governments of the mid-1990s effectively redefined the French nation along neo-racist lines, treating immigrant and regional cultural and religious differences as potentially subversive.

This retrenchment of imagined and physical national borders is further related to larger debates provoked by France's economic and political integration into the European Community. The rise of ethnoparticularist national sentiment in France has had as much to do with base economic, political, and cultural fears of immigrant difference as it has had with a more general uncertainty over France's role in a borderless Europe. For small farmers and shopkeepers inhabiting regions not particularly affected by immigration patterns, the socioeconomic threat implied by the withdrawal of French protectionism derives primarily from east of the Rhine, and not south of the Mediterranean. Nonetheless, their tacit if not electoral support for Euroskeptic parties like the Front National—exemplified most dramatically in Le Pen's accession to the second round of the 2002 presidential elections—lends support to the growth of anti-immigration policies and serves indirectly to radicalize immigrant identity politics that today constitute the major challenge to the sovereign integrity of the French nation-state.

Pan-Ethnic Unity

The interaction between a unifying Europe and postcolonial immigration has productive implications beyond its challenge to state sovereignty. For, while the weakening of inter-European borders has implied the strengthening of extra-European ones, the parallel growth of supranational European bodies, like the European Court or the European Parliament, has actually served in many cases to protect the rights of immigrant and refugee populations. On the one hand, this has occurred through common agreements to smooth out national differences in citizenship and naturalization legislation, changes which have encouraged nations like Germany, with immigrant incorporation and citizenship policies based on heredity (*jus sanguinis*), to adopt more lenient policies based on residence (*jus soli*) (cf. Brubaker 1992; Soysal 1994). On the other hand, these European institutions have provided forums for immigrant groups themselves to initiate change. Already in 1994, non-European immigrant groups from across Europe jointly appealed to the European Parliament for independent representation as the "Thirteenth Nation" in an EU of then twelve states (Kastoryano 1994).

More recently, Berber groups based in Europe, representing populations throughout North Africa and the diaspora, have likewise addressed letters, petitions, and speeches to the United Nations, UNESCO, and the European Parliament demanding the official recognition and teaching of Berber culture in individual countries like Algeria and France. For instance, on 24 July 2002, representatives of the CMA addressed the UN Commission on Human Rights Working Group on Autochthonous Peoples at its twentieth annual session in Geneva. In light of the 2001 violent confrontations between government forces and residents of Kabylia, the CMA asked that the group "demand that different states recognize the Amazighs' right to self-determination, as a means of protecting their cultural identity and preventing or resolving conflicts with the states." In preparation for this

session, the representatives solicited specific proposals using the various
Internet mailing lists and bulletin boards, particularly Amazigh-Net and
soc.cult.berber, that have for the last five years served as forums for political
and cultural debate among Berber populations resident throughout the world.
Such discussion aided in the forging of virtual transnational solidarity regardless of any actual political outcomes of the session.

If immigrant groups in France and beyond appear to have followed the
inspiration of the French regionalist movement in utilizing Europe as a court
of appeals against individual nation-states, such a tactical overlap has been
by no means incidental. Since the mid-1990s, immigrant causes in France
have directly united their struggles with those of various ethnolinguistic
activist groups in Europe. From its inception in the early 1980s, the yearly
Festival of Breton People organized by the Breton Democratic Union has
invited artists and artisans from other French regions, from across the Channel, and from former North African colonies (McDonald 1989: 151). Additionally, the Breton Douarnenez film festival devoted its 1994 and 1996
programs to "Berbers" and "Immigrant Communities" respectively. The
1994 festival, in bringing together Berber activists and artists from throughout Europe, actually served as the birthplace of what would become the
CMA. Similarly, the 1996 event, in featuring films produced by Algerians in
France, Turks in Germany, and Pakistanis in Britain, as well as offering
lectures and debates on regional and immigrant rights, provided the space
for immigrant organizations to interact and compare their struggles. While
Breton films were still shown in these festivals, they took a peripheral place
to the focus group's endeavors.

Likewise, immigrant groups in France have similarly begun to open
their conferences and festivals to regional minority groups in Europe. The
MCB-France's 1996 commemoration of the Berber Spring was a particularly poignant example of this performed solidarity. While the room was
decked with Kabyle flags and maps, and while the majority of interventions
addressed aspects of Berber identity and the place of Tamazight in France
and Algeria, the Occitans attempted to relate these questions to the larger
issue of minoritized languages in the French metropole. In particular, Jean-
François Blanc, director of one of the oldest Occitan cultural organizations,
the Institute of Occitan Studies, centered his discussion on a critique of the
nation-state as an instrument of homogenization. He warned Berber activists that the seeming support given by the Algerian government for Berberity
by the creation of the HCA might prove fleeting. He concluded that "the
[Occitan] experience with regards to the central state shows that we cannot
count on it." If Occitan activists modeled themselves on Algerian revolu-
tionaries during the wars of decolonization, in the postcolonial period they
were holding themselves up as models to be followed.

In this way, the joint action of non-commensurable immigrant and regionalist groups in France has largely predicated itself on a critique of the

Poster of the 1996 Film Festival of Douarnenez (Brittany)
dedicated to "Immigrant Communities in Europe."

nation-state as an agent of homogenization and cultural destruction. In a
pamphlet distributed across Paris and its *banlieues* five months after the
conference—on the eve of the referendum of an Algerian constitution that,
as Blanc had predicted, betrayed Berberophone populations by once again
reiterating Arabic as the national language of Algeria—the MCB-France
levied its definitive disavowal of traditional state structures. According to
the pamphlet, "The rupture with the concept of the nation-state, 'one language, one culture, one school,' elsewhere paradoxically defended until now

by a large number of militants, is today a necessity." What remained was to work through decentralized, transnational bodies, like the imagined Berber homeland of Tamazgha or, alternately, a unified Europe.

But which Europe? For Occitan militant Robert Lafont, only a "Europe of regions" would suffice, for a "Europe of states" had only aided and abetted member states in the persecution of regionalist groups accused of state subversion (Alcouffe et al. 1979: 102). The contemplated "Europe of regions" remains an unfulfilled promise, seemingly forever deferred but potentially of dramatic consequence for the topography of European sovereignty. As French regionalist activist Alain Sibé mused, "The reality of today's Europe has transformed our geopolitical situation. We were on the periphery. We can become, if we want, axes, pivotal regions" (1988).

Conclusion

The place of ethnoracial, religious, and linguistic difference in the French nation-state has been profoundly ambivalent and marked by the play of structural nostalgia. From the colonization of Algeria through the postcolonial present, state and subaltern actors have simultaneously avowed and disavowed—produced and erased—subnational categories of French and Algerian identity. Rather than the primordial "others" of the nation-state, Islam and Berberity as contemporary cultural logics and categories of political subjectivity are the products of complex historical processes of construction, elaboration, appropriation, and contestation. Discursive formations like the "Kabyle Myth" and the "Islamalgam" underwrite how ethnic and religious identities have been historically represented and embodied in complex symbolic figures like Zinedine Zidane, Khaled Kelkal, Azouz Begag, and Lounès Matoub. They similarly pervade such symbolically charged spaces as the Kabyle domestic *axxam*, the *tajmaât* village assembly, the *cité* housing project, and the secular school system. These people and spaces come to signify idealized pasts—a "time before time"—as well as a set of alternately anticipated and feared futures of national unity or breakup. They are thus sites of contestation over the nature of Frenchness, over the place of Muslim and Berber particularism within republican universalism, over the legitimacy of Islam and Berberity as elements of French and Algerian modernity. It is these processes of contention, as they occur simultaneously on both sides of the Mediterranean, that constitute the transpolitics with which this book is concerned.

How can we understand the impact of Algerian transpolitics on the political and cultural life of the French nation-state? Islam and Berberity, as historically constructed categories of religious and ethnic difference, outline the social and political reality of nearly two million Algerian immigrants and their children in contemporary France. As cultural logics, they shape everyday performances including bodily comportment, language use, residence patterns, intergenerational relations, literary taste, interior decoration, and ritual forms. As identity diacritics, they enable various forms of cultural politics and political engagement both within France and across the Mediterranean. They frame the enactment of the Algerian civil war on French soil, as well as a variety of local actions, from cultural and neighborhood activism to novel writing, to municipal and national electioneering. The April 2001 political campaign and electoral success in Toulouse of the Franco-Kabyle rap-pop musical group Zebda—funded through the group's sales of global disco hits, Marxist revolutionary anthems, and collaborations with Kabyle singer-activist Idir—attests to the multidimensionality of allegiances and sites of immigrant politics in France.

Moreover, Algerian transpolitics effects transformations in French public life writ large. Islam and Berberity are not merely attributes of Algerian denizens of France, but categories through and against which the French nation-state as a whole has been dialectically determined. The simultaneous colonial elaboration of Islamic religion, Berber ethnicity, and French nationality as variously commensurate and incommensurate modalities of personal identity and group solidarity has found itself repeatedly revisited and renegotiated as the French presence in Algeria has been replaced by an Algerian presence in France, as France has reoriented itself from empire to Europe. In the context of a newly unified Europe, Algerian transpolitics calls into direct question the cultural makeup of French nationality and citizenship, the particularist and universalist dimensions of the French nation-state as a political form. In the face of the growth of such transnational social formations, national sovereignty is increasingly at stake.

Transnational Social Formations

The discussion of diasporic Algerian cultural politics in France necessitates a re-evaluation of the nation, infranation, and transnation as discrete, mutually exclusive categories of sociopolitical allegiance and belonging. Diasporas and transnational social movements have become constitutive features of the contemporary political landscape, as well as salient keywords within a burgeoning academic register that seeks to challenge state-centered realist theories of political action. More than ever, global networks of "flows and fluxes" of goods, ideas, and people seem to constitute the definitive feature of the modern world-system (cf. Appadurai 1996: 27–47; Schiller et al. 1992, 1994; Robertson 1992; Sassen 1998; Tsing 2000). These motions, as mediated by technologies of high-speed communication, create new boundaries that are not necessarily defined in national terms. Such new technologies outline both the infranational physical neighborhoods of the *cités* in France and transnational virtual communities of diasporic Berbers united through Internet mailing lists and web surfing.

The creation of these infranational and transnational boundaries results in the formation of new categories of political subjectivity, of new formulations of solidarity and belonging across spatial and ethnic divides, of "new patriotisms" (Appadurai 1996: 158–177; Hall 1991): Boukhedenna's fantasized passport marked "Nationality: Immigrant," or the World Amazigh Congress's index of a multistate Berber homeland of "Tamazgha." Indeed, these new modalities of transnational political belonging may signal an emerging "crisis of the nation-state" and the entrance of the world into a "postnational" phase of politics (Appadurai 1996: 19; Schiller et al. 1994). However, tolling the death knell of the nation-state may be both premature and misleading. The danger of characterizing contemporary politics as postnational is that it potentially underwrites a simplistic Hegelian teleological schema by which the "transnational" becomes the latest evolutionary stage in the perfection of human political society. Algerian transpolitics in France attests to a more complex reality.

The transnational, as a category of Franco-Algerian political action and an articulation of political solidarity, is neither some more global version of the national nor some alternate sphere of meaning completely removed from the national. Rather, it should be understood as simultaneously both and neither; it is related to the nation-state in some intimate way, while itself being constituted in the nation-state's limits. Transnational politics—whether exemplified in immigrant and regionalist actors' recourse to the supranational institutions of the UN and the EU for national political status or legal rights, or in their articulation of a spatially non-contiguous "Thirteenth Nation" or Berber Tamazgha—clearly defy national boundaries while at the same time being predicated on them. They provide a powerful recourse for localized groups seeking to challenge the authority of national governments while at the same time constraining those groups' actions in that the very political forms and supranational bodies with which they negotiate are themselves the product and purview of extant nation-states. In other words, the very existence and functioning of transnational social formations within France or elsewhere does not in and of itself imply a "crisis of the nation-state." If such a crisis exists, then it is but the latest manifestation in a long dialectic in which the nation and its internal and external excesses have been mutually engaged.

Immigrant transpolitics have nonetheless been directly implicated in particular transformations in the cultural logics of French and Algerian state national sovereignty. Algerian transnational social movements based on Islam and Berberity situate themselves at the interstices within the French and Algerian nation-states' homonymous configuration of ethnos, territory, and state (cf. Ruggie 1993). While posed as a universal template of political belonging, the French republic has been historically based on a profound mystification of time and space, on a particular fantasy of a single people (or *ethnos*) mapped onto a single geographical space as governed by a single political authority. However, each of these triangular, dyadic axes—linking ethnos and state, ethnos and territory, and state and territory—represent ongoing historical projects of construction and are hence always already unstable, all the more so under conditions of extreme social upheaval such as the current civil war in Algeria. It is along such ruptures that Algerian transpolitics operates.

Ethnos and State

In the first place, the fantasized fungibility of ethnos and sovereignty is belied by the ambivalent incorporation of cultural particularity into universalist frameworks of citizenship from colonial times to the present. The growth of postcolonial Algerian immigrant groups in France has particularly underlined fractures within French nationalist ideologies that unilineally unite nationality and citizenship, that hyphenate nations and states. In parallel with Kabyle manifestations in Algeria for the officialization of Tamazight as a national language, the Beur Movement in early 1980s France articulated a claim of their veritable "right to difference" posed in a language of universal rights. Drawing inspiration from each other's successes, Kabyle Algerians and Algerian French have taken liberal universalism to its logical end, attempting to break free of the bonds of assimilation while affirming their political rights as citizens. Being French, according to this reformulation of political subjectivity, need not imply accepting the Gauls as one's ancestors.

To a large extent, this invocation of cultural difference as a universal human right extended from the ruling socialist party's promulgation of a "plural France" and its experiments with multicultural policies during the early 1980s. While a number of the Beur Movement's social actions were designed to combat practical problems involved with life in the suburban *cités*—repairing dilapidated housing projects or providing after-school tutoring for local youth—its cultural and literary production focused more directly on the reappropriation of immigrant cultural histories marginalized in official versions of French unity. Moreover, Beur activists organized and participated in a series of anti-racist political marches and demonstrations for racial equality and civic rights, rights which they felt were denied de facto under French integration policies. Throughout, they declared their hybrid cultural particularity as neither fully French nor Algerian, as "mutants torn from the 'McDonalds couscous-steak-fries society'" (Kettane 1986: 19).

The Beur challenges to the unity of French nationality and citizenship, of ethnos and state, provoked a two-part response. The claim to cultural difference as a universal human right was co-opted by neo-racist groups who affirmed the inviolability of ethnic particularity under the rubric of "France for the (truly) French." Citizenship, accordingly, was resutured to national identity. In parallel, the claims of a "right to difference" were countered by even more universalist invocations of a "right to resemblance," an extreme form of liberalism that, in the words of Julia Kristeva (1993), would envision "nations without nationalism." As such, a set of putatively postnational identity politics, as well as the responses to them, have reopened a set of debates concerning the nature of universalism as a constitutive feature of French nationalism. Transnational processes of migration and cultural exchange thus serve to redefine, as well as simply challenge, national discourses.

Ethnos and Territory

In the second place, Algerian transpolitics has situated itself at the unstable intersection of ethnos and territory within national formations. While the nation-state is premised on the isomorphic identity of a unitary people and a single geographic space, many Algerians in France have constructed hybrid political subjectivities and allegiances, often holding dual citizenship and participating politically to one degree or another in both France and Algeria. Eschewing any cultural referents to a single place or country of origin, they quite literally operate between national entities with no aim to reterritorialize or to form a separate state.

Likewise, the transnational Berberist movement situates itself simultaneously within and between territorial boundaries. With no official status in North Africa, Berberophones have globally participated in a spatially transient World Amazigh Congress (CMA). While the CMA discursively enacts a postnational, non-contiguous Berber world, or Tamazgha, that unites members resident in North Africa and abroad, it is pragmatically organized along national lines, with an administrative structure that mimics the executive and legislative branches of nation-states, with representatives elected from each national entity. Indeed, alliances and conflicts within the CMA have largely followed such national lines, occurring particularly between Moroccan and Algerian member associations. Moreover, the CMA's activities have been largely oriented toward a world of nation-states and borrow directly from the language of universalism: whether it be publicizing the violation of Touareg human rights in Niger, or petitioning the UN and EU to underwrite claims for the official recognition of the Berber language in Morocco and Algeria (Maddy-Weitzman 2001; Silverstein 2003).

Further, Algerian transnational social formations challenge the bundling of ethnos and territory within contemporary nation-states in terms of the ways immigrant and regionalist groups have actively forged alliances with other groups with whom they may share very little in common outside of their minoritized status. Beur and Berber activists have in different contexts declared themselves transnationally in solidarity with the struggles of Palestinian refugees and Israelis. They have also joined forces with other non-European immigrant groups throughout Europe and have variously created mutual aid societies in hopes of achieving some form of official representation as a "Thirteenth Nation" within the European Union (Kastoryano 1994: 170). Indeed, in the mid-1990s there occurred a burgeoning interaction between the transnational Berber cultural movement and localized Breton and Occitan militant organizations, with both groups allying their demands for the French ratification of the European Charter institutionalizing their respective idioms as "minority languages" of France. In other words, while organized and solidified transnationally, the ground on which such transpolitics has occurred is clearly national in scope.

Territory and State

In the third place, Algerian transnational politics has played on the instabilities of unifying ideologies of territory and the state within national formations, on the increasing non-contiguity of state polities. With a large number of their nationals living in diasporic settings, the Algerian state has been forced to direct a great deal of its political energy abroad. Already during the Algerian war, France was administratively delineated by the revolutionary FLN as the "seventh *wilaya* (province)" of fund-raising, recruiting, and military action (Haroun 1992). After independence, the FLN attempted to encapsulate its overseas citizens as a single diasporic group, seeking to manage their religious, political, and cultural lives through the medium of its European representative, the Amicale. Since the constitutional reforms of 1989, this outreach to Algerians in Europe has been fragmented by the legalization of multiple political parties of Islamist, Berberist, feminist, and Marxist ilk that have each established their overseas agencies that not only electioneer, but also organize conferences, demonstrations, and educational activities. In yet another postcolonial irony, one could argue that France has become a primary site for conducting Algerian politics.

However, such a putative postnational politics is largely enacted in forms recognizable and legitimated by French political structures. On the one hand, certain North African Islamist jurists and orators, recognizing the large number of Muslim practitioners in the Hexagon, have reterritorialized France as part of the transnational *dar al-islam* (realm of Islam/peace), in opposition to the non-Muslim *dar al-harb* (realm of war) in Islamic geography. Underlining such a characterization, transnational Islamist social movements have appropriated globally circulating technologies and media—from newsprint to cassette recording to the World Wide Web—in order to forge a sense of simultaneity of identity and purpose among believers worldwide (cf. Eickelman and Anderson 1999).

On the other hand, Muslim leaders in France have generally operated within the moral and political frameworks of the French state. Institutionalizing themselves as cultural associations, Islamic groups in France have been greatly involved in local community life, providing religious, economic, and policing services for disenfranchised suburban immigrant housing projects, much as they had in the poorer urban quarters of pre–civil war Algeria. While in Algeria such grassroots community organization was eventually perceived as a threat to state authority and violently dismantled in a series of heavy-handed actions that largely precipitated the 1990s civil war, in France such local Muslim organization was often logistically and economically subsidized by local municipal governments more than happy to have help in the administration of these economically impoverished areas. Such initial support, however, proved to be only ambivalently granted, as the French state carefully monitored the thin line between social action and politics, and tended to intervene—with mass arrests of suspected Islamist "terrorists"—whenever it believed an autonomous *dar al-islam* was being erected on French soil.

Nation, Intranation, Transnation

Thus, the French nation-state functions as one possible imagined community among others, as one very particular mapping of people (as homogenized) onto territory (as bounded) onto power (as unitary and bureaucratic). Perpetually needing to reimagine itself, it remains in continual dialogue and mutual dependence with its infranational and transnational others. Its power only assured when recognized globally, the French government has been a key player in the establishment of transnational regulatory bodies such as the UN and the EU that are imbued with the power to intercede in the affairs of sovereign states. Likewise, in order to reinforce their internal authority, French state actors have historically engaged in techniques of categorization and enumeration—including mapping, censuses, statistical and ethnographic studies, and development projects—that have had the paradoxical result of fixing the very regional boundaries and reifying the very ethnic, linguistic, and religious differences that they may have ultimately wished to suppress.

The result of these necessary and natural functions of the French nation-state has been more and more the organization of intranational groups across national borders that have begun to make political claims directly to transnational bodies. While these developments do not necessarily imply the decline and fall of the nation-state, they do imply that new spaces are opening up for the enacting of power which in many ways unseat the nation-state's unique claim to hegemony in global politics and which furthermore challenge its internal hyphenation (cf. Appadurai 1996: 161–177). Claims of Berber and Beur distinctiveness, largely based in the reappropriation of colonial and nationalist narratives, have simultaneously forced a re-evaluation of France's and Algeria's individual negotiations of state power and ethnic difference, as well as their collective articulation of territorial borders and state sovereignty. In these ways, nation, infranation, and transnation function as mutually dependent and dialectically constituted categories of subjectivity, bases of sovereignty, and modalities of political action.

In this respect, events and genres like the Beur novel, suburban urbanism, the headscarf affair, and the World Amazigh Congress are total social phenomena that simultaneously have political, cultural, and socioeconomic dimensions and that operate in a transnational space of discourse and practice that unites France and Algeria, Europe and North Africa. While operating within such conditions of cross-border flows and fluxes of ideas, commodities, and people, these processes have been largely productive of sets of national and intranational—religious, ethnic, and linguistic—categories that have largely conditioned the constitution of gendered and generational subjectivities and hierarchies among Algerians and Franco-Algerians in France. Moreover, such categories have engendered a diverse set of transpolitics, from the creation of associations based on generation and locality, to sports play and novel writing.

Algerian transpolitics in France charts a close relation between cultural production and changing modes of political contestation. Most significantly for the contemporary period, there has occurred a series of shifts in the imagination of internal and external boundaries, as the contours of the French political imaginary alternately expand and contract to encompass a colonial empire or a unified Europe. For both Franco-Algerian and regional groups alike, these changes have outlined new possibilities for the enactment of civil society. From electioneering to jointly petitioning the Council of Europe, French citizens of minoritized ethnic, religious, or linguistic identity have been able to articulate a cultural politics that reaches beyond the confines of assimilation to French republican norms. While this transnationalization has on occasion abetted the growth of religious or ethnic extremisms, it has more often encouraged the expansion of minority rights and tolerance.

In both their functioning in a transnational space and demands for infranational particularity, Algerian transpolitics thus calls into question the unitary authority of the nation-state to monolithically couple people, territory, and power. However, since the political strategies and identity categories underwriting this challenge have been culled and adapted from the very techniques of classification and enumeration, from the processes of industrialization and centralization employed by the nation-state to exert and extend its own dominance, one must see the contemporary contestation in large part as a product of the nation-state's own internal contradictions. In what Zygmunt Bauman (1991) has termed the "ambivalence of modernity," France and Algeria each find themselves engaged in ongoing processes of political and cultural reinvention, in a protracted conflict surrounding the unresolved hyphenation of national particularism and civic universalism, of nation and state. Algerian transpolitics represents an important element and agent in these contemporary struggles.

Most importantly, the ambivalence of modernity is not simply a feature of Algeria in France, but rather characteristic of the larger world that anthropologists take as their object of study. The pervasiveness of high-speed technologies of communication means that local life in even the most out-of-the-way places is increasingly dependent on and in dialogue with dynamics and developments occurring beyond the boundaries of the community. Anthropologists' privileged interlocutors are not only cultural specialists in the narrow sense of being master speakers of a local cultural idiom, but are most often engaged in processes of cultural representation, translation, and objectification for, and with agents of, the national government, non-governmental organizations, and supranational institutions. To put it a different way, anthropology's much-touted local perspective is always already embedded in a set of global discourses and processes. For anthropology to become more local, it thus must become more global. However, this "global," outside of a scholarly abstraction, only exists as locally instantiated and can but be studied as such. Reciprocally, then, for anthropology to become more global it must simultaneously become more local.

All of which is to gloss Bernard Cohn's famous statement about the interdependence of anthropological and historical inquiry, that "anthropology can become more anthropological in becoming more historical" (1987: 42). For anthropology's object of study is constituted across time as well as space. To be exact, the dialogue between local and global perspectives is itself determined within a history of colonialism and postcoloniality in which both anthropological and local scripts of culture have been formed and transformed. Making this historical dialogue the object of scholarly inquiry reveals the play of transpolitics in everyday social life, not only in terms of the ways in which transnational concerns imbue everyday struggles, but also in terms of how seemingly delimited practices such as sports play, novel writing, and religious dress become themselves objects of politics. *Algeria in France* calls our attention to these larger processes that characterize the world we inhabit and study.

Notes

1. Immigration Politics in the New Europe

1. Such reticence was in contrast to the large international media coverage of anti-Semitic violence in France in 2002–2003 in the wake of the al-Aqsa Intifada and the U.S. war in Iraq.

2. The last issue has proved especially important for Turkish residents, as giving up Turkish citizenship means, according to Turkish law, forfeiting their rights to own property in Turkey.

3. For a nuanced and revealing history of French immigration policy and scholarship, focusing on how immigrant difference has been written out of French history, see Green (1991) and Noiriel (1988).

4. Algerians were additionally subject to a separate 1973 statute by which children of Algerian immigrants born in France after 1962 to parents born in Algeria under French colonialism (i.e., when Algeria was legally three states [*départements*] of France) were considered full French citizens at birth. This provision retrospectively treated their parents as if they were French citizens. In point of fact, Algerian Muslims were granted a degree of French citizenship only after World War II, and then with only partial representation and partial rights.

5. These revisions, known collectively as the "Pasqua Laws" after the conservative minister of the interior, also revoked the special provisions for Algerians. The Pasqua Laws were rescinded after the election of the socialist Lionel Jospin as prime minister in 1996.

6. "Does not the manifest tolerance of the ethnicities and religions that are included in the notion of British subject, which does not invite them to share an *esprit général* but claims to respect their particularities, end up immobilizing the latter and perpetuating the racial or religious wars that are shaking up the Commonwealth as well as the United Kingdom?" (Kristeva 1993: 12). Schnapper adds, "In countries founded on the principle of collective [as opposed to individual] integration, we witness the formation of ethnic quarters" (1992: 97).

7. Such nostalgia, as Marilyn Ivy suggests, is decidedly modern, a product of nation formation (Ivy 1995).

2. Colonization and the Production of Ethnicity

1. For a general discussion of North African Muslim heteropraxy, focused primarily on Morocco, see Geertz (1968) and Gellner (1969). For a critique of this

approach, see Hammoudi (1997) and Messick (1993). For a detailed historical account of precolonial Algeria, see Valensi (1969).

2. The dey Hussein was reported to have yelled "Leave! Roman (*roumi*), son of a dog. Leave! Leave!" and to have slapped the consul across the face with his fly swatter (Garrot 1910: 648).

3. For a detailed discussion of the differences between strategies of assimilation and integration, see Wright (1997: 327).

4. "Teachers have been invited to consider themselves as the agents and collaborators of the commandants and to inspire themselves from their advice. After the military conquest, the French language and idea have become the new weapons (*armes*) with which to enter into the fray (*mener le bon combat*)" (Anon. 1924: 252).

5. For a critical reading of the French "civilizing mission" as it played itself out in the Pacific, see Bullard (2000). For a discussion of processes of disenchantment in another colonial context, see Bourdieu (1979) and Mitchell (1988).

6. For an erudite history of the Berber peoples from antiquity to the present, see Brett and Fentress (1996). For a nuanced anthropological history of colonial and postcolonial Kabylia, see Mahé (2001).

7. Abdellah Hammoudi (1993: 15–32; 1997: 98–133) has brilliantly discussed French anthropologists of Berber ritual and political structures as "pioneers" of colonialism in Morocco. See Said (1993: 97–110) for a larger discussion of the role of European scholars and intellectuals in maintaining the "cultural integrity of Empire."

8. The appellation "Kabyle Myth" was first formulated by Charles-Robert Ageron (1960) in his seminal article, "La France, a-t-elle un politique kabyle?" ("Does France have a Kabyle policy?"). He identified the myth of Kabyle superiority as operating primarily from 1840 to 1870, though with antecedents going back to 1826 (before the French occupation) and corollary attitudes continuing into the twentieth century. What changed, according to the author, was the assumption of the assimilability of the Kabyles (cf. Guilhaume 1992: 236–241; Lucas and Vatin 1975: 45). For a detailed description of the myth, see Lorcin (1995) and Sayad (1992).

9. See Assia Djebar (1980) for a postcolonial literary dramatization-cum-eruption of Delacroix's harem scene. For a further discussion of French colonial desire and scopic regimes in North Africa, see Apter (1999, esp. 99–112). For a detailed discussion of the "women's question" in colonial and postcolonial Algeria, and a critique of Fanon and Alloula's patri-nationalist writings, see Lazreg (1994).

10. Early racial interpretations of the French Revolution by the Abbé de Sièyes, for instance, linked the Third Estate with the biblical Gauls overthrowing the Aryan Frankish aristocracy. Whether France was intrinsically Gaulish or Frankish became a subject of wide academic controversy for nearly a century. Later, the romantic historian Jules Michelet situated the originality of France in the very mélange of these races with others (cf. Citron 1994).

11. Assertions of a culturally unified Mediterranean have been appropriated into anthropological studies of the region, in part via the bridging work of Fernand Braudel (1972)—himself a product of the late colonial period—in part through an obsession with cultural features like the "honor-shame syndrome" as a unifying trope for the region (cf. Peristiany 1965; Gilmore 1987). Michael Herzfeld has largely debunked such "master symbols," demonstrating how they are reified within an-

thropological discourse and contribute to a de facto hardening of stereotypes within the region itself (1984: 439–443).

12. Abdelmalek Sayad (1994a) has levied a thoroughgoing critique of this position, demonstrating that the Kabyles' propensity to spatial displacement was the direct result of colonial upheavals.

13. The law of 26 June 1889 granted automatic French citizenship to children of non-French Europeans ("foreigners") born in Algeria, and further cleared administrative impediments to the naturalization of their parents. The celebration of the miscegenated Latin race should not mask the fact that a fervent internal racism against "foreigners" and "neos" (new citizens) did exist within the colony, with certain nativist politicians decrying the existence of a "foreign peril" in the new arrivals (Ageron 1991: 62; Guilhaume 1992: 221–222).

14. In Morocco, the colonial government issued the so-called Berber "dahir" of 1930 in which the tribal populations were administratively divided from Arab ones and were allowed to be governed by their own customary tribunals and courts of appeal instead of the Islamic shari'a courts (cf. Hammoudi 1997: 113–123).

15. François Mitterrand, then minister of the interior, stated in a speech given on 5 November 1954 during an official visit to the Aurès: "Algeria is France. And France will not recognize any other authority there but its own" (cited in Manceron and Remaoun 1993: 24).

16. For a discussion of the ongoing relevance and normativity of these foundational ideological struggles over the content of Algerian nationalism, see Moussaoui (2001).

17. Informally, Tamazight maintained a vibrant existence in Algeria, and even grew in strength with the work of standardization accomplished primarily in the diaspora but also underground in Algeria itself. For a provocative analysis of Algeria's postindependence linguistic struggles, see Khatibi (1990) and the essays collected in Berger (2002).

18. Pamphlet entitled "20 avril 1995: 15 ans de lutte ininterrompue" by the RCD-Immigration. The "eternal Jugurtha" refers to an epic poem by Jean Amrouche published in 1943 in which the Berber chieftain was presented as an "emblem of absolute liberty" for later generations of militants (Yacine 1995: 102).

3. Spatializing Practices

1. In one of the earliest studies of "foreigners" (*étrangers*) in France, Georges Mauco wrote, "The nationalities where criminality is the highest are those that most suffered from uprooting (*déracinement*) and whose adaptation is most difficult because of highly accentuated ethnic and civilizational differences" (1933: 269). See Wihtol de Wenden (1991: 103–106) for an extended discussion of this period in French immigration discourse. See Noiriel (1988: 159–163) for a discussion of *déracinement* as an analytical model in French migration studies.

2. While similar grand-scale plans were proposed for Algeria (and Algiers in particular) in the 1930s by Henri Prost, Le Corbusier, and others, none were adopted (Çelik 1997: 70–86). Nonetheless, urban apartheid was established, with European cities built alongside the "indigenous" *medinas* and *casbahs,* creating what Frantz Fanon would decry as a "world divided into compartments" (1963: 38–39).

3. For a detailed study of the growth and industrial development of Paris's southern suburbs (esp. Ivry, Vitry, and Choisy), see Bastié (1964: 137–160).

4. For stimulating ethnographic and sociological studies of the *banlieues,* see Dubet and Lapeyronnie (1992), Lepoutre (1997), and Petonnet (1982). For a comparison between the Parisian *banlieue* and the Chicago "ghetto," see Wacquant (1994).

5. The first line was built in 1837 connecting Paris to west-suburban Pecq. By the end of Louis Napoleon's reign in 1870, 18,000 kilometers of rail had been laid, all of which converged on Paris's seven train stations (Saint-Lazare, Montparnasse, Est, Nord, Lyon, Austerlitz, and Orsay/Invalides).

6. See also Mohammed Zerroug's beautiful film *Vivre au Paradis* ("Living in Paradise") (1999), set in the Nanterre *bidonville* during the Algerian war. For an ethnography of the Nanterre *bidonville,* see Sayad and Dupuy (1995).

7. The French state's destruction of the FLN's network in France also took on more directly violent forms, as Parisian police opened fire on protesters during a 17 October 1961 FLN-sponsored demonstration in Paris to protest against newly imposed curfew laws, resulting in the death of nearly 200 Algerian men (Amicale des Algériens en Europe 1987; Stora 1991: 92–108).

8. After World War II, this mixed company would be reformed into the Public Office for Low-Rent Housing (OPHLM)). Today, the HLM designation applies to all public housing in France, whether controlled by the state, mixed public-private companies, or individual industries.

9. In a schematic plan for the forty-two-hectare garden city in Suresnes, legend indicators are given for social centers, apartment complexes, individual houses, baths, schools, health and nutritional centers, retirement homes, day care facilities, playing fields, single workers' dormitories, homeless shelters, assembly halls, automobile garages, and a church. Factories and administrative buildings are similarly portrayed in the design (HLM Aujourd'hui 1989).

10. Nearly a million French and Cagayous colonists, as well as more than 100,000 Jews and close to 200,000 *harkis* (or "repatriated French Muslims" in the official discourse), migrated from Algeria to France around the close of the war (Liauzu 1996: 105–111).

11. After 1996, this system began to be reformed, with more and more HLM operations being appropriated by the state, and the mandatory 1 percent employer contribution being phased out.

12. For a pointed examination of the situation of marginalization (*galère*) of *cité* youth, see Dubet (1987).

13. For studies of the settlement process, see Costa-Lascoux and Temime (1985), De Rudder (1992), Desplanques and Tabard (1991), Hargreaves (1995), and Tribalat (1991).

14. The northern suburbs of Paris have been historically known colloquially as the *banlieue rouge,* a solid constituency of the French Communist Party (PCF). This continued link of the PCF to the Parisian northern suburbs is today symbolized by its holding of an annual Humanity Festival in the large park of La Courneuve.

15. For an analysis of the symbolic importance of "chez soi" in the constitution of immigrant subjectivity, see Noiriel (1988: 215–217).

16. The sociologist Françoise Gaspard (personal communication) recounted a similar episode from a *cité* in the Parisian suburb of Dreux concerning a conflict between two groups of youths from adjoining areas known locally as "Moroccans" and "Harkis," racialized denominations that supposedly corresponded to the ar-

eas' original, but not current, residents. The conflict emerged over admittance to a party held in a building on the territory of one of the groups. The national newspaper, *Libération*, on the sole basis of an interview with police, reported the event as an *émeute*, a report ridiculed by local community organizers with whom Gaspard spoke shortly thereafter.

17. These numbers would increase by the June 1996 re-presentation of the plan before the National Assembly, from twenty duty-free zones to thirty-five, and from 546 sensitive urban areas to 744 (*Le Monde* 19 June 1996). For astute discussions of *banlieue* exclusion and violence, see Dubet and Lapeyronnie (1992), Wacquant (1994), and Wieviorka (1996; 1999).

18. For a reflexive anthropology of the Parisian *métro*, see Augé (2002).

19. For an extended discussion of ghettocentrism and the politics of locality in French hip-hop, see Silverstein (2002b).

4. Islam, Bodily Practice, and Social Reproduction

1. For a general discussion of the relationship between football and French national consciousness, see Bromberger (1998) and Hare (2003). For a detailed discussion of the PSG and its increasingly *banlieue*-based supporters, see Hare (2003: 78–88).

2. Nike eventually abandoned the campaign after the powerful anti-racist organization, the Movement Against Racism and for the Friendship of All Peoples (MRAP), called for a boycott of its products and pavilion. Nike replaced the *République populaire* advertisements with simple portraits of its internationally sponsored players.

3. For a history of immigration and French football, see Beaud and Noiriel (1990).

4. For an ancillary discussion of the relation of the U.S. news coverage of the 1979 Iranian revolution and the subsequent hostage crisis to the production of essentialized images of Islam as amalgamated to categories of fanaticism and terrorism, see Said (1981).

5. Notable exceptions to this portrayal include Cesari (1994; 1998); Kepel (1991); and Morsy (1993).

6. The 1996 Toubon and Debré laws would later link these two aspects of the plan, as they declared that all aid given to illegal immigrants would be punishable as a breach of state security under anti-terrorist laws.

7. This contrasts with the lack of territorialization that Pascal Chantelat et al. (1996: 91–93) detected in their study of street football and basketball in the suburbs of Lyon.

8. Séverine Labat, interview in *Le Monde*, 13 October 1995. Even official football clubs have made a place for religion. The PSG youth teams based in the *banlieues* have altered their schedules to account for the fasting of their Muslim players during Ramadan (Hare 2003: 87).

9. While Islamic theology gives primacy to the soul (*nafs*) over the body (*jasad*) (Chebel 1984), sports practice is publicly sanctioned and financially supported throughout the Muslim world.

10. For parallel discussions and interpretations of the "headscarf affair," see Auslander (2000), Bloul (1994), Beriss (1990), Cesari (1998), Hargreaves (1995: 125–131), and Terrio (1999).

11. As late as April 2003, conservative Prime Minister Jean-Pierre Raffarin called on French legislators to revisit the 1989 high court decision and ban all Muslim headscarves from schools.

12. In fact, Bayrou did not mention the *foulard* by name, unlike Jospin, who cited headscarves particularly but did not in any way differentiate them from other signs of religious belonging. By using the term "signs," Bayrou left the question open to school administrators who could then interpret any gesture or object (not just an article of clothing or jewelry) as "ostentatious."

13. For a chronicle and analysis of media representations of the headscarf, see Battegay and Boubeker (1993) and Perotti and Toulat (1990).

14. For a discussion of the relationship of schoolgirls to the American national fantasy, see Berlant (1997).

15. In 1994, under the new leadership of an African Muslim, SOS-Racisme changed its position entirely, declaring itself against "the wearing of any sign of religion in school" (*Le Monde* 27 October 1994).

5. The Generation of Generations

1. For a close reading of Sayad's dialectical model of Algerian emigration as a general approach to rural-urban migration, see Noiriel (1988: 148–187).

2. For younger generations, the residence permit (*carte de séjour*) has taken on a similar role as an instrument of surveillance that symbolizes their marginal existence in France.

3. For a parallel discussion of descent, land inheritance, emigration, and status conflict in Berberophone Morocco, see Berque (1962), Hart (1996), Ilahiane (2001), McMurray (2001), and Montagne (1930).

4. For discussions of "race" and "racism" in France, see Lamont (2000), Noiriel (1988), Schain et al. (2002), Sternhell (1983), Taguieff (1991), and Wihtol de Wenden (1991). For a detailed discussion of violence in France, see Wieviorka (1999).

5. For an anthropological analysis of anti-immigrant exclusionary violence in Europe, see Stolcke (1995). For a critical reinterpretation of the violence as national *inclusion* of marginalized *beaufs,* see Turner (1995).

6. The Barre/Bonnet law, passed in December 1979, enabled the detention and expulsion without trial of non-citizens in violation of immigration laws. The Stoléru Circular, officially enacted in June 1980, expanded the previous legislation by sanctioning the expulsion of legal aliens unemployed for a six-month period. While these laws were annulled in 1981 by President Mitterrand, the deportations continued apace under the auspices of even tougher legislation against undocumented immigrants.

7. The word *verlan* itself is a microcosm for the game, as it is an inversion of *l'envers,* the French term for "inverse." Other popular examples include *renoi* for *noir* ("Black"), *feuj* for *juif* ("Jew"), and, of course, *çéfran* for *français* ("French"). For a sociolinguistic analysis of *verlan,* see Lefkowitz (1991).

8. These measures included the creation of a National Commission for Urban Social Development (CNDSQ) and the establishment of "Special Education Sections" (SES) for immigrant children. The latter, unfortunately, tended to handicap rather than facilitate the students' progress toward the baccalaureate exam.

9. Official associations in France were established under a 1901 law that out-

lined the organizational and financial structures necessary for an association, as a non-profit entity, to receive government funds. The 1938 legislation prohibiting immigrant associations emerged from the socialist Popular Front government that feared the manipulation of Italian and German immigrant groups by cross-border fascist parties.

10. This formulation inverted Charles de Gaulle's famous defense of an imperial France "from Dunkerque to Tamanrasset."

11. A derogatory term for an Algerian, likely from the slang expression for a coal miner (*bougna*) used in the north of France where many Algerians once labored.

12. In a 1992 speech in Amiens, Le Pen commented on the slogan of the 1984 march, "France is like a moped: a mélange is required to make it run," adding, "Yes, but above four percent you blow the motor" (*Le Monde* 22 January 1996: 6).

6. Beur Writing and Historical Consciousness

1. For discussions of Boudjellal's work, see Douglas and Malti-Douglas (1994: 198–216) and McKinney (1997).

2. For a detailed history and parallel discussion of Beur writing, see Hargreaves (1991; 1997). For a poststructuralist reading of several of the genre's key texts, see Laronde (1993). My analysis is based on a close reading of more than twenty-five works by Beur authors.

3. For in-depth discussions of the history of North African literature as national narratives, see Apter (1999), Bensmaïa (2003), Bounfour (1994), Khatibi (1968), and Woodhull (1993).

4. Leila Sebbar explicitly explores such hybridity in her characterization of her protagonist in *Le Chinois vert d'Afrique* (1984) as the genealogical product of an Arabo-Sino-Turco-Vietnamese union living in France (see Laronde 1993: 177). For a more general discussion of Sebbar's oeuvre, see Kaplan (2001).

5. Mireille Rosello (1998) has provided an important analysis of Beur authors' confrontation of extant stereotypes.

7. Transnational Social Formations in the New Europe

1. For good histories and political analyses of the conflict in Algeria that Stora (2001), for one, has called "the second Algerian War," see Carlier (1995), Colonna (1995), Quandt (1998), and Roberts (2003). For a discussion of the epistemologies of conspiracy employed by Algerians to make sense of the conflict, see Silverstein (2002a).

2. Mouvement Culturel Berbère (Paris), "Lettre ouverte aux candidats à la présidence de la République," 3 April 1995.

3. RCD-Immigration, "20 avril 1995: 15 ans de lutte ininterrompue."

4. "In effect, roughly $2/3$ of the Maghreb's exterior commerce takes place with the EEC, $3/4$ with Europe, $4/5$ with the Western world, and only $1/5$ with the rest of the globe" (Khader 1995: 81).

5. For further articulations and analyses of a renewed French-Mediterranean space, see Balta (1992).

6. For a larger discussion of European discourse and institutions on immigrant and regional cultural rights, see Soysal (1994: 136–162).

Bibliography

Abouda, Mohand. 1985. *Axxam (Maisons kabyles): Espaces et fresques murales.* Goussainville: M. Abouda.

Abou-Sada, Georges, and Helène Millet. 1986. *Générations issues de l'immigration.* Paris: Editions de l'Arcantère.

Abu-Lughod, Janet. 1980. *Rabat: Urban Apartheid in Morocco.* Princeton, N.J.: Princeton University Press.

Abu-Lughod, Lila, ed. 1998. *Remaking Women: Feminism and Modernity in the Middle East.* Princeton, N.J.: Princeton University Press.

Achour, Christiane. 1993. The Quest for Identity: Proper Names and Narrators in Algerian Life-Histories. In *French and Algerian Identities from Colonial Times to the Present.* Edited by Alec Hargreaves and Michael J. Hefferman, pp. 203–215. Lewiston, N.Y.: Edwin Mellen Press.

Addi, Lahouari. 1996. Colonial Mythologies: Algeria in the French Imagination. In *Franco-Arab Encounters.* Edited by L. Carl Brown and Matthew S. Gordon. Beirut: American University of Beirut.

Ageron, Charles-Robert. 1991. *Modern Algeria: A History from 1830 to the Present.* Trenton, N.J.: Africa World Press.

———. 1960. La France a-t-elle un politique kabyle? *Revue historique* 223: 311–352.

Aïchoune, Farid. 1991. *Nés en banlieue.* Paris: Ramsay.

———, ed. 1985. *La Beur Génération.* Paris: Sans Frontière/Arcantère.

Aïssou, Abdel. 1987. *Les Beurs, l'école, et la France.* Paris: Editions l'Harmattan.

Al-Madani, Tawfiq. 1986 [1927]. *Qartâjanna fî arba'a 'usûr.* Algiers: Enterprise Nationale du Livre.

———. 1963 [1932]. *Kitâb al-Jazâ'ir.* Cairo: Dar al-Ma'arif.

Alcouffe, Alain, Pierre Lagarde, and Robert Lafont (1979): *Pour l'Occitanie.* Toulouse: Domaine Occitan Privat.

Allen, Sheila, and Marie Macey. 1990. Race and Ethnicity in the European Context. *British Journal of Sociology* 41 (3): 375–393.

Alloula, Malek. 1986. *The Colonial Harem.* Translated by Myrna Godzich and Wlad Godzich. Minneapolis: University of Minnesota Press.

Altschull, Elizabeth. 1995. *Le voile contre l'école.* Paris: Seuil.

Amalou, Florence. 1998a. Nike à l'école de la propagande totalitaire. *Le Monde,* 14 June.

———. 1998b. Adidas a déjà (presque) gagné sa coupe. *Le Monde,* 12 July.

Amicale des Algériens en Europe, ed. 1987. *17 octobre 1961. Mémoire d'une communauté*. Paris: Actualité de l'Emigration.

Ammi, Mustapha. 1985. Paroles de Beurs. In *La Beur Génération*. Edited by Farid Aïchoune. Paris: Sans Frontière/Arcantère.

Amselle, Jean-Loup. 2003. *Affirmative Exclusion: Cultural Pluralism and the Rule of Custom in France*. Ithaca, N.Y.: Cornell University Press.

———. 1998. *Mestizo Logics: Anthropology of Identity in Africa and Elsewhere*. Stanford, Calif.: Stanford University Press.

Anderson, Benedict. 1991. *Imagined Communities*. London: Verso.

Anonymous. 1924. La politique berbère du Protectorat. *Algérie française, Renseignements coloniaux* (July): 214–255.

Anonymous. 1881. *Guide de l'émigrant par un colon*. Paris: Agence Territoriale Algérienne.

Anonymous. 1873. *Les Arabes et la colonisation en Algérie*. Paris: Pougin.

Anonymous. 1836. *Colonisation de la régence d'Alger*. Paris: Société d'Afrique.

Appadurai, Arjun. 1996. *Modernity at Large: Cultural Dimensions of Globalization*. Minneapolis: University of Minnesota Press.

Apter, Emily. 1999. *Continental Drift: From National Characters to Virtual Subjects*. Chicago: University of Chicago Press.

Arnaud, Pierre. 1997. *Les athlètes de la République: Gymnastique, sport et idéologie républicaine, 1870–1914*. Paris: Harmattan.

Asad, Talal. 1993. *Genealogies of Religion: Discipline and Reasons of Power in Christianity and Islam*. Boston: Johns Hopkins University Press.

———. 1973. Two European Images of Non-European Rule. In *Anthropology and the Colonial Encounter*. Edited by Talal Asad. Atlantic Highlands, N.J.: Humanities Press.

Audisio, Gabriel. 1935. *Jeunesse de la Méditerranée*. Paris: Gallimard.

Augé, Marc. 2002. *In the Metro*. Trans. Tom Conley. Minneapolis: University of Minnesota Press.

Auslander, Leora. 2000. Bavarian Crucifixes and French Headscarves: Religious Signs and the Postmodern European State. *Cultural Dynamics* 12 (3): 183–209.

Axel, Brian, ed. 2002. *From the Margins: Historical Anthropology and Its Futures*. Durham, N.C.: Duke University Press.

Bahloul, Joelle. 1992. *La maison de mémoire. Ethnologie d'une demeure judéo-arabe en Algérie*. Paris: Editions Metailie.

Bakhtin, Mikhail M. 1981. *The Dialogic Imagination*. Trans. Caryl Emerson and Michael Holquist. Austin: University of Texas Press.

Balibar, Etienne, and Immanuel Wallerstein. 1991. *Race, Nation, Class: Ambiguous Identities*. New York: Verso.

Balta, Paul, ed. 1992. *La Méditerranée réinventée. Réalités et espoirs de la coopération*. Paris: La Découverte.

Barker, Martin. 1981. *The New Racism*. London: Junction Books.

Barré, Virginie. 1985. Fugueuses d'Aubervilliers. In *La Beur Génération*. Edited by Farid Aïchoune. Paris: Sans Frontière/Arcantère.

Barou, Jacques, ed. 1993. *Mémoire et intégration*. Paris: Syros.

Barthes, Roland. 1972. Myth Today. In *Mythologies*. New York: Noonday Press.

Basfao, Kacem, and Jean-Robert Henry. 1991. Le Maghreb et l'Europe: Que faire de la Méditerranée? *Vingtième Siècle* 32: 43–51.

Bastié, Jean. 1964. *La croissance de la banlieue parisienne*. Paris: Presses Universitaires de France.

Battegay, Alain, and Ahmed Boubeker. 1993. *Les images publiques de l'immigration*. Paris: CIEMI/Harmattan.

Bauböck, Rainer. 1991. Migration and Citizenship. *New Community* 18 (1): 27–48.

Bauman, Zygmunt. 1991. *Modernity and Ambivalence*. Ithaca, N.Y.: Cornell University Press.

Bazin, René. n.d. *Charles de Foucauld explorateur du Maroc, ermite au Sahara*. Paris: Plon.

Beaud, S., and Gérard Noiriel. 1990. L'immigration dans le football. *Vingtième-Siècle* (April–June): 83–96.

Beer, William R. 1980. *The Unexpected Rebellion: Ethnic Activism in Contemporary France*. New York: New York University Press.

Begag, Azouz. 1989. *Béni ou le Paradis Privé*. Paris: Seuil.

———. 1986. *Le gone du Chaâba*. Paris: Seuil.

Begag, Azouz, and Abdellatif Chaouite. 1990. *Ecarts d'identité*. Paris: Seuil.

Belghoul, Farida. 1986. *Georgette!* Paris: Barrault.

Benaïssa, Aïcha, and Sophie Ponchelet. 1990. *Née en France. Histoire d'une jeune beur*. Paris: Payot.

Benguigui, Yamina. 1996. *Femmes d'Islam*. Paris: Albin Michel.

Benmatti, N. A. 1982. *L'habitat du tiers monde. Cas de l'Algérie*. Algiers: SNED.

Bennabi, Malek. 1948. *Les conditions de la renaissance. Problèmes d'une civilisation*. Algiers: Mosquée des Etudiants de l'Université d'Alger.

Bensmaïa, Réda. 2003. *Experimental Nations*. Trans. Alyson Waters. Princeton, N.J.: Princeton University Press.

Benyahia, Mohamed Sadek. 1970. Les mutations psychologiques dans la révolution algérienne. *Révolution africaine* 316: 26.

Berger, Anne-Emmanuelle, ed. 2002. *Algeria in Others' Languages*. Ithaca, N.Y.: Cornell University Press.

Beriss, David. 1992. To Not Be French: Counter-Discourses of Antillean Identity in France. Ph.D. dissertation, Department of Anthropology, New York University.

———. 1990. Scarves, Schools, and Scapegoats: The Headscarf Affair. *French Politics and Society* 8 (1).

Berlant, Lauren. 1997. *The Queen of America Goes to Washington City: Essays on Sex and Citizenship*. Durham, N.C.: Duke University Press.

Berque, Jacques. 1962. *Le Maghreb entre deux guerres*. Paris: Seuil.

Bertholon, Lucien. 1913. Sociologie comparée des Achéens d'Homère et des Kabyles contemporains. In *Recherches anthropologiques dans la Berbérie orientale, Tripolitainie, Tunisie, Algérie*, vol. 1. Edited by Lucien Bertholon and E. Chantre. Lyon: A. Rey.

———. 1898. Notice sur l'origine des Berbères de souche européenne. *Congrès de l'Association Française de l'Avancement des Sciences* 1: 533–541.

Bertrand, Louis. 1934. *Un grand Africain. Le maréchal de Saint-Arnaud*. Paris: Fayard.

———. 1930 (1889). *Le sang des races. Le cycle africain*. Paris: Albin Michel.

———. 1921. *Les villes d'or. Algérie et Tunisie romaines*. Paris: Fayard.

Bhabha, Homi. 1990. DissemiNation: Time, Narrative, and the Margins of the Modern Nation. In *Nation and Narration*. London: Routledge.

Birks, J. S., and C. A. Sinclair. 1979. The International Migration Project: An Enquiry into the Middle East Labour Market. *International Migration Review* 13 (1): 122–135.

Bischoff, D., and W. Teubner. 1990. *Zwischen Einburgerin und Ruckkehr. Auslanderpolitik und Auslanderrecht der Bundesrepublik Deutschland*. Berlin: Hitit Verlag.

Bloul, Rachel. 1994. Veiled Objects of (Post-)Colonial Desire: Forbidden Women Disrupt the Republican Fraternal Sphere. *Australian Journal of Anthropology* 5 (1–2): 113–123.

Bodley, R. V. C. 1926. *Algeria from Within*. London: Hutchinson & Co.

Böhning, W. R. 1991. Integration and Immigration Pressures in Western Europe. *International Labour Review* 130 (4): 445–458.

Borgé, Jacques, and Nicolas Viasnoff. 1995. *Archives de l'Algérie*. Milan: Editions Michèle Trinckvel.

Borjas, George. 1989. Economic Theory and International Migration. *International Migration Review* 23 (3).

Bouamama, Saïd, Hadjila Sad-Saoud, and Mokhtar Djerdoubi. 1994. *Contribution à la mémoire des banlieues*. Paris: Editions du Volga.

Boubakeur, Dalil. 1995. *Charte du culte musulman en France*. Paris: Editions du Rocher.

Boubeker, Ahmed, and Mogniss H. Abdallah. 1993. *Douce France. La saga du mouvement Beur*. Paris: Im'media.

Boubeker, Ahmed, and Zakya Daoud. 1993. Radiographie de la plus grande ZUP de France. In *Banlieues . . . intégration ou explosion?* Edited by Catherine Wihtol de Wenden and Zakya Daoud. Special edition of *Panoramiques* II (12): 21–24.

Bouderon, Roger, and Pierre de Perette. 1988. *Histoire de Saint-Denis*. Toulouse: Privat.

Boudjedra, Rachid. 1992. *FIS de la haine*. Paris: Denoël.

———. 1975. *Topographie idéale pour une agression caracterisée*. Paris: Denoël.

Boudjellal, Farid. 1995. *Jambon-Beur. Les couples mixtes*. Toulon: Soleil.

———. 1990. *Juif-Arabe*. Toulon: Soleil.

———. 1988. *Ramadân (l'Oud III)*. Paris: Futuropolis.

———. 1985. *Le Gourbi (l'Oud II)*. Paris: Futuropolis.

———. 1983. *L'Oud*. Paris: Futuropolis.

Boukhedenna, Sakinna. 1987. *Journal. "Nationalité: immigré(e)."* Paris: Harmattan.

Boulot, Serge, and Danielle Boyzon-Fradet. 1988. *Les immigrés et l'école. Une course d'obstacles*. Paris: CIEMI/Harmattan.

Bounfour, Abdellah. 1994. *Le noeud de la langue. Langue, littérature et société au Maghreb*. Aix-en-Provence: Edisud.

Bouraoui, Nina. 1990. *La voyeuse interdite*. Paris: Seuil.

Bourdieu, Pierre. 2000. Making the Economic Habitus: Algerian Workers Revisited. *Ethnography* 1 (1): 17–41.

———. 1991. *Language and Symbolic Power*. Cambridge, Mass.: Harvard University Press.

———. 1984. *Distinction: A Social Critique of the Judgement of Taste*. Cambridge, Mass.: Harvard University Press.

————. 1979. *Algeria 1960*. Trans. Richard Nice. Cambridge: Cambridge University Press.

————. 1977. *Outline of a Theory of Practice*. Trans. Richard Nice. Cambridge: Cambridge University Press.

————. 1963a. The Attitude of the Algerian Peasant toward Time. In *Mediterranean Countrymen: Essays in the Social Anthropology of the Mediterranean*. Paris: Mouton.

————. 1963b. Etude sociologique. In *Travail et travailleurs en Algérie*. Edited by Maier Darbel et al. Paris: Mouton.

————. 1962. De la guerre révolutionnaire à la révolution. In *L'Algérie de demain*. Edited by François Perroux. Paris: Presses Universitaires de France.

Bourdieu, Pierre, and Jean-Claude Passeron. 1990. *Reproduction in Education, Society, and Culture*. Trans. Richard Nice. London: Sage.

Bourdieu, Pierre, and Abdelmalek Sayad. 1964. *Le déracinement*. Paris: Minuit.

Bouzid, Kara. 1984. *La Marche*. Paris: Sinbad.

Braudel, Fernand. 1985 (1977). *La Méditerranée. L'espace et l'histoire*. Paris: Flammarion.

————. 1972. *The Mediterranean and the Mediterranean World in the Age of Philip II*. 2 vols. New York: Harper and Row.

Brémond, Général Edouard. 1942. *Berbères et Arabes. La Berbérie est un pays européen*. Paris: Payot.

Brenner, Marie. 2003. France's Scarlet Letter. *Vanity Fair* (June): 106–128.

Brett, Michael, and Elizabeth Fentress. 1996. *The Berbers*. Oxford: Blackwell.

Bromberger, Christian. 1998. *Passions ordinaires. Du match de football au concours de dictée*. Paris: Bayard.

Brubaker, Rogers. 1992. *Citizenship and Nationhood in France and Germany*. Cambridge, Mass.: Harvard University Press.

Bullard, Alice. 2000. *Exile to Paradise: Savagery and Civilization in Paris and the South Pacific, 1790–1900*. Stanford, Calif.: Stanford University Press.

Burdy, Jean-Paul, and Jean Marcou. 1995. Textes officiels français sur la laïcité. *Cahiers d'études sur la Méditerranée orientale et le monde turco-iranien* 19: 298–311.

Burlen, Katherine. 1987. Sciences du logement et gestion sociale des populations. In *La banlieue oasis. Henri Sellier et les cités-jardins, 1900–1940*. Edited by Katherine Burlen. Saint-Denis: Presses Universitaires de Vincennes.

Busset, Maurice, et al. 1929. *Maroc et l'Auvergne*. Paris: Imprimerie Nationale.

Camps, Gabrielle. 1984. *L'Encyclopédie berbère*. Vol. 1. Aix-en-Provence: Edisud.

Carette, Ernest. 1848. *Etudes sur la Kabilie proprement dite*. Paris: Imprimerie Nationale.

Carlier, Omar. 1995. *Entre Nation et Jihad. Histoire sociale des radicalismes algériens*. Paris: Presses de la Fondation Nationale des Sciences Politiques.

————. 1984. Note sur la crise berbériste de 1949. *Annuaire de l'Afrique du Nord* 22: 347–371.

Castles, Stephen. 1984. *Here for Good: Western Europe's New Ethnic Minorities*. London: Pluto Press.

Castro, Roland. 1998. Allez la France Mondiale! *Libération*, 10 July.

Catani, Maurizio. 1986. Le transnational et les migrations. Individualisation et interaction entre systèmes de valeurs. *Peuples Méditerranéens* 35–36: 149–164.

Cauhapé, Véronique. 1996. Le CSA autorise Beur FM à émettre sur 106.7 24 heures sur 24. *Le Monde,* 26 March: 28.

CCI/Centre Georges Pompidou. 1984. *Enfants d'immigrés maghrébins.* Paris: Centre de Création Industrielle.

Çelik, Zeynep. 1997. *Urban Forms and Colonial Confrontations: Algiers under French Rule.* Berkeley: University of California Press.

Cesari, Jocelyne. 1998. *Musulmans et républicains. Les jeunes, l'islam et la France.* Brussels: Complexe.

———1994. *Être musulman en France. Associations, militants et mosquées.* Paris: Karthala/IREMAM.

Chaker, Salem. 1990. *Imazighen ass-a (Berbères dans le Maghreb contemporain).* Algiers: Bouchène.

———. 1985. Berbérité et emigration kabyle. *Peuples Méditerranéens* 31–32: 217–224.

Chantelat, Pascal, Michel Fodimbi, and Jean Camy. 1996. *Sports de la cité. Anthropologie de la jeunesse sportive.* Paris: Harmattan.

Charef, Mehdi. 1989. *Le harki de Meriem.* Paris: Mercure de France.

———. 1983a. *Le thé au harem d'Archi Ahmed.* Paris: Mercure de France.

———. 1983b. La Nouvelle Culture des immigrants: d'abord ne pas oublier. *La Croix.*

Chatterjee, Partha. 1995. *The Nation and Its Fragments.* Princeton, N.J.: Princeton University Press.

Chebel, Malek. 1984. *Le corps dans la tradition au Maghreb.* Paris: Presses Universitaires de France.

Chevallier, Gabrielle. 1934. *Clochemerle.* Paris: Presses Universitaires de France.

Chevrillon, André. 1927. *Les Puritains du désert.* Paris: Plon.

Citron, Suzanne. 1994. Imaginaire de la nation française, xénophobie, et racisme. In *L'immigration américaine. Exemple ou contre-exemple pour la France.* Edited by Sylvio Ullmo, pp. 55–63. Paris: Harmattan.

Clancy-Smith, Julia. 1996. The Colonial Gaze: Sex and Gender in the Discourses of French North Africa. In *Franco-Arab Encounters.* Edited by L. Carl Brown and Matthew S. Gordon. Beirut: American University of Beirut.

———. 1994. *Rebel and Saint: Muslim Notables, Popular Protest, Colonial Encounters (Algeria and Tunisia, 1800–1904).* Berkeley: University of California Press.

Clifford, James. 1994. Diasporas. *Cultural Anthropology* 9 (3): 302–338.

Cobban, Alfred. 1965. *A History of Modern France.* Vol. 3: *1871–1962.* New York: Penguin Books.

———. 1961. *A History of Modern France.* Vol. 2: *1799–1871.* New York: Penguin Books.

Cohn, Bernard. 1987. *An Anthropologist among Historians, and Other Essays.* Delhi: Oxford University Press.

Collot, Claude. 1987. *Les institutions de l'Algérie durant la période coloniale (1830–1962).* Paris: Editions du CNRS.

Colonna, Fanny. 1995. *Les Versets de l'invincibilité. Permanence et changements religieux dans l'Algérie contemporaine.* Paris: Presses de la Fondation Nationale des Sciences Politiques.

———. 1983. Présentation. In *Formation des cités chez les populations sédentaires de l'Algérie*, by Emile Masqueray. Aix-en-Provence: Edisud.

———. 1975. *Instituteurs algériens, 1883–1939.* Paris: Presses de la Fondation Nationale des Sciences Politiques.

Comaroff, Jean. 1985. *Body of Power, Spirit of Resistance.* Chicago: University of Chicago Press.

Comaroff, Jean, and John Comaroff. 1997. *Of Revelation and Revolution.* Vol. 2. Chicago: University of Chicago Press.

———. 1992. *Ethnography and the Historical Imagination.* Boulder: Westview Press.

Costa-Lascoux, Jacqueline. 1992. Comparentives au délà des frontières. *Migrants-Formations* 90 (numéro spécial).

Costa-Lascoux, Jacqueline, and Emile Temime, eds. 1985. *Les Algériens en France. Genèse et devenir d'un migration.* Paris: Publisud.

Coulon, Alain. 1992. *Connaissance de la guerre d'Algérie.* Paris: Université de Paris-VIII.

Dahmani, Areski. 1988. Le point de vue. *Alternatives Economiques* (October 1988): 25.

Dakhlia, Jocelyne. 1990. *L'oubli de la cité. La mémoire collective à l'épreuve du lignage dans le Jérid tunisien.* Paris: La Découverte.

Daoud, Zakya. 1993a. Brève histoire de la politique de la ville. In *Banlieues . . . intégration ou explosion?* Edited by Catherine Wihtol de Wenden and Zakya Daoud. Special edition of *Panoramiques* II (12): 136–139.

———. 1993b. Le chomage? In *Banlieues . . . intégration ou explosion?* Edited by Catherine Wihtol de Wenden and Zakya Daoud. Special edition of *Panoramiques* II (12): 72–75.

———. 1993c. Mantes, ma jolie. In *Banlieues . . . intégration ou explosion?* Edited by Catherine Wihtol de Wenden and Zakya Daoud. Special edition of *Panoramiques* II (12): 25–28.

———. 1993d. Qui fait quoi? In *Banlieues . . . intégration ou explosion?* Edited by Catherine Wihtol de Wenden and Zakya Daoud. Special edition of *Panoramiques* II (12): 140–143.

———. 1993e. Le logement? In *Banlieues . . . intégration ou explosion?* Edited by Catherine Wihtol de Wenden and Zakya Daoud. Special edition of *Panoramiques* II (12): 76–80.

Daumas, General Eugène. 1855. *Moeurs et coutumes d'Algérie.* Paris: Hachette.

Daumas, Eugène, and M. Fabar. 1847. *La Grande Kabylie. Etudes historiques.* 2 vols. Paris: Hachette.

De Certeau, Michel. 1984. *The Practice of Everyday Life.* Berkeley: University of California Press.

Dély, Renaud. 1998. Zidane, icone de l'intégration. *Libération,* 10 July.

Demontès, Victor. 1922–1930. *L'Algérie économique.* 3 vols. Algiers: Gouvernement Général d'Algérie, Direction de l'Agriculture, du Commerce, et de la Colonisation.

———. 1906. *Le peuple algérien. Essais de démographie algérienne.* Algiers: Gouvernement Général d'Algérie, Direction de l'Agriculture, du Commerce, et de la Colonisation.

De Neveu, Edouard. 1846. *Les Khouan. Ordres religieux chez les musulmans d'Algérie.* Paris: Guyot.

De Rudder, Véronique. 1992. Immigrant Housing and Integration in French Cities. In *Immigrants in Two Democracies: French and American Experience.* Edited by Donald L. Horowitz and Gérard Noiriel, pp. 247–267. New York: New York University Press.

———. 1990. De Varsovie à Barbès. *Différences.* Special edition of MRAP.

Désir, Harlem. 1987. *SOS-Désirs.* Paris: Calmann-Lévy.

Desplanques, Guy, and Nicole Tabard. 1991. La localisation de la population étrangère. *Economie et statistiques* 242: 51–62.

Desporetes, Gérard. 1998. Hommes, femmes, blancs, blacks, beurs . . . L'équipe finaliste du Mondial, modèle d'intégration réussie. *Libération,* 10 July.

De Tocqueville, Alexis. 1847 [1991]. Rapport sur l'Algérie. In Alexis de Toqueville, *De la colonie en Algérie,* pp. 151–179. Brussels: Complexe.

———. 1841 [1991]. Travail sur l'Algérie. In Alexis de Toqueville, *De la colonie en Algérie,* pp. 57–150. Brussels: Complexe.

———. 1837 [1991]. Lettre sur l'Algérie. In Alexis de Toqueville, *De la colonie en Algérie,* pp. 37–56. Brussels: Complexe.

Dietler, Michael. 1994. "Our Ancestors the Gauls": Archaeology, Ethnic Nationalism, and the Manipulation of Celtic Identity in Modern Europe. *American Anthropologist* 96 (3): 584–605.

Di Lucio, C., H. Sarlin, and P. Iton. 1938. *Géographie de l'Algérie.* Paris: Delalain.

Dine, Philip. 1994. *Images of the Algerian War: French Fiction and Film, 1954– 1992.* Oxford: Clarendon Press.

Direche-Slimani, Karima. 1992. Histoire de l'émigration kabyle en France au XXᵉ siècle: Réalités culturelles et reappropriations identitaires. Diplôme de troisième cycle, dirigé par Salem Chaker. Université de Provence-Aix-Marseille I.

Djebar, Assia. 1980. *Femmes d'Alger dans leur appartement.* Paris: Des Femmes.

Djura. 1993. *La saison des narcisses.* Paris: Michel Lafon.

———. 1990. *Le voile du silence.* Paris: Michel Lafon.

Docteur X. 1891. *Simples réflexions d'un colon algérien.* Paris: Hennequin.

Donadey, Anne. 1996. "Une Certaine Idée de la France": The Algeria Syndrome and Struggles over "French" Identity. In *Identity Papers: Contested Nationhood in Twentieth-Century France.* Edited by Steven Ungar and Tom Conley. Minneapolis: University of Minnesota Press.

Douglas, Allen, and Fedwa Malti-Douglas. 1994. *Arab Comic Strips.* Bloomington: Indiana University Press.

Dubet, François. 1987. *La galère: jeunes en survie.* Paris: Fayard.

Dubet, François, and Dominique Lapeyronnie. 1992. *Les quartiers d'exil.* Paris: Seuil.

Dunning, Eric, and Chris Rojek, eds. 1992. *Sport and Leisure in the Civilizing Process.* Toronto: University of Toronto Press.

Duret, Pascal. 1996. *Anthropologie de la fraternité dans les cités.* Paris: Presses Universitaires de France.

Durkheim, Emile. 1915. *The Elementary Forms of Religious Life.* New York: Basic Books.

Eickelman, Dale. 1977. Time in a Complex Society: A Moroccan Example. *Ethnology* 16 (1): 39–55.

Eickelman, Dale, and Jon Anderson. 1999. *New Media in the Muslim World.* Bloomington: Indiana University Press.

El Moudjahid. 1959. Extraits de *Formation civique et morale du contigent,* ouvrage édité par le Ministère Français de la Défense Nationale, 5ᵉ bureau, 15 January: 132–133.

El Tayeb, Salah El Din El Zein. 1987. *The National Ideology of the Radical Algerians and the Formation of the FLN, 1924–1954.* Durham, N.C.: Center for Middle Eastern and Islamic Studies.

El Yazan, Driss. 1985. Les Beurs entre la mémoire et le débat. In *La Beur Génération.* Edited by Farid Aïchoune. Paris: Sans Frontières/Arcantère.

Elias, Norbert. 2000 [1939]. *The Civilizing Process.* Oxford: Blackwell.

Etienne, Bruno. 1994. *L'Islam en France.* Paris: CNRS.

Etienne, Mona, and Eleanor Leacock. 1980. *Women and Colonization: Anthropological Perspectives.* New York: Praeger.

Fabian, Johannes. 1983. *Time and the Other: How Anthropology Makes Its Objects.* New York: Columbia University Press.

Fabre, Thierry. 1992. France-Algérie: Questions de mémoire. In *Le Maghreb, l'Europe et la France.* Edited by Kacem Basfao and Jean-Robert Henry, pp. 353–360. Paris: CNRS.

Fanon, Frantz. 1965. Algeria Unveiled. In *A Dying Colonialism,* pp. 35–67. New York: Grove Press.

———. 1963. *The Wretched of the Earth.* New York: Grove Weidenfeld.

Farbiaz, Patrick. 1998. Le "tautisme," ou quand le peuple s'invite sur scène. *Libération,* 24 July.

Favret, Jeanne. 1968. Relations de dépendance et manipulation de la violence en Kabylie. *L'Homme* 8 (4): 1–25.

Feraoun, Mouloud. 1954. *Le fils du pauvre.* Paris: Seuil.

Ferrié, Jean-Noël, and Gilles Boëtsch. 1992a. L'immigration comme domaine de l'anthropologie. *Anthropologie de l'immigration.* Cahiers de l'IREMAM 2. Aix-en-Provence: IREMAM.

———. 1992b. Du Berbère aux yeux clairs à la race eurafricaine. La Méditerranée des anthropologues physiques. In *Le Maghreb, L'Europe et la France.* Edited by Kacem Basfao and Jean-Robert Henry, pp. 191–207. Paris: Editions du CNRS.

Finifter, Germaine. 1986. *Nous venons d'Algérie.* Paris: Syros.

Fontaine, André. 1957. *L'Algérie, terre de contrastes et de conflits. Etude de géographie physique, humaine et économique à l'usage des classes du second degré et des cours élémentaires.* Oran: Fouque.

Ford, Caroline. 1991. *Creating the Nation in Provincial France.* Princeton, N.J.: Princeton University Press.

Gallissot, René. 1992. Pluralisme culturel en Europe: identités nationales et identité européenne. De l'intellectuel métis au métissage culturel de masses. *Information sur les Sciences Sociales* 31 (1): 117–127.

———. 1986. L'état-relais à partir de l'exemple algérien. La transnationalisation à l'oeuvre sous le modèle de l'Etat national. *Peuples Méditerranéens* 35–36: 247–256.

———. 1985. *Misère de l'antiracisme. Racisme et identité nationale: le défi de l'immigration.* Paris: Acantère.

Garçon, José. 1998. La dérive sanglante des milices en Algérie. *Libération,* 15 April.

Garrot, Henri. 1910. *Histoire générale de l'Algérie.* Bastion Nord: Voutes.

Gaspard, Françoise, and Farhad Khosrokhavar. 1995. *Le foulard et la République.* Paris: La Découverte.

Gaspard, Françoise, and Claude Servan-Schreiber. 1984. *La fin des immigrés.* Paris: Seuil.

Gautier, Emile-Félix. 1931. Le cadre géographique de l'histoire de l'Algérie. In *Histoire et historiens de l'Algérie.* Paris: Alcan.

———. 1922. *Structure de l'Algérie.* Paris: Société d'Editions Géographiques et Scientifiques.

Geertz, Clifford. 1968. *Islam Observed: Religious Development in Morocco and Indonesia.* Chicago: University of Chicago Press.

Gellner, Ernest. 1983. *Nations and Nationalism.* Ithaca, N.Y.: Cornell University Press.

———. 1972. Introduction. In *Arabs and Berbers: From Tribe to Nation in North Africa.* Edited by Ernest Gellner and Charles Micaud. Lexington, Mass.: Lexington Books.

———. 1969. *Saints of the Atlas.* London: Weidenfeld and Nicholson.

Genevois, H. 1962. *Contribution à l'étude ethnologique du Maghreb: la famille. Notes remises dans la région de Michelet.* Fort National: Fichier de Documentation Berbère.

Gillette, Alain, and Abdelmalek Sayad. 1976. *L'immigration algérienne en France.* Paris: Entente.

Gilmore, David, ed. 1987. *Honor and Grace and the Unity of the Mediterranean.* Washington, D.C.: American Anthropological Association.

Gilroy, Paul. 1991 [1987]. *"There Ain't No Black in the Union Jack."* Chicago: University of Chicago Press.

———. 1990. The End of Anti-Racism. *New Community* 17 (1): 71–83.

Gilsenan, Michael. 1982. *Recognizing Islam: Religion and Society in the Modern Arab World.* New York: Pantheon.

Giordan, Henri. 1982. *Démocratie culturelle et droit à la différence. Rapport présenté à Jack Lang, ministre de la Culture.* Paris: La Documentation Française.

Goodman, Jane. 2002. Writing Empire, Underwriting Nation: Discursive Histories of Kabyle Berber Oral Texts. *American Ethnologist* 29 (1): 86–122.

Grandguillaume, Gilbert. 1983. *Arabisation et politique linguistique au Maghreb.* Paris: Maisonneuve et Larose.

Green, Nancy. 1991. L'immigration en France et aux Etats-Unis. Historiographie comparée, *Vingtième Siècle* 29 (January–March): 67–82.

Grillo, Ralph. 1985. *Ideologies and Institutions of Urban France: The Representation of Immigrants.* New York: Cambridge University Press.

Gross, Joan, David McMurray, and Ted Swedenburg. 1994. Arab Noise and Ramadan Nights: Rap, Rai, and Franco-Maghrebi Identity. *Diaspora* 3 (1): 3–39.

Guéant, Claude. 1995. Des responsables extrémistes cherchent à utiliser certains jeunes délinquants. Interview in *Le Monde,* 12 September.

Guernier, Eugène. 1952. *L'Apport de l'Afrique à la pensée humaine.* Paris: Payot.

———. 1950. *La Berbérie, l'Islam, et la France.* Paris: Editions de l'Union Française.

Guilhaume, Jean-François. 1992. *Les mythes fondateurs de l'Algérie française.* Paris: Harmattan.

Guiral, Pierre. 1955. L'opinion marseillaise et les débuts de l'entreprise algérienne. *Revue Historique* 214 (July–September): 9–34.

Habermas, Jürgen. 1992. Citizenship and National Identity: Some Reflections on the Future of Europe. *Praxis-International* 12 (1): 1–19.

Haddab, Mustafa. 1984. Histoire et modernité chez les réformistes algériens. In *Connaissances du Maghreb: Sciences sociales et colonisation.* Edited by Jean-Claude Vatin, pp. 387–400. Paris: CNRS.

Haddour, Azzedine. 1993. Algeria and Its History: Colonial Myths and the Forging and Deconstructing of Identity in *Pied-Noir* Literature. In *French and Algerian Identities from Colonial Times to the Present.* Edited by Alec Hargreaves and Michael J. Hefferman, pp. 77–94. Lewiston, N.Y.: Edwin Mellen Press.

Halbwachs, Maurice. 1980 [1950]. *Collective Memory.* New York: Harper and Row.

Hall, Stuart. 1991. Old and New Identities, Old and New Ethnicities. In *Culture, Globalization and the World System: Contemporary Conditions for the Representation of Identity.* Edited by Anthony D. King. Binghamton: SUNY Press.

Hamelin, M. 1833. *Notice sur Alger.* Paris: Dentu.

Hammar, Tomas. 1990. *Democracy and the Nation State.* Brookfield, Vt.: Grower Publishing Company.

———, ed. 1985. *European Immigration Policy: A Comparative Study.* Cambridge: Cambridge University Press.

Hammoudi, Abdellah. 2000. Pierre Bourdieu et l'anthropologie du Maghreb. *Awal* 21: 11–16.

———. 1997. *Master and Disciple: The Cultural Foundations of Moroccan Authoritarianism.* Chicago: University of Chicago Press.

———. 1993. *The Victim and Its Masks: An Essay on Sacrifice and Masquerade in the Maghreb.* Chicago: University of Chicago Press.

Handler, Richard. 1988. *Nationalism and the Politics of Culture in Quebec.* Madison: University of Wisconsin Press.

Handler, Richard, and Daniel Segal. 1993. Introduction: Nations, Colonies and Metropoles. *Social Analysis* 33: 3–8.

Hannerz, Ulf. 1992. *Cultural Complexity.* New York: Columbia University Press.

———. 1980. *Exploring the City: Inquiries toward an Urban Anthropology.* New York: Columbia University Press.

Hanoteau, Louis, and Aristide Letourneux. 1871. *La Kabylie et les coutumes kabyles.* Paris: Imprimerie Nationale.

Harbi, Mohammed. 1980. Nationalisme algérien et identité berbère. *Peuples Méditerranéens* 11: 31–37.

Hare, Geoff. 2003. *Football in France: A Cultural History.* Oxford: Berg.

Hargreaves, Alec G. 1997. *Immigration and Identity in Beur Fiction: Voices from the North African Community in France,* 2nd ed. New York: Berg.

———. 1995. *Immigration, "Race," and Ethnicity in Contemporary France.* New York: Routledge.

———. 1991. *Voices from the North African Immigrant Community in France.* New York: Berg.

Hargreaves, Alec, and Mark McKinney. 1997. *Post-Colonial Cultures in France.* New York: Routledge.

Haroun, Ali. 1992. *Le septième wilaya.* Paris: Seuil.

Hart, David M. 1996. Segmentary Models in Morocco. *Journal of the Royal Anthropological Institute* 2 (4): 721–722.

Harvey, David. 1989. *The Condition of Postmodernity.* Oxford: Blackwell.

Harzoune, Mustapha, and Belkacem Tatem, eds. 1991. *Le voyage du Kabyle. Mémoires de l'immigration algérienne en France.* Paris: Im'média.

Hebdige, Dick. 1979. *Subculture: The Meaning of Style.* London: Methuen.

Herder, Johann Gottfried. 1968 (1792). *Reflections on the Philosophy of the History of Mankind.* Chicago: University of Chicago Press.

Herzfeld, Michael. 1997. *Cultural Intimacy.* London: Routledge.

———. 1984. The Horns of the Mediterranean Dilemma. *American Ethnologist* 11 (3): 439–454.

HLM Aujourd'hui. 1989. Un siècle d'habitat social, cent ans de progrès. Supplement to n. 13. Paris: Union Nationale des Fédérations d'Organismes d'HLM.

Hobsbawm, E. J. 1990. *Nations and Nationalism since 1780: Programme, Myth, Reality.* Cambridge: Cambridge University Press.

Hocquenghem, Guy. 1979. *La beauté du métis.* Paris: Ramsay.

Holmes, Douglas R. 2000. *Integral Europe: Fast-Capitalism, Multiculturalism, Neofascism.* Princeton, N.J.: Princeton University Press.

Horowitz, Donald L., and Gérard Noiriel. 1992. *Immigrants in Two Democracies: French and American Experience.* New York: New York University Press.

Houari, Leïla. 1985. *Zeida de nulle part.* Paris: Harmattan.

Huntington, Samuel. 1996. *The Clash of Civilizations and the Remaking of the World Order.* New York: Simon and Schuster.

Ibrahimi, Ahmed Taleb. 1973. *De la décolonisation à la révolution culturelle, 1962–1972.* Algiers: SNED.

Iguedelane, El-Hadi. 1996. Anthropologie de l'espace kabyle. Le village de Tizouyar. Diplôme d'étude approfondie en anthropologie sociale et ethnologie, dirigé par Tassadit Yacine. Ecole des Hautes Etudes en Sciences Sociales.

Ilahiane, Hsain. 2001. The Social Mobility of Haratine and the Re-working of Bourdieu's *Habitus* on the Saharan Frontier, Morocco. *American Anthropologist* 103 (2): 380–394.

Imache, Tassadit. 1995. *Le dromadaire de Bonaparte.* Paris: Actes Sud.

Institut du Monde Arabe. 1992. *Mémoire et enseignement de la guerre d'Algérie. Actes du colloque.* Paris: Centre de documentation de l'IMA.

Issawi, Charles. 1987. *An Arab Philosophy of History. Selections from the Prolegomena of Ibn Khaldun of Tunis (1332–1406).* Princeton, N.J.: The Darwin Press.

Ivy, Marilyn. 1995. *Discourses of the Vanishing: Modernity, Phantasm, Japan.* Chicago: University of Chicago Press.

Jacques, André. 1985. *Les déracinés. Refugiés et migrants dans le monde.* Paris: La Découverte.

Jameson, Fredric. 1986. Third World Literature in the Era of Multinational Capital. *Social Text* 15: 65–88.

Jazouli, Adil. 1992. *Les années banlieues.* Paris: Seuil.

———. 1986. *L'action collective des jeunes maghrébins de France.* Paris: CIEM/ Harmattan.

Joffrin, Laurent. 1998. Plaidoyer pour le football. *Libération,* 10 June.

Julien, Charles-André. 1963. L'insurrection de Kabylie (1870–1871). In *Preuves* (December): 60–66.

Kaddache, Mahfoud. 1973. L'utilisation du fait berbère comme facteur politique dans l'Algérie coloniale. In *Proceedings of the First Congress of Mediterranean Studies of Arabo-Berber Influence*. Algiers: SNED.

Kalouaz, Ahmed. 1986. *Point kilométrique 190*. Paris: Harmattan.

Kaplan, Nicole. 2001. Re-visualising Beur Identity in Sebbar's Trilogy. *The Journal of North African Studies* 6 (4): 27–46.

Kastoryano, Riva. 1994. Mobilisations des migrants en Europe: du national au transnational. *Revue Européenne des Migrations Internationales* 10 (1): 169–180.

Kelley, Robin D. G. 1996. Kickin' Reality, Kickin' Ballistics: Gangsta Rap and Postindustrial Los Angeles. In *Droppin' Science: Critical Essays on Rap Music and Hip Hop Culture*. Edited by William Eric Perkins. Philadelphia: Temple University Press.

Kepel, Gilles. 1991. *Les banlieues de l'Islam*. Paris: Seuil.

Kettane, Nacer. 1986. *Droit de réponse à la démocratie française*. Paris: La Découverte.

———. 1985. *Le sourire de Brahim*. Paris: Denoël.

Khader, Bichara. 1995. *Le Grand Maghreb et l'Europe. Enjeux et perspectives*. Paris: Publisud.

Khatibi, Abdelkebir. 1990. *Love in Two Languages*. Trans. Richard Howard. Minneapolis: University of Minnesota Press.

———. 1968. *Le roman maghrébin*. Paris: Maspero.

Khellil, Mohand. 1994. Kabyles en France. Un apperçu historique. *Hommes et Migrations* 1179: 12–18.

———. 1984. *La Kabylie, ou l'ancêtre sacrifié*. Paris: Harmattan.

———. 1979. *L'exil kabyle*. Paris: Harmattan.

Kriegel, Annie. 1978. Generational Difference: The History of an Idea. *Daedalus* 107 (4): 23–38.

Kristeva, Julia. 1993. *Nations Without Nationalism*. New York: Columbia University Press.

Lacheraf, Mostefa. 1953. *La Colline oubliée* ou les consciences anachroniques. *Le Jeune Musulman*, 13 February.

Lafont, Robert. 1967. *La révolution régionaliste*. Paris: Gallimard.

Lallaoui, Mehdi. 1993. *Du bidonville aux HLM*. Paris: Syros.

———. 1986. *Les Beurs de Seine*. Paris: Arcantère.

Lamand, Francis. 1986. *L'Islam en France*. Paris: Albin Michel.

Lamont, Michèle. 2000. *The Dignity of Working Men: Morality and the Boundaries of Race, Class, and Immigration*. Cambridge, Mass.: Harvard University Press.

Larcher, Emile. 1903. *Traité élémentaire de législation algérienne*. Vol. 1. Paris: Rousseau.

Laronde, Michel. 1993. *Autour du roman beur*. Paris: Harmattan.

Lazreg, Marnia. 1994. *The Eloquence of Silence: Algerian Women in Question*. New York: Routledge.

Lebovics, Herman. 1994. Creating the Authentic France: Struggles over French Identity in the First Half of the Twentieth Century. In *Commemorations: The Politics of National Identity*. Princeton, N.J.: Princeton University Press.

———. 1992. *True France: The Wars over Cultural Identity, 1900–1945*. Ithaca, N.Y.: Cornell University Press.

Lefkowitz, Natalie. 1991. *Talking Backward, Looking Forwards: The French Language Game Verlan*. Tübingen: Gunter Narr Verlag.

Le Glay, Général. 1921. L'école française et la question berbère. *Bulletin de l'Enseignement Publique au Maroc* 33bis: 1–15.

Lepoutre, David. 1997. *Coeur de banlieue: codes, rites et langages.* Paris: O. Jacob.

Liauzu, Claude. 1996. *Histoire des migrations en Méditerranée occidentale.* Brussels: Complexe.

Lipietz, Alain. 1998. Le carnaval social. *Libération,* 29 July.

Lorcin, Patricia M. E. 1995. *Imperial Identities: Stereotyping, Prejudice and Race in Colonial Algeria.* London: I. B. Tauris.

Low, Setha, ed. 1999. *Theorizing the City: The New Urban Anthropology Reader.* New Brunswick, N.J.: Rutgers University Press.

Loy, John, and Gerald S. Kenyon, eds. 1969. *Sport, Culture and Society.* London: Macmillan.

Lucas, Philippe, and Jean-Claude Vatin. 1975. *L'Algérie des anthropologues.* Paris: François Maspero.

Lyons, Thomas. 2001. Ambiguous Narratives. *Cultural Anthropology* 16 (2): 183–201.

MacGaffey, Janet, and Rémy Bazenguissa-Ganga. 2000. *Congo-Paris: Transnational Traders on the Margins of the Law.* Bloomington: Indiana University Press.

MacClancy, Jeremy, ed. 1996. *Sport, Identity and Ethnicity.* London: Berg.

MacMaster, Neil. 1997. *Colonial Migrants and Racism: Algerians in France, 1900–1962.* New York: St. Martin's Press.

———. 1993. Patterns of Emigration, 1905–1954: "Kabyles" and "Arabs." In *French and Algerian Identities from Colonial Times to the Present.* Edited by Alec Hargreaves and Michael J. Hefferman. Lewistown, N.Y.: Edwin Mellen.

———. 1991. The "Seuil de Tolérance": The Uses of a "Scientific" Racist Concept. In *Race, Discourse and Power in France.* Edited by Maxim Silverman. Brookfield, Vt.: Grower Publishing Co.

Maddy-Weitzman, Bruce. 2001. Contested Identities: Berbers, "Berberism" and the State in North Africa. *The Journal of North African Studies* 6 (3): 23–47.

Mahé, Alain. 2001. *Histoire de la Grande Kabylie, XIXe–XXe siècles.* Paris: Bouchène.

Mahfoufi, Mehenna. 1994. La chanson kabyle en immigration: une retrospective. *Hommes et Migrations* 1179: 32–39.

Malinowski, Bronislaw. 1922. *Argonauts of the Western Pacific.* London: Routledge.

Malkki, Liisa. 1992. National Geographic: The Rooting of Peoples and the Territorialization of National Identity among Scholars and Refugees. *Cultural Anthropology* 7: 24–44.

Manceron, Gilles, and Hassan Remaoun. 1993. *D'une rive à l'autre. La guerre d'Algérie de la mémoire à l'histoire.* Paris: Syros.

Mannheim, Karl. 1952. The Problem of Generations. In *Essays on the Sociology of Knowledge,* pp. 276–320. New York: Oxford University Press.

Marchal, C. 1901. Intervention. In *Congrès international de sociologie coloniale, 6–11 août 1900.* Paris: Rousseau.

Maréchal, Élle. 1994. Charles Pasqua plaide pour un islam de France. *Le Figaro* 2 (October).

Marti, Claude. 1975. *Homme d'Oc.* Paris: Stock.

Marx, Karl. 1963. *The Eighteenth Brumaire of Louis Bonaparte.* New York: International Publishers.

Masqueray, Emile. 1886. *Formation des cités chez les populations sédentaires de l'Algérie*. Paris: Ernst Leroux.

Massignon, Louis. 1930. Cartes de la répartition des kabyles dans la région parisienne. *Revue des Etudes Islamiques* 2.

Matoub, Lounès. 1995. *Rebelle*. Paris: Stock.

Mattelart, Armand. 1996. *The Invention of Communication*. Minneapolis: University of Minnesota Press.

Mauco, Georges. 1933. Les étrangers en France. *La Revue de Paris* 40 (4): 834–856.

Maunier, René. 1922. Leçon d'ouverture d'un cours de sociologie algérienne. *Hespéris* 11: 93–107.

McDonald, Maryon. 1989. *"We are not French!" Language, Culture and Identity in Brittany*. London: Routledge.

McDougall, James. 2003. Myth and Counter-Myth: "The Berber" as National Signifier in Algerian Historiographies. *Radical History Review* 86: 66–88.

McKinney, Mark. 1997. *Métissage* in Post-Colonial Comic Strips. In *Post-Colonial Cultures in France*. Edited by Alec G. Hargreaves and Mark McKinney. London: Routledge.

McMurray, David. 2001. *In and Out of Morocco: Smuggling and Migration in a Frontier Border Town*. Minneapolis: University of Minnesota Press.

Meillassoux, Claude. 1981. *Maidens, Meals, and Money*. Cambridge: Cambridge University Press.

Merad, Ali. 1967. *Le réformisme musulman en Algérie, 1925–1940. Essai d'histoire sociale et religieuse*. Paris: Mouton.

Merakchi, Nadia. 1985. Des Beurs dans l'animation. In *La Beur Génération*. Edited by Farid Aïchoune. Paris: Sans Frontière/Arcantère.

Mercier, Ernst. 1871. Ethnographie de l'Afrique septentrionale. Notes sur l'origine du peuple berbère. *Revue Africaine* 40: 420–433.

Mercier, Gustave. 1954. L'exploration scientifique de l'Algérie. In *La découverte de l'Algérie. Initiation à l'Algérie*. Paris: Maisonneuve.

Mernissi, Fatima. 1987. *Beyond the Veil: Male and Female Dynamics in a Modern Muslim Society,* revised ed. Bloomington: Indiana University Press.

Messaoudi, Khalida. 1995. *Une Algérienne debout*. Paris: Flammarion.

Messick, Brinkley. 1993. *The Calligraphic State: Textual Domination and History in a Muslim Society*. Berkeley: University of California Press.

Milliot, Louis. 1932. *Les institutions kabyles*. Paris: Librarie Orientaliste Paul Geuthner.

Mitchell, Timothy. 1988. *Colonising Egypt*. Cambridge: Cambridge University Press.

Montagne, Robert. 1930. *Les Berbères et le Makhzen dans le sud du Maroc*. Paris: Felix Alcan.

Morizot, Jean. 1985. *Les Kabyles: propos d'un témoin*. Paris: CHEAM.

Morsy, Magali. 1993. *Demain, l'Islam de France*. Paris: Editions Mame.

Mosse, George L. 1985. *Nationalism and Sexuality: Middle-Class Morality and Sexual Norms in Modern Europe*. Madison: University of Wisconsin Press.

Moussaoui, Abderrahmane. 2001. Du danger et du terrain en Algérie. *Ethnologie Française* 31: 51–59.

Naïr, Sami. 1995. L'Europe à l'assaut commercial de la Méditerranée. *Le Monde,* 4 October.

Neveu, Catherine. 2000. European Citizenship, Citizens of Europe and European Citizens. In *An Anthropology of the European Union*. Edited by Irène Bellier and Thomas M. Wilson. Oxford: Berg.

Nini, Soraya. 1993. *Ils disent que je suis une beurette*. Paris: Fixot.

Noiriel, Gérard. 1988. *Le creuset français. Histoire de l'immigration XIXe–XXe siècle*. Paris: Seuil.

Nora, Pierre, ed. 1984. *Les lieux de mémoire*. Paris: Gallimard.

Odinot, Paul. 1924. Les Berbères. *La Géographie* 41 (2): 137–149.

Ozouf, Mona. 1988. *Festivals and the French Revolution*. Cambridge, Mass.: Harvard University Press.

Parti Socialiste. 1981. *La France au pluriel*. Paris: Entente.

Peristiany, Jean G., ed. 1965. *Honor and Shame: The Values of Mediterranean Society*. London: Weidenfeld and Nicolson.

Perotti, Antonio, and Pierre Toulat. 1990. Immigration et médias. Le 'foulard' surmédiatisé? *Migrations-Société* 12 (2): 9–46.

Petonnet, Colette. 1982. *Ethnologie des banlieues*. Paris: Galilée.

Piore, Michael J. 1979. *Birds of Passage: Migrant Labor and Industrial Societies*. Cambridge: Cambridge University Press.

Pitt-Rivers, Julian A. 1961 (1954). *The People of the Sierra*. Chicago: University of Chicago Press.

———. 1960. Social Class in a French Village. *Anthropological Quarterly* 33: 1–13.

Poinard, Michel. 1992. L'insaisissable objet d'un recherche 'à problèmes.' *Migrants-Formations* 90 (numéro spécial).

Pomel, Auguste. 1871. *Des races indigènes de l'Algérie et du rôle que leur reservent leurs aptitudes*. Oran: Veuve Dagorn.

Power, Jonathan. 1979. *Migrant Workers in Western Europe*. Oxford: Pergamon.

Prost, Antoine. 2002. *Republican Identities in War and Peace: Representations of France in the Nineteenth and Twentieth Centuries*. Oxford: Berg.

Pujadas, David, and Ahmed Salam. 1995. *La tentation du Jihad*. Paris: J. C. Lattès.

Quandt, William B. 1998. *Between Ballots and Bullets: Algeria's Transition from Authoritarianism*. Washington, D.C.: Brookings Institution Press.

———. 1972. The Berbers in the Algerian Political Elite. In *Arabs and Berbers: From Tribe to Nation in North Africa*. Edited by Ernest Gellner and Charles Micaud. Lexington, Mass.: Lexington Books.

Quellien, Narcisse. 1899. *Chansons et danses des Bretons*. Paris: Maisonneuve et Leclerc.

Quéméré, Jean-Marc. 1986. Les interventions des Fonds européens de développement régional en Bretagne. In *Bretagne 2000*, ed. Fañch Elegeot, pp. 61–74. Plabennec (France): Tud Ha Bro.

Rabinow, Paul. 1989. *French Modern: Norms and Forms of the Social Environment*. Cambridge, Mass.: MIT Press.

Radio Beur. 1988. *Octobre à Alger*. Paris: Seuil.

Rambaud, Alfred. 1892. L'éducation française des Musulmans d'Algérie. *La revue bleue,* 10 September: 321–328.

Rarrbo, Kamel. 1995. *L'Algérie et sa jeunesse. Marginalisations sociales et désarroi culturel*. Paris: Harmattan.

Raulin, Anne. 2000. *L'ethnique est quotidien: diasporas, marchés et cultures metropolitaines*. Paris: Harmattan.

Reclus, Elisée. 1876. *Nouvelle géographie universelle. La terre et les hommes.* Paris: Hachette.

Renan, Ernest. 1990 [1882]. What Is a Nation? In *Nation and Narration.* Edited by Homi Bhabha. London: Routledge.

Rex, John. 1985. *Ethnic Identity and Mobilisation in Britain.* CRER, Monographs in Ethnic Relations (5).

Richter, Melvin. 1963. Tocqueville on Algeria. *Review of Politics* 25: 37–38.

Rinn, Louis. 1889. *Les origines berbères. Etude linguistique et ethnologique.* Algiers: Jourdan.

———. 1884. *Marabouts et Khouan. Etude sur l'Islam en Algérie.* Algiers: Jourdan.

Rivière-Platt, Nell, ed. 1993. *French Approaches to the Urban Crisis. A Study Program on Urban Problems in France for United States Specialists, December 2–5, 1992.* Paris: The French-American Foundation.

Roberts, Hugh. 2003. *The Battlefield: Algeria, 1988–2002.* London: Verso.

Robertson, Roland. 1992. *Globalization: Social Theory and Global Culture.* London: Sage.

Rodier, Claire, and Dominique Lahalle. 1988. *Code de la nationalité française. Pour le retrait du projet de reformes.* Paris: MRAP.

Rogers, Susan Carol. 1991. *Shaping Modern Times in Rural France.* Princeton, N.J.: Princeton University Press.

Rosello, Mireille. 2001. *Postcolonial Hospitality: The Immigrant as Guest.* Stanford, Calif.: Stanford University Press.

———. 1998. *Declining the Stereotype: Ethnicity and Representation in French Cultures.* Hanover, N.H.: University Press of New England.

Rosenzweig, Luc. 1998. Le Zidane de la boulangerie. *Libération,* 9 July.

Rouse, Roger. 1991. Mexican Migration and the Social Space of Post-Modernism. *Diaspora* 1 (1): 8–23.

Ruedy, John. 1992. *Modern Algeria: The Origins and Development of a Nation.* Bloomington: Indiana University Press.

Ruel, Anne. 1991. L'invention de la Méditerranée. *Vingtième Siècle* 32: 7–14.

Ruggie, John Gerard. 1993. Territoriality and Beyond: Problematizing Modernity in International Relations. *International Organization* 47 (1): 139–173.

Ryan, Cédric. 1998. Sous le maillot, le marcel. *Le Monde,* 9 July.

Safran, William. 1991. State, Nation, National Identity, and Citizenship: France as a Test Case. *International Political Science Review* 12 (3): 219–238.

Sahli, Mohammed C. 1953. La colline du reniement. *Le Jeune Musulman,* 2 January.

Sahlins, Marshall. 1988. Cosmologies of Capitalism: The Trans-Pacific Sector of the "World System." *Proceedings of the British Academy* 74: 1–51.

Said, Edward. 1993. *Culture and Imperialism.* New York: Vintage.

———. 1981. *Covering Islam.* New York: Pantheon Books.

Sakouhi, Fethi. 1996. L'insertion par le sport des jeunes d'origine maghrébine des banlieues en difficulté. *Migrations-Société* 8 (45): 81–100.

Sassen, Saskia. 1998. *Globalization and Its Discontents.* New York: New Press.

Sayad, Abdelmalek. 2000. El Ghorba: From Original Sin to Collective Lie. *Ethnography* 1 (2): 147–171.

———. 1999. *La double absence. Des illusions de l'émigré aux souffrances de l'immigré.* Paris: Seuil.

———. 1994a. Aux origines de l'émigration kabyle ou montagnarde. *Hommes et Migrations* 1179: 6–11.

———. 1994b. La mode de génération des générations "immigrés." *L'Homme et la Société* 111–112: 155–174.

———. 1992. Minorités et rapport à l'État dans le monde méditerranéen: le "mythe kabyle." In *Connaissance de l'Islam,* pp. 135–181. Paris: Syros.

———. 1977. Les trois 'âges' de l'émigration algérienne en France. *Actes de la Recherche en Sciences Sociales* 15: 59–79.

Sayad, Abdelmalek, and Eliane Dupuy. 1995. *Un Nanterre algérienne, terre de bidonvilles.* Paris: Autrement.

Schain, Martin, Aristide Zolberg, and Patrick Hossay. 2002. *Shadows over Europe: The Development of the Extreme Right in Western Europe.* New York: Palgrave.

Schiller, Nina Glick, Linda Basch, and Cristina Szanton-Blanc. 1994. *Nations Unbound: Transnational Projects, Postcolonial Predicaments, and Deterritorialized Nation-States.* Langhorne, Pa.: Gordon and Breach.

———. 1992. *Towards a Transnational Perspective on Migration: Race, Class, Ethnicity and Nationalism Reconsidered.* New York: New York Academy of Sciences.

Schnapper, Dominique. 1992. *L'Europe des immigrés: essai sur les politiques d'immigration.* Paris: F. Bourin.

Sebbar, Leila. 1996. *La jeune fille au balcon.* Paris: Seuil.

———. 1984. *Le Chinois vert d'Afrique.* Paris: Stock.

———. 1982. *Shérazade.* Paris: Stock.

Segal, Daniel, and Richard Handler. 1992. How European Is Nationalism? *Social Analysis* 32: 1–15.

Serageldin, Ismail, James Socknat, Stace Birks, Bob Li, and Clive Sinclair. 1983. *Manpower and International Labor Migration in the Middle East and North Africa.* Oxford: World Bank/Oxford University Press.

Servier, André. 1923. *L'Islam et la psychologie du musulman.* Paris: Challamel.

———. 1913. *Le Péril de l'avenir. Le nationalisme musulman en Egypte, en Tunisie, en Algérie.* Constantine: Boet.

Shavit, Yacov. 1994. Mediterranean History and the History of the Mediterranean: Further Reflection. *Journal of Mediterranean Studies* 4 (2): 313–329.

Shils, Edward. 1957. Primordial, Personal, Sacred and Civil Ties. *British Journal of Sociology* 8 (2): 130–145.

Sibé, Alain. 1988. *Nations dépendantes, France métropolitaine.* Biarritz: J&D Editions.

Silverman, Maxim. 1992. *Deconstructing the Nation: Immigration, Racism, and Citizenship in Modern France.* London: Routledge.

———, ed. 1991. *Race, Discourse and Power in France.* Brookfield, Vt.: Grower Publishing Co.

Silverstein, Paul. 2003. Martyrs and Patriots: Ethnic, National, and Transnational Dimensions of Kabyle Politics. *Journal of North African Studies* 8 (1): 87–111.

———. 2002a. An Excess of Truth: Violence, Conspiracy Theory, and the Algerian Civil War. *Anthropological Quarterly* 75 (4): 641–672.

———. 2002b. "Why Are We Waiting to Start the Fire?": French Gangsta Rap and the Critique of State Capitalism. In *Black, Blanc, Beur: Rap Music and Hip-Hop Culture in the Francophone World.* Edited by Alain-Philippe Durand. Lanham, Md.: Scarecrow Press.

——. 2002c. Stadium Politics: Sport, Islam, and Amazigh Consciousness in France and North Africa. In *With God on Their Side: Sport in the Service of Religion.* Edited by Tara Magdalinski and Timothy J. L. Chandler. London: Routledge.

——. 2002d. France's *Mare Nostrum:* Colonial and Post-Colonial Constructions of the French Mediterranean. *The Journal of North African Studies* 7 (4): 1–22.

——. 1999. Franco-Algerian War and Remembrance: Discourse, Nationalism, and Post-Coloniality. In *Francophone Studies: Discourse and Multiplicity.* Edited by Kamal Salhi. Exeter: Elm Bank Publications.

Sivinandan, A. 1993. Europe: Variations on a Theme of Racism. *Race and Class* 32 (3): R5–R6.

Smith, Anthony D. 1986. *The Ethnic Origins of Nations.* Oxford: Basil Blackwell.

Société de l'Afrique. 1836. *Colonisation de la régence d'Alger.* Paris: Société de l'Afrique.

Soulignac, François. 1993. *La banlieue parisienne. Cent cinquante ans de transformations.* Paris: La Documentation Française.

Soysal, Yasemin. 1996. Boundaries and Identity: Immigrants in Europe. EUI Working Paper EUF no. 96/3. San Domenico, Italy: Badia Fiesolana.

——. 1994. *The Limits of Citizenship: Migrants and Post-National Membership in Europe.* Chicago: University of Chicago Press.

Sternhell, Zeev. 1983. *Ni droite ni gauche. L'idéologie fasciste en France.* Paris: Seuil.

Stolcke, Verena. 1995. Europe: New Boundaries, New Rhetorics of Exclusion. *Current Anthropology* 36 (1).

Stoler, Ann Laura. 2002. Developing Historical Negatives: Race and the (Modernist) Vision of the Colonial State. In *From the Margins: Historical Anthropology and Its Futures.* Edited by Brian Keith Axel, pp. 156–181. Durham, N.C.: Duke University Press.

——. 1995. *Race and the Education of Desire: Foucault's History of Sexuality and the Colonial Order of Things.* Durham, N.C.: Duke University Press.

Stora, Benjamin. 2001. *La guerre invisible. Algérie, années 90.* Rabat: Centre Tarik Ibn Zyad.

——. 1995a. Algérie: absence et surabondance de mémoire. *Esprit* (January): 62–67.

——. 1995b. *L'Algérie en 1995. La guerre, l'histoire, la politique.* Paris: Michalon.

——. 1995c. Jeunes de l'immigration algérienne. Memoires de guerre. *Peuples Méditerranéens* 70–71: 293–308.

——. 1992. *Aide-mémoire de l'immigration algérienne (1922–1962).* Paris: CIEMI/ Harmattan.

——. 1991. *La gangrène et l'oubli. La mémoire de la guerre d'Algérie.* Paris: La Découverte.

Stuart, John. 1996. Zimbabwean Soccer. In *Sport, Identity and Ethnicity.* Edited by John MacClancy. London: Berg.

Swedenburg, Ted, and Smadar Lavie, eds. 1996. *Displacement, Diaspora, and Geographies of Identity.* Durham, N.C.: Duke University Press.

Système d'Observation Permanente des Migrations (SOPEMI). 1973–1992. *Tendances des migrations internationales.* Paris: OCDE.

Tadjer, Akli. 1984. *Les ANI du "Tassili."* Paris: Seuil.

Taguieff, Pierre-André. 1991. *Face au racisme.* Paris: La Découverte.

Talha, Larbi. 1989. *Le salariat immigré devant la crise.* Paris: CNRS.

Tamba, Saïd. 1992. Imaginaire et immigration. A la mémoire de l'ami d'outre Atlantique. *Information sur les Sciences Sociales* 31 (1): 153–157.

Tauxier, H. 1862–1863. Etudes sur les migrations des tribus berbères avant l'islamisme. *Revue Africaine* 18: 35–37.

Terrio, Susan J. 2000. *Crafting the Culture and History of French Chocolate*. Berkeley: University of California Press.

———. 1999. Crucible of the Millennium? The Clovis Affair in Contemporary France. *Comparative Studies in Society and History* 41 (3): 438–457.

Tessier, Octave. 1865. *Napoléon III en Algérie*. Paris: Chalamel.

Todorov, Tzvetan. 1991. Tocqueville et la doctrine coloniale. In Alexis de Toqueville, *De la colonie en Algérie*, pp. 9–36. Brussels: Complexe.

Touati, Hassan. 1997. Algerian Historiography in the Nineteenth and Twentieth Centuries: From Chronicle to History. In *The Maghrib in Question: Essays in History and Historiography*. Edited by Michelle Gall and Kenneth Perkins, pp. 84–94. Austin: University of Texas Press.

Touraine, Alain. 1992. Vraie et fausse intégration. *Le Monde,* 29 January.

Touraine, Alain, François Dubet, Zsuzsa Hegedus, and Michel Wieviorka. 1981. *Le pays contre l'État. Luttes occitanes.* Paris: Seuil.

Tribalat, Michèle. 1998. Ce jour est magique, il incarne l'idéal du creuset français. *Libération,* 10 July.

———. 1991. *Cent ans d'immigration. Etrangers hier, Français d'aujourd'hui.* Paris: PUF/INED.

Tsing, Anna. 2000. The Global Situation. *Cultural Anthropology* 15 (3): 327–360.

Turner, Terence. 1995. Comment on Verena Stolcke, "Europe: New Boundaries, New Rhetorics of Exclusion." *Current Anthropology* 36 (1).

Turner, Victor. 1967. Betwixt and Between: The Liminal Period in *Rites de Passage*. In *The Forest of Symbols: Aspects of Ndembu Ritual*. Ithaca, N.Y.: Cornell University Press.

Ungar, Steven, and Tom Conley, eds. 1996. *Identity Papers: Contested Nationhood in Twentieth-Century France*. Minneapolis: University of Minnesota Press.

Valensi, Lucette. 1969. *Le Maghreb avant la prise d'Alger, 1790–1830*. Paris: Flammarion.

Van der Veer, Peter, ed. 1995. *Nation and Migration: The Politics of Space in the South Asian Diaspora*. Philadelphia: University of Pennsylvania Press.

Van Vollenhoven, Joost. 1903. *Essai sur le fellah algérien*. Paris: Rousseau.

Vinocur, John. 1999. Just a Soccer Star, After All. *New York Times,* 14 March.

Wacquant, Loïc. 1994. Urban Outcasts: Color, Class, and Place in Two Advanced Societies. Ph.D. dissertation, University of Chicago.

Weber, Eugen. 1976. *Peasants into Frenchmen*. Stanford, Calif.: Stanford University Press.

Werbner, Pnina. 1996. "Our Blood Is Green": Cricket, Identity and Social Empowerment among British Pakistanis. In *Sport, Identity and Ethnicity*. Edited by James MacClancy, pp. 87–111. London: Berg.

Wieviorka, Michel. 2002. Race, Culture and Society: The French Experience of Muslims. In *Muslim Europe or Euro-Islam: Politics, Culture, and Citizenship in the Age of Globalization*. Edited by Nezar AlSayyad and Manuel Castells. London: Lexington Books.

———. 1999. *Violence en France*. Paris: Seuil.

——. 1996. Violence, Culture and Democracy: A European Perspective. *Public Culture* 8: 329–354.

——. 1993. Mémoire, histoire et intégration. In *Mémoire et Identité*. Edited by Jacques Barou. Paris: Syros.

Wihtol de Wenden, Catherine. 1991. North African Immigration and the French Political Imaginary. In *Race, Discourse and Power in France*. Edited by Maxim Silverman. Brookfield, Vt.: Grower Publishing Co.

——. 1990. Naissance d'une "Beurgeoisie." *Migrations-Société* 2 (8): 9–16.

——. 1988. Une citoyenneté concrète. *Cahiers de l'Orient* 11: 115–135.

Wilpert, Czarina. 1991. Migration and Ethnicity in a Non-Immigration Country: Foreigners in a United Germany. *New Community* 18 (1).

Woodhull, Winifred. 1993. *Transfigurations of the Maghreb: Feminism, Decolonization, and Literature*. Minneapolis: University of Minnesota Press.

Wright, Gwendolyn. 1997. Tradition in the Service of Modernity: Architecture and Urbanism in French Colonial Policy, 1900–1930. In *Tensions of Empire: Colonial Cultures in a Bourgeois World*. Edited by Frederick Cooper and Ann Laura Stoler, pp. 322–345. Berkeley: University of California Press.

——. 1991. *The Politics of Design in French Colonial Urbanism*. Chicago: University of Chicago Press.

Wylie, Lawrence. 1957. *Village in the Vaucluse*. Cambridge, Mass.: Harvard University Press.

Wysner, Glora M. 1945. *The Kabyle People*. New York: Privately printed.

Yacine, Kateb. 1956. *Nedjma*. Paris: Seuil.

Yacine, Tassadit. 1995. La revendication berbère. *Intersignes* 10: 95–106.

Zehraoui, Ahsène. 1994. *L'immigration: de l'homme seul à la famille*. Paris: CIEMI/Harmattan.

Zidane, Zinedine. 1998. *Zidane-Dugarry, mes copains d'abord*. Paris: Mango-Sport.

Zonabend, Françoise. 1980. *La mémoire longue. Temps et histoires au village*. Paris: Presses Universitaires de France.

Index

Abbas, Ferhat, 68, 69
Abd al-Qadir, Emir, 42, 46, 47
Adidas, 125, 127, 136
Action Française, 82
Ad-Da'wa mosque, 131, 134
adrum (patriliny), 80, 82, 84, 158. *See also* generations
Agence Im'media, 164, 203
Aït Ahmed, Hocine, 70, 214
Aït-Menguellat, Lounis, 71, 137, 168
Algerian civil war, 1–3, 74–75, 122, 128, 152–53, 169, 215, 224; and Berberism, 181–82, 220–23, 238–40; in Beur literature, 188, 203, 207–12; in France, 5–8, 9–11, 16, 175–78; as identity crisis, 74–75; and Islamism, 48, 54, 130, 133–35, 146, 149–50, 174, 178–80, 183, 216, 242–43; and terrorism, 14. *See also* Algerian war
Algerian People's Party (PPA), 68, 69
Algerian war, 3, 35, 242; and Arab-Berber divide, 67–70; in Beur literature, 184–85, 206–209; and French regionalism, 73–74; gender relations in, 147–48; and generations, 154, 157, 167; memory of, 204; resettlement during, 81, 83–84, 91–92, 94, 107
al-Madani, Tawfiq, 68–69
Alsace-Lorraine: and regionalism, 231; colonial emigration from, 43–44, 89
Amara, Saleiha, 165, 166, 175
Amicale of Algerians in Europe, 165–66, 242
Amrouche, Taos, 71, 199
Anderson, Benedict, 9, 39, 243
anti-racism, 20–22, 25–34, 127, 146, 152, 211–12, 251n2; and Beur Movement, 159–66, 167–70, 172–73, 186–87, 193–

203, 240–41; and Beur writing, 211–12; in the New Europe, 20–22, 25–34. *See also* Front National; SOS-Racisme
Appadurai, Arjun, 8, 10, 34, 124, 126, 238–39, 243–44
Arab-Berber divide, 14, 46–58, 67–74, 216–22, 227–28, 237–40, 249n14; appropriation by Berber Cultural Movement, 45, 63–64, 66–67, 74–75, 214–15, 241–42. *See also* Kabyle Myth
Arabization, 14, 39, 70, 115, 180–81, 216. *See also* Arabo-Islamism
Arabo-Islamism, 3, 37, 67–70, 74–75, 84, 224
arch (tribe), 43, 47, 54–58, 68
Argenteuil, xi, 13, 76–77, 89, 96, 107–108, 116, 182, 227
Armed Islamic Group (GIA), 1, 108, 133, 147, 215–17, 218–19
assimilation, 25–30, 31–34, 47–52, 66–67, 188–90, 202–203, 229, 240–41, 243–45; and education, 20–21, 53–55, 58, 60–62, 75, 77–79, 123–25, 178–80, 202, 205; and second-generation identity, 8–10, 169–73, 187, 201–205
Association Gutenberg, 160, 164
Association of Algerian Muslim *'Ulama* (AUMA), 68–70
Association of the New Immigrant Generation (ANGI), 164, 165, 167, 175
Association SOS Avenir Minguettes, 160–62
associations, xi, 11–13, 18–19, 71–72, 76–77, 79, 108–109, 115–19, 122, 152, 226–31, 252n9; and Berber Cultural Movement, 37–38, 67, 175, 213–15, 241–44; and Beur Movement, 15, 163–73, 174–83, 185–87, 199, 205, 216–19, 222, 240; and *cités*, 6, 9, 104–106, 131–

Paul A. Silverstein is Assistant Professor of Anthropology at Reed College.